Learning Modern C++ for Finance
Foundations for Quantitative Programming

Daniel Hanson

Learning Modern C++ for Finance

by Daniel Hanson

Published by O'Reilly Media, Inc., 1005 Gravenstein Highway North, Sebastopol, CA 95472.

O'Reilly books may be purchased for educational, business, or sales promotional use. Online editions are also available for most titles (*http://oreilly.com*). For more information, contact our corporate/institutional sales department: 800-998-9938 or corporate@oreilly.com.

Acquisitions Editor: Amanda Quinn
Development Editor: Jeff Bleiel
Production Editor: Ashley Stussy
Copyeditor: Sharon Wilkey
Proofreader: Kim Cofer

Indexer: WordCo Indexing Services, Inc.
Interior Designer: David Futato
Cover Designer: Karen Montgomery
Illustrator: Kate Dullea

November 2024:   First Edition

Revision History for the First Edition

2024-11-04:   First Release

See *http://oreilly.com/catalog/errata.csp?isbn=9781098100803* for release details.

978-1-098-10080-3

LSI

In loving memory of my parents.

Table of Contents

Preface

The modern features that have been added to the C++ Standard beginning with C++11 in 2011 have been truly remarkable and transformative. Consider the following additions through 2017, which can be of immediate benefit to financial C++ developers, and in most cases are very easy to incorporate into code:

- Move semantics, allowing transfer of object ownership without the performance overhead of copying (C++11)

- Smart pointers, which dramatically reduce problems associated with raw pointers (C++11 and C++14)

- Parallel standard algorithms that require only an additional parameter yet can speed up code by magnitudes (C++17)

- Random number generation from common distributions (C++11)

- Task-based concurrency, which can run tasks in parallel by simply replacing a couple of lines of code (C++11)

Updated versions of the C++ Standard have been released every three years since C++11, leading to the subsequent standard C++20 and the most recent C++23. In particular, these more recent features are also now available:

- A new date class, critical for fixed income applications (C++20)

- Concepts, making template-based generic programs simpler to debug and more expressive (C++20)

- Range adaptors, enabling the composition of algorithms in a modern functional form, while cutting out "the middleman" of inefficient object copying (C++20 and C++23)

- Modules—say goodbye to `#include` and hello to safer code (C++20)

All the modern features mentioned here, plus coverage of popular open source C++ libraries such as Eigen (linear algebra) and the Boost libraries, are provided within this book, with a focus on relevant financial applications.

In computer science and financial engineering curricula (at least throughout the United States), however, as well as in popular online credential programs in quantitative finance, C++ education largely appears to be living in the past. Many courses still seem to be based on the 2003 Standard, referred to as C++03. This is a common complaint I have heard from many students in the CppCon (*https://oreil.ly/JDAFa*) (annual C++ conference) Student Program, and from a few of my own master's students who took undergraduate C++ courses before entering the computational finance program in which I taught at the University of Washington through 2022. Some students said that professors refused to update their syllabi, while others said that professors wanted to teach modern C++, but their departments wouldn't allow it.

So I tried to write the book with this audience in mind: those who have had some introductory-level experience with C++ but who wish to learn more about modern methods relevant to the implementation of financial models. It is also feasible for those with experience in other programming languages to work through this book, in tandem with an introductory book such as *C++ Primer*, 5th edition (*https://oreil.ly/z12jO*), by Stanley B. Lippman et al. (Addison-Wesley, 2012), or *Teach Yourself C++ in One Hour a Day*, 9th edition (*https://oreil.ly/5siYU*), by Siddhartha Rao (Sams, 2022). I also highly recommend *The C++ Standard Library: A Tutorial and Reference*, 2nd edition (*https://oreil.ly/51GHg*), by Nicolai M. Josuttis (Addison-Wesley, 2012), as a reference book for both beginners and advanced readers. You may note that the links provided here are to the electronic editions available on the O'Reilly Learning Platform (*https://learning.oreilly.com/home/*). Other references cited throughout the book will be linked to this platform where available.

One more excellent resource is the *Back to Basics* series of talks from the annual CppCon C++ conference, which is freely available on the conference YouTube channel (*https://www.youtube.com/user/CppCon*). If you wish to learn more about a particular topic, chances are a *Back to Basics* talk is available.

This book assumes readers have knowledge of the following topics. If you are new to C++ or if it has been a while, you might want to specifically review these or keep a reference book handy such as those noted previously:

- Basic exception handling
- `static_cast<.>`
- Basic class design in general—and in particular `public`, `protected`, and `private` member functions and data members
- Static data members and member functions

- cout and console output
- Header and implementation files
- The difference between #include<*blah*> and #include "*blah*.h"
- The standard `vector` container
- Code debugging with an integrated development environment (IDE)
- Compiling and linking an executable program

Also, because financial modeling involves math, a basic-level knowledge of the following topics is also assumed, in certain chapters:

- Probability theory and statistics
- Basic numerical root–finding methods
- Linear algebra and matrix decompositions
- Black-Scholes option pricing and the associated Brownian motion stochastic process

Navigating This Book

This book is organized roughly as follows:

- Chapter 1, "An Overview of C++" provides an overview of C++, beginning with a brief history of C++ in finance, and the shift toward modern C++, beginning with C++11. It also covers the separation of the core language and the C++ Standard Library, followed by key modern updates to the language that will be used throughout the remainder of the book, such as automatic type deduction, range-based `for` loops, scoped enumerations, and lambda expressions. It also includes coverage of basic mathematical features within the core language and the Standard Library. It concludes with a discussion about coding style and standards, and those that will be followed in this book.

- Chapter 2, "Writing User-Defined Classes with Modern C++ Features" and Chapter 3, "Inheritance, Polymorphism, and Smart Pointers" are focused on object-oriented features in C++, and modern additions that have changed (and have helped improve) the methods once commonly employed in C++ for implementing composition and inheritance. Chapter 2 is primarily concerned with composition, namely the storage of a private data member that is itself an object, and how move semantics introduced in C++11 can make this more efficient by avoiding object copy at construction of the enclosing object. It also covers the new C++20 three-way operator (also called the *spaceship operator*), which greatly streamlines implementation of equality and inequality operators.

Chapter 3 begins with modern features that better facilitate inheritance and dynamic polymorphism. It then shifts back to composition, where the subobject member is now a pointer resource, and how smart pointers help eliminate the problems associated with raw pointers. Composition and inheritance are then tied together in a modern context where the resource is a smart pointer to a polymorphic object. Financial examples in both chapters are related to option pricing.

- Chapter 4, "The Standard Template Library Part I: Containers and Iterators" and Chapter 5, "The Standard Template Library Part II: Algorithms and Ranges" cover what has traditionally been called the *Standard Template Library (STL)*. This is a set of standard containers—including the vector container and others—plus iterators that allow you to traverse these containers, and algorithms that perform operations on elements in a container. STL containers and iterators are covered in Chapter 4, while the algorithms are covered in Chapter 5. Chapter 5 also contains a discussion of C++20 and C++23 extensions of algorithms in the more expressive form of ranges, and furthermore how ranges relate to range views and range adaptors. As you will see, these can be used in a functional programming context for composing a sequence of algorithms such that the performance overhead from copying data and generating temporary container objects can be avoided.

- Chapter 6, "Random Number Generation and Concurrency" begins with a discussion of random number generation from known probability distributions, another new Standard Library feature released in C++11. Standard normal random variates in particular are key to continuous-time financial models, while the random values from a Poisson distribution are often used in modeling tick data for testing live trading strategies. Two examples are presented. The first is the shuffle algorithm combined with a C++11 random engine to generated Monte Carlo scenarios of equity lines to measure the risk associated with the volatility of maximum drawdown in a trading strategy. The second is a Monte Carlo model for valuing European options with barriers, where random variates from a standard normal distribution are used in a discretized Brownian motion process. The chapter then changes focus to concurrency and parallelism, first with examples of parallel STL algorithms, introduced with C++17. These are mostly overloads of existing algorithms, but with an additional execution policy parameter, which means significant performance increases can be had by simply including an extra argument. The chapter concludes with a return to the Monte Carlo option pricing example, but using the Standard Library async(.) function and future class, which help facilitate generating each Monte Carlo scenario as a parallel task, again resulting in significant increases in the magnitude of speed for larger numbers of scenarios and time steps.

- Chapter 7, "Dates and Fixed Income Securities" introduces the new C++20 date functionality in the Standard Library, and how date functions and validations typically required for fixed income trading can be incorporated into code. Discussion then proceeds to wrapping this functionality in a user-defined date class that can be used in the design of a yield curve class and a bond class, and how these can all be used together to price a coupon-paying bond. This includes coverage of potentially tedious but important details that are crucial for fixed income trading but are often left out of related textbooks and course syllabi.

- Chapter 8, "Linear Algebra" is devoted to linear algebra in C++. A common technique used in C++ linear algebra library development is expression template programming, so a gentle introduction to this topic is provided before moving on to the open source, third-party C++ linear algebra library called Eigen. This will include applications to fund tracking (regression), valuing basket options (Cholesky decomposition), and yield curve dynamics (principle component decomposition). The chapter concludes with a look ahead to linear algebra capabilities in the C++ Standard Library, particularly the mdspan multidimensional array reference from C++23, and the standard interface based on the Basic Linear Algebra Subprograms (BLAS) slated for C++26.

- Chapter 9, "The Boost Libraries" covers some of the peer-reviewed, open source Boost libraries. A fair amount of content from Boost has found its way into the C++ Standard over the years (in similar but not necessarily identical form), while other Boost libraries remain orthogonal to the Standard but can be applied to problems that arise in finance. In particular, the set of statistical distributions from the Boost Math Toolkit library provides the probability density function (PDF), cumulative distribution function (CDF), and percentile function for each of 34 "textbook" distributions. The Boost MultiArray library provides a generic multidimensional array that can be adapted for binomial (and trinomial) lattice option pricing models, and the Boost Accumulators library contains efficient incremental descriptive statistical computations on dynamic sets of data that are well suited for keeping track of performance metrics in trading backtests. Each of these is covered in the chapter.

- Chapter 10, "Modules and Concepts" covers two more recent features included in C++20: modules and concepts. Modules unfortunately have gotten off to a slow start, with some compilers only recently nearing completion of their implementation. On the other hand, they bring a more modern touch to C++ software design and implementation, with cleaner and safer code, increased productivity, and in some cases reduced compile times. Furthermore, it is my opinion that once modules become more mainstream, they will provide a huge benefit to those learning C++, as they will be able to get up and running more quickly. In contrast, concepts have been quickly adopted by developers and were a long awaited enhancement. Concepts give programmers more control over template programming, particularly pinpointing compile-time errors that in preceding years might be buried among an avalanche of cryptic errors. They also lend clarity to code, in a sense helping it to be better self-documenting. Concepts can be user-defined, while a robust set of predefined concepts, based on C++11 type traits, is provided by the Standard Library as of C++20.

- Five appendices are provided at the end of the book for readers who might be interested in a deeper dive into more advanced and historical topics.

Conventions Used in This Book

The following typographical conventions are used in this book:

Italic

Indicates new terms, URLs, email addresses, filenames, and file extensions.

`Constant width`

Used for program listings, as well as within paragraphs to refer to program elements such as variable or function names, databases, data types, environment variables, statements, and keywords.

`Constant width italic`

Shows text that should be replaced with user-supplied values or by values determined by context.

This element signifies a general note.

This element indicates a warning or caution.

Using Code Examples

As you will see, there are numerous code examples throughout the book. These are available for download from GitHub (*https://github.com/QuantDevHacks/Learning ModCppFinance*), such that you can compile and run them on your local machine. You are free to use this code as you wish, per the reasonable conditions of the Mozilla Public License, v. 2.0. Supplemental information to accompany the repository may also be posted from time to time.

It is important to note that these code examples are intended to introduce you to modern C++ features and open source libraries, and to show you ways in which you could use them. They are not meant to be simply part of a cookbook or production-ready code. The priority is to help you learn, so that from there you can use the material creatively in your own applications.

There is always the chance, especially with the initial release of the software, that it contains errors or inconsistencies, so for this, apologies in advance. If you do run across a problem, please feel free to log an issue on the companion GitHub site.

If you have a technical question or a problem using the code examples, please send email to *support@oreilly.com*.

This book is here to help you get your job done. In general, if example code is offered with this book, you may use it in your programs and documentation. You do not need to contact us for permission unless you're reproducing a significant portion of the code. For example, writing a program that uses several chunks of code from this book does not require permission. Selling or distributing examples from O'Reilly books does require permission. Answering a question by citing this book and quoting example code does not require permission. Incorporating a significant amount of example code from this book into your product's documentation does require permission.

We appreciate, but generally do not require, attribution. An attribution usually includes the title, author, publisher, and ISBN. For example: "*Learning Modern C++ for Finance* by Daniel Hanson (O'Reilly). Copyright 2025 Daniel Hanson, 978-1-098-10080-3."

If you feel your use of code examples falls outside fair use or the permission given above, feel free to contact us at *permissions@oreilly.com*.

O'Reilly Online Learning

O'REILLY® For more than 40 years, *O'Reilly Media* has provided technology and business training, knowledge, and insight to help companies succeed.

Our unique network of experts and innovators share their knowledge and expertise through books, articles, and our online learning platform. O'Reilly's online learning platform gives you on-demand access to live training courses, in-depth learning paths, interactive coding environments, and a vast collection of text and video from O'Reilly and 200+ other publishers. For more information, visit *https://oreilly.com*.

How to Contact Us

Please address comments and questions concerning this book to the publisher:

O'Reilly Media, Inc.
1005 Gravenstein Highway North
Sebastopol, CA 95472
800-889-8969 (in the United States or Canada)
707-827-7019 (international or local)
707-829-0104 (fax)
support@oreilly.com
https://oreilly.com/about/contact.html

We have a web page for this book, where we list errata, examples, and any additional information. You can access this page at *https://oreil.ly/learningModCPlus Plus_finance*.

For news and information about our books and courses, visit *https://oreilly.com*.

Find us on LinkedIn: *https://linkedin.com/company/oreilly-media*.

Watch us on YouTube: *https://youtube.com/oreillymedia*.

Acknowledgments

I would like to sincerely thank a number of people for their help in completing this book.

Patrice Roy was one of the original technical reviewers, but he agreed to stay on to patiently answer a lot of my questions about deeper technical details and matters concerning proposals that have gone before the ISO C++ committee. He also contributed specific material to Chapters 4, 5, and 6. Ken Adams provided considerable help in providing both C++ and financial modeling examples that eventually became material for this book, and he also coauthored Chapter 7, covering dates, date calculations, and fixed income trading applications.

Technical reviewers Kurt Guntheroth and Vittorio Romeo also provided useful and candid feedback. This book is a much better product thanks to their input earlier on. My editor, Jeff Bleiel, helped me get through earlier stumbles and encouraged me to keep going and focus on the final product, and he also provided invaluable recommendations that will make this book more consistent and readable. Also, thanks to acquisitions editor Amanda Quinn, production editor Ashley Stussy, and copy editor Sharon Wilkey at O'Reilly.

Two former students—whom I now consider my friends—Steven Zhang and Chris Alpert, graciously reviewed a later draft of the book and sample code from the perspective of the target audience. They caught issues and errors that required attention, as well as suggested different phrasing in places that should make the content clearer to readers.

Rob Verran provided some very nice real-world examples of how shared pointers could be used in trading system applications, in Chapter 3. Mark Hoemmen and Andrew Lumsdaine provided additional reviews of Chapter 8, and Mark was also kind enough to answer several rounds of questions related to the new linear algebra–related features that have gone into C23 (mdspan) and C26 (BLAS interface). John Spraker also reviewed some of the mathematical details in this chapter and caught a few points that required corrections and clarification. Thaddeus Tarpey likewise reviewed some of the mathematics related to the Boost Statistical Distributions discussion in Chapter 9. Ruibo Zhang provided a final review of the math in Chapters 8 and 9, and he also interestingly adopted portions of the book for implementing simulations in C++ of stochastic processes used in cancer modeling, his area of research.

Two more people who, while not directly involved with writing this book, deserve special thanks and mention. I truly thank my wife, Yoshie, for her patience and encouragement, and also for keeping me properly watered and fed through the ordeal. Also many thanks to R. Douglas Martin, professor emeritus of the departments of Applied Mathematics and Statistics at the University of Washington, without whose mentorship over the past two decades, the opportunities and experiences that led to my being able to write this book would never have existed.

To all mentioned here, I cannot fully express how much I appreciate your help and support. My sincere thanks and deepest gratitude.

CHAPTER 1

An Overview of C++

This chapter presents an overview of C++, beginning with a brief history—including its early popularity in quantitative finance—and the start of its modern era marked by major enhancements in 2011, released as C++11. Prior to C++11, the last release was in 2003 (C++03), which was an update mainly addressing bug fixes following the first C++ release that was compliant with the International Organization of Standardization (ISO (*https://www.iso.org/home.html*)) in 1998 (C++98). The modernization that began with C++11 has continued with further innovations added to the core language, and its companion, the C++ Standard Library, every three years, bringing us to the current C++23 version.

You will also be introduced to useful new language features that will be used in subsequent chapters, as well as convenient math-related updates to the Standard Library. Finally, we will look at common class, function, and variable naming conventions, and point out those that will be used throughout this book.

C++ and Quantitative Finance

C++ started its rapid growth in the financial sector around the mid-1990s. Many of us who were in the industry around this time had been raised on Fortran, which was used for writing numerical routines and scientific applications. While Fortran and its supporting libraries (BLAS, LAPACK, IMSL) were well-developed in terms of mathematical and linear algebra support, the language lacked support for *object-oriented programming*, the inclusion of which was considered C++'s big advantage among financial developers at the time. Of course, C++ supports more than object-oriented programming, as is discussed later in this chapter.

Financial modeling in the abstract naturally comprises components that interact with one another. For example, pricing even a simple derivatives contract based on foreign exchange and interest rates would typically require the following:

- The yield curve for each currency
- A market rate feed of live foreign exchange rate quotes
- Volatility curves and/or surfaces for option pricing and calculating risk measures
- A set of derivative pricing methods, such as closed-form solutions and numerical approximations

Each of these components can be represented by an object, and C++ provides the means for creating these objects and managing their relationships to one another.

Banks and other financial institutions also needed a way to generate risk reports at both a regional and global scale. This was a significant challenge for companies with trading operations spread across the major financial centers around the world such as New York, London, and Tokyo. At the start of each trading day, risk reporting was required for a firm's headquarters in, say, New York that took into account the portfolios maintained both locally and globally. This could be a computationally intensive task, but the performance of C++ made it possible and was yet another significant factor in its early adoption in the financial industry.

Following the turn of the century, newer object-oriented languages, such as Java and C#, made software development a somewhat easier and faster process, while more-efficient processors became less expensive. However, the same features in these languages that enabled quicker deployment (such as built-in managed memory, garbage collection, and intermediate compilation) could also introduce overhead in terms of runtime performance. Management decisions on which language to adopt often came down to a trade-off between more-rapid development and runtime efficiency. However, even if one of these language alternatives were employed, computationally intensive pricing models and risk calculations were—and still are—often delegated to existing C++ libraries and called via an interface. It should also be noted that C++ offers certain compile-time optimizations that are not available in these other programming languages.

C++11: The Modern Era Is Born

In 2011, the ISO C++ Committee (*https://isocpp.org*) (usually just called *the Committee*) released a substantial revision that addressed long-needed modernization. In particular, C++11 provided these welcome abstractions that are immediately useful to quantitative developers:

- Random number generation from a variety of probability distributions
- Lambda expressions encapsulating mathematical functions that can also be passed as arguments to other functions
- Basic task-based concurrency that can parallelize computations without the need for manual thread management
- Smart pointers that can help prevent memory-related program crashes and undefined behavior

These topics and more are discussed in the chapters ahead.

In this chapter and throughout the book, you will sometimes see the term *undefined behavior*. This is referenced throughout the C++ Standard as well, and it means behavior for which no guarantees are provided. In common parlance, this means the code is not "playing by the rules," and that the program is broken. So, if your code is at risk of causing undefined behavior, the simple advice is "do not do that."

Following C++11, new releases with more and more modern features addressing the demands of financial and data science industries are being rolled out on a three-year cadence, with the most recent release being C++23. This book primarily covers developments through C++20, but it will also discuss some new items in C++23, as well as a few proposed coming attractions in C++26 that should be of interest to financial developers.

Proprietary and high-frequency trading firms have been at the forefront of adopting C++11 and later standards, because the speed of acting on market and trading book signals in statistical strategies can mean a profound difference in profit and loss. Modern C++ is also in keen demand for implementing computationally intensive derivative pricing models utilized by traders and risk managers at investment banks and hedge funds.

For more coverage of the broader history and evolution of C++ into the modern era, *C++ Today: The Beast is Back* (*https://oreil.ly/ZHjnQ*) by Jon Kalb and Gašper Ažman (O'Reilly, 2015) is highly recommended. It should also be noted that with the publication of, and more attention to, the ISO C++ Core Guidelines (*https://oreil.ly/Kc69F*) and *ISO C++ Coding Standards* (*https://oreil.ly/P6CK0*), C++ development can now be more reliable and efficient than in years past. The Core Guidelines in particular are referenced with some frequency throughout this book.

Open Source Mathematical Libraries

Another welcome development over the past decade has been the proliferation of robust open source mathematical libraries written in standard C++ that therefore do not require the time-consuming C-language interface gymnastics of the past. Primary among these are the Boost libraries, the Eigen and Armadillo linear algebra libraries, and machine learning libraries such as TensorFlow and PyTorch. We will discuss Boost and Eigen further as the book proceeds.

Some Myths about C++

Here are some of the more infamous false beliefs that have been perpetuated about C++:

Knowledge of C is necessary for learning C++.
   While the C++ Standard retains most of the C language, it is entirely possible to learn C++ without knowledge of C, as you will see in the material that follows. Clinging to C style can, in fact, hinder learning the powerful abstractions and potential benefits of C++.

C++ is too difficult.
   OK, yes, this has some truth, as C++ is undoubtedly a rich language that provides plenty of the proverbial rope with which to hang ourselves, and indeed it can at times be the source of nontrivial frustration. However, by leveraging *modern* features of the language, it is entirely possible to become productive as a quantitative financial developer in C++ more quickly compared to relying on legacy C++03 methods.

Memory leaks are always a problem in C++.
   With smart pointers available since C++11—one of the more prominent *modern* features—most code should not need to play with raw pointers or memory allocation. Along with other Standard Library features such as standard algorithms (covered in Chapter 5), this no longer needs to be an issue in most financial-modeling implementations.

Compiled Versus Interpreted Code

C++ is a *compiled* language: commands typed into a file by us mere mortals are first translated into a set of binary instructions, or *machine code*, that a computer processor will understand. This is in contrast to nontyped and interpreted quantitative languages such as Python, R, and MATLAB, where each line of code must be reprocessed each time it is executed, thus slowing execution time for larger applications, especially those with heavy reliance upon iterative (looping) statements.

This is by no means a knock on these languages. Their power is evident in their popularity for rapid implementations and visualizations of models arising in quantitative fields such as finance, data science, and biosciences, where their available mathematical and statistical functions are often already compiled in C, C++, or Fortran. However, financial programmers may be well aware of models that would require days to run in an interpreted language, but only a matter of minutes or seconds when reimplemented in C++.

An effective approach is to use interpreted mathematical languages with C++ in a complementary fashion. Computationally intensive models code could be written in a C++ library and then called either interactively or from an application in Python or R, for example. C++ efficiently takes care of the number crunching, while the results can be used inside powerful plotting and other visualization tools in Python and R that are not available in the C++ Standard Library.

Another advantage of organizing financial models in a C++ library is the code is written once and maintained in a single repository. This way, a common set of code can be deployed across many departments, divisions, and even international boundaries, and called via interfaces from applications written in different frontend languages. This helps ensure consistent numerical results throughout the organization, which can be particularly advantageous for regulatory compliance purposes.

Popular open source C++ integration packages are available for both R and Python (namely, Rcpp (*https://oreil.ly/8QpEJ*) and pybind11 (*https://oreil.ly/9saMd*), respectively). MATLAB also provides options for C++ interfaces, although nontrivial license fees can be required for their add-on features.

The Components of C++

Standard C++ releases at a high level consist of two components: language features and the C++ Standard Library. Together, the Standard C++ language and the Standard Library are commonly referred to as *the Standard*.

C++ Language Features

C++ language features mostly overlap with the following essential operators and constructs you would find in other programming languages:

- Fundamental integer and floating-point numerical types
- Conditional branching: `if`/`else` statements and `switch`/`case` statements
- Iterative constructs: `for` loops and `while` loops
- Standard mathematical and logical operators for numerical types: addition, subtraction, multiplication, division, modulus, and inequalities

C++ language features support at least four of the major programming paradigms: procedural programming, object-oriented programming, generic programming, and functional programming. A short list of specific related features are, respectively, as follows:

- Free functions, also referred to as nonmember functions (of a class)
- Classes and inheritance
- Templates
- Lambda expressions (since C++11)

Each is utilized throughout the book, beginning with this chapter.

Finally, the C++ language provides a plethora of fundamental numerical and logical types. Those that we will primarily use are as follows:

- `double` (double precision) for floating-point values
- `int` for positive and negative integers
- `unsigned int` (or alternatively just `unsigned`) for nonnegative integers
- `bool` for boolean representation (`true` or `false`)

Ranges for each of the numerical types can vary across platforms, but on modern compilers, the types noted here are mostly sufficient for modern financial applications. You can find a comprehensive guide that provides these ranges and details on cppreference.com (*https://oreil.ly/q0DdU*). This website is an essential resource for any C++ developer.

The C++ Standard Library

A *software library* is essentially a set of functions and classes that are called by an application or system. Library development—both open source and commercial—now dominates modern C++ development compared to standalone applications that were more popular in previous decades. Subsequent chapters cover some of the popular open source options that are useful for computational work. The most important C++ library, however, is the *Standard Library*, which is shipped with most modern compilers.

The C++ Standard Library "enable(s) programmers to use general components and a higher level of abstraction without losing portability rather than having to develop all code from scratch."[1] Up through C++23, highly useful library features for financial modeling include the following:

- Single-dimension container classes, particularly the dynamically resizeable vector class
- A wide set of standard algorithms that operate on these containers, such as sorting, searching, and efficiently applying functions to a range of elements in a container
- Standard real-valued mathematical functions such as square root, exponential, and trigonometric functions
- Complex numbers and related arithmetic operations
- Random number generation from a set of standard probability distributions
- Task-based concurrency that can provide return values from functions run in parallel
- Smart pointers that abstract away the dangers associated with memory allocation and management
- A string class to store and manage character data

Use of Standard Library components requires the programmer to explicitly import them into the code, as they reside in a separate library rather than within the core language. The idea is similar to importing a NumPy array into a Python program or loading an external package of functions into an R script. In C++, this is a two-step process, starting with including the header files (with the #include preprocessor directive) containing the Standard Library functions and classes we wish to use, and then scoping these functions with the Standard Library namespace name, std, often pronounced as "stood" by C++ developers.

As a quick first example, let's create a vector of int values and a string object, and output them to the console from a simple executable program inside the main() function:

```cpp
#include <vector>     // vector class
#include <string>     // string class
#include <iostream>   // cout

int main()
{
    std::vector<int> x{1, 2, 3};
    std::string s{"This is a vector:"};
```

---

1 Nicolai M. Josuttis, *The C++ Standard Library: A Tutorial and Reference* (*https://oreil.ly/lIV2L*) (Addison-Wesley, 2012), Chapter 1.

```
    std::cout << s << x[0] << ", " << x[1] << ", " << x[2] << "\n";
}
```

Note that the Standard Library classes vector and string, and the console output cout, are scoped with the Standard Library std namespace. If you wish to save yourself typing std::, you can employ using statements, preferably within individual function scopes, although placed at the top of a file can be acceptable in certain limited situations, such as writing small sets of test functions:

```
#include <vector>        // vector class
#include <string>        // string class
#include <iostream>      // cout

int main()
{
    using std::vector, std::string, std::cout;

    vector<int> v{1, 2, 3};
    string s{"This is a vector:"};
    cout << s << v[0] << ", " << v[1] << ", " << v[2] << "\n";
}
```

The output is not surprisingly as follows:

```
This is a vector: 1, 2, 3
```

The using statement is required only once, with the three Standard Library components following on the same line. This is a newer feature as of C++17. For examples in this book, it will often be assumed that using statements have been applied to commonly used Standard Library classes and functions such as vector, string, and cout. Also, it should be noted that cout is generally not used in production code. We will use it as a placeholder where a result in reality would more likely be passed to a GUI or database interface, or another section of code.

Importing the std namespace into the global namespace with

using namespace std;

is sometimes found in code to replace the individual using statements or explicit scoping with the std namespace. However, this is not considered good practice, as it can result in naming clashes at compile time. You can find more details in the ISO C++ Coding Standards FAQ entry, "Should I use using namespace std in my code?" (*https://oreil.ly/lPnJw*).

Uniform initialization (also called *braced initialization*), used in some of the preceding examples, was also introduced in C++11:

```
vector<int> v{1, 2, 3};

string s{"This is a vector:"};
```

This is a useful feature in general that is discussed in "Uniform Initialization" on page 13. For further convenience, you will see later that the template parameter can be dropped in certain cases, using another newer feature called *class template argument deduction*, or *CTAD* for short.

To close out this introductory discussion of the Standard Library, one more type to be aware of is `std::size_t` (*size type*). Rather than being part of the core language, it is contained in the Standard Library and "is defined to be an unsigned integer with enough bytes to represent the size of any type."[2] It is not as much a distinct type as it is an alias for one of the existing unsigned integral types, so it might be `unsigned int` on some platforms and `unsigned long` on others. Per its definition, it will always be at least as large as the return type for the size of a `vector`.

The size type of a `vector` is also a platform-dependent unsigned integral type, which in some cases might be the same as `size_t` but not necessarily so. However, because `size_t` will be at least as large, the value returned from the `size()` member function is often just implicitly converted:

```
#include <vector>
#include <cstdlib>         // std::size_t


. . .

std::vector<int> v{1, 2, 3};

std::size_t v_size = v.size();
```

As you will see soon, however, with modern features of C++ such as `auto` and range-based `for` loops, this issue has become more of an artifact.

Some New Language Features Since C++11

This section covers some useful features and syntax introduced since C++11 (inclusive). Although it has been over 10 years since C++11 hit the scene, it unfortunately is still not covered in many university and quantitative finance programs, let alone later releases such as C++17.

---

2 Christopher Di Bella, "Why do some C++ programs use `size_t`?" (*https://oreil.ly/_P-CM*), Quora.

The auto Keyword

C++11 introduced the `auto` keyword that can automatically deduce a variable or object type. Here are simple examples:

```
auto k = 1;          // int
auto x = 419.53;     // double
```

In this case, k is deduced as an `int` type, and x a `double` type.

Programmers have varied opinions on the use of `auto`, but many still prefer to explicitly state fundamental types such as `int` and `double` to avoid ambiguity. This is the style followed in this book.

The `auto` keyword becomes more useful when the return type is reasonably obvious from the context. As you will see in Chapter 3, a unique or a shared pointer can be created with the Standard Library function `make_unique<T>(.)` or `make_shared<T>(.)`:

```
auto call_payoff = std::make_unique<CallPayoff>(75.0);
auto mkt_data = std::make_shared<LiveMktData>("CattleFutures");
```

In the first case, `make_unique<CallPayoff>` makes it fairly obvious that a unique pointer to a `CallPayoff` object is being created (with a strike of 75). In the second, `make_shared<LiveMktData>` says it is creating a shared pointer to a `LiveMktData` object (providing cattle futures prices). These are sufficiently expressive and a lot easier to maintain than what would be required otherwise:

```
std::unique_ptr<CallPayoff> call_payoff = std::make_unique<CallPayoff>(75.0);
std::shared_ptr<LiveMktData> mkt_data =
    std::make_shared<LiveMktData>("CattleFutures");
```

It is also handy if the return type is a long and nested class template type, such as from a function as follows:

```
std::map<std::string, std::complex<double>> map_of_complex_numbers(. . .)
{
    // . . .

    std::map<std::string, std::complex<double>> map_key_string_val_complex;

    // . . .

    return map_key_string_val_complex;
}
```

Then, instead of the pre-C++11 way

```
std::map<std::string, std::complex<double>> cauchys_revenge =
    map_of_complex_numbers(. . .);
```

we can more cleanly and clearly call the function and define the result by using `auto`:

```
auto cauchys_revenge = map_of_complex_numbers(. . .);
```

Range-Based for Loops

Prior to C++11, iterating through a `vector` would involve using the index as the counter, up to the number of its elements:

```
vector<double> v{1.0, 2.0, 3.0, 4.0, 5.0};

for(std::size_t i = 0; i < v.size(); ++i)
{
    // Do something with v[i]
}

// For example:
for (std::size_t i = 0; i < v.size(); ++i)
{
    cout << v[i] << " ";
}
```

Alternatively, you can also use an iterator-based `for` loop, which was also available before C++11:

```
for (auto iter = v.begin(); iter != v.end(); ++iter)
{
    cout << *iter << " ";
}
```

In some cases, this form can be more convenient, as you will see in later examples. As an aside here, note that the `auto` keyword means we can save ourselves from first having to explicitly specify the iterator type, such as with this:

```
for (std::vector<double>::iterator iter = v.begin(); iter != v.end(); ++iter)
{
    // . . .
}
```

Range-based for *loops*, introduced in C++11, can make this code more elegant and functional. Instead of explicitly using the `vector` index, a range-based `for` loop simply says, "for every element x in v, do something with it," similar to what you would find using Python or R:

```
for (double x : v)
{
    cout << x << " ";
}
```

Range-based `for` loops can also be used in applying operations to the elements of a `vector`. As an example, we could calculate the sum of the elements in the vector v:

```
double sum = 0.0;
for (double x : v)
{
    sum += x;
}
```

With this, we are done. No worries about making a mistake with the index, and the code more obviously expresses what it is doing. The C++ Core Guidelines, in fact, tell us to prefer using range-based `for` loops (*https://oreil.ly/zvKke*) with `vector` objects, as well as with other standard containers that are discussed in Chapter 4.

The reference operator `&` can also be used in range-based `for` loops, similarly to functions:

```
for (double& x : v)
{
    x *= x;
}

// vector v is now 1, 4, 9, 16, 25

vector<string> sorry_dave{"Open", "the", "pod", "bay", "doors", "HAL"};
for (const string& s : sorry_dave)
{
    cout << s << " ";
}
```

The output is:

```
Open the pod bay doors HAL
```

The using Keyword

Another way to ease the pain with cryptic template types prior to C++11 was to use a `typedef`. Revisiting the preceding complex map example, we could define an alias, `complex_map`:

```
typedef std::map<std::string, std::complex<double>> complex_map;
```

Beginning with C++11, the `using` statement was extended to perform the same task, but in a more natural syntax:

```
using complex_map = std::map<std::string, std::complex<double>>;
```

The Core Guidelines recommend preferring `using` over `typedef`, first because of improved readability: "With `using`, the new name comes first rather than being embedded somewhere in a declaration."[3] There are also considerations with respect to advanced template methods, although these are beyond the scope of this book.

Uniform Initialization

C++11 introduced *uniform initialization*, also called *braced initialization*. There are several use cases, beginning with the simple case of initializing a numeric variable:

```
int i{100};
```

This isn't terribly interesting, as it simply replaces writing `int i = 100;`. However, what if we had the following?

```
double x = 92.09;

int k = x;        // Compiles, possibly with a warning
```

This will compile, albeit *possibly* (but not guaranteed) with a warning to the effect that the decimal part of x will be truncated, leaving k holding 92 alone. With uniform initialization, the compiler would issue a *narrowing conversion* error and halt the build, thus preventing unexpected results at runtime. This is a good thing, as it's better to catch errors at compile time rather than runtime:

```
int n{x};        // Compiler ERROR: narrowing conversion
```

An alternate equivalent form of uniform initialization is to put an equals sign between the variable name and the left brace:

```
int i_alt = {100};
vector<int> v = {1, 2, 3};
```

The particular style for using braced initialization adopted for this book, however, is braced initialization *without* the equals sign.

Uniform Initialization of a vector

In the case of a `vector`, uniform initialization requires an exception to the rule. Going by the previous discussion alone, you would probably expect the following to create a vector u of two integers:

```
vector<int> u{2};
```

However, as you saw prior to the current discussion, this will actually initialize a vector with one `int` element, 2. To create a vector v of two elements, you would still

---

3 "Prefer using over typedef for defining aliases" (*https://oreil.ly/zJsge*), ISO C++ Core Guidelines.

need to use the old parenthetical form to indicate that the 2 is a constructor argument and not a data value:

```
vector<int> v(2);
```

This may seem strange at first, but Chapter 4 and Appendix D provide some detailed reasons behind it.

Formatting Output

A new feature in the Standard Library as of C++20 worth mentioning is a new `std::format(.)` function that can format character and numerical data into a text format and return it as a `string` object.

For example, suppose we have two variables u and v that have been assigned some values:

```
double u = 1.5;
double v = 4.2;
```

If we want to output these values with the variable name labels, we could write something like the following:

```
cout << "u = " << u << ", v = " << v << "\n";
```

The output to the screen would then be as follows:

```
u = 1.5, v = 4.2
```

Chaining the chevrons together, however, can become tiresome. Instead, we can now use `format(.)` as follows:

```
#include <format>
. . .

string output = std::format("\nu = {0}, v = {1}\n", u, v);
cout << output;
```

This says to put the value held by u in the first (zero-indexed) position after "u = ", and then the value v in the following position. The output is then similar to before:

```
u = 1.5, v = 4.2
```

For those who are familiar with C#, you may notice this usage is similar in form to `Console.WriteLine(.)`.

Alternatively, as the `format(.)` function returns a `string` type, it can just be placed inside the cout statement:

```
using std::format;
cout << format("nu = {0}, v = {1}\n", u, v);
```

This gives us the following:

```
u = 1.5, v = 4.2
```

When the order is from left to right, however, the index values can be dropped, and the output results will be the same as shown in the preceding example:

```
cout << format("u = {}, v = {}\n", u, v);
```

In some cases, however, the index values are needed:

```
#include <cmath>     // To be covered in more detail later in this chapter

// . . .

cout << format("u = {0}, v = {1}, sin({0}) + {1} = {2}\n",
    u, v, std::sin(u) + v);
```

The order is then preserved in the output:

```
u = 1.5, v = 4.2, sin(1.5) + 4.2 = 5.197495
```

To reiterate, console output in production code would be rare, if ever, but it can be useful as a tool when learning C++ on its own. As such, it is used throughout the book for demonstrating output results.

Going forward, we will often assume a `using` statement exists so we can drop the `std::` scope when applying `format(.)` in code examples, similar to `vector`, `string`, and `cout` as noted earlier.

Class Template Argument Deduction

C++17 introduced *class template argument deduction (CTAD)*. Similar to `auto`, it will deduce the type of a template parameter based on the data being initialized. So, in place of the earlier example

```
std::vector<int> v_01{1, 2, 3};
```

we could instead drop the `int` template parameter to arrive at the same result:

```
std::vector v_02{1, 2, 3};
```

These examples are again trivial, using just hardcoded values, but CTAD in more realistic situations can lighten the notation and make your code more readable. You will see such examples later in the book, particularly in Chapter 8 when working with the multidimensional array view `std::mdspan`, a notable new feature in C++23.

Enumerated Constants and Scoped Enumerations

Prior to C++11, *enumerated constants* (more commonly called *enums* for short) were a great means of making it clearer for us mere mortals to comprehend integer codes by representing them as named constants. Using enums could also be far more efficient for the machine to process integers rather than passing bulkier `std::string` objects that take up more memory. And finally, errors caused by typos in quoted characters and stray strings could be avoided.

The C++11 Standard improved on this further with *scoped enumerations* (using `enum class`). These remove ambiguities that can occur with overlapping integer values when using regular enum constants, while preserving the advantages.

In what follows, the motivation for preferring the more modern scoped enumerations over integer-based enums is presented.

Enumerated constants

To start with an example, we could create an enum called `OptionType` that will represent the types of option deals that are allowed in a simple trading system, such as European, American, Bermudan, and Asian. The `enum` name (`OptionType`) is declared; then, inside the braces, the particular constant values are defined, separated by commas. By default, each will be assigned an integer value starting at zero and incremented by one (consistent with zero-based indexing in C++). The closing brace must be followed by a semicolon. In code, to illustrate, we could write the following:

```
enum OptionType
{
    European,   // default integer value = 0
    American,   // = European + 1 = 1, etc...
    Bermudan,   // = 2
    Asian       // = 3
};
```

Just to verify each corresponding integer value, output it to the screen:

```
cout << " European = " << European << "\n";
cout << " American = " << American << "\n";
cout << " Bermudan = " << Bermudan << "\n";
cout << " Asian = " << Asian << "\n";
cout << " American + Asian = " << American + Asian << "\n";
```

Checking the output, we get this:

```
European = 0
American = 1
Bermudan = 2
Asian = 3
American + Asian = 4
```

Potential conflicts with enums

As discussed at the outset, for any enum type, the default integer assignments start at zero and then are incremented by one for each value. Therefore, it is possible that two enumerated constants from two different types could be numerically equal. For example, suppose we define two enum types, called Football and Baseball, representing the defensive positions in each sport. By default, the baseball positions start with 0 for the pitcher and are incremented by one for each in the list. The same goes for the (American) football positions, starting with defensive tackle. The integer constants are provided in the comments:

```
enum Baseball
{
    Pitcher,        // 0
    Catcher,        // 1
    First_Baseman,  // 2
    Second_Baseman, // 3
    Third_Baseman,  // 4
    Shortstop,      // 5
    Left_Field,     // 6
    Center_Field,   // 7
    Right_Field     // 8
};

enum Football
{
    Defensive_Tackle, // 0
    Edge_Rusher,      // 1
    Defensive_End,    // 2
    Linebacker,       // 3
    Cornerback,       // 4
    Strong_Safety,    // 5
    Free_Safety       // 6
};
```

Then, we could compare Defensive_End and First_Baseman:

```
if (Defensive_End == First_Baseman)
{
    cout << "Defensive_End == First_Baseman\n";
}
else
{
    cout << "Defensive_End != First_Baseman\n";
}
```

Our result would be nonsense:

```
Defensive_End == First_Baseman
```

This is because both positions map to an integer value of 2. A quick fix, and one that was often employed prior to C++11, would be to reindex each set of enums:

```
enum Baseball
{
    Pitcher = 100,
    Catcher,        // 101
    First_Baseman,  // 102
    . . .
};

enum Football
{
    Defensive_Tackle = 200,
    Edge_Rusher,    // 201
    Defensive_End,  // 202
    . . .
};
```

Now, if we compare `Defensive_End` and `First_Baseman`, they will no longer be equal, because 202 ≠ 102. Still, large codebases might have hundreds of enum definitions, so it would not be out of the question for an overlap to slip in and cause errors. Enum classes, introduced in C++11, eliminate this risk.

Scoped enumerations with enum classes

Using modern C++, a more robust approach obviates manually manipulating enumeration integer values. The other benefits of enums still remain, such as avoiding cryptic raw numerical codes or relying on `string` objects, but the numerical conflicts like those shown in the previous examples are avoided by using a *scoped enumeration*, accomplished with an enum *class*, a new language feature in C++11. As an example, we could define bond and futures contract categories, as shown here:

```
enum class Bond_Type
{
    Government,
    Corporate,
    Municipal,
    Convertible
};

enum class Futures_Contract
{
    Gold,
    Silver,
    Oil,
    Natural_Gas,
    Wheat,
    Corn
};
```

Attempting to compare enumerators from two enum classes, such as a `Corporate` bond and a `Natural_Gas` futures position, will now result in a compiler error. For example, the following will not even compile:

```
if(Bond_Type::Corporate == Futures_Contract::Silver)
{
    // . . .
}
```

This works to our advantage, as again it is much better to catch an error at compile time rather than chase it at runtime. The Core Guidelines now maintain that we should prefer using enum classes rather than enumerated constants, to "minimize surprises."[4]

It is still possible to cast scoped enums to integer index values if desired. For example, each of `Bond::Corporate` and `FuturesContract::Silver` is the second member in its respective enum class, so by default each can be cast to a value of 1 (zero-indexed), even though they are not comparable:

```
cout << format("Corporate Bond index: {}\n",
static_cast<int>(Bond_Type::Corporate));
    cout << format("Natural Gas Futures index: {}\n",
        static_cast<int>(Futures_Contract::Natural_Gas));
```

The output is shown here:

```
1
3
```

It is also possible to explicitly assign particular index values in an `enum class`, if desired. For example:

```
// Explicitly set each index value:
enum class Futures_Contract
{
    Gold         = 100,
    Silver       = 102,
    Oil          = 104,
    Natural_Gas  = 106,
    Wheat        = 108,
    Corn         = 110
};
```

These integers can then be recovered by casting to `int` types:

```
// silver_int = 102
auto silver_int = static_cast<int>(Futures_Contract::Silver);
```

---

4 "Prefer class enums over *plain* enums" (*https://oreil.ly/vnGs9*), ISO C++ Core Guidelines.

```
// natural_gas_int = 106
auto natural_gas_int = static_cast<int>(Futures_Contract::Natural_Gas);
```

But again, there is no risk of equivalence with an enumerator from another enum class, as this is prevented by the compiler. In some cases, however, having numerical representations can be convenient, as you will see in later chapters.

Finally, enums in general, and enum classes in particular, are natural complements to switch/case statements. The following code outlines an example with a scoped enum:

```
void switch_statement_scoped_enum(Bond_Type bnd)
{
    switch (bnd)
    {
    case Bond_Type::Government:
        std::cout << "Government Bond..." << "\n";
        // Do stuff...
        break;
    case Bond_Type::Corporate:
        cout << "Corporate Bond..." << "\n";
        // Do stuff...
        break;
    case Bond_Type::Municipal:
        cout << "Municipal Bond..." << "\n";
        // Do stuff...
        break;
    case Bond_Type::Convertible:
        cout << "Convertible Bond..." << "\n";
        // Do stuff...
        break;
    default:
        cout << "Unknown Bond..." << "\n";
        // Check the bond type...
        break;
    }
}
```

Lambda Expressions

A *lambda expression* is often referred to as an *anonymous function object*, a term ostensibly coined from its original design proposal (*https://oreil.ly/Sxm3m*) back in 2006. Also known in the vernacular as a *lambda function*, or just a plain *lambda*, it can define a function (or more precisely, a *functor*, to be discussed in the next chapter) on the fly within the body of another function. Additionally, a lambda can be passed as an argument into another function. This last property is what makes them so powerful for use within standard algorithms, which again are covered in Chapter 5.

Lambda expressions are a welcome addition to the modern C++ arsenal. Introduced first in C++11, various enhancements were made in each subsequent release, including the most recent C++20 Standard. You can find a helpful summary of the evolution of these improvements in in Jonathan Boccara's blog post, "The Evolution of Lambdas in C++14, C++17, and C++20" (*https://oreil.ly/OdvWi*).

To begin the discussion, a lambda expression that prints out good old "Hello World!" can be written as follows inside an enclosing function:

```
void hello_world()
{
    auto f = []
    {
        std::cout << "Hello World!" << "\n";
    };

    f();
}
```

A lambda can also take in function arguments by using optional parentheses, a la a regular C++ function:

```
auto g = [](double x, double y)
{
    return x + y;
};

double z = g(9.2, 2.6);    // z = 11.8
```

Note three points at this stage.

First, by default, a lambda's return type is deduced following the same rules as those used for `auto` variables; that is, their return type is the type of the expression used for the `return` statement. However, we do have the option of indicating an explicit return type is an option, as follows:

```
auto g = [](double x, double y) -> double
{
    return x + y;
};
```

When the return type is readily obvious, however, the explicit type is typically dropped.

Second, be sure to place a semicolon at the end of the lambda block. When placed on a single line as in the first example, the lambda is somewhat obvious as it looks just like any other one-line C++ statement. However, the semicolon can be easily overlooked if your lambda implementation spans several lines, in which case your code will fail to compile.

Third, in cases of no function arguments, such as in the first example, the parentheses are generally optional (except, technically speaking, for special cases we need not be concerned with in this book), but the square brackets are mandatory in order to define a lambda. The square brackets in the previous examples are empty, but in general they provide the capture of the lambda expression.

The *capture* of a lambda expression does what it says: it captures (nonstatic) external variables, including objects, allowing them to be used inside the body of the lambda. The capture data may be taken in by value or by non-const reference, with the latter option potentially resulting in modification.

For example, suppose we have a vector of real numbers, u. We want to add a constant shift value to each element and then multiply each shifted value by a scalar alpha. We could write a lambda expression that captures u by reference, shift by value, and then takes alpha in as an argument. If written this way, u can be modified inside the lambda:

```
vector u{1.0, 1.5, 2.0, 2.5, 3.0, 3.5};
double shift = 0.25;
auto shift_scalar_mult = [&u, shift](double alpha)
{
    for (double& x : u)
    {
        x = alpha * (x + shift);
    }
};

shift_scalar_mult(-1.0);
```

In this example, u is modified to its new state, which is also reflected externally after the lambda is exited, because it is being captured by reference. After running this code, u will contain the values –1.25, –1.75, –2.25, –2.75, –3.25, and –3.75.

The capture in general can contain an arbitrary number of variables, but you need to be sure not to designate a single variable by both value and reference; for example, putting

```
[u, &u, shift]
```

in the preceding capture would result in a compiler error.

Wildcards in Lambda Captures

Using the wildcard [=] or [&] as a lambda capture will allow any preceding external variable or object to be captured by value or reference, respectively. There is some debate among C++ developers whether this is good practice, however. Probably the best way to summarize this salient point of view is to paraphrase from *Effective Modern C++:*[5]

- Using [&] can result in dangling references and undefined behavior.
- Using [=] could cause problems due to unexpected copying of pointers, including smart pointers.
- Avoiding these defaults can increase the probability of catching problems at compile time rather than at runtime.

These admonitions are observed in this book.

Mathematical Operators, Functions, and Constants in C++

Standard mathematical operators for numerical types are available as language features in C++. Common mathematical functions (such as cosine and exponential) plus a newer set of special functions are provided in the C++ Standard Library rather than in the core language.

Standard Arithmetic Operators

Addition, subtraction, multiplication, and division of numerical types are provided in C++ with the operators +, -, *, and /, respectively, as usually found in other programming languages. Furthermore, the modulus operator, %, is also defined for integral types (int, unsigned, long, etc.). Some examples are as follows:

```
// integers:
int i = 8;
int j = 5;
int k = i + 7;
int v = j - 3;
int u = i % j;

// double precision:
double x1 = 3.06;
double x2 = 8.74;
double x3 = 0.52;
double y = x1 + x2;
double z = x2 * x3;
```

---

5 Item 31 of *Effective Modern C++* (*https://oreil.ly/kzLpS*) by Scott Meyers, (O'Reilly, 2014), 217, 220.

The order and precedence of arithmetic operators are the same as found in most other programming languages, as well as middle school math for that matter:

- Order runs from left to right:

    ```
    i + j - v
    ```

    Using the preceding integer values would result in 8 + 5 – 2 = 11.

- Multiplication, division, and modulus take precedence over addition and subtraction:

    ```
    x1 + y / z
    ```

    Using the preceding double-precision values would result in the following:

    $$3.06 + \frac{11.8}{4.5448} = 3.06 + 2.5964 = 5.6564$$

    Use parentheses to change the precedence:

    ```
    (x1 + y) / z
    ```

    This would yield the following:

    $$\frac{14.86}{4.5448} = 3.2697$$

- Compound assignment operators are also included. For example,

    ```
    x1 = x1 + x2;
    ```

    can be replaced with addition assignment:

    ```
    x1 += x2;
    ```

The remaining operators -, *, /, and % also have their respective versions of compound assignment operators: -=, *=, /=, and %=.

Mathematical Functions in the Standard Library

Many of the usual mathematical functions we find in other languages are provided in the C++ Standard Library and have the same or similar syntax. Table 1-1 provides a non-exhaustive list of those commonly used in computational applications; x, y, and z are assumed to be double-precision variables.

Table 1-1. Commonly used Standard Library mathematical functions

C++	Description
cos(x)	Cosine of x
sin(x)	Sine of x
tan(x)	Tangent of x
exp(x)	Exponential function e^x
log(x)	Natural logarithm $ln(x)$
sqrt(x)	Square root of x
cbrt(x)	Cube root of x
pow(x, y)	x raised to the power of y
hypot(x, y)	Computes $\sqrt{x^2 + y^2}$
hypot(x, y, z)	Computes $\sqrt{x^2 + y^2 + z^2}$ (since C++17)
erf(x)	Computes the error function $\frac{2}{\sqrt{\pi}} \int_0^x e^{-u} \, du$

A comprehensive list of common mathematical functions is available on cppreference.com (*https://oreil.ly/B0t_n*).

As these are contained in the Standard Library rather than as language features, the cmath header file must be included in order to use them, with the functions scoped by the std:: prefix:

```
#include <cmath>      // Put this at top of the file.

double trig_fcn(double theta, double phi)
{
    return std::sin(theta) + std::cos(phi);
}

// Or, alternatively

double zero_coupon_bond(double face_value, double int_rate, double year_fraction)
{
    using std::exp;
    return face_value * exp(-int_rate * year_fraction);
}
```

Two points to note regarding <cmath> functions are as follows. First, C++ has no power operator. Unlike other languages, which typically indicate an exponent by a ^ or a ** operator, this does not exist as a C++ language feature (the operator ^ does exist but is not used for this purpose). Instead, we need to call the Standard Library std::pow(.) function in <cmath>. When computing polynomials, however, it may be more efficient to apply factoring per Horner's method and reduce the number of multiplicative operations, as described in Section 8.1 of *From Mathematics* *to Generic Programming* (*https://oreil.ly/aYPTt*) by Alexander Stepanov and Daniel Rose (Addison-Wesley, 2014). For example, if we wish to implement the function

$$f(x) = 8x^4 + 7x^3 + 4x^2 - 10x - 6$$

it can be written in C++ as

```
double f(double x)
{
    return x * (x * (x * (8.0 * x + 7.0) + 4.0 * x) - 10.0) - 6.0;
}
```

rather than

```
double f(double x)
{
    return 8.0 * std::pow(x, 4) + 7.0 * std::pow(x, 3) +
       4.0 * std::pow(x, 2) + 10.0 * x - 6.0;
}
```

As implementation of `std::pow` is vendor-specific, performance results may vary. There may also be differences due to compiler optimizations. However, Horner's method does reduce the number of operations, and as such it is often preferred.

For a noninteger exponent, say,

$$g(x,y) = x^{-1.368x} + 5.311y$$

there is no available alternative to using `std::pow(.)`:

```
double g(double x, double y)
{
    return std::pow(x, -1.368 * x) + 5.311 * y;
}
```

Second, you might be able to use some of these functions without `#include <cmath>`. This is unfortunately one of the quirks in C++ due to its long association with C; however, the moral of the story is quite simple: to keep C++ code ISO-compliant, and thus help ensure compatibility across different compilers and operating system platforms, we should always use `#include <cmath>` and scope the math functions with `std::`.

A prime example is the absolute value function. In some C++ Standard Library implementations, the default (global namespace) abs(.) function might be a carry-over from math.h that was implemented only for integer types in C. To calculate the absolute value of a floating-point number in math.h, we would need to use the fabs(.) function. However, std::abs(.) is overloaded for *both* integer and floating-point (e.g., double) arguments and should be preferred.

It is also the case that the <cmath> functions have been evolving separately from their C counterparts, including optimizations particular to C++. This is one more reason to prefer the Standard Library versions. The *GNU C++ Library Manual* explains:[6]

> The standard specifies that if one includes the C-style header (<math.h> in this case), the symbols will be available in the global namespace and perhaps in namespace std:: (but this is no longer a firm requirement). On the other hand, including the C++-style header (<cmath>) guarantees that the entities will be found in namespace std and perhaps in the global namespace.

So, long story short: use #include <cmath> and scope math functions with std::.

Mathematical Special Functions

Mathematical special functions include Legendre polynomials, Hermite polynomials, Bessel functions, and the exponential integral. These were added to the Standard Library in C++17, and they also require inclusion of the <cmath> header. These functions are often employed in physics, but as quantitative finance has a strong historical ties to the physics world, you may come across them in advanced derivatives modeling. In one of the most well-known and cited papers on options pricing, "Valuing American Options by Simulation: A Simple Least-Squares Approach" (*https://oreil.ly/sW010*) by Francis A. Longstaff and Eduardo S. Schwartz, both Legendre and Hermite polynomials can be used as a basis (among others) for the underlying model.

Further discussion is beyond the intended scope of this book, but you can find more details about the special math functions on cppreference.com (*https://oreil.ly/JOHy9*).

Standard Library Mathematical Constants

A handy addition to the C++20 Standard Library is a set of commonly used mathematical constants, such as the values of π, e, and $\sqrt{2}$. Some of those that may be convenient for quantitative finance applications are shown in Table 1-2.

---

6 Paolo Carlini et al., *The GNU C++ Library Manual* (*https://oreil.ly/e9b5x*), "The C Headers and namespace std."

Table 1-2. Standard Library mathematical constants

C++ constant	Definition
e	e
pi	π
inv_pi	$\frac{1}{\pi}$
inv_sqrt_pi	$\frac{1}{\sqrt{\pi}}$
sqrt2	$\sqrt{2}$

To use these constants, we must first include the `<numbers>` header in the Standard Library. Each must be scoped with the `std::numbers` namespace. For example, to implement the function

$$f(x) = \frac{1}{\sqrt{2\pi}}\Big(sin(\pi x) + cos\big(\tfrac{y}{\pi}\big)\Big)$$

we could write this:

```
#include <cmath>
#include <numbers>
. . .
double math_constant_fcn(double x, double y)
{
    using namespace std::numbers;

    double math_inv_sqrt_two_pi =
        inv_sqrtpi / sqrt2;

    return math_inv_sqrt_two_pi * (std::sin(pi * x) +
        std::cos(inv_pi * y));
}
```

This way, whenever π is used in calculations, for example, its value will be consistent throughout the program, rather than leaving it up to different programmers on a project who might use approximations out to varying precisions, resulting in possible inconsistencies in numerical results.

In addition, the value of $\sqrt{2}$, which can crop up somewhat frequently in mathematical calculations, does not have to be computed with

```
std::sqrt(2.0)
```

each time it is needed. The constant

```
std::numbers::sqrt2
```

holds the double-precision approximation itself. While perhaps of trivial consequence in terms of one-off performance, repeated calls to the std::sqrt function millions of times in computationally intensive code would potentially have some effect.

 While not essential to know at this point, it is worth mentioning that these constants are fixed at compile time rather than computed with each call runtime, using a C++11 designation called constexpr.

As a closing note, it is somewhat curious that the set of mathematical constants provided in C++20 include the value $\frac{1}{\sqrt{3}}$, but not $\frac{1}{\sqrt{2}}$ or $\frac{1}{\sqrt{2\pi}}$, despite the latter two being far more commonly present mathematical and statistical functions, including those used in finance. These latter two are, however, included in the Boost Math Toolkit library, covered in Chapter 9.

Naming Conventions

Guidelines on code formatting and variable naming are quite important when writing critical production code in financial systems, in a feature-rich language such as C++. Bugs, runtime errors, and program crashes are much more easily avoided or addressed if the source code is written in a consistent, clean, and maintainable state.

So far, we have just been plowing ahead with examples without discussing this topic. The examples have been fairly simple so far, but as code gets more involved, it is a good idea to step back and conclude this chapter with a brief discussion about naming conventions and coding style, and the style guidelines that are used in this book. More importantly, in real-life financial C++ development work, the code you work with and write will take a quantum leap in complexity, so these issues become a necessity.

To review some fundamentals from introductory C++, variable, function, and class names can be any contiguous combination of letters and numbers, subject to the following conditions:

- Names must begin with a letter or an underscore; leading numerals are not allowed (nonleading numerals are). Leading underscores, however, are best avoided (see the Note that follows).

- Other than the underscore character, special characters such as @, =, and $ are not allowed.

- Spaces are not allowed. Names must be contiguous.

- Language keywords are reserved and are not allowed to also be names, such as `double`, `if`, and `while`.

You can find a complete listing of reserved keywords on cppreference.com (*https:// oreil.ly/oMmJg*).

 Technically speaking, names beginning with an underscore are legal; however, in reality, they are often reserved for implementations of the C++ Standard and so are typically discouraged (*https:// wg21.link/n4868*) per Section 5.10 of the C++ Standard, Working Draft. Some variable naming styles (for example, as exhibited in the Google C++ Style Guide (*https://oreil.ly/h8uhm*)) do prescribe *trailing* underscores for private class members—for example, `member_variable_`. This meaning of a trailing underscore will also be adopted for code examples used in this book.

Single-letter variable and function names are fine for simple examples and plain mathematical functions. However, for quantitative financial models implementation, and for trading and risk systems, it will usually be better to pass function arguments with more descriptive names. Function and class names should also provide some indication of what they do. Furthermore, it is important to decide as a group or company on a set of naming and style rules in order to enhance code maintainability and reduce the risk of bugs getting into the code.

Several naming styles have been common over the years:

Lower camel case
> The first word is lowercase, and the first letter of the following words is capitalized: `optionDelta`, `riskFreeRate`, `efficientFrontier`

Upper camel case, aka Pascal case
> The first letter of each word is uppercase: `OptionDelta`, `RiskFreeRate`, `EfficientFrontier`

Snake case
> Each word is lowercase, separated by an underscore character: `option_delta`, `risk_free_rate`, `efficient_frontier`

Lower camel and snake cases are typically found in C++ function and variable names, and class names are usually in upper camel form. Users should adopt the style of their team and in general be comfortable with each style. In this book, we will use snake case for function and variable names, and upper camel for class names. As noted earlier, trailing underscores will be used for private member variables and member functions; here's an example:

```
class Blah
{
    public:
        Blah(double x, . . .);
        void calc_blah(double y) const;

        . . .

    private:
        double x_;

        double do_something_();
};
```

When single characters are used for integral counting variables, using the Fortran convention of letters i through n is still common, although this is not required. We will also adopt this practice for the most part.

For an example of how *not* to write code, "How to Write Unmaintainable Code: Ensure a Job for Life ;-)" (*https://oreil.ly/RpQ6g*) by Roedy Green provides a humorous but not irrelevant viewpoint. To quote Homer Simpson, "It's funny because it's true" (d'oh).

Summary

C++ is broadly divided into two components: language features and the Standard Library. Taken together, they are typically referred to as *the Standard*, and the major compiler vendors (particularly "the big three," Microsoft Visual Studio (*https://oreil.ly/Kz06Z*), LLVM Clang (*https://clang.llvm.org/*), and GNU gcc (*https://gcc.gnu.org/*)) also include their respective Standard Library distributions with their compiler releases. Implementation of the Standard Library is mostly left up to the individual vendor, as long as they comply with the ISO Standard requirements.

There is some history behind the rise and fall in popularity of C++ in financial software development, and its subsequent resurgence. After some struggles competing with Java and C#, C++ started to experience a bit of a renaissance in this domain with the release of C++11. With subsequent releases every three years—currently C++23—new features and inexpensive abstractions have supplanted a lot of coding that once had to be done from scratch, resulting in cleaner code when used effectively. Some of these, such as the auto keyword, range-based for loops, scoped enums, lambda expressions, and mathematical constants, were discussed here. Further specific examples as applied to financial software follow in subsequent chapters.

Further Resources

A recommended resource for learning more about good modern C++ programming style guidelines is Chapter 3 (*https://oreil.ly/JEYMV*) of the freely available online book *C++ Best Practices* by Jason Turner. Its content is also relevant to topics covered in Chapters 2 and 3 of this book.

If you're interested in Python/C++ integration with pybind11, Steven Zhang has created some straightforward examples on GitHub (*https://oreil.ly/igNwY*) to help you get started.

For more information on getting started with Rcpp and integrating reusable C++ code in R packages, a series of blog posts (*https://oreil.ly/JsKWu*) by the author were published in 2020. The link provided points to the final post in the series, from which links to each post can be found, starting from the beginning.

CHAPTER 2

Writing User-Defined Classes with Modern C++ Features

User-defined classes have been a mainstay in financial C++ development from the beginning, because instruments and data (such as bonds, options contracts, and rate curves) can be naturally represented by objects. One useful feature that has existed prior to C++11 is the overloading of the parentheses () operator, which enables an object to be utilized as a *function object*, or *functor*. In general, functors are objects that "behave like functions, but, like objects, can manage additional data."[1] As you will see, this is particularly convenient when we might need to find the root of a function, such as when calculating the implied volatility of a traded options contract.

A newer form of a functor, called a *lambda expression* (also known as a *lambda function* or just a *lambda*), was added to the language with C++11, as previously discussed in Chapter 1. This chapter covers lambdas in further detail, with examples of how they can be used for refactoring functionality into a single location and thus reduce code duplication. Lambdas can also be passed as function arguments. Functors, including lambda expressions, will also be key within the context of *Standard Template Library (STL) algorithms*, covered in Chapter 5.

Move semantics were another major addition to the C++11 Standard, allowing an often significant efficiency gain by *transferring possession* of a constructor input argument to its respective member variable. This chapter also covers in-class initialization of member data in a header file, the default keyword, and the *three-way operator*, also commonly called the *spaceship operator*, which was first released in C++20. Each of these modern additions can improve reliability and maintainability in class design.

---

1 Nicolai Josuttis, *Object-Oriented Programming in C++* (Wiley, 2002), 542, section 9.2.2.

A Black-Scholes Class

The Black-Scholes model might sometimes seem like the "Hello World!" of quantitative finance programming, but we can use it to review some important points about writing user-defined classes, as well as illustrate more-modern additions to the C++ Standard, such as lambda expressions, a fixed-length array container (`std::array`), and enum classes.

To start, recall that the Black-Scholes pricing formula applies to calculating the value V of an (equity) option with strike price X, where the underlying spot (share) price is S. Trading of the option is assumed to start at some time $t = 0$, with expiration at some time $T > 0$, with time measured in units of years, or as a year fraction. The option can be valued at any time t where $0 \leq t \leq T$, at which point the remaining time to expiration is thus $T - t$. A nicely presented version that lends itself well to implementation in code can be found in *Option Theory*, upon which the following is based:[2]

$$V = \phi\left[Se^{-q(T-t)}N(\phi d_1) - Xe^{-r(T-t)}N(\phi d_2)\right]$$

where

$\phi = 1$ for a call option, -1 for a put option

$q =$ the continuous annual dividend rate

$r =$ the continuous annual risk-free interest rate

$\sigma =$ the annual volatility

$N(x)$ is the standard normal cumulative distribution function (CDF),

and d_1 and d_2 are defined as follows:

$$d_1 = \frac{log\left(\frac{S}{X}\right) + \left(r - q + \frac{1}{2}\sigma^2\right)(T-t)}{\sigma\sqrt{T-t}}$$

$$d_2 = d_1 - \sigma\sqrt{T-t}$$

---

2 Peter James, *Option Theory* (Wiley, 2003), section 5.2.

Representing the Payoff

Before proceeding to the class design, we can appeal to an enum class to represent the payoff of an option, a call, or a put. Recall from Chapter 1 that it is possible to associate integer values with each scoped enumerator while still ensuring that they remain noncomparable with enumerators of other enum classes. This way, we can obtain the values ± 1 "for free":

```
enum class PayoffType
{
    Call = 1,
    Put = -1
};
```

We can recover the value of ϕ by casting the scoped enum to an integer:

```
auto payoff_type = PayoffType::Call;
// . . .

int phi = static_cast<int>(payoff_type);        // phi = 1
```

This value can then be used in the pricing formula.

Writing the Class Declaration

We can now propose the following declaration for the class:

```
#include <array>    // std::array (introduced in C++11, see the NOTE that follows)

class BlackScholes
{
public:
    // default dividend = 0
    BlackScholes(double strike, double spot, double time_to_exp,
        PayoffType payoff_type, double rate, double div = 0.0);

    double operator()(double vol);

private:
    std::array<double, 2> compute_norm_args_(double vol);

    double strike_, spot_, time_to_exp_;
    PayoffType payoff_type_;
    double rate_, div_;
};
```

The constructor will take in each of the required arguments except for the volatility, which will be used as an argument by the () operator to compute and return the price. This will allow us to reuse the class later in order to compute the implied volatility numerically. In this example, a default value of 0 has been set for the dividend rate in the constructor declaration.

The private member function `compute_norm_args_(double vol)` will calculate the d_1 and d_2 values, and it will return them in a fixed two-element `std::array` container. These will then be used as arguments in the standard normal CDF to compute $N(d_1)$ and $N(d_2)$ in the Black-Scholes pricing formula.

A `std::array` container is an array with the number of elements fixed at compile time. It was added to the Standard Library in C++11. In this example, this array will contain the values d_1 and d_2 in the Black-Scholes formula, so it is returned as a `std::array <double, 2>` type, where the 2 refers to the number of elements it contains. Chapter 4 provides more details but this explanation should give you enough information to work through the present example.

Writing the Class Implementation

We can start by implementing the constructor, as follows:

```
BlackScholes::BlackScholes(double strike, double spot, double time_to_exp,
    PayoffType payoff_type, double rate, double div) :
    strike_{strike}, spot_{spot}, time_to_exp_{time_to_exp},
    payoff_type_{payoff_type}, rate_{rate}, div_{div}
```

Note that in general, it is good practice per the Core Guidelines to ensure that all member data is initialized at construction (*https://oreil.ly/hD0la*), as shown in the constructor initializer list (*https://oreil.ly/K4CiK*) following the colon in the implementation. Also, each member variable should be initialized in the order in which it is declared; otherwise, it "can make it hard to see order-dependent bugs."[3]

Valuation of the option then begins with the parentheses operator, as defined next, taking in the volatility as input. The steps numbered (1) through (8) are described following this code block.

```
double BlackScholes::operator()(double vol)
{
    using std::exp;
    // phi, as in the James book (reference {5}):
    const int phi = static_cast<int>(payoff_type_);      ❶

    if (time_to_exp_ > 0.0)                              ❷
    {
        auto norm_args = compute_norm_args_(vol);        ❸
        double d1 = norm_args[0];
        double d2 = norm_args[1];
```

---

3 "Discussion: Define and initialize data members in the order of member declaration" (*https://oreil.ly/Mdv22*), ISO C++ Core Guidelines, May 11, 2024.

```
        auto norm_cdf = [](double x)                              ❹
        {
            return (1.0 + std::erf(x / std::numbers::sqrt2)) / 2.0;
        };

        double nd_1 = norm_cdf(phi * d1);               // N(d1) ❺
        double nd_2 = norm_cdf(phi * d2);               // N(d2)
        double disc_fctr = exp(-rate_ * time_to_exp_);  ❻

        return phi * (spot_ * exp(-div_ * time_to_exp_)
            * nd_1 - disc_fctr * strike_ * nd_2);       ❼
    }
    else
    {
        // std::max in <algorithm> (to be covered in Chapter 5)
        return std::max(phi * (spot_ - strike_), 0.0);  ❽
    }
}
```

❶ The value of ϕ (phi) in the Black-Scholes formula is recovered by casting the payoff type enumerator to its constant integer equivalent.

❷ The nontrivial case for pricing an option is before it has expired (`time_to_exp_ > 0.0`). In this case, the Black-Scholes formula is applied.

❸ We calculate the values of d_1 and d_2, which will be used as arguments in the standard normal CDF. These are stored in the `array<double, 2>` container `norm_args` and accessed by using the usual square bracket operator.

❹ $N(d_1)$ and $N(d_2)$ are then determined by invoking the *error function* (*https://oreil.ly/lGF4z*) `erf(.)` that is available to us in `<cmath>` (discussed in Chapter 1)

$$N(x) = \frac{1 + \mathrm{erf}\left(\frac{x}{\sqrt{2}}\right)}{2}$$

where

$$erf(z) = \int_0^z e^{-t^2} dt$$

We could have implemented this with brute force:

```
        double nd_1 = 1.0 + std::erf( (phi * d1) / std::numbers::sqrt2;   // N(d1)
        double nd_2 = 1.0 + std::erf( (phi * d2) / std::numbers::sqrt2;   // N(d2)
```

However, although perhaps a seemingly trivial example, mistakes can happen, such as accidentally using a minus sign instead of a plus sign when computing nd_2:

```
// This is OK:
double nd_1 = 1.0 + std::erf( (phi * d1) / std::numbers::sqrt2;    // N(d1)

// Error: minus sign
double nd_2 = 1.0 - std::erf( (phi * d2) / std::numbers::sqrt2;    // N(d2)
```

Instead, we can make the code cleaner by factoring out this expression into a *lambda expression* (again, introduced in Chapter 1), thus avoiding problems like that shown just previously:

```
auto norm_cdf = [](double x)
{
    return (1.0 + std::erf(x / std::numbers::sqrt2)) / 2.0;
};
```

❺ A lambda expression allows us to place what is essentially a function as a statement inside another function. In the present example, it furthermore helps eliminate duplicate code. It can be called just like any other function:

```
double nd_1 = norm_cdf(phi * d1);      // N(d1)
double nd_2 = norm_cdf(phi * d2);      // N(d2)
```

❻ Finally, the discount factor from T back to time t (time_to_exp_ = $T - t$) is computed.

❼ The preceding intermediate results are then placed in the Black-Scholes formula, with the result returned as the calculated option price.

❽ In the event the option is expired, its value is simply the raw payoff. Note that by using the enum class PayoffType and assigning its designated integer equivalent to phi_, we avoid several extra lines comprising an if/else statement.

As examples, consider an in-the-money (ITM) call function at expiration, and an out-of-the-money (OTM) put option with time remaining. In the real world, data would be obtained via an interface, but let's simulate it as follows:

```
double strike = 75.0;
auto payoff_type = PayoffType::Call;
double spot = 100.0;
double rate = 0.05;
double vol = 0.25;
double time_to_exp = 0.0;
```

First, calculate the value of the ITM call, assuming the default dividend rate of zero. In this case, control drops to line ❸, which just calculates and returns the payoff value at expiration:

```
// ITM Call at expiration (time_to_exp = 0):
BlackScholes bsc_itm_exp{strike, spot, rate, time_to_exp, payoff_type};

double value = bsc_itm_exp(vol);    // $25
```

If time remains until expiration, the program will progress from steps ❸ to ❼ to calculate the Black-Scholes formula price. In this example, we will assume that three months ($T - t = 0.25$) remain until expiration; and just for fun, we will also assume an annualized dividend rate of 7.5% for the underlying equity:

```
// OTM put with time remaining:
time_to_exp = 0.25;
double dividend = 0.075;
payoff_type = PayoffType::Put;

BlackScholes bsp_otm_tv{strike, spot, time_to_exp, payoff_type, rate, dividend};
value = bsp_otm_tv(vol);             // = 0.04487
```

The results are $25 for the ITM call (at expiration) and approximately $0.05 for the OTM put (with time value remaining).

Using a Functor for Root Finding: Implied Volatility

Functors become convenient in numerical analysis applications, such as root finding. A common case in computational finance is calculating the implied volatility of an option, given its market price, as there is no closed-form solution. This is the motivation for making the functor in the BlackScholes class a function of the option volatility.

As an example, we can apply the well-known secant method (*https://oreil.ly/KFHb_*) to determine the root of the function

$$f = V(\sigma; \phi, S, r, q, t, T) - V_m$$

where V_m is the observed market price of the option. The values to the right of the semicolon as mathematical arguments of the function V can be considered fixed values (parameters in the mathematical sense), while allowing σ to vary.

The secant method says for a function $y = f(x)$, where f is a twice continuously differentiable function, we can find a root of f by using the iteration

$$x_{i+1} = x_i - f(x_i) \frac{x_i - x_{i-1}}{f(x_i) - f(x_{i-1})}$$

given two initial guesses for the volatility (x_0 and x_1), provided it converges.

Because a `BlackScholes` object maintains the state of its parameters and computes its option value in terms of volatility, implementing the secant method becomes a simpler and cleaner task, avoiding a long list of individual option valuation parameters in the implied volatility function. Also, because an option value is monotonically increasing with respect to volatility, there can only be one root. We could then implement the secant method to locate this root, as follows, with the individually numbered steps again described after the code:

```cpp
#include <cmath>     // std::nan(.) (explained in the discussion that follows)

double implied_volatility_with_lambda(const BlackScholes& bsc,
    double opt_mkt_price, double x0, double x1, double tol,
    unsigned max_iter)                                          ❶
{
    auto diff = [&bsc, opt_mkt_price](double x)
    {
        return bsc(x) - opt_mkt_price;
    };

    double y0 = diff(x0);                                       ❷
    double y1 = diff(x1);

    double impl_vol = 0.0;
    unsigned count_iter = 0;
    for (count_iter = 0; count_iter <= max_iter; ++count_iter)  ❸
    {
        // x0, x1: store previous and updated volatility values
        // through each iteration.

        // y0, y1: store previous and updated values of
        // BSc opt price - opt mkt price.

        if (std::abs(x1 - x0) > tol)
        {
            impl_vol = x1 - (x1 - x0) * y1 / (y1 - y0);

            // Update x1 & x0:
            x0 = x1;
            x1 = impl_vol;
            y0 = y1;

            // Use lambda expression instead of y1 = bsc(x1) - opt_mkt_price:
            y1 = diff(x1);
        }
        else
        {
            return x1;          // (convergence) ❹
        }
    }
}
```

```
        return std::nan("");        //  (does not converge) ❺

}
```

❶ The function first takes in a `BlackScholes` object that holds the parameters of *V* previously discussed, followed by the option price `opt_mkt_price` (usually as observed in the market) for which we want to compute the implied volatility. The remaining input values are the two initial guesses (`x0` and `x1`), followed by a convergence tolerance value `tol` and maximum number of iterations `max_iter`.

❷ The initial function values `y0` and `y1` can be obtained by first calling the functor on the `bsc` object at each of `x0` and `x1`, and then subtracting the market option price. Rather than code the same subtraction operation twice,

```
        double y0 = bsc(x0) - opt_mkt_price;
        double y1 = bsc(x1) - opt_mkt_price;
```

a lambda expression named `diff(.)` is used, for reasons similar to those discussed within the context of the Black-Scholes model implementation previously.

❸ `diff(.)` is also called from within the secant method iteration that follows, with `x0` and `x1` assigned to the updated "initial" values x_i and x_{i+1}. This will continue until either the maximum number of iterations is hit, or

❹ it converges to the implied volatility per the given tolerance `tol` and returns the root (`x1`).

❺ Otherwise, if the loop reaches the maximum number of iterations before reaching convergence, `std::nan("")` (in `<cmath>`), representing *"not a number"* as a `double` type, is returned, indicating an error condition. There are error-handling methods perhaps more suitable for production code, such as using `std::numeric_limits` (*https://oreil.ly/8s2SS*), but rather than dive into those particulars, `std::nan("")` should be adequate for this example.

As an example, suppose we have an ITM call option with the following contract and market data, again with a positive dividend rate (and again pretending this is coming from a system interface, not hard-coded data):

```
double strike = 95.0;
double mkt_opt_price = 6.2;        // Current option price quoted in the market
auto payoff_type = PayoffType::Call;
double spot = 100.0;
double rate = 0.05;
double dividend = 0.07;
double time_to_exp = 0.25;
```

Then, construct a `BlackScholes` object using this data:

```
BlackScholes bsc_impl_vol{strike, spot, rate, time_to_exp, payoff_type};
```

Next, choose two initial guesses for the secant method:

```
double init_vol_guess_1 = 0.1;
double init_vol_guess_2 = 0.15;
```

And set the tolerance and maximum number of iterations:

```
double tol = 1e-6;
unsigned max_iter = 1000;
```

Now, supply `bsc_impl_vol` and the two initial guesses, along with the current market price of the option, as arguments in the implied volatility root-finding function:

```
double impl_vol = implied_volatility(bsc_impl_vol, mkt_opt_price,
    init_vol_guess_1, init_vol_guess_2 , tol, max_iter);
```

We can first test whether the result is not a number by using the boolean `std::isnan(.)` function, also in `<cmath>`. If the first condition is true, we have convergence, in which case the implied volatility value is displayed, as well as verification that we can recover the market option price by calculating the Black-Scholes price at this same volatility level, as follows:

```
if (!std::isnan(impl_vol))
{
    cout << format("Call ITM, time to expiration = {}, ", time_to_exp);
    cout << format("Implied vol = {}\n", impl_vol);

    double opt_val = bsc_impl_vol(impl_vol);
    cout << format("Value of option at implied vol = {}, ", opt_val);
    cout << format("Market option price = {}\n", mkt_opt_price);
}
else
{
    // Handle the case where the secant method fails to converge --
    // one option would be to throw an exception,
    // but more simply for this example:
    cout << "No convergence to implied volatility\n";
}
```

In this case, we get convergence, and hence the following approximate output:

```
Call ITM, time to expiration = 0.25, implied vol = 0.18501
Value of option at implied vol = 6.20000, market option price = 6.2
```

Move Semantics and Special Member Functions

Object-oriented programming in C++03, especially when designing user-defined classes, required special attention to four special member functions on a class:

- Default constructor
- Copy constructor
- Copy assignment operator
- Destructor

Defaults for each were (and still are) provided by the compiler. *Move semantics*, another major enhancement in C++11, allow us to transfer ownership of an object, as opposed to copying it, thus avoiding a potentially nontrivial performance hit due to object copy. Move semantics have become convenient for financial programming, as often only the transfer of ownership is actually required, obviating the need for two copies of the same object.

With move semantics came two new special member functions, the *move constructor* and the *move assignment operator*, analogous to the copy constructor and copy assignment operator. In addition, new and more straightforward ways of disabling or declaring a special member function as its default were also added as language features in C++11.

This section also presents C++11 features regarding the default constructor. Updated features since C++11 related to the copy constructor, copy assignment operator, and destructor will be discussed within a more relevant context in Chapter 3.

Data Members and Performance Considerations

A frequent problem in pre-C++11 development was something simple: initializing and storing a *subobject member* of an *enclosing* object. A decision would come down to safety versus speed. The safe approach would incur the cost of object copy, while opting for speed could open a program up to runtime problems.

As an example, at a high level, suppose we have a live trading analytics tool to compute metrics used to determine intraday patterns, and assume that it takes in large sequences of live market data. We can sketch out a (simple) class that takes in the data as a `vector` and uses it for this purpose:

```
class PatternAnalytics
{
public:
    PatternAnalytics(const std::vector<double>& data_in, . . .);
    double moving_average(. . .) const;
    double exponential_moving_average(. . .) const;
    double relative_strength_index(. . .) const;
```

```
private:
    std::vector<double> data_;

};
```

In this case, a `PatternAnalytics` instance would be the enclosing object, and its `data_` member would be the subobject member. In its current form, a `vector` (say, `data`) could be passed to the constructor as a reference to a `const` `vector` (or `const` reference, as it is often referred to for short), which avoids the copy penalty from binding to the constructor argument value. However, the initialization of the `data_` member in the implementation of the constructor will result in an object copy:

```
// Constructor implementation (initialization will involve object copy):
PatternAnalytics::PatternAnalytics(const std::vector<double>& data_in, . . .) :
    data_{data_in}, . . .
{
    // . . .
}
```

On the upside, the `PatternAnalytics` object would have exclusive *ownership* of its `data_` member, but for a large `vector`, the copy penalty at initialization could be significant.

Prior to C++11, programmers would sometimes prevent object copying by instead defining the subobject `prices_` member as a `const` reference:

```
class PatternAnalytics
{
public:
    PatternAnalytics(const std::vector<double>& data_in, . . .);
    // . . .

private:
    // Now stored as a reference to an external vector:
    const std::vector<double>& data_;

};
```

Designed this way, an enclosing `PatternAnalytics` object would be *non-owning*. While this approach will likely prevent performance hits due to object copy, it can introduce other problems. In particular, it creates the potential for the `data_` member being modified from outside the `PatternAnalytics` object. Worse, if in a multithreaded context, the `PatternAnalytics` object could end up referring to a destroyed object. Another issue is *shallow copy*, where two `PatternAnalytics` objects end up sharing the same `data_` vector.

Under controlled circumstances, the performance reward might have been deemed worth the risk. However, it would be even better to have the `PatternAnalytics` object retain exclusive ownership of its `data_` member, but without the overhead of an object copy. This is now possible with *move semantics*, introduced in C++11.

An Introduction to Move Semantics

Let's start with an example to present the basics of what it means when an object is moved. Suppose we have a class called `SimpleClass` that simply stores a single `int` value as a member:

```
class SimpleClass
{
    public:
        SimpleClass(int k);
        int get_val() const;        // Accessor function, aka a "getter"
        void reset_val(int k);      // Mutator function, aka a "setter"


    private:
        int k_;
};

// Implementation:
SimpleClass::SimpleClass(int k) :k_{k} {}
int SimpleClass::get_val() const
{
    return k_;        // Private member on SimpleClass
}

void SimpleClass::reset_val(int k)
{
    k_ = k;
}


// Elsewhere (e.g. in main() function), create an instance:
SimpleClass sc_01{78};
```

If we need an additional but identical `SimpleClass`, we can of course copy it, using the default copy constructor provided by the compiler:

```
SimpleClass another_sc{sc_01};        // Copy constructor
```

In general, this can come with the overhead of object copy. In this particular case, because the data member is simply an `int`, the performance hit would be nil. If we had one or more large objects as data members, such as a large `vector`, the penalty would become significant.

Suppose instead we won't need the original object after the duplicate is created. In this case, we can more efficiently *move* the original to the target instead of copying, a feature introduced in C++11. Again, in the general sense, the motivation is to eliminate the performance penalty of object copy. It is accomplished by invoking an object's *move constructor*.

Returning to the trivial SimpleClass example to demonstrate the mechanics, we first need to include the <utility> header in the Standard Library, which allows us to use the std::move(.) function as the input parameter for the move constructor:

```
#include <utility>

// . . .

SimpleClass move_sc_01{std::move(sc_01)};      // Move constructor called
```

Alternatively, the move constructor would be called if we replaced the previous line of code to the following, using the = operator, as move_sc does not yet exist:

```
SimpleClass move_sc_01 = std::move(sc_01);       // Move constructor called
```

Similar to the copy constructor in this example, here the default move constructor on SimpleClass has been called. What essentially happens is all the member data on the moved object is taken away from it and placed in the moved-to object, "stolen," in a sense. So, in this case, if we accessed the k_ value on move_sc_01, it would return 78. The mechanics behind std::move(.), however, do not actually move anything from sc_01 to move_sc_01. Rather, std::move(sc_01) casts sc_01 to an *rvalue reference*—namely, an "argument from which we may move."[4] The term *rvalue* traditionally stems from it being an "anonymous temporar[y] that can appear only on the righthand side of an assignment."[5] In the context of C++, this can also extend to the righthand side of other operators.

This is opposed to the terms *lvalue* and *lvalue reference*, which relate to the same references we have known and loved prior to C++11:

```
SimpleClass sc_02{12};           // sc_02 is an lvalue
SimpleClass& sc_lval = sc_02;    // sc_lval is an lvalue reference
```

As function parameters, rvalue references are indicated by a double ampersand operator. If we were to implement the SimpleClass move constructor, its signature would be of this form:

```
SimpleClass(SimpleClass&& to_be_moved);
```

The signature of a copy constructor, in contrast, uses a const lvalue reference as its parameter:

```
SimpleClass(const SimpleClass& to_be_copied);
```

---

4 Bjarne Stroustrup, *A Tour of C++* (*https://oreil.ly/2EATE*), 3rd edition (Addison Wesley, 2022), section 6.2.2.

5 Nicolai Josuttis, *The C++ Standard Library* (*https://oreil.ly/yT14P*), 2nd edition (Addison-Wesley, 2012), 20, section 3.1.5.

A default *move assignment operator* is also provided by the compiler, allowing us to move a new `SimpleClass` object to one that exists (`move_sc`) a priori:

```
SimpleClass sc_03{23};

// move_assignment_target.k_ = 53:
SimpleClass move_assignment_target{53};

// move_assignment_target.k_ now = 23:
move_assignment_target = std::move(sc_03);
```

Be aware that attempting to create an rvalue reference to a non-rvalue object—that is, an object not cast to a temporary movable state—will not compile:

```
SimpleClass&& sc_err = sc_03;        // Compiler error!
```

The topic of rvalues and lvalues can descend into a lengthy and complex discussion rather quickly, so this explanation has been kept brief and related specifically to the task at hand—namely, how to *use* move semantics. If you wish to read deeper into the subject, it is covered in robust detail in Section 13.6.1 of C++ *Primer* (*https://oreil.ly/QcmrY*), 5th edition, by Stanley B. Lippman et al. (Addison-Wesley, 2012).

Finally, an obvious question might be, what happens to a *moved-from* object? Suppose we create a `SimpleClass` object `sc_04` and move it to a different `SimpleClass` object called `move_sc_04`:

```
SimpleClass sc_04{41};
SimpleClass move_sc_04{std::move(sc_04)};
```

 In this book, we will primarily be concerned with default move operations and will not require implementation of the move constructor or the move assignment operator. The important point here is to understand how to *use* default move operations in order to move objects rather than copy them. Default move operations will return in the next chapter as well.

Implementation of a user-defined move constructor and move assignment operator come with extra considerations and a discussion about writing exception-safe code. These points are beyond the scope of this book, but if you are interested in learning more, see Appendix C for examples extended from Chapter 3.

In this case, `sc_04` is the *moved-from* object. As to what happens to it, the answer is it remains in a *valid but indeterminate state*, as it is not automatically destroyed. We have two options for moved-from objects. You can reuse them if you reassign to them first as shown here for `sc_04`; then, you know their state:

```
sc_04 = SimpleClass{216};            // Reassign to sc_04
int sum = sc_04.get_val() + 100;     // sum = 316
```

Otherwise, you can just let them destroy themselves as they go out of scope.

Initialization of Constructor Arguments with std::move(.)

This now brings us back to the motivation mentioned at the outset: finding an efficient way to initialize a subobject member of an enclosing object, while allowing the latter to retain exclusive ownership of the former. For demonstration, we will continue with our toy example, initializing a SimpleClass subobject member and storing it on an Enclose class. This particular example provides no real performance gain but will extend to situations where performance does become an issue, as you will see at the end of this section.

An enclosing class can be designed to take in a constructor argument the "old way," by const reference, as well as by rvalue and std::move(.), by including two constructors:

```
class Enclose
{
public:
    Enclose(const SimpleClass& sc);        // Constructor 1
    Enclose(SimpleClass&& sc);             // Constructor 2

    SimpleClass get_sc() const;            // Accessor

private:
    SimpleClass sc_;
};


// Implementation:
Enclose::Enclose(const SimpleClass& sc) :sc_{sc} {}           // Constructor 1
Enclose::Enclose(SimpleClass&& sc) :sc_{std::move(sc)} {}     // Constructor 2

SimpleClass Enclose::get_sc() const                           // Accessor
{
    return sc_;
}
```

The first constructor, again, is nothing new:

```
SimpleClass sc_enc{100};
Enclose enc{sc_enc};
```

Here, the sc_enc argument is passed by const reference, and then a full object copy is made in the initialization of the subobject member sc_ in the first constructor.

Alternatively, object copy can be avoided by passing an rvalue reference to sc_enc with std::move(.), and then the initialization of sc_ results in the move constructor on SimpleClass being called once:

```
Enclose enc_move{std::move(sc_enc)};
```

A commonly preferred approach, however, has emerged that can yield essentially equivalent results with just a single constructor. In this case, the sc parameter is written to take in its argument by value, but the member initialization is performed by move:

```
class EncloseSingleConstructor
{
public:
    EncloseSingleConstructor(SimpleClass sc);
    SimpleClass get_sc() const;

private:
    SimpleClass sc_;
};



// Constructor implementation:
EncloseSingleConstructor::EncloseSingleConstructor(SimpleClass sc) :
    sc_{std::move(sc)}{}
```

Proceeding naively:

```
SimpleClass sc_enc{100};
EncloseSingleConstructor enc_sing_ctor{sc_enc};
```

This results in one copy of sc_enc being generated when bound to the constructor argument, but the initialization of sc_ is done by move. In terms of performance, this is on par with a const reference constructor argument initializing the sc_ member by value (copy), as was the case with Constructor 1 in the previous Enclose class.

We can then do better (in nontrivial cases) by passing an rvalue reference:

```
EncloseSingleConstructor enc_move_sing_ctor{std::move(sc_enc)};
```

In this case, there are two move operations. The first occurs when the move constructor is called on the sc constructor parameter, and the second occurs when initializing the sc_ member. As move operations are extremely cheap, this in general would not affect performance significantly compared to a constructor of an enclosing class with an explicit rvalue reference parameter, such as Constructor 2 of the earlier Enclose class.

Note, however, that as a moved-from object, sc_enc is now in a valid but indeterminate state, very different from if it were used in the previous copy constructor case, where it would remain in its original state. More specifically, if you had a function f(.) with signature

```
void f(SimpleClass sc);
```

and were to call it passing sc_enc as an argument after constructing enc_sing_ctor, and then were to do the same after constructing enc_move_sing_ctor, chances are the function would behave differently in each case. The same admonition holds as before: either reassign `sc_enc` or let it destroy itself as it goes out of scope.

Now, returning to the sketch of the `PatternAnalytics` class, let's look at simply constructing the object with a `vector` constructor argument containing 1,000 market data (`double` type) elements:

```
vector<double> data{38.6832, 3.94, 68.6824, 24.8948, 79.5146, . . . , 149.847};
```

Then, let's write a constructor that loads the data and uses move semantics for initializing the subobject member `data_`:

```
PatternAnalytics::PatternAnalytics(std::vector<double> data_in /*, . . .*/) :
    data_{std::move(data_in)} {}
```

Our first option is to pass the `data` vector by value:

```
PatternAnalytics pass_by_value{data};
```

In this case, a copy of `data` is created when it is bound to the `data_in` constructor parameter by value, while initialization is performed by move semantics. A `vector` is equipped with both default copy and move constructors.

Alternatively, we can pass by move, and then again initialization will be performed using move semantics:

```
PatternAnalytics pass_by_move{std::move(data)};
```

In tests using Visual Studio 2022 on a laptop even with just two physical cores, the results were rather stunning. Instantiating `PatternAnalytics` 10,000 times by value and by move, the average times in milliseconds over five runs each were as follows: 4.0441 ms for pass by value and 0.3672 ms for pass by move. That's a speed increase of just over 10 times.

The upshot here is that in nontrivial cases, binding constructor arguments and initializing subobject members with move semantics can be far less expensive than requiring a copy of the object, while still ensuring the safety provided by granting the enclosing object with exclusive control over its member data.

Anonymous Temporary Objects and Move Semantics

An anonymous temporary object—an rvalue rather than an rvalue reference—can also be passed to a function by using move semantics. Suppose we have this function:

```
void r_val_ref(SimpleClass&& sc)
{
    cout << "r_val_ref (&&):  k = " << sc.get_val() << "\n";
}
```

If we know that we will not need to reuse the `SimpleClass` object being input, we could call this function with an anonymous temporary (rvalue) argument, making it more concise. Note that because the temporary `SimpleClass{20}` object is already an rvalue, `std::move(.)` is not used:

```
r_val_ref(SimpleClass{20});          // rvalue argument
```

Note that this is different from the earlier case of a named `SimpleClass` object being cast to an rvalue *reference*:

```
SimpleClass move_sc{30};
int m = 2 * move_sc.get_val();       // Use object before function call

r_val_ref(std::move(move_sc));       // rvalue reference to named object argument
```

In this latter case, the same caveats apply to `move_sc` as before, as it is in a valid but indeterminate state after `std::move(.)` is applied in the `r_val_ref(.)` function call.

Return Value Optimization

Given the efficiencies that can be gained with move semantics, we might be tempted to return objects from functions by move:

```
// Don't do this:
SimpleClass f(int n)
{
    return std::move(SimpleClass{n});
}

// or this:
SimpleClass g(int n)
{
    SimpleClass sc{n};
    return std::move(sc);
}
```

Per the Core Guidelines (*https://oreil.ly/kn05E*), this is not good practice and can result in suboptimal results. Instead, we should simply return the object as usual, as guaranteed copy elision (*https://oreil.ly/7FExK*) takes care of the optimization for us.

This means that if we instead write the functions as follows

```
SimpleClass f(int n)
{
    return {n};      // Same as 'return SimpleClass{n}',
                     // using uniform initialization and
                     // automatic type deduction, introduced in C++11.
}

SimpleClass g(int n)
{
    SimpleClass sc{n};
    return sc;
}
```

then invoking the function calls

```
SimpleClass scf = f(2);
SimpleClass scg = g(3);
```

would be essentially the same as writing this:

```
SimpleClass scf{2};
SimpleClass scg{3};
```

That is, no extra SimpleClass copies are generated when returning the object from f(.) or g(.). In the case of f(.), this is referred to as *return value optimization* (*RVO*), and in the case of g(.), it is called *named return value optimization (NRVO)* as the named object sc is created first before being returned.

This copy elision was permitted (under more specific conditions) beginning with C++11 but was not mandatory, although many compilers already provided it. The Standard began requiring it beginning with C++17 and under more general conditions. As with just about everything else in C++, subtleties and exceptions exist, in particular those involving returns from different conditional control paths. Jonathan Boccara's Fluent C++ blog (*https://oreil.ly/mpY1C*) provides a straightforward post that should help fill in these details.

Default Constructor

If no user-defined constructor is provided on a class, we can use a default constructor provided by the compiler:

```
class Minimal
{
public:
    // No constructor declared.
    // The compiler provides a default constructor.

    int do_something(int k) const;

};
```

A Minimal instance is then constructed by the default constructor provided by the compiler:

```
Minimal min{};
int did_something = min.do_something(42);
```

If a user-defined constructor is added, however, the compiler-provided default constructor is automatically disabled. If a default constructor is still needed, the programmer becomes responsible for providing it. Prior to C++11, if we needed a default constructor to initialize member data, we had to supply the initialization in its implementation. For example, supposing a member variable x_ needed to be initialized as 0 in the Minimal class, it would be updated as something like the following:

```
class Minimal
{
public:
    Minimal(int x);            // x_{x};
    Minimal();                 // x_{0};
    int do_something(int k) const;
    int do_something_with_x() const;

private:
    int x_;
};

// User-defined constructor:
Minimal::Minimal(int x) x_{x} {}

// User-defined default constructor
Minimal::Minimal() : x_{0} {}

int Minimal::do_something(int k) const
{
    // . . .
}


int Minimal::do_something_with_x() const
{
    // . . .
}
```

Since C++11, however, the default constructor can just be set to `default` in the header, which explicitly instructs the compiler to generate the same default constructor as it automatically provided when there was no user-defined constructor. Then, in-class member initialization, as shown next, can take care of setting the default value of `x_`. This results in a more modern style:

```
class Minimal
{
public:
    Minimal(int x);            // x_{x};
    Minimal() = default;       // Can use default keyword      ❶
    void do_something(int k) const;
    void do_something_with_x() const;

private:
    int x_{0};                 // in-class member initialization ❷
};
```

More specifically:

❶ The default constructor is explicitly defined as its compiler-provided default. This also means that one fewer constructor requires implementation, and thus one fewer thing that can go wrong (particularly in more realistic and involved cases compared with this minimal class example).

❷ x_ is initialized in its declaration.

The Core Guidelines tell us to prefer in-class initialization (*https://oreil.ly/Vy9An*) when one or more members need to be initialized with a literal value. This ensures consistent behavior when there might be more than one constructor requiring a default value, leading to cleaner code while also being the most efficient form. In addition, a positive resulting effect is it helps ensure that all data members get initialized at construction, another best practice discussed earlier in this chapter.

Since the release of C++11, the default keyword can also be used in other cases to instruct the compiler to generate default behavior, as you will see in the next section and in the next chapter.

Three-Way Comparison Operator (Spaceship Operator)

Suppose we have a Fraction class that takes in two integers and stores them as members n_ and d_, representing the numerator and denominator:

```
class Fraction
{
public:
    Fraction(int n, int d);    // initializes n_{n}, d_{d}


private:
    int n_, d_;

};
```

To simplify this example, assume that these values are nonnegative and that the denominator is not 0. For our purposes, these conditions can be enforced using the assert(.) function (*https://oreil.ly/q1Q7Z*), declared in the <cassert> header, as shown in the implementation of the constructor. This will halt execution if either case is violated. We can also simplify the fraction by finding the greatest common divisor with the std::gcd(.) function, which became available in the set of <numeric> algorithms with C++17 (Chapter 5 provides more details about numeric algorithms).

```
// Implementation of the constructor:
#include <cassert>
#include <numeric>

Fraction::Fraction(int n, int d) :n_{n}, d_{d}
{
    assert((n < 0) || (d <= 0));        // Inherited from C; no std:: scope.
```

```
// Simplify fraction:
int frac_gcd = std::gcd(n, d);
n_ /= frac_gcd;
d_ /= frac_gcd;

if (n_ == d_)
{
    n_ = 1;
    d_ = 1;
}
}
```

Suppose now we create two `Fraction` instances, a and b:

```
Fraction a{1, 2};
Fraction b{3, 4};
```

Then, say we were to try to compare them:

```
if(a == b)
{
    // Do something. . .
}

if(a > b)
{
    // do something. . .
}
```

The compiler would complain, as it doesn't know what *equality* or *greater than* means for a user-defined class. Therefore, we need to define these operators ourselves.

Prior to C++11, definitions of all six comparison operators (==, !=, <, <=, >, and >=) were required in order to cover every contingency:

```
bool operator == (const Fraction& rhs) const;
bool operator != (const Fraction& rhs) const;
bool operator < (const Fraction& rhs) const;
bool operator > (const Fraction& rhs) const;
bool operator <= (const Fraction& rhs) const;
bool operator >= (const Fraction& rhs) const;
```

From a logic point of view, if == and < were defined, the remaining implementations could be expressed in terms of these two operators. However, separate implementations of all six were still required in the code, even if the remaining four were based on the first two. With C++20, this is now streamlined with the introduction of the *three-way operator*, aka the *spaceship operator*, <=>. Now, all we need to do is provide == and <, and we're essentially done.

Returning to the `Fraction` class, the equality operator is a simple matter of defining == as `default`. The `default` keyword in this context instructs the compiler to provide the default behavior for the equality of two objects. Each member will be compared with the respective member on the object being compared: the numerators are compared, and then denominators are compared. If each pair is equal, the operator returns true. If at least one comparison is not equal, the operator will return false. Conversely, the default definition of the == operator also now automatically defines the != operator:

```
#include <compare>

class Fraction
{
public:
    Fraction(int n, int d);

    // Defines both "==" and "!=":
    bool operator == (const Fraction& rhs) const = default;

private:
    int n_, d_;

};
```

The remaining inequality operators (both exclusive and inclusive) can be defined by the spaceship operator (<=>), for which the Standard Library <compare> header is required. However, rather than a bool return type, std::strong_ordering is used for integer values (more about this shortly).

A compiler-provided default is provided for <=> as well, but it doesn't help us in this case as it defines member-by-member lexicographic comparison. Say, for example, we were to write this:

```
#include <compare>

class Fraction
{
public:
    Fraction(int n, int d);
    bool operator == (const Fraction& rhs) const = default;

    // This default will give incorrect results:
    std::strong_ordering operator <=> (const Fraction& rhs) const = default;

private:
    int n_, d_;

};
```

We would get nonsensical results such as the following, resulting in a true condition:

$\frac{2}{3} < \frac{4}{6}$, because $4 > 2$

$\frac{1}{2} < \frac{1}{5}$, because the numerators are equal, and 5 > 2

For this reason, we first need to drop the `default` setting in the header file:

```
// Remove the default setting:
std::strong_ordering operator <=> (const Fraction& rhs) const;
```

We then also need to write our own implementation, which can be done by defining and checking the less-than (<) condition first. If not true, the next step will be to check for equality based on the definition of == already established. If neither of these is true, the result must be greater than (>). These return types are indicated by the `strong_ordering` values `less`, `equivalent`, and `greater`, respectively:

```
std::strong_ordering Fraction::operator <=>(const Fraction& rhs) const
{
    if(n_ * rhs.d_ < rhs.n_ * d_)
    {
        return std::strong_ordering::less;
    }
    else if (*this == rhs)        // Check if the active object is equal to rhs
    {
        return std::strong_ordering::equivalent;
    }
    else
    {
        return std::strong_ordering::greater;
    }
}
```

With definitions for both == and <=> in place, we can then apply any of the six comparative operators as usual:

```
Fraction f_01{1, 5};
Fraction f_02{1, 2};

if(f_01 <= f_02)
{
    // <=> now properly evaluates the inequality 1/5 < 1/2
    // . . .
}
else
{
    // . . .
}
```

Using the `strong_ordering` return type means any two values can be compared, as is the case for integral types in C++. The Standard Library also has a `std::partial_ordering` type that should be used for floating-point types such as `double` and `float`. This is because a floating type (e.g., `double`) can hold noncomparable assignments such as infinity and *NaN* (not a number). It should also be noted that two floating types should never be compared directly in defining `==`. Instead, equivalence in this case—say, of two `double` values x and y—should be determined by whether y falls within a certain tolerance of x.

We can use third return type, `weak_ordering`, for cases such as comparing strings (although not limited to this example), where case-insensitive but otherwise like characters are considered equivalent. You can find a thorough comparison of these return categories in Section 4.3.3 of *C++20: Get the Details* by Rainer Grimm (Leanpub, 2023).

The usual ordering required for financial applications would probably be based on a numerical type (e.g., `double`) already defined in the language. However, one place where overloads for `==` and `<=>` can be handy is in the design of a date class, where ordering and date arithmetic is based on the number of days since an epoch (such as 1970-01-01, the Unix epoch). Chapter 7 covers this topic within the context of a user-defined date class.

Lambda Expressions and User-Defined Class Members

Returning now to the topic of lambda expressions, one last point to cover is capturing object member data and member functions in a lambda expression. Suppose we have a class that computes the values of a quadratic function of the form

$$ax^2 + bx + c$$

for a given vector of real numbers

$$x_1, x_2, \cdots, x_n$$

with the coefficients a, b, and c of the function stored as member variables. A public member function `generate_values(.)` will compute the value of the function for each element in a `vector<double>` argument and return the results in another vector:

```
#include<vector>
class QuadraticGenerator
{
public:
    QuadraticGenerator(double a, double b, double c);    // a_{a}, b_{b}, c_{c}
    std::vector<double> generate_values(const std::vector<double>& v);

private:
    double a_, b_, c_;
};
```

Inside the generate_values(.) function, we can separate out the function evaluation into a lambda expression that gets called each time from a range-based for loop iterating over v. To do this, we need the member variables a_, b_, and c_. We could list these individually in the capture, but it is also possible to gain access to all member data (and member functions) by inserting the this pointer (*https://oreil.ly/F6b3R*)—which points to the active object—in the lambda capture instead:

```
std::vector<double> QuadraticGenerator::
        generate_values(const std::vector<double>& v)
{
    auto quadratic_value = [this](double x)
    {
        return x * (a_ * x + b_) + c_;
    };

    std::vector<double> y;

    for (double x : v)
    {
        y.push_back(quadratic_value(x));
    }

    return y;
}
```

In certain thread-based situations, it is possible that instead of the this pointer, a copy of the active object, *this, might be necessary as the lambda capture argument. This was enabled later in C++17, so that quadratic_value(.) could instead be written as follows:

```
auto quadratic_value = [*this](double x)
{
    return x * (a_ * x + b_) + c_;
};
```

This is mentioned here just for completeness. Specific examples would introduce complexities of multithreaded programming that are a topic for more advanced books. Our examples will primarily use the former case of capturing the this pointer rather than *this.

Summary

The topics presented in this chapter may have come across as a "various and sundry" list of mostly newer features that can be employed when writing user-defined classes, so it will probably help to recap what has been discussed.

Recall that a functor is an object that behaves like a function but that also can hold state by exposing at least one user-defined overload of `operator ()`. A functor can be a useful tool in quantitative programming, such as for root finding to compute the implied volatility of an option.

A lambda expression, introduced in Chapter 1, is another form of a functor that was added to the Standard in C++11. In this chapter, you saw how a lambda can advantageously be defined on the fly inside another function, and how it can help in refactoring code that is called multiple times. One simple example was the `norm_cdf` lambda in the `BlackScholes` class implementation. Lambda expressions can also capture the `this` pointer to an active object (or the dereferenced `*this` instead if desired), providing the lambda with access to any data member or member function on the active object. As a side note of topics to come, both function objects and lambdas can be passed as an argument to a function or an STL algorithm, as you will see in Chapter 5.

Move semantics allow the transfer of ownership of objects, such as of arguments to functions and in initializing subobject members at construction. In nontrivial cases, this can significantly reduce the performance overhead of object copy while avoiding the problems that can result from older methods such as passing pointers or storing members by reference. You will see more practical examples in subsequent chapters.

The `default` keyword makes it clear and obvious up front that a special member function is to assume its compiler-provided default. As one specific example, combined with in-class member initialization, `default` can obviate the need to implement a default constructor. In-class member initialization provides several benefits that help reduce the risk of bugs, particularly as a complement to a defaulted constructor. It also helps ensure that all member data is initialized at construction.

Another useful example of the `default` keyword was the default member-by-member equality definition for the `==` operator. The three-way comparison operator, commonly referred to as the spaceship operator, allows you to implement all six equality and comparison operators in terms of `==` and `<`, as shown in the `Fraction` class example, so that it is no longer required to define each in a separate implementation.

Additional References

Nicolai M. Josuttis, *C++ Move Semantics: The Complete Guide* (Leanpub, 2022), chapter 2.

Mark S. Joshi, *C++ Design Patterns and Derivatives Pricing*, 2nd edition (Cambridge, 2008), 142–144, section 9.2.

"Implied Volatility in C++ Using Template Functions and Interval Bisection" (*https://oreil.ly/-kZMf*), Quantstart.

Nicolai M. Josuttis, *Object-Oriented Programming in C++* (Wiley, 2002), 126, section 4.1.

Chris Gregg, Lecture slides from CS 106B (*https://oreil.ly/iSK83*) Stanford University (another example of a `Fraction` class).

CHAPTER 3

Inheritance, Polymorphism, and Smart Pointers

Historically, C++ has been a popular language in the finance industry because it supports *object-oriented programming*, which leverages relationships and interactions among objects. Dependencies between objects are broadly divided into two categories: *composition* (a "has-a" relationship) and *inheritance* (an "is-a" relationship). Here are two examples related to financial programming:

- An options contract *has a* payoff.
- A call payoff *is a* type of payoff.

More financial examples of has-a relationships (composition) include the following:

- A Treasury bill *has a* day count basis.
- A coupon-paying bond *has a* first coupon date, penultimate coupon date, and maturity date.

And as for additional is-a relationships (inheritance), the financial world has cases such as these:

- Each of Actual/365, Actual/360, and 30/360 *is a* day count basis.
- A mortgage pass-through security, a collateralized mortgage obligation (CMO), an interest-only strip, or a principal-only strip *is a* mortgage-backed security.

Composition was touched upon in Chapter 2, where an enclosing object was composed with a subobject member. In addition, you saw how move semantics, introduced in C++11, allows the enclosing object to have exclusive control over this member without incurring the cost of object copy. Using `std::move` just in the initialization of the `data` vector in the sketch of the `PatternAnalytics` example resulted in over a tenfold increase in speed. Move semantics will continue to play an important role within this chapter as well.

Regarding inheritance, C++11 introduced new contextual keywords such as `override` and `final` to catch errors at compile time when object inheritance is used. This way, previously common runtime errors associated with inheritance are prevented from ever seeing the light of day and wreaking potentially serious havoc in mission-critical financial systems. Related examples will also follow.

Finally, some objects might interact but might not be related in either the has-a or is-a sense. This is called *association*. Here are two examples:

- An option pricing model class uses market data and contract data.
- A coupon-paying bond class uses a yield curve to compute its valuation.

In each case, the data objects could be taken in as input data to a valuation member function but not stored as member data. This also means they would not inherit from the valuing object.

In this chapter, you will be introduced to some useful modern features related to composition and inheritance that came into the Standard as of C++11 and after. You will then see how they can be applied to improve upon the C++03 coding style that was commonly used in the past for inheritance and composition.

This will lead into a realistic financial use case, starting in "Resource Ownership with Raw Pointers" on page 70, where an option class is composed with a payoff member whose type—call or put—is inherited from a base class and determined polymorphically at runtime. This will be followed by an introduction to *smart pointers*, again introduced in C++11, which are safer alternatives to the `new` and `delete` operators for memory allocation and cleanup. We will then reprise the option and payoff example in "Managing Resources with Unique Pointers" on page 91, where a *unique pointer*, a particular type of smart pointer, can provide for safer, cleaner, and even more efficient code.

Discussion of modern best practices will be emphasized as we proceed, with reference to the Core Guidelines. A "Back to Basics" talk on object-oriented programming (*https://oreil.ly/yc43i*), presented by Jon Kalb at CppCon 2019, provides informative and more in-depth coverage on this topic and is recommended viewing. More than just back to basics, this talk is actually more forward looking with respect to modern C++.

Technically speaking, the term *polymorphism* in this chapter refers to *dynamic polymorphism* (also called *runtime polymorphism*), whereby the specific type of a derived object does not need to be known until runtime. In contrast, *static polymorphism* can help improve performance at runtime but comes with limitations, involves the additional complexity and sophistication of template programming, and results in possibly increased compile times.

The focus of this chapter is on the dynamic case. For more information on static polymorphism, an important topic for more advanced C++ programmers, a good source is Section 18.2 (*https://oreil.ly/ojQbu*) of the C++ book *Templates: The Complete Guide*, 2nd edition, by David Vandevoorde et al. (Addison-Wesley, 2017).

Polymorphism

A common example of *polymorphism* is of a base Shape class from which two concrete shape classes, such as Circle and Rectangle are *derived*. This is also referred to as *inheriting* from the base class, using alternative but also common terminology.

To start, suppose our Shape class has two *virtual functions* (*https://oreil.ly/BIJDR*). The first, what_am_i(), will return a string containing the name of a particular shape (in this case, "Circle" or "Rectangle") or simply "Shape" if called on a base object:

```
class Shape
{
public:

    virtual std::string what_am_i() const;   // Returns "Shape"
    virtual double area() const = 0;
    virtual ~Shape() = default;               // Note: virtual default destructor
};
```

The area() function is *pure virtual*, indicated by the = 0 in its declaration. This sets up a contract that mandates its implementation on derived classes while having no implementation of its own on the base class. This makes the Shape an *abstract base class* that cannot be instantiated without a derived object, such as a Circle or a Rectangle. Figure 3-1 shows the Unified Modeling Language (UML) representation of this class hierarchy.

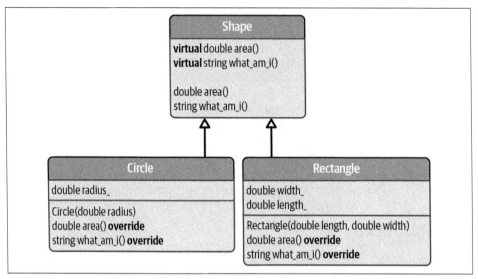

Figure 3-1. Abstract base class and inheritance

Note two details at this point:

- A virtual default destructor is also declared, using the `default` keyword. This ensures that destructors on derived objects are also called before the destructor on a base object is invoked. This is particularly important because a pointer to a base object is often used (as will be discussed shortly) to handle an object derived from its base. This will be taken as given throughout the chapter, but the reasons for its importance are shown in an example in Appendix A.

- One further advantage of making a base class abstract is it prevents a pesky problem that can arise in object-oriented programming: object slicing (*https://oreil.ly/bkgjc*). Appendix B provides an example.

The declaration for the Circle class can be written as follows, with the C++11 keywords `override` and `final` to be explained in context:

```
class Circle final : public Shape
{
public:
    Circle(double radius);
    std::string what_am_i() const override;    // Returns "Circle"
    double area() const override;

private:
    double radius_;
};
```

Similarly, the declaration for `Rectangle` follows:

```
class Rectangle final : public Shape
{
public:
    Rectangle(double length, double width);
    std::string what_am_i() const override;    // Returns "Rectangle"
    double area() const override;

private:
    double length_, width_;
};
```

Note here the presence of the C++11 `final` and `override` keywords. The `final` keyword now in C++ is essentially the same as `final` in Java, or `sealed` in C#, which prevents deeper inheritance chains that should be avoided when possible. Any attempt to do so will, by design, be thwarted by a compiler error. The `final` keyword can also help improve performance through devirtualization, as explained in a 2022 blog post by Niall Cooling (*https://oreil.ly/EXKry*).

The `override` keyword explicitly indicates in its declaration that a function is overriding a virtual function of the same name. What follows is an example of a problem that this solves. Suppose in the preceding `Circle` class, the `what_am_i()` function name was intended to override the virtual function on the base class but was mistakenly declared and implemented as `what_i_am()`, and with no `override` keyword:

```
class Circle final : public Shape
{
public:
    Circle(double radius);
    std::string what_i_am() const;    // Problem!  Should be what_am_i()
    double area() const override;

private:
    double radius_;
};

// In class implementation:
std::string Circle::what_i_am() const
{
    return "Circle";
}
```

Suppose further that a `Circle` instance is created, and we call the `what_am_i()` member function:

```
Circle circle{1.0};

cout << circle.what_am_i() << "\n";
```

The code would compile and run, but the output to the screen would be `Shape` rather than `Circle`. In contrast, if the `override` keyword were present,

```
std::string what_i_am() const override;
```

a compiler error would also be generated, saying there is no virtual function `what_i_am()` on the base class to override, which is more desirable than incorrect runtime behavior that can cause serious problems in more complex real-world software applications. The results would be similar for the `Rectangle` class.

For completeness, the implementations for each class are as follows. Note that the `override` keyword is not used in a separate implementation; it is specified only in the declaration:

```
// Shape implementation
std::string Shape::what_am_i() const
{
    return "Shape";
}

// Circle implementation
Circle::Circle(double radius) :radius_{radius} {}

std::string Circle::what_am_i() const          // override
{
    return "Circle";
}

double Circle::area() const                     // override
{
    return std::numbers::pi * radius_ * radius_;
}

// Rectangle implementation
Rectangle::Rectangle(double length, double width) :
        length_{length}, width_{width} {}

std::string Rectangle::what_am_i() const     // override
{
    return "Rectangle";
}

double Rectangle::area() const                  // override
{
    return length_ * width_;
}
```

In the previous chapter, we looked at initializing and storing a subobject member on an `Enclose` object, more formally referred to as the *composition* of two objects. An extension of this can arise whereby the enclosing class is composed with a pointer (of some form, to be discussed later in the chapter) to an object of a derived type, such as `Circle` or `Rectangle` inheriting from a `Shape` (abstract) base class. This pointed-to derived object is an example of a *resource*, and the goal would be to provide the `Enclose` class with *ownership* of this resource. Definitions of these terms will be provided momentarily; for now, suffice it to say that because the resource requires allocation and management in heap memory, providing this ownership will now necessitate extra work and consideration.

Suppose, as a simple example, the `Enclose` class had a function that would expand or contract the area of a shape by a certain scale factor. A preliminary sketch of the class might then be something like the following:

```
class Enclose
{
public:
    Enclose(const Shape& shape)
    {
        // . . .
    }

    double scale_area(double scale) const
    {
        return scale * shape_->area();
    }

private:
    Shape* shape_;
};
```

Figure 3-2 is a high-level UML diagram showing this owner-resource design.

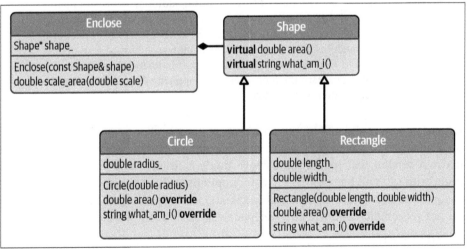

Figure 3-2. In this composition example, a resource points to an object of a derived type

The challenging part comes next in establishing this ownership, as it involves pointers and allocated memory, and thus requires special care, as will be discussed next. After the following introduction to modern smart pointers, however, we will show how the solution can be updated in cleaner and safer code.

Resource Ownership with Raw Pointers

Suppose we have an object representing an option, and it needs to hold its payoff as a data member, but the payoff—call or put—will not be known until runtime. This scenario is based on an example presented in Chapter 4 of C++ *Design Patterns and Derivatives Pricing*, 2nd edition, by Mark S. Joshi (Cambridge University Press), which was published in 2008 before enhancements such as smart pointers, move semantics, and keywords such as `override`, `default`, and `delete` (to be discussed) became available in the C++11 Standard.

For its time, however, this book presented an easily comprehensible and straightforward example that set a polymorphic payoff object on a containing option contract class such that the actual payoff—call or put—was not known until runtime. This design obviated the need for an `if...then` condition to set the payoff, and thus resulted in cleaner code. It furthermore presented a design enabling option information to be stored in a common and reusable object that remains separate from the pricing model.

 On a somber note, Joshi passed away at a young age in 2017 (*https://oreil.ly/80y32*). His contributions to the financial field were substantial, with the publication of two additional books on mathematical finance, over 70 published research papers, and development of practical open source utilities for C++ financial developers. Although his C++ design patterns book was published a few years prior to C++11, it remains a fine text for financial programmers wishing to learn the fundamentals of applying C++ object-oriented design patterns in practice.

Returning to our discussion, we will begin with a similar example that illustrates the challenges in establishing resource ownership, and then gradually build out an updated version that incorporates more modern features and methods. This will begin with call and put payoffs for equity options that are derived from an abstract `Payoff` base class. The proposed class declarations are shown here, but note that these are not yet complete and will be developed over the discussion that follows:

```
class Payoff
{
public:
    virtual double payoff(double price) const = 0;
    virtual ~Payoff() = default;    // Remember to include a
```

```
                                  // virtual default destructor
                                  // on the base class.

    // . . . More left to do
};

class CallPayoff final : public Payoff
{
public:
    CallPayoff(double strike);
    double payoff(double price) const override;

    // . . . More left to do


private:
    double strike_;
};

class PutPayoff final : public Payoff
{
public:
    PutPayoff(double strike);
    double payoff(double price) const override;

    // . . . More left to do


private:
    double strike_;
};
```

The pure virtual `payoff()` member function on the `Payoff` base class mandates its implementation on each derived class. It will return the payoff value for a given spot underlying price, as shown in each derived implementation:

```
#include <algorithm>           // std::max


// --- CallPayoff implementation ---
CallPayoff::CallPayoff(double strike) :strike_{strike} {}

double CallPayoff::payoff(double spot) const
{
    return std::max(spot - strike_, 0.0);
}

// . . .


// --- PutPayoff implementation ---
PutPayoff::PutPayoff(double strike) :strike_{strike} {}
```

```
double PutPayoff::payoff(double spot) const
{
    return std::max(strike_ - spot, 0.0);
}

// . . .
```

Next, suppose we have an `OptionInfo` class that will hold the time to expiration in units of years (or a year fraction), as well as information about its payoff. The idea here is to hold information needed to value an option into a reusable class separate from a collection of pricing models that will require this information as input.

The particular type of payoff, call or put, is to be determined dynamically at runtime. This will again require indirection, meaning the payoff would need to be stored as either a (const) reference or a pointer to a `Payoff`. Using a `const` reference, we could run into the same problems of shallow copy and possible modification of the object outside the enclosing object, as seen in Chapter 2. Using a pointer, a programmer might naively choose to take in a pointer to a `Payoff` as a constructor argument and assign it to the `payoff_ptr_` member:

```
class OptionInfo
{
public:
    // This will be a problem:
    OptionInfo(const Payoff* payoff, double time_to_exp);

    double option_payoff(double spot) const;
    double time_to_expiration() const;

private:
    Payoff* payoff_ptr_;
    double time_to_exp_;
};
```

In this case, however, we will not only have the same issues as with a `const` reference member, but moreover things could go very wrong if the pointer gets deleted from outside the active enclosing object. For example:

```
Payoff* call_payoff = new CallPayoff{25.0};    // Call with strike = 25
OptionInfo opt_info(call_payoff, 0.5);         // Time to exp = six months

delete call_payoff;                            // OOPS!
```

Now, `opt_info` points to a deleted object on the heap. This is not good.

Another issue arises if the memory that is allocated and pointed to by `call_payoff` is never cleaned up before `opt_info` goes out of scope when a function using it is exited:

```
void f(. . .)
{
    Payoff* call_payoff = new CallPayoff{25.0};     // Call with strike = 25
    OptionInfo opt_info(call_payoff, 0.5);

    // . . .

    // Function exits, delete never called on call_payoff

}
```

In this case, we will be exposed to memory leaks and undefined behavior. This is also not good.

To avoid these issues, we would like to somehow grant an `OptionInfo` object sole ownership of its `payoff_ptr_` member. In general terminology, a pointer data member is a type of *resource*. As described in *Effective C++*, a resource "is something that, once you're done using it, you need to return to the system. If you don't, bad things happen. In C++ programs, the most commonly used resource is dynamically allocated memory (if you allocate memory and never deallocate it, you've got a memory leak)."[1] In addition to a pointer, a resource could also refer to a file that can be opened and closed, or a thread in a parallelized application.

The solution is to apply the *resource acquisition is initialization (RAII)* programming technique, which says *the lifetime of a resource is guaranteed to be tied to its owner*. When an owning object goes out of scope, RAII says that the owner is responsible for destroying its resource and returning the memory it occupied to the system.

A more specific explanation is as follows:

> Modern C++ avoids using heap memory as much as possible by declaring objects on the stack. When a resource is too large for the stack, then it should be owned by an [enclosing] object. As the object gets initialized, it acquires the resource it owns. The object is then responsible for releasing the resource in its destructor. The owning object itself is declared on the stack. The principle that objects own resources is also known as "resource acquisition is initialization," or RAII.[2]

If you are interested in a refresher regarding stack and heap memory, you can refer to an informative discussion on Stack Overflow, "What and where are the stack and heap?" (*https://oreil.ly/D91BC*).

In the example that follows, `OptionInfo` will be designed to *own* a resource derived from its abstract base class `Payoff`. The resource type, a `CallPayoff` or `PutPayoff`,

---

1 Scott Meyers, *Effective C++* (*https://oreil.ly/KsGer*), 3rd edition (Addison-Wesley, 2005), Chapter 3.

2 "Object Lifetime and Resource Management (RAII)" (*https://oreil.ly/F1oiP*), Microsoft Learn, November 6, 2022.

will be determined at runtime and *handled* by a pointer to a Payoff. Supposing the payoff type is a CallPayoff, the enforcement of RAII can then be broken into satisfying two specific requirements:

1. payoff_ptr_ will be initialized with the heap memory address holding the respective CallPayoff resource at the construction of its owning OptionInfo instance.

2. This resource will persist throughout the lifetime of its owner, and it will be destroyed only when the destructor on its owning OptionInfo object is called.

Using Clone Methods

Prior to C++11 and the advent of smart pointers in the Standard, a common approach to implementing RAII in cases such as this example would often start by implementing *clone* methods on the resource classes. These member functions would then generate a pointer to a *copy* of the active derived object (in our case, a call or put payoff).

This works by overriding a pure virtual clone() method on each derived payoff class, as shown in the following declaration of the base class and the CallPayoff class, again based on the example from the Joshi book. You can find a more general discussion of clone() methods in Chapter 3 of the classic text *Design Patterns: Elements of Reusable Object-Oriented Software* by Erich Gamma, Richard Helm, Ralph Johnson, and John Vlissides (Addison-Wesley, 1994), which is often referred to as the *Gang of Four* book because of its four authors.

```
class Payoff
{
public:
    virtual double payoff(double price) const = 0;
    virtual Payoff* clone() const = 0;      // New (pure virtual) member function
    virtual ~Payoff() = default;
};

class CallPayoff : public Payoff
{
public:
    CallPayoff(double strike);
    double payoff(double price) const override;
    CallPayoff* clone() const override;      // New overriding member function


private:
    double strike_;
};
```

The declaration of the PutPayoff class would be similar.

In the `clone()` implementation, the active `CallPayoff` object creates a copy of itself (`*this`) in heap memory and returns a pointer to it. This pointer will then become the member on the owning `OptionInfo` object pointing to the `Payoff` resource:

```
CallPayoff* CallPayoff::clone() const
{
    return new CallPayoff(*this);
}
```

The value of the call payoff is obtained from the `payoff(.)` function:

```
double CallPayoff::payoff(double spot) const
{
    return std::max(spot - strike_, 0.0);    // #include <algorithm>
}
```

The implementation of the `payoff(.)` function for `PutPayoff` is again similar, with `strike` and `spot` reversed in the `max(.)` function argument. Usage of a clone method is sometimes mnemonically referred to as a "virtual constructor" (*https://oreil.ly/5K04S*) (an idiom), as it will construct an object, but an object whose type is determined at runtime using polymorphism.

As a side note, as indicated in the code comment, inclusion of the Standard Library header `<algorithm>` is required for the `std::max(.)` function. Chapter 5 covers Standard Library algorithms (also known as "STL algorithms") in more detail.

Creating an Instance of OptionInfo

The `Payoff` resource is then *acquired* by an `OptionInfo` object at construction, with its `payoff_ptr_` member initialized with the heap memory address it will point to. Instead of taking in a pointer to a `Payoff`—as was naively attempted in the earlier strawman example—the constructor argument is replaced with a const reference parameter to a `Payoff`:

```
OptionInfo(const Payoff& payoff, double time_to_exp);
```

Initialization in the constructor will then call the `clone()` virtual function from the reference to whichever payoff type argument is present, and then initialize `payoff_ptr_` as either a `CallPayoff` or `PutPayoff`:

```
OptionInfo::OptionInfo(const Payoff& payoff, double time_to_exp):
    payoff_ptr_{payoff.clone()}, time_to_exp_{time_to_exp} {}
```

This way, the memory acquisition to contain the `Payoff`-derived instance occurs only when the owning `OptionInfo` object is constructed, thus preventing it from being deleted or modified externally. This completes a necessary condition for our RAII requirement 1.

As for the payoff value of the option, it can then be easily obtained from the owning OptionInfo by providing an accessor that calls the payoff() member function on the dereferenced payoff_ptr_ resource, given the spot price of the underlying security as its input parameter:

```
double OptionInfo::option_payoff(double spot) const
{
    return payoff_ptr_->payoff(spot);
}
```

The remaining accessor, returning the time to expiration, is trivial:

```
double OptionInfo::time_to_expiration() const
{
    return time_to_exp_;
}
```

Preventing Shallow Copy

So far, you have seen how a clone method can be used to allocate a resource, satisfying a necessary condition for our RAII requirement 1 at the time the owning object is created. However, this would not be sufficient.

As it stands right now, if for some reason a copy of an OptionInfo were attempted, the default copy constructor would be called, resulting in a shallow copy sharing the same Payoff resource. This violates RAII, in that the lifetime of the shared resource may now depend on two owners. This means we need to address what happens when the copy constructor or copy assignment operator on OptionInfo is called.

The easy solution is to just disallow copying, and this is consistent with practical cases sometimes found when valuing an asset or derivative. An OptionInfo object with an accompanying payoff would be created once, passed to a pricing model, and then left to go out of scope. If a trader or analyst needs to revalue the option, a new option object can be created and then be passed into the same pricing model function.

In the C++03 state of the world, we would usually disable the copy constructor and the copy assignment operator by declaring them private:

```
class OptionInfo
{
public:
    OptionInfo(const Payoff& payoff, double time_to_exp);
    ~OptionInfo();

    double option_payoff(double spot) const;
    double time_to_expiration() const;

private:
    Payoff* payoff_ptr_;
```

```
    double time_to_exp_;

    // If we don't need to copy the object, declare
    // copy operations private (prior to C++11):
    OptionInfo(const OptionInfo& rhs);
    OptionInfo& operator =(const OptionInfo& rhs);
};
```

Technically speaking, however, although declaring the special copy operations private will prevent them from being accessed externally, it would still be possible to implement a private copy constructor that could be invoked internally, and similarly a private copy assignment operator. Consider the following modified version of the SimpleClass example from Chapter 2:

```
// Modified version of SimpleClass:
class SimpleClassPrivateCopy
{
public:
    SimpleClassPrivateCopy(int k);
    int get_val() const;
    void reset_val(int k);
    void copy_mischief(int k);

private:
    int k_{0};

    // Copy constructor and copy assignment operator disabled
    // externally by declaring them private:
    SimpleClassPrivateCopy(const SimpleClassPrivateCopy& rhs);
    SimpleClassPrivateCopy& operator =(const SimpleClassPrivateCopy& rhs);
};
```

This prevents external copying, but it would still be possible to implement a private copy constructor that could be invoked internally, and similarly a private copy assignment operator:

```
// Copy constructor can still be implemented even if declared private:
SimpleClassPrivateCopy::
    SimpleClassPrivateCopy(const SimpleClassPrivateCopy& copy):
        k_{copy.k_} {}

// Copy assignment operator, also private
SimpleClassPrivateCopy& SimpleClassPrivateCopy::operator =
    (const SimpleClassPrivateCopy& copy)
{
    k_ = copy.k_;
    return *this;
}
```

In addition, nothing prevents the definition of a public member function that creates a copy internally, even though the copy constructor is private:

```
void SimpleClassPrivateCopy::copy_mischief(int k)
{
    SimpleClassPrivateCopy scpc{k};

    // Copy generated here; active object is modified:
    SimpleClassPrivateCopy scpc_copy{scpc};

    // . . .
}
```

Similarly, the private copy assignment operator could also be invoked indirectly.

The `delete` keyword, introduced in C++11, can instead be utilized to explicitly disable copy operations, both externally and internally, and is thus preferred in modern C++:

```
class OptionInfo
{
public:
    OptionInfo(const Payoff& payoff, double time_to_exp);
    ~OptionInfo();

    double option_payoff(double spot) const;
    double time_to_expiration() const;

    // Copy operations disabled both externally and internally:
    OptionInfo(const OptionInfo& rhs) = delete;
    OptionInfo& operator =(const OptionInfo& rhs) = delete;

    // . . .

private:
    Payoff* payoff_ptr_;
    double time_to_exp_;
};
```

By disabling the copy operations, plus incorporating clone methods, we have essentially satisfied the first RAII requirement. Later, we will look at copying becoming a functional requirement. But for now, we have a viable solution to the problem that also happens to be commonly used in programming pricing models.

Finally, if an object holds a raw pointer member, invoking the default move constructor or move assignment operator is also dangerous. So for now, with `OptionInfo`, we can prevent these problems as well by also disabling the special move member functions, again using `delete`:

```
class OptionInfo
{
public:

    // . . .
```

```
// Move operations are discussed later; just disable for now as well:
OptionInfo(OptionInfo& rhs) = delete;
OptionInfo& operator =(OptionInfo&& rhs) = delete;

// . . .
};
```

Implementing the OptionInfo Destructor

One more important step is needed in order to satisfy requirement 2 in our RAII example. Consider what would happen if an `OptionInfo` object were to go out of scope in its current form: its default destructor would be called, but the memory containing the payoff member would not be deallocated and returned to the system. For this reason, it is necessary to supplant the default destructor with a user-defined destructor that deallocates the memory pointed to by `payoff_ptr_`.

Only one line of code is required in the destructor—namely, invoking the `delete` operator—but failure to implement it would run the risk of unreleased memory resources (memory leaks) and undefined behavior at runtime. The declaration and implementation of the destructor are shown here:

```
// Declaration of the destructor:
public:
    . . .
    ~OptionInfo();

// Destructor implementation:
OptionInfo::~OptionInfo()
{
    delete payoff_ptr_;
}
```

The memory occupied by the `Payoff` resource is then released when the owning `OptionInfo` object is no longer needed. With this step, along with initializing the resource by using its `clone()` function, and disabling the copy constructor and copy assignment operator (as well as the move operations), both conditions of RAII are met.

Pricing an Option

So why are we going through all this? Ultimately, we want to construct an `OptionInfo`, complete with a `Payoff` resource, that can be used (by association) inside a numerical option pricing model. As suggested at the outset, the name `OptionInfo` indicates a separation of the information a model might need with a pricing model that uses this information in its calculations.

One example is a binomial lattice model that requires the payoff and time to expiration at each node based on a set of projected share prices. Other market data such as volatility, the dividend rate, and the risk-free interest rate, along with the desired number of time steps for the lattice, are also taken in as constructor parameters of, say, a `BinomialLattice` object, as sketched out in the following declaration:

```
enum class OptType
{
    European,
    American
};


class BinomialLattice
{
    public:
        BinomialLattice(const OptionInfo& opt, double vol, double int_rate,
            unsigned time_steps, double div_rate);

        double calc_price(double spot, OptType opt_type);
};
```

The price is then obtained from the `calc_price(.)` member function that takes in the underlying spot price and the option type (e.g., European or American). A full implementation of a binomial lattice model is covered in Chapter 9.

The same `OptionInfo` class could then also be reused in other numerical pricing models, such as Monte Carlo–based models. The primary goal of this chapter, as you've hopefully seen so far, is developing the assembly of option information, including its payoff, which can then be safely passed to the desired numerical pricing method, as shown in Figure 3-3.

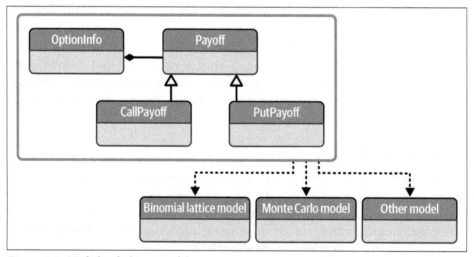

Figure 3-3. High-level object model

That is, we are currently concentrating on designing and composing the code inside the rectangular outline, at top-left in the figure.

Putting it all together in a high-level example for now, we will create a `CallPayoff` object with a strike of, say, 75. We will then use it to construct an `OptionInfo` with, for example, half a year remaining until expiration:

```
CallPayoff call_payoff{75.0};
OptionInfo call_opt{call_payoff, 0.5};
```

Then, the value of an American call option with a strike of 75 and six months until expiration could be calculated using a `BinomialLattice` object by providing it with the market data arguments for the annual volatility and risk-free rates, the number of time steps desired for the lattice, and the annual continuous dividend rate of the underlying equity. The `calc_price(.)` member function is responsible for the valuation, given the spot share price for the underlying equity, quoted at 85, for example, and the option type:

```
BinomialLattice binomial_lattice{call_opt, 0.25, 0.04, 100, 0.02};
double opt_val = binomial_lattice.calc_price(85.0, OptType::American);
```

Note that the `BinomialLattice` doesn't care whether the option is a call or a put, as the `call_opt` argument bound to its `OptionInfo` constructor argument is solely responsible for generating the payoff type. This is determined polymorphically at runtime, which will subsequently be invoked inside the lattice model.

This avoids tight coupling of the classes representing the payoff, the option, and the pricing model, which in turn allows for code reuse, one of the most important and fundamental motivations for utilizing object-oriented programming. One more notable point to recall is that `OptionInfo` is designed, per RAII, to clean up after itself by deleting its `payoff_ptr_` resource in the destructor, meaning the model code implemented within `BinomialLattice` is free of this responsibility.

Implementing Copy Operations

You saw earlier that disabling copying was a quick and simple fix for avoiding shallow copy, which would be perfectly fine in some situations. In other cases, however, we might need to take a copy of an object, such as in a trade entry system that might have multiple deals with the same or partially overlapping contract data being entered. Perhaps more importantly, this leads into a discussion of best practices related to special member functions to be taken up shortly.

But first, to ensure a *deep copy* (*https://oreil.ly/YfvWI*) and thus also still comply with RAII, we need to write our own implementations of the copy constructor and copy assignment operator. This means we first need to remove the `delete` settings previous employed:

```
Class OptionInfo
{
public:

    // . . .

    OptionInfo(const OptionInfo& rhs);
    OptionInfo& operator =(const OptionInfo& rhs);

    // . . .

};
```

Implementation of the copy constructor then requires initializing each data member individually from the object being copied. Initializing `time_to_exp_` is trivial, but we again need to create a copy of the `Payoff` member on the heap and define a new pointer to it. Most of this work is done already in the virtual `clone()` method on each derived payoff object type, so there's not much to implementing the copy constructor:

```
OptionInfo::OptionInfo(const OptionInfo& rhs):
    payoff_ptr_{rhs.payoff_ptr_->clone()},
    time_to_exp_{rhs.time_to_expiration()} {}
```

It might seem that the copy assignment operator would follow fairly similarly, but in reality certain issues do not make it quite that easy. Suppose we proceed naively, as follows. Before reassigning the `payoff_ptr_` member, we need to free the memory that the incumbent is pointing to, by calling the `delete` operator:

```
OptionInfo& OptionInfo::operator =(const OptionInfo& rhs)
{
    // naive implementation
    delete payoff_ptr_;
    payoff_ptr_ = rhs.payoff_ptr_->clone();
    time_to_exp_ = rhs.time_to_expiration();
}
```

The problem here is we will potentially encounter an attempt to assign an object to itself. The following case is trivial, but sometimes self-assignment can be mistakenly obscured and not so obvious:

```
OptionInfo opt_01{. . .};
opt_01 = opt_01;
```

In this case, the `payoff_ptr_` member on `opt_01` would be deleted. In general, calling a member function on a deleted object could result in undefined behavior, which might result in a system crash, and possibly even worse, data corruption propagating into a database.

One solution you might come across is to first check whether a copy of the same object is being attempted:

```
OptionInfo& OptionInfo::operator =(const OptionInfo& rhs)
{
    // Need to check if attempting to copy same object:
    if (this != &rhs)
    {
        delete payoff_ptr_;
        payoff_ptr_ = rhs.payoff_ptr_->clone();
        time_to_exp_ = rhs.time_to_expiration();
    }
    return *this;
}
```

If rhs and the active object (*this) are not the same, the payoff_ptr_ resource is deleted, and the individual assignment operator for each data member is invoked.

However, when working with pointers, it is a fact of life that things can go wrong. In particular, if the memory cannot be allocated by the clone() function, a std::bad_alloc exception will be thrown, and the active OptionInfo object will be left with an invalid payoff_ptr_ resource. Also, although self-assignment would rarely occur, the if statement needs to be executed every time copy assignment is used.

There is, however, a happy ending. As stated in *Effective C++*, "Making operator= exception-safe typically renders it self-assignment-safe, too."[3] This can be effected by employing the *copy-and-swap idiom*, which consists of writing a swap(.) member function, within which the std::swap(.) function, available in the Standard Library <utility> header, swaps each data member one by one. It is "a common mechanism for coping with the possibility of assignment to self."[4]

std::swap(.) does what its name suggests: it swaps the states of two objects. A trivial example with int values shows the basics of how this works:

```
#include <utility>

// . . .

int a = 1, b = 2;
std::swap(a, b);      // Now a = 2 and b = 1
```

std::swap(.) is also safe when swapping two pointers, as only the memory addresses are being exchanged. No memory reallocation is occurring, so we need not be concerned with any deletions or memory leaks.

---

3 Meyers, *Effective C++* (*https://oreil.ly/k8Jo9*), Chapter 2, Item 11.

4 Meyers, *Effective C++* (*https://oreil.ly/HR8AT*), Chapter 4, Item 24.

The swap(.) member function works as follows. First, declare it as a new void member function on OptionInfo that takes in the object to be copied by non-const reference, so that it is modifiable:

```
void swap(OptionInfo& rhs);
```

Then, inside the implementation, apply the std::swap(.) function for each data member:

```
void OptionInfo::swap(OptionInfo& rhs)
{
    using std::swap;
    swap(payoff_ptr_, rhs.payoff_ptr_);
    swap(time_to_exp_, rhs.time_to_exp_);
}
```

As long as the class has both a copy constructor and destructor (with cleanup of any member resources) defined, the copy-and-swap idiom can be applied. As we have already implemented these for OptionInfo, we are good to go. Also, as noted previously, there is no risk in swapping pointer memory addresses (in this case, the payoff_ptr_ pointers), and swapping the fundamental double types for time_to_exp_ is completely safe. As a result, no exceptions will be thrown by our swap(.) member function.

 The swap(.) member function could be declared with the C++11 noexcept keyword, which indicates a function will not throw an exception. For more details, see "Managing Resources with Unique Pointers" on page 91.

Now, to complete the copy part of the copy-and-swap idiom, we can rewrite the implementation of the copy assignment operator in terms of the copy constructor and the swap(.) member function, as shown next. We will first make an anonymous copy of the object argument with the copy constructor, and apply our swap(.) method on this copy. The active object then holding the new payoff and time to expiration will be returned as *this, while the copy holding the swapped-out data dies gracefully thanks to the destructor defined on OptionInfo. Here's the code:

```
OptionInfo& OptionInfo::operator =(const OptionInfo& rhs)
{
    OptionInfo{rhs}.swap(*this);
    return *this;
}
```

Recalling that the swap(.) member function will not throw an exception, the worst possible case—albeit unlikely—would be a failure to allocate the memory for the payoff_ptr_ member in the OptionInfo copy constructor initialization. But even here, an exception would be thrown inside the copy constructor (and could be handled locally), but not inside the definition of the copy assignment operator. A copy of the active object would fail to be generated, but its original state would be maintained.

As a result, the *strong exception guarantee* is enforced. This means that "if an exception is thrown from within [a function] f, then the state of all objects that f modifies will be restored to the state they had before f was called."[5] And, the original issues with self-assignment are averted as well.

The (Old) Rule of Three

The previous section illustrates an example of the *rule of three* that was common practice prior to C++11, before the era of move operations and smart pointers. It says that if any one of a destructor, copy constructor, or copy assignment operator is declared, then we should explicitly declare the other two (or alternatively just disable the copy operations and implement the destructor).

The implication is that if any of these has been implemented, a member resource probably needs special attention (in particular, where a raw pointer member points to allocated memory, as in the example just presented). In the first case, no copying was required, so we just disabled the copy constructor and copy assignment operator in the declaration, but we did implement the destructor so that when an enclosing OptionInfo object went out of scope, the memory pointed to by its Payoff resource was properly deallocated. When copying was assumed to be a requirement, the special copy functions—as well as the destructor—were implemented.

In either case, all three special member functions played a part in preventing memory leaks and/or shallow copies, and thus also complied with RAII.

This rule of three is the predecessor of the *rule of five* that came into being after the release of C++11, with the extra two rules pertaining to the move constructor and move assignment operator. Before returning to this topic, however, we will first look at smart pointers, as these will also be relevant for what follows.

Introducing Smart Pointers

Smart pointers, which eliminate a lot of the risks associated with raw pointers and heap memory allocation, were introduced in C++11. One of these, the *unique pointer* (std::unique_ptr), represents sole (unique) ownership of the pointee. More specifically, it assures that only *one* unique pointer to a particular memory location can exist at one time. It is an example of a very low-cost abstraction, as little to no appreciable difference in performance results (in release mode compilation at least) compared to

---

5 Matt Austern, "Standard Library Exception Policy" (*https://oreil.ly/N3bYx*), ISO C++ proposal N1077, 1997.

a conventional raw pointer. Possession of a unique pointer is transferred using move semantics, since a unique pointer represents single ownership of the pointee, and as such a unique pointer cannot be copied.

Along with unique pointers, two other smart pointers, *shared pointers* and *weak pointers*, were introduced in C++11. These also help prevent problems associated with standard raw pointers when used to allocate and manage memory. In fact, as stated in the Core Guidelines, a unique or shared pointer should be preferred over a raw pointer when possible in order "to avoid forgetting to delete objects."[6]

Our discussion of smart pointers will primarily focus on unique pointers, and they will be the primary go-to smart pointers for this book. In "Managing Resources with Unique Pointers" on page 91, we will then discuss how to swap them in for the raw pointers in the earlier version of the RAII example. Unique pointers provide a safer alternative while also providing a performance improvement by obviating object copy in the constructor of the owning object. You will see this when we return to our payoff and option example in the concluding section of this chapter.

We will also have a look at shared pointers, but these should be used only when shared ownership of a resource is required, such as with an object that provides live updated market data that is shared by multiple trading tasks. Shared pointers are also used in multithreading situations in which a pointed-to object is shared by at least two threads and you don't know which one will be responsible for the object's destruction.

A weak pointer is used for breaking cyclic dependencies that can arise where the reference count of a shared pointer never reaches zero. This is a more advanced topic that is mentioned here only for completeness.

Unique Pointers

A *unique pointer* has sole (unique) ownership of a pointed-to object. It cannot be copied, but possession can be transferred with move semantics. The Core Guidelines recommend using a unique pointer as a general rule when a raw pointer would be otherwise needed. More specifically, again referring to the Core Guidelines, using a unique pointer "is the simplest way to avoid leaks. It is reliable, it makes the type system do much of the work to validate ownership safety, it increases readability, and it has zero or near zero run-time cost."[7]

A unique pointer is defined by a class template in the Standard Library, indicated by `std::unique_ptr<T>`, with template parameter T. For introductory

---

6 "Use `unique_ptr` or `shared_ptr` to avoid forgetting to `delete` objects created using new" (*https://oreil.ly/2PPU5*), ISO C++ Core Guidelines.

7 "Use a `unique_ptr<T>` to hold pointers" (*https://oreil.ly/3Nu3a*), ISO C++ Core Guidelines.

examples, consider a simple case of pointers to `string` objects. The generally recommended method to create a unique pointer is to use the function template `std::make_unique<T>(.)`, subsequently added to the Standard Library with C++14, as shown in the next code example. Like a raw pointer, a unique pointer can be declared and defined separately in two lines (e.g., for separate declaration and initialization as an object member), or combined in one line (otherwise typically preferred to avoid wasted cycles) by using `auto` for implicit typing, as the righthand side of the assignment makes it obvious what is being created. The Standard Library `<memory>` header needs to be included to use smart pointers:

```
#include <memory>      // For Standard Library smart pointers
#include <utility>     // std::move

std::unique_ptr<string> ptr_01;
// . . .
ptr_01 = std::make_unique<string>("To err is human");

// Alternatively (and better when possible), on one line:
auto ptr_02 =
    std::make_unique<string>("To moo, bovine");
```

The actual string object can be obtained by dereferencing the unique pointers in the usual way, with the * operator:

```
cout << format("Contents of ptr_01: {}\n", *ptr_01);
cout << format("Contents of ptr_02: {}\n", *ptr_02);
```

The output is:

```
Contents of ptr_01: To err is human
Contents of ptr_02: To moo, bovine
```

Next, we can transfer ownership of the allocated memory to a different unique pointer, say, `ptr_03`. This is accomplished using move semantics:

```
auto ptr_03 = std::move(ptr_02);
```

The unique pointer `ptr_02` is set to a null state, as `ptr_03` now assumes exclusive ownership of the second `std::string` object. Attempting to output `*ptr_02` or use it elsewhere can result in a runtime error. Although unique pointers provide a safe yet efficient means of managing allocated heap memory, this shows that you still need to exercise caution at times when using them, as this is a problem that can slip through the cracks undetected at compile time and quite possibly crash your program.

If there ever is any possible doubt, you can check whether a pointer is indeed valid by checking whether it is null. This can be done the same way as you would with a raw pointer:

```
if (ptr_02)
{
```

```
    cout << format("ptr_02 is not null\n");
}
else
{
    cout << format("ptr_02 is null\n");
}
```

Attempting to dereference `ptr_02` without checking first:

```
auto s = *ptr_02;    // ptr_02 is null -- DON'T do this!
```

can result in (grave) undefined behavior as noted earlier, although depending on your compiler settings, you might at least get a compile-time *warning* first.

Assigning new data to the pointed-to memory is also the same as with raw pointers, by dereferencing the pointer first:

```
*ptr_01 = "To bark is canine";
*ptr_03 = "To purr, feline";
```

Finally, if a unique pointer is no longer needed before going out of scope, it can be deleted and set to null explicitly with its `reset()` member function:

```
ptr_01.reset();
if (!ptr_01)
{
    cout << "ptr_01 is null" << "\n";    // Will be displayed
}
```

An equivalent result can be obtained by setting a unique pointer equal to `nullptr`, another keyword introduced in C++11:

```
ptr_03 = nullptr
if (!ptr_03)
{
    cout << "ptr_03 is null" << "\n";    // Will be displayed
}
```

It should be noted, however, that if you find yourself resetting or nulling out a unique pointer before a function exits, it might be an indication that your function is too long.

Shared Pointers

In contrast to a unique pointer—which, as indicated by its name, is *uniquely* responsible for a pointed-to object in memory—a *shared pointer* can share this responsibility with another shared pointer. Although similar to a raw pointer, a shared pointer is a safer alternative because the pointed-to memory will not be released until the last remaining shared pointer to a given shared pointee goes out of scope. This is made possible behind the scenes by *reference counting*, which keeps count of the number of active shared pointers to a common block of heap memory. The pointed-to object will persist until the count reaches zero, and only at this point will the memory be deallocated, thus preventing a memory leak and possible undefined behavior at runtime.

Similar to a unique pointer, a shared pointer can be created by invoking the `make_shared(.)` function. This can again be performed in two separate lines, or on one line (with `auto`, and again, typically preferred), as shown here:

```
std::shared_ptr<std::string> sp_one;
// . . .
sp_one = std::make_shared<string>("To err is expected");

// Single line
auto sp_two =
    std::make_shared<string>("To nap is supine");
```

Like a raw pointer, the pointed-to objects are again accessed by dereferencing:

```
cout << format("Contents of sp_one: {}\n", *sp_one);
cout << format("Contents of sp_two: {}\n", *sp_two);
```

The output is:

```
Contents of sp_one: To err is expected
Contents of sp_two: To nap is supine
```

To see how reference counting works here, we can first call the `use_count()` member function on `shared_ptr`. The following displays a value of 1, as at this stage only one pointer is pointing to the `string` object in heap memory:

```
cout << format("How many pointers are there to sp_one? {}\n",
    sp_one.use_count());    // count = 1
```

With a shared pointer, we can create multiple pointers to the same object, similarly to a raw pointer:

```
auto sp_one_2 = sp_one;
auto sp_one_3 = sp_one_2;
```

Now, `use_count()` will return a value of 3 if called on any of these shared pointer objects. Unlike a raw pointer, however, there is no `delete` operator. Instead, if the `reset()` function is called on `sp_one_2`, then that pointer becomes null, and the reference count will fall to 2:

```
sp_one_2.reset();

auto count = sp_one.use_count();    // = 2
```

If the code examples here for `shared_ptr` were inside a function, then when `sp_one` and `sp_one_3` go out of scope at the end of a function block, both would be destroyed, and the memory occupied by the pointed-to `string` object would be deallocated as the reference count hits 0.

For an example of using shared pointers in a financial setting, common commercial trading system software allows a trader to enter trades, monitor and revalue positions, and run risk analysis on trading books. Each of these tasks, visualized on a workstation in separate application windows, can be open concurrently, and multiple windows might be open at the same time. They will also typically rely on live market data (read-only), provided by an internal service or external vendor, updated in real time from a price feed. A shared pointer pointing to an object containing the requested data would be created with the first task, followed by additional shared pointers for subsequent tasks.

With the same set of market data being used in multiple places, you don't want to delete the memory until all the various windows have finished using the data. Several windows might use market data in a trading system, including, for instance:

- A daily chart (e.g., a graph of stock price over time)
- An order entry window that might show the level 1 price (top of book) and level 2 (depth of book) prices
- A position window with profit/loss (P/L) value calculations
- A risk checker that might be configured with a risk rule to prevent limit orders from being sent with limit prices that are too far away (e.g., >10% away) from the current market price

A shared pointer might also point to a trade execution. Trading systems calculate and display partial execution records (aka *partial fills*) for an order. A few windows would display this information in different ways:

- The average price of each order, which needs to be recalculated from the child orders each time a new partial fill comes in
- A list of the executions themselves, so the trader can drill down on the parent order to see how and when it was filled
- A positions window, which keeps a running total of the user's position, typically aggregated by symbol and account number
- An execution for an order can also be canceled after it has happened, if it were deemed incorrect for some reason and would need to be reversed out of the displays and calculations mentioned in the preceding points

Although shared pointers provide the very significant safety advantages noted here, there are two caveats to consider. First, shared pointers have greater performance overhead than raw pointers and unique pointers, so some cost/benefit analysis would be in order rather than proceeding naively. Second, shared pointers are also often found in multithreaded applications with data that is no longer just read-only, and the underlying object is shared by two or more threads. In general, certain precautions need to be in place when working with multithreaded code, and in particular, conditioning on the value of use_count() is not usable in this case. You can find details on the proper use of shared pointers in multithreaded applications, a more advanced topic, in Chapters 3 and 4 of C++ *Concurrency in Action* (*https://oreil.ly/ RLCtx*) by Anthony Williams (Manning, 2019).

Managing Resources with Unique Pointers

Returning now to the payoff and option example, we can improve the version discussed in "Resource Ownership with Raw Pointers" on page 70 rather significantly by managing the Payoff resource with a unique pointer (introduced previously) and move semantics (discussed in the previous chapter). The benefits will be safer and more efficient code, while still retaining the benefits of RAII.

As before, let's begin with the case not requiring copying. In this case, because of the presence of a unique pointer member, the compiler prevents copying from ever happening at all, thus avoiding associated problems surfacing at runtime. From there, we will look at a sketch this time of a Monte Carlo pricing model application, and then conclude with a discussion of special copy functions used when a unique pointer data member is present.

Just Move It

Suppose now we go ahead and replace the Payoff pointer member on an OptionInfo object with a unique pointer. To start, we can get a good idea of what it will look like by writing out the OptionInfo class declaration. The interface is clear, and the intended semantics are evident:

```
#include <memory>      // std::unique_ptr

class OptionInfo
{
public:
    OptionInfo(std::unique_ptr<Payoff> payoff, double time_to_exp);
    double option_payoff(double spot) const;
    double time_to_expiration() const;

private:
    std::unique_ptr<Payoff> payoff_ptr_;
    double time_to_exp_;
};
```

Note also that no destructor is declared, because a `unique_ptr` automatically takes care of memory deallocation for us when an enclosing `OptionInfo` object goes out of scope. The compiler-provided default destructor is sufficient now, and thus we eliminate problems associated with forgetting to delete a raw pointer.

To initialize the `payoff_ptr_` member, move semantics are applied in its initialization, as shown here:

```
OptionInfo::OptionInfo(std::unique_ptr<Payoff> payoff, double time_to_exp) :
    payoff_ptr_{std::move(payoff)}, time_to_exp_{time_to_exp} {}
```

As a result, we don't need to call the `clone()` function on the `Payoff` derivation, since we are just moving a unique pointer. Now, two very nice corollaries thus emerge:

- No copy of the payoff object is generated from clone functions, meaning more-efficient code.

- Less can go wrong, as no manual memory allocation is involved at construction, and we have no risk of forgetting to delete the resource in the destructor.

The definitions of the constructor and the payoff for a call option are the same as in the raw pointer version, so we are left with the same class implementation as before, sans a `clone()` member function (for now):

```
CallPayoff::CallPayoff(double strike) :strike_{strike} {}

double CallPayoff::payoff(double price) const
{
    return std::max(spot - strike_, 0.0);
}
```

The put payoff is again similar, except for the spot and strike prices being reversed.

Returning to the updated `OptionInfo` class, the `option_payoff(.)` member function implementation is then also exactly the same as before, as the syntax for dereferencing a unique pointer is the same:

```
double OptionInfo::option_payoff(double spot) const
{
    return payoff_ptr_->payoff(spot);
}
```

So now, we can construct an `OptionInfo` object without generating a copy of the payoff object. One approach is to create a unique pointer to the particular payoff type and then apply `std::move(.)` in the constructor argument:

```
auto call_payoff = std::make_unique<CallPayoff>(75.0);
OptionInfo call_opt{std::move(call_payoff), 0.5};
```

Alternatively, this can be written in one line with an anonymous temporary unique pointer created by `std::make_unique` at construction of the enclosing `OptionInfo` object:

```
OptionInfo call_opt{std::make_unique<CallPayoff>(75.0), 0.5};
```

Also notable is we don't have to worry about shallow copies either, as the compiler prevents an attempt to copy an object with a `unique_ptr` member, which is again a good thing as opposed to encountering problems at runtime:

```
OptionInfo call_copy{call_opt};      // Will not compile!
```

As such, we don't need to explicitly disable the copy operations.

On the other hand, because a unique pointer is movable, moving an `OptionInfo` object is completely legal, by simply using the default move constructor,

```
OptionInfo call_move{std::move(call_opt)};
```

or the move assignment operator:

```
OptionInfo call_move_assgn{std::make_unique<CallPayoff>(85.0), 0.45};
// . . .
call_move_assgn = std::move(call_move);
```

To recap, by replacing the pre-C++11 cloned initialization method with a unique pointer and move semantics, we get the following:

- More-efficient code, as object cloning is not necessary for initialization of the payoff (replaced by *moving* a unique pointer)
- Safer code that prevents undefined behavior and memory leaks commonly associated with raw pointers
- No implementation of the destructor is required, as the code went from explicitly managing a resource to delegating that responsibility to a `unique_ptr` object
- Prevention of shallow copies at compile time
- Safe use of the compiler-provided default move constructor and move assignment, with no user-defined implementation required

And ultimately, we retain compliance with RAII, as the two requirements are met, but in a slightly different and improved way:

- `payoff_ptr_` is initialized by *transferring unique control* of the heap memory address holding the respective `CallPayoff` resource at construction of its owning `OptionInfo` instance.

- This resource will persist throughout the lifetime of its owner, and it will be destroyed *automatically* only when the default destructor on the owning `OptionInfo` is called.

In other words, when using a unique pointer, the lifetime of the `CallPayoff` resource is still tied to the lifetime of its owning `OptionInfo` object, as required by RAII. In addition, we obtain the preceding benefits compared to the version in "Resource Ownership with Raw Pointers" on page 70.

Using the Result in a Pricing Model

In the raw pointer version using a "virtual constructor," we concluded with a sketch of an example using a binomial lattice pricing model. Just to provide a little variety, we can apply our modernized version (with copy operations again deleted, for now) to the case of a Monte Carlo option pricing model, with a proposed declaration as follows (again, this is a high-level sketch; an implementation example is presented in Chapter 6):

```
MCOptionValuation
{
public:
    MCOptionValuation(OptionInfo&& opt,
        double vol, double int_rate, int time_steps,
        double div_rate);

    double calc_price(double spot, int unif_start_seed, int num_scenarios);

private:
    OptionInfo opt_;

    . . .

};
```

Note the `OptionInfo` argument type can be used as a Monte Carlo pricing model constructor argument just as it would with a modestly updated binomial lattice class. In general, this means that the `OptionInfo` class can be written just once and reused with multiple pricing models. It carries with it the information about its payoff (owning a call or put resource) and the time left to expiration, meaning the model object itself is indifferent to these settings when it is constructed.

All market data other than the underlying spot price is again taken into the model object constructor, along with the user-supplied argument for the number of time steps for each simulation. The underlying spot argument is also again delayed until the option value is calculated with the `calc_price(.)` member function, where the remaining user arguments for the random seed and number of simulated scenarios are set.

On a side note, in contrast to a lattice model, the basic Monte Carlo method cannot handle American options because of possible early exercise, so there is no OptType parameter in the calc_price(.) member function. Monte Carlo simulation does, however, require a starting seed value and the number of random equity price path scenarios. For a Monte Carlo–based model that does evaluate optimal early exercise, the Longstaff and Schwartz least squares Monte Carlo model (*https://oreil.ly/_KAJs*), also noted in Chapter 1, is often cited.

The common themes between the Monte Carlo and binomial lattice cases are that we can ultimately use the same OptionInfo type—carrying only its associated payoff member and time to expiration—while the remaining market data is required only at construction of a pricing model object and when the calc_price(.) member function is called. This means we can separate out the division of labor among the different classes and reuse them within the context of pricing models, without having to duplicate code. This hopefully demonstrates a key motivation behind object-oriented programming, and why it has remained popular in financial software development.

If Copy Operations Are Required

For pricing model applications such as those shown in the preceding examples, copy operations on a class are often not necessary. And again, with a unique_ptr member present, an attempt to use the default copy constructor will conveniently fail at compile time, preventing any related undefined behavior from ever occurring.

On the other hand, as before, sometimes copying is a requirement. For this, we need an updated clone() function, but now only for the copy constructor. This gives us the following declarations:

```
class Payoff
{
public:
    virtual double payoff(double price) const = 0;
    virtual std::unique_ptr<Payoff> clone() const = 0;
    virtual ~Payoff() = default;
};

class CallPayoff final : public Payoff
{
public:
    CallPayoff(double strike);
    double payoff(double price) const override;
    std::unique_ptr<Payoff> clone() const override; // clone() here returns a
                                                    // unique_ptr<Payoff>,
                                                    // not unique_ptr<CallPayoff>

private:
    double strike_;
```

```
};

class PutPayoff final : public Payoff
{
public:
    PutPayoff(double strike);
    double payoff(double price) const override;
    std::unique_ptr<Payoff> clone() const override;  // clone() here returns a
                                                      // unique_ptr<Payoff>,
                                                      // not unique_ptr<PutPayoff>

private:
    double strike_;
};
```

Clone methods, revisited

While cloning the payoff will remain unnecessary at construction of a modernized OptionInfo object, it will be needed for its copy constructor. One semantic difference exists: its return type of the payoff resource will be a unique_ptr<Payoff> type rather than a raw pointer to a particular derived payoff (CallPayoff, PutPayoff), as in general, a unique_ptr<Derived> can be moved into a unique_ptr<Base> object.

The updated clone() method, with implementation shown here for a call payoff, returns a unique_ptr to a copy of the active object in memory:

```
std::unique_ptr<Payoff> CallPayoff::clone() const
{
    return std::make_unique<CallPayoff>(*this);
}
```

Implementing the put payoff would be similar.

Implementation of the updated copy operations

We can now update the OptionInfo class with a user-defined copy constructor, using the new clone() methods on the derived payoff classes. Our modernized class will also require a copy assignment operator, but this will now follow quite easily because of the work already completed in the raw pointer version using the copy/swap idiom.

Before proceeding, note two points. First, in the updated declaration that follows, the swap(.) function is now being declared with the C++11 noexcept keyword, which specifies that the function will not throw an exception. We know this is true, as established earlier, because simply swapping memory addresses and built-in numerical types will not throw. The noexcept declaration also carries other benefits to be discussed shortly.

Second, formulating the updated OptionInfo class is still a work in progress, as there are considerations regarding the special move member functions required to make this example complete. This second point is covered in "The rule of zero/the rule of five" on page 98, but for now, just understand that what immediately follows is again not yet complete.

As the updated declaration now stands, we have the following:

```
class OptionInfo
{
public:
    // Note: Still a work in progress, not yet complete . . .
    OptionInfo(std::unique_ptr<Payoff> payoff, double time_to_exp);
    double option_payoff(double spot) const;
    double time_to_expiration() const;
    void swap(OptionInfo& rhs) noexcept;

    OptionInfo(const OptionInfo& rhs);            // Copy constructor
    OptionInfo& operator =(const OptionInfo& rhs);   // Copy assignment

    // More to come . . .

private:
    std::unique_ptr<Payoff> payoff_ptr_;
    double time_to_exp_;
};
```

Implementation of the copy constructor is pretty much painless and similar to the previous raw pointer version while again satisfying our RAII requirements. The difference mainly lies with the updated clone() method on payoff_ptr_ that returns a unique pointer to be moved, rather than a raw pointer:

```
OptionInfo::OptionInfo(const OptionInfo& rhs) :
    payoff_ptr_{rhs.payoff_ptr_->clone()},
    time_to_exp_{rhs.time_to_expiration()} {}
```

As for the copy assignment operator, the syntax is exactly the same as in the raw pointer version, with the addition again of a swap() method that uses std::swap(.) to swap each of the data members individually. This works with unique pointers as well. Note that the noexcept keyword is also required for the implementation of the swap() member function (and in general if a function is declared noexcept):

```
#include <utility>

// . . .

void OptionInfo::swap(OptionInfo& rhs) noexcept
{
    using std::swap;
    swap(payoff_ptr_, rhs.payoff_ptr_);
    swap(time_to_exp_, rhs.time_to_exp_);
}

OptionInfo& OptionInfo::operator =(const OptionInfo& rhs)
```

```
{
    OptionInfo{rhs}.swap(*this);
    return *this;
}
```

This will again prevent problems associated by self-assignment by adhering to the strong exception guarantee.

The noexcept designation as applied to the implementation of the swap(.) member function does not technically affect the function's behavior, as it already is guaranteed not to throw an exception. However, it does add clarity to the code so that other developers will easily understand its intent.

Suppose, for example, that a line throwing a std::runtime_error somehow gets carelessly placed in the swap(.) implementation. Depending on your compiler and its settings, it *might* issue a warning. At runtime, because the function has broken its contract marked noexcept, the program will terminate at that point:

```
void OptionInfo::swap(OptionInfo& rhs) noexcept
{
    using std::swap;
    swap(payoff_ptr_, rhs.payoff_ptr_);
    swap(time_to_exp_, rhs.time_to_exp_);

    // For demonstration -- DO NOT DO THIS!
    // Program will be terminated.
    throw std::runtime_error{"Error: Sloppy programming!"};
}
```

One more important benefit of declaring a function noexcept is it also frees the compiler from "produc[ing] additional code that also hampers optimizations."[8]

The rule of zero/the rule of five

As noted in the preceding section, we are not quite completely done, as implementing the copy member functions will affect the behavior of the default move special member functions.

Recall from the version of OptionInfo with a raw pointer Payoff member, we discussed the rule of three from the pre-C++11 era, which indicates that if any one of the copy constructor, copy assignment operator, or destructor is defined, then user-defined versions of the remaining two should also be present (including the option of disabling the copy constructor/assignment operator). With the addition of move constructors and move assignment operators in C++11, this means two more

---

8 Nicolai M. Josuttis, *The C++ Standard Library: A Tutorial and Reference* (*https://oreil.ly/1DtCT*), 2nd edition (Addison-Wesley, 2012), section 3.1.7.

special member functions need to be considered. As such, the situation becomes more complex, with default behavior dependent on which of the five is/are defined:

- If either the copy constructor or copy assignment operator is defined (or both), the compiler-provided default move operations are disabled.
- If the destructor is defined, we get the same result.

Even worse, the code will compile and run, but move operations will be replaced by their copy counterparts, meaning any optimizations expected from using move semantics will be silently voided at runtime. Some compilers may issue a warning, but others do not, so this is another case of a problem possibly going undetected.

For these reasons, the *rule of five* supplants the rule of three, as follows: if any one of these five special functions is defined, include definitions for the remaining four. This can include just declaring them as `default` or `delete` where appropriate, and leaving generation of the implementations to the compiler.

To ensure that default move operations behave as we would expect, when the copy operations are user-defined, we need to explicitly set the move operations to `default`, and for good measure the destructor as well, even though responsibility for deallocating the memory pointed to by `payoff_ptr_` has been delegated to its `unique_ptr` type:

```
class OptionInfo
{
public:
    OptionInfo(std::unique_ptr<Payoff> payoff, double time_to_exp);
    double option_payoff(double spot) const;
    double time_to_expiration() const;
    void swap(OptionInfo& rhs) noexcept;

    OptionInfo(const OptionInfo& rhs);                  // User-defined
    OptionInfo& operator =(const OptionInfo& rhs);      // User-defined

    // Remaining Rule of Five:

    // Default move constructor
    OptionInfo(OptionInfo&& rhs) = default;

    // Default move assignment
    OptionInfo& operator =(OptionInfo&& rhs) = default;

    // Default destructor
    ~OptionInfo() = default;

private:
    std::unique_ptr<Payoff> payoff_ptr_;
    double time_to_exp_;
};
```

The rule of five has two corollaries in the Core Guidelines that are also germane here:

If you can avoid defining these five special class functions, do.

    This was the case for the `OptionInfo` version, where no user-defined copy functions were implemented. This is called the *rule of zero*, and it should be preferred when possible.

If you `default` or `delete` any copy, move, or destructor function, `default` or `delete` them all.

    The Core Guidelines explain:

> The semantics of copy, move, and destruction are closely related, so if one needs to be declared, the odds are that others need consideration too. Declaring any copy/move/destructor function, even as `default` or `delete` will suppress the implicit declaration of a move constructor and move assignment operator. Declaring a move constructor or move assignment operator, even as `=default` or `=delete` will cause an implicitly generated copy constructor or implicitly generated copy assignment operator to be defined as deleted. So as soon as any of these are declared, the others should all be declared to avoid unwanted effects like turning all potential moves into more expensive copies, or making a class move-only.[9]

Two informative blog references that provide more details on the rule of zero/rule of five appear on Jonathan Boccara's Fluent C++ site (*https://oreil.ly/6wHQh*) and Rainer Grimm's Modernes C++ (*https://oreil.ly/nuFVq*).

As noted in Chapter 2, this book focuses on using the default move constructor and default move assignment operator, as these are sufficient for our needs in subsequent chapters. If you are interested, however, in user-defined cases, Appendix C provides introductory examples.

Summary

The main focus of this chapter was to show how more modern methods—namely, employing `std::unique_ptr`—can make handling a memory resource on an owning object safer and more efficient, with little to no performance penalty. In our example of RAII using raw pointers, RAII provided safer code, but it came with a performance cost due to the copy penalty when acquiring and initializing the `Payoff` resource.

By introducing unique pointers and using move semantics to implement RAII in a modern context, we eliminated the copy penalty while obtaining additional benefits

---

9 "If you define or =delete any copy, move, or destructor function, define or =delete them all" (*https://oreil.ly/ gnbK4*), ISO C++ Core Guidelines.

in terms of safer and cleaner code. The rule of five, which has the two newer special move member functions in play, introduced new considerations compared to the older rule of three. However, at the same time, with a unique pointer handling the `Payoff` resource on the owning `OptionInfo` class, defining the destructor as `default` was sufficient. This removed the risk of forgetting to manually code in the release of its memory resource. In the case of not implementing the special copy functions, we could just observe the rule of zero rather than the full rule of five.

Object-oriented programming remains a viable choice even as more attention in the C++ world is being devoted to functional and generic programming. And if you are inclined to dive into generic programming with templates, some of the same high-level object-oriented programming concepts can still be relevant. In any case, handling a derived resource by an owning object is still likely to be common in financial programming.

Shared pointers—the other smart pointers covered in this chapter—provide a safer alternative to conventional raw pointers, allowing multiple pointers to the same object but with reference counting. This can help prevent the associated problems with raw pointers: memory leaks, dangling pointers, and undefined behavior lurking about. However, a trade-off with performance needs to be taken into consideration, and additional considerations are necessary when a shared pointer is used within a multithreaded context.

Further Resources

For more information on the strong exception guarantee, *The C++ Programming Language*, 4th edition, by Bjarne Stroustrup (Addison-Wesley, 2013), Section 13.2, "Exception Guarantees" (*https://oreil.ly/5y7-1*) is especially helpful, specifically the bullet point "The strong guarantee for key operations."

For a more in-depth look at the rule of five (plus the default constructor), a Bloomberg speaker series lecture by Howard Hinnant (*https://oreil.ly/UctQ2*) (the primary author of the new date classes in C++20, covered in Chapter 7) is very informative. The table shown at 23:22 shows how the different combinations of special member function declarations can affect others. To avoid surprises, the upshot is if the intention is to use the constructor-provided defaults for each, use the rule of zero. Otherwise, use the rule of five.

CHAPTER 4

The Standard Template Library Part I: Containers and Iterators

The *Standard Template Library*, also commonly referred to as the *STL*, is a subset of C++'s Standard Library that houses a set of container classes, including `std::vector`, that will be discussed in this chapter. The STL also provides a group of algorithms applicable to those containers and other containers—including your own—that follow the same coding conventions.

The STL is a revolutionary design brought to the world by Alexander Stepanov, David Musser, and Meng Lee. It was officially integrated into the C++ Standard library in the 1990s, as described in "C++ in 2005" (*https://oreil.ly/5OXuY*) by Bjarne Stroustrup. This "library within a library" combines algorithms and containers to form a whole that is significantly larger than the sum of its parts. Technically speaking, as Scott Meyers points out in the introduction to *Effective STL*, there is "no official definition of *the STL*, and different people mean different things when they use the term."[1] However, it is used throughout the C++ vernacular to represent the container classes, iterators, and algorithms.

You have already seen that a `vector` on its own is quite useful and versatile. It is the workhorse of the STL and the container of choice for most financial modeling applications (as well as for many other application domains). For this reason alone, it is worth getting familiar with the `vector` class in more detail, but in doing so, you will also find it easier to then understand how other STL containers work.

---

1 Scott Meyers, *Effective STL* (*https://oreil.ly/WGsAr*) (Addison-Wesley, 2001).

What makes STL containers so powerful is their relationship with STL *algorithms*. Algorithms work on an abstraction called *iterators*, rather than on containers themselves:

- Containers define how data is organized.
- Iterators describe how organized data can be traversed.
- Algorithms describe what you can do on the data.

At a high level, algorithms let you traverse an STL container, and they can apply a function to each member, or a subset thereof, efficiently replacing iterative `for` and `while` statements in a single statement. Since algorithms are expressed in terms of iterators, not in terms of containers, you can write a single algorithm and leverage its impact on a whole set of containers at once.

STL containers such as a `vector` are generic in the sense that they can hold a homogeneous set of (almost) any arbitrary type—indicated as a template parameter—be it a plain numerical type such as `double` or a class type such as `BlackScholes` (from Chapter 2), as long as these types conform to the requirements of the functions we seek to apply to them. Such containers can also handle polymorphic objects as pointers to a common interface base class, in which case three programming paradigms converge: functional, with STL algorithms; generic, using STL container class templates; and object-oriented, at least under some definitions of that term, whereby the elements are pointers to polymorphic objects. In modern C++, as you saw in Chapter 3, unique pointers provide a safe yet efficient alternative to the raw pointers of yore, and these can also be held as elements in an STL container.

In this chapter, we will first work through an overview/review of templates, as these are the *T* in *STL*. STL containers and iterators will follow. Chapter 5 demonstrates how iterative tasks over container elements can be expressed more efficiently and safely with STL algorithms, compared to loops. Most of the material presented in these two chapters will focus primarily on C++ itself as opposed to applications in finance, but it will set us up for more applied examples in the remaining chapters.

Templates

Templates in C++ are like blueprints for functions and classes. They facilitate generic programming in C++, enabling a function or class to be designed for arbitrary types, as opposed to individual versions written for each type that can end up duplicating code to a large degree. The following examples of a generic function and of a generic class will give you insight on how templates work in C++.

To start, let's go back to the case of a `vector`, which is a common example of a class template. Like other containers, it can hold a homogeneous collection of an arbitrary type by specifying the type as a template parameter inside the angle brackets:

```
// A vector of real numbers:
vector<double> v{1.0, 2.0, 3.0};

// A vector of BlackScholes objects:
vector<BlackScholes> opts
{
    {100.0, 106.0, 0.04, 0.5, PayoffType::Call},
    {110.0, 106.0, 0.04, 0.5, PayoffType::Put},
    {95.0, 106.0, 0.032, 0.25, PayoffType::Call},
    {105.0, 106.0, 0.032, 0.02, PayoffType::Put},
    {115.0, 106.0, 0.045, 1.5, PayoffType::Put}
};
```

The `vector` class is generic in the sense that it doesn't care what type of object it is holding.

Going a step further, to better understand how templates work, we will next look at how to implement user-defined function and class templates.

Using Function Templates

Recalling the `Fraction` class from Chapter 2, we can add a definition of the * operator, and accessors for the numerator and denominator, in order to help demonstrate *function templates*. The previous inclusions of the < and spaceship operators will also be used shortly in an example involving class templates. The updated header file could be written as follows:

```
class Fraction
{
public:
    Fraction(unsigned n, unsigned d);
    bool operator === (const Fraction& rhs) const = default;
    std::strong_ordering operator <=> (const Fraction& rhs) const;

    // operator * has been added for current chapter:
    Fraction operator *(const Fraction& rhs) const;
    unsigned n() const;                // return n_ (numerator)
    unsigned d() const;                // return d_ (denominator)

private:
    unsigned n_, d_;

};
```

The two accessors returning the numerator and denominator are trivial, and for the *
operator, we can return the fraction product:

```
Fraction Fraction::operator *(const Fraction& rhs) const
{
    return {n_ * rhs.n_, d_ * rhs.d_};
}
```

Suppose now you need to square integer, real, and Fraction types. Proceeding
naively, as C++ is a strongly typed language, you could write three separate functions:

```
// integers:
int int_square(int k)
{
    return k * k;
}

// real numbers (double):
double dbl_square(double x)
{
    return x * x;
}

// Fraction:
Fraction frac_square(const Fraction& f)
{
    return f * f;    // operator* on Fraction is defined
}
```

However, all three can be replaced by a single function template:

```
template <typename T>
T tmpl_square(const T& t)
{
    return t * t;
}
```

Squaring an integer or double-precision value is trivial, as the numerical arguments
imply their types, int and double, respectively:

```
int sq_int = tmpl_square(4);          // tmpl_square(const int&)
double sq_real = tmpl_square(4.2);    // tmpl_square(const double&)
```

Applying the function to a Fraction is more interesting, because we no longer have
the built-in arithmetic operators, as we do with numerical types. The object type
needs to be specified somehow, and this can be done in a couple of ways. One is to
construct a Fraction object and pass it into the function:

```
Fraction frac{2, 3};
Fraction sq_frac = tmpl_square(frac);    // tmpl_square(const Fraction&)
```

The second option is to use uniform initialization, where the constructor arguments alone suffice. But here, we need to specify the template parameter; otherwise, the tmpl_square(.) function will have no way of knowing the type being passed:

```
auto sq_frac_unif = tmpl_square<Fraction>({2, 3});
```

In each case, $\frac{4}{9}$ will be returned:

```
// Use the accessors to get the numerator and denominator in each case:
cout << format("Square of fraction {}/{} is {}/{}\n",
    frac.numer(), frac.denom(), sq_frac.numer(), sq_frac.denom());

cout << format("Square of fractions using unif initialization = {}/{}\n",
    sq_frac_unif.numer(), sq_frac_unif.denom());
```

The output is:

```
Square of fraction 2/3 is 4/9
Square of fraction using unif initialization = 4/9
```

The function template does not care what the specific type T is, as long as the multiplication operator is defined. If it is not, such as in attempting to square a Circle object (Chapter 3), the code would not compile:

```
// operator* not defined for Circle.
// Will not compile!

Circle circ{1.0};
double area = tmpl_square(circ);
```

 Although it is generally good when errors are detected by the compiler, with template code, compiler error output can get long and somewhat cryptic, making it more painful to locate the source of the problem in the code, particularly in more realistic settings with expanded code complexity. Fortunately, we have new ways of alleviating this, particularly C++20 concepts, which are presented in Chapter 10.

Using Class Templates

A *class template* is syntactically similar to a function template except that a template parameter applies to the entire class. For example, here is a class template that will hold two private members of the same type, and provide a public member function that computes the minimum of the two:

```
// Class Declaration:
template <typename T>
export class MyPair
{
```

```
public:
    MyPair(const T &first, const T &second) :a_(first), b_(second) {}
    T get_min() const;

private:
    T a_, b_;
};

// Class implementation:
template <typename T>
MyPair<T>::MyPair(T first, T second) :a_(first), b_(second) {}

template <typename T>
T MyPair<T>::get_min() const
{
    return a_ < b_ ? a_ : b_;
}
```

As long as the less-than operator < is defined for type T, the code will compile. For two int types, the inequality definition is provided by the language; no problem here:

```
MyPair<int> mp_int{10, 26};
int min_int = mp_int.get_min();            // OK, returns 10
```

Using the simple Fraction class defined in Chapter 2, the inequality was defined within the class, so we are OK here as well:

```
MyPair<Fraction> mp_frac{{3, 2}, {5, 11}};
Fraction min_frac = mp_frac.get_min();     //  Returns 5/11
```

Attempting to call the get_min() member function when the template parameter type does not support the inequality, such as again with the Circle class, the result will be a compile-time error:

```
// Will not compile!

MyPair<Circle> fail{{1.5}, {3.0}};
fail.get_min(); // no operator< for Circle
```

We could have expressed the body of MyPair<T>::get_min() as

```
T retval;              // ❶
retval = a < b? a : b;  // ❷
return retval;
```

However, this would have required that T expressed a copy assignment operator ❷ as well as a default constructor ❶, whereas our suggested implementation does not impose these requirements. When writing generic code, it is often useful to consider what we ask of the types for which our code will be instantiated and strive to ask only for what we really require, nothing more. This widens the set of types for which our code will be applicable.

Compiling Template Code

Templates are primarily written in header files, because templates guide the compiler as to how code should be generated. You can think about templates as being like a pattern for a suit. Nothing will happen until the tailor selects the material to be used (analogous to the type), and then cuts it and stitches it together. A tailor could even say, "In general, this is how I do things, but for you, I have something special in mind." For templates, this is called a *specialization*.

For each type that a function or class template uses in its template parameter, a specialization is generated by the compiler, resulting in additional binary code for each. Suppose we write the same three lines of code as in the earlier example:

```
int sq_int = tmpl_square(4);
double sq_real = tmpl_square(4.2);
auto sq_frac_unif = tmpl_square<Fraction>({2, 3});
```

Putting these three lines in your code will cause the compiler to generate three versions (specializations) of tmpl_square(.), one for type int, one for type double, and one for Fraction.

Similarly, creating instances of MyPair objects as before will result in compiled code for each of the int, double, and Fraction specializations:

```
MyPair<int> mp_int{10, 6};
MyPair<double> mp_dbl{4.22, 55.1115};
MyPair<Fraction> mp_frac{{3, 2}, {5, 10}};
```

Of course, had we written these respective functions and classes individually with parameter type overloading, we would have arrived at the same solution. Templates save us the trouble of manually writing that code.

Additional benefits of templates include facilitating generic programming, as well as potentially improving runtime performance. The downside is that templates can increase build times quite significantly with template-heavy codebases, although this situation has improved since C++11. The introduction of modules in C++20 in some respects has also helped reduce build times, discussed in Chapter 10.

We can also use default template parameters to make user code simpler to express. Returning to the MyPair class that holds two elements of the same type T, we could default this template parameter to a double type:

```
template <typename T = double>
class MyPair
{
public:
    MyPair(T first, T second);
    T get_min() const;

private:
```

```
    T a_, b_;
};
```

Then, if we want a `MyPair` object to hold two `double` types, we can omit the explicit type name from inside the angle brackets:

```
MyPair<> real_pair{19.73, 10.26};
double min_val = real_pair.get_min();        // 19.73
```

Class templates can take in more than one parameter type. For example, the `MyPair` class template could have taken in two template parameters not necessarily of the same type:

```
template <typename T, typename U>
class MyPair
{
public:
    MyPair(T first, U second);
    // . . .

private:
    T a_;
    U b_;
};
```

Another example is the `std::map<K, V>` class template, an associative STL container covered in "Associative Containers" on page 128. Templates can also involve compile-time integral values, such as with the fixed-size sequential STL container `std::array<T, N>`, where N is a positive integer, which will also be discussed in this chapter (you might also recall that you got a sneak preview of this container type in Chapter 2). Templates can even accept templates as parameters—which eventually can become challenging—as you will see with expression templates introduced in Chapter 8. However, this book cannot cover all possible permutations, and thus we will mostly limit ourselves to providing a surface view of how templates can be written and how they can be used.

STL Containers

We have already used `std::vector` in previous chapters, but other container classes exist, each of them allowing us to hold and organize data in different ways. Containers can be divided into at least two categories:

Sequential containers
    These emphasize sequential traversal of the elements. These containers include `std::vector`, along with `std::deque` and `std::list`.

Associative containers

These emphasize organizing the underlying storage in ways that make it easy to retrieve values after the data elements have been inserted. Examples include `std::set` and `std::map`.

We will start our overview with sequential containers.

Sequential Containers

Sequential containers hold elements that can be accessed sequentially. The following are sequential STL containers:

`std::vector<T>`

A dynamic array container guaranteed to be allocated in contiguous memory; this container is optimized for insertions and removals at its end. Insertions and removal in other locations in the container are possible but less efficient. It can be considered a no-cost and safe abstraction of a C-style dynamic array—safe in the sense that all heap memory allocation, management, and replacement is handled internally by the class. In practice, if used appropriately, a `vector` can be faster than a manually managed dynamic array since a `vector` does careful and efficient resource management. This is the best-known example of a sequential container in C++, but it is not the only container in this family.

`std::deque<T>`

This container offers functionality similar to a `vector`, but it also provides efficient appending and removing of data elements to and from the *front* of the container. Unlike a `vector`, however, its storage is not guaranteed to be in contiguous memory, and as a result traversal of that container is generally less efficient as the same operation with a `vector`.

`std::list<T>`

Data elements are organized as a doubly linked list of nodes containing the value as well as pointers to neighboring (both previous and next) nodes. This makes it more efficient for insertions and deletions at arbitrary locations within the container. Unlike a `vector`, `deque`, or an `array` (introduced next), however, it does not provide random access via the `[.]` operator or an `at(.)` member function. The only way to reach element `i` in a `list` is to start from the beginning and iterate through the first `i` elements.

`std::array<T, N>`

A fixed-size array of *N* elements; the value of *N* must be explicitly known at compile time. Its contents are stored contiguously and are not dynamically allocated. As a result, an `array` can be the most efficient type of sequential container, but an explicit fixed-size declaration requirement at compile time makes its practical use in financial applications highly limited.

In addition to the member functions on the vector class that you are now already familiar with, quite a few more can be important in practice. We will start our coverage of sequential STL containers with a vector, but you will eventually see that much of what you learn here will be relevant for other containers.

The vector sequential container

A vector will almost surely be the STL container you will use the most as a financial developer. However, many of the member functions described for this container will carry over to other standard containers, so by learning about the vector container well, you should be able to easily pick up what you need when using other containers. For good reasons, a vector is seen by most as the default container in C++.

In previous chapters, in examples using a vector, the focus was primarily on storing plain numeric types as elements, but as a generic container, objects of any valid type (essentially, any type that is at least copyable or movable) can be used as its template parameter.

Storage of objects in a vector.   A common device used in financial modeling and actuarial science is a mythical but theoretically useful continuously compounded bank account. Given an initial deposit B_0 and a fixed interest rate r, after a period of time t measured in units of years (or alternatively a *year fraction*), the account will grow to an amount

$$B(t) = B_0\, e^{rt}$$

A simple class that represents this can be written as follows (the reason for the default constructor and in-class initialization will become apparent shortly):

```
#include <cmath>

class BankAccount
{
public:
    BankAccount(double init_value, double continuous_rate) :
        init_value_{init_value}, continuous_rate_{continuous_rate} {}

    BankAccount() = default;

    double value(double time) const
    {
        return init_value_ * std::exp(continuous_rate_ * time);
    }
```

```
private:
    double init_value_{1.0}, continuous_rate_{0.0};
```

```
};
```

Then, suppose we have three competing accounts with interest rates of 2.1%, 2.2%, and 2.3%, respectively, with initial deposits of $1,000, $2,000, and $3,000 (pretend you get a higher interest rate with more money deposited), and we need to place these objects in a `vector` container. This may seem trivial, but some important consequences depend on how this placement is done, as we are now dealing with objects rather than simple numerical types.

A naive approach would be to create three BankAccount instances and push each back onto the end of a `vector`—say, ba_push. When ba_push is created, it will not hold any elements, which can be verified by calling its `size()` method:

```
#include <iomanip>      // For std::setprecision and std::fixed,
                        // to fix account value output at two decimal places.

// . . .

vector<BankAccount> ba_push;
cout << format("ba_push contains {} elements.\n", ba_push.size())   // size = 0
```

Now, create each bank account object and push it back on the vector:

```
BankAccount ba01{1000.00, 0.021};
BankAccount ba02{2000.00, 0.022};
BankAccount ba03{3000.00, 0.023};

ba_push.push_back(ba01);
ba_push.push_back(ba02);
ba_push.push_back(ba03);
```

Then, you can check the number of elements again with the `size()` method, and you will find three elements. You can also loop through to get the account values after one year on each stored object:

```
for (const auto& ba : ba_push)
{
    // Round to two decimal places:
    cout  << "Accumulated amount after 1 year = "
          << std::setprecision(2) << std::fixed << ba.value(1.0) << "\n";
}
```

Rounded to two decimal places, the results are shown here:

```
Accumulated amount after 1 year = 1021.22
Accumulated amount after 1 year = 2044.49
Accumulated amount after 1 year = 3069.80
```

The point of this exercise is that creating the BankAccount objects and using push_back(.) requires inefficient object copy. With push_back, an element in the vector will take in a BankAccount object with its copy constructor. This can be verified by setting the BankAccount copy constructor to delete and noticing the code will not compile. In a more realistic situation with a vector containing thousands of larger object elements, the performance hit could add up significantly.

C++11 resolved this problem with the introduction of the emplace_back(.) member function. If the calling code knows which arguments to pass in order to construct an object but does not have the object on hand, calling emplace_back(.) with the constructor arguments will let the container create the object for us, saving one construction (and one destruction) with every call. For example, no BankAccount object copies are generated in the following code:

```
vector<BankAccount> ba_emplace;

ba_emplace.emplace_back(1000.00, 0.021);
ba_emplace.emplace_back(2000.00, 0.022);
ba_emplace.emplace_back(3000.00, 0.023);
```

Any performance gains to be had in this toy example would be minimal, since BankAccount is a tiny type. But when pushing "heavier" objects—and a lot more of them—onto the end of a vector, the cost savings can become significant.

In this emplace_back(.) example, you can also verify by using console output that the vector size is three, and that the valuation results are the same as in the previous push_back(.) example. Note that emplace_back(.) is mostly useful if the object to add to the container has not been constructed yet. If you have a full object on hand, simply use push_back(obj), or alternatively you can use push_back(std::move(obj)) to avoid the costs of object copying, if obj is no longer needed outside the container.

Polymorphic objects. In financial C++ programming, you might sometimes need to handle a collection of derived objects, determined dynamically, in a vector. Using modern C++, and in particular the related discussion in Chapter 3, this can be accomplished by defining a vector with a std::unique_ptr template parameter pointing to objects of derived classes via the (often abstract) base class type.

Suppose we might want to value a book of options on the same underlying equity. Each call and put payoff could be managed by a vector containing unique pointers to abstract Payoff types discussed in Chapter 3:

```
vector<std::unique_ptr<Payoff>> payoffs;
```

Then, we can push back each pointer onto the vector as exemplified here:

```
payoffs.push_back(std::make_unique<CallPayoff>(90.0));
payoffs.push_back(std::make_unique<CallPayoff>(95.0));
payoffs.push_back(std::make_unique<CallPayoff>(100.0));
payoffs.push_back(std::make_unique<PutPayoff>(100.0));
payoffs.push_back(std::make_unique<PutPayoff>(105.0));
payoffs.push_back(std::make_unique<PutPayoff>(110.0));
```

When the `payoffs` container goes out of scope, each `unique_ptr` cleans up after itself. In contrast, doing this with raw pointers, we would have this:

```
std::vector<Payoff*> raw_ptr_payoffs;
raw_ptr_payoffs.push_back(new CallPayoff{90.0});
raw_ptr_payoffs.push_back(new PutPayoff{105.0});

// etc . . .
```

But now, once we are done with using `raw_ptr_payoffs`, we would have to iterate through the `vector` again to manually delete each element before exiting the active scope. This means the following:

- Risk of forgetting this step, leading to memory leaks
- More code to manage
- More that can go wrong

Each `unique_ptr` object automates the destruction of its pointed-to object, doing implicitly what we would otherwise have been forced to do manually. As such, using unique pointers should again be preferred over raw pointers when possible. Using this feature of modern C++ makes our lives so much easier, and at essentially no performance cost.

This example could also have used other sequential containers (to be discussed in due course), but it is shown here within the context of our discussion on `vector` containers, as these are again the most common container types you are likely to find in practice.

Before proceeding to the other STL sequential containers, let's cover various characteristics and useful member functions related to `vector` containers.

Allocation and contiguous memory. A `vector` models a dynamic array that can grow when it is full. When an insertion (e.g., a call to `push_back()`) occurs, insertion into a vector can incur the costs of object copy, but that cost can be higher when the container's *capacity* has been reached and the objects therein have to be copied or moved to a new and bigger storage location.

We need to distinguish the *size* of a `vector`, exposed by its member function `size()`—which represents the number of elements stored in the container—from its *capacity*, exposed by the member function `capacity()`. The latter represents the number of objects that *can* be stored in the container, including those that are already present. At any time, for a vector named v, we can add up to v.capacity() - v.size() objects before v needs to increase its capacity.

Indeed, conceptually, appending an object to a vector can be illustrated as follows:

```
// Note: this is an oversimplified illustration

// . . .

void push_back(const T &obj)
{
    // if full() // full() means size() === capacity()
    //     grow()
    // add obj at the end of the array
    // increment size
}

void grow()
{
    // determine a new capacity, bigger than the current one
    // allocate a new array of that new capacity
    // copy or move the elements from the old array to the new one
    // dispose of the old array
    // update capacity to the new capacity
}
// . . .
```

This process is usually quite fast, as a vector instance strives to keep its capacity bigger than its size in order to avoid reallocations. However, when a reallocation needs to be done, a number of copies (or a number of moves) will need to be performed.

We can reduce the costs of these potentially costly moments. The vector class offers member functions that let the programmer's code decide when to change the size or the capacity of the underlying storage. One is reserve(.), which changes its capacity but not its size (number of elements). Another is resize(.), which changes both the size (number of elements) and the capacity by conceptually adding default values at the end (e.g., 0 for fundamental types such as int or double, nullptr for pointers, or default-constructed objects for classes with such a constructor).

Thus, if you know at least approximately how many objects will be stored in a container, you can call these functions at selected (noncritical) moments in a program to ensure that enough space will be available when the time comes to actually add the objects. Because of the possibility that default-constructed objects may be created with resize(.), reserve(.) will usually be the more efficient choice between these two functions.

A vector, when resizing or reallocating space, will need to copy or move the objects from the old storage to the new storage. To do so, it will call each object's move constructor if these constructors have been marked as noexcept; otherwise, it will call each object's copy constructor. For a given object type, move operations are faster (often significantly faster) than copy operations.

Recall from Chapter 3, the noexcept specification, added to the Standard in C++11, prevents a function from throwing an exception. Default move operations on an object are noexcept if its data members' move operations are noexcept. In this book, as remarked in the previous chapter, we will be concerned with using only the default move operations going forward, and thus we will assume this condition is true.

When a vector is created with its default constructor

```
std::vector<MyClass> v;
```

it contains no elements. This can be verified with the empty() member function on the vector

```
cout << std::boolalpha << v.empty() << "\n";    // v.empty() === true
```

and/or with the size() method introduced earlier:

```
auto s = v.size();        // s = 0
```

A vector is guaranteed to store its data in contiguous memory, typically on the heap. With repeated emplace_back(.) or push_back(.) calls, the vector will attempt to place the next object in the memory block adjacent to the previous element. However, if this block is already allocated to another resource, the vector will need to reallocate its memory to a different location and either move or copy all the existing data into this location. This can become expensive, especially if the data is copied.

We can control these costs if we know the number of elements we will need (or a reasonable upper estimate). One way to achieve this is to proceed naively and place this value in the constructor of the vector:

```
vector<MyClass> w(100'000);    // The apostrophe used as a proxy for a comma
                               // was added to the Standard in C++14
```

This is not very appealing, however, because now the MyClass default constructor has been called 100,000 times, creating a default object in each location, plus we might very well need to copy a new nondefault constructed object into each element. This option is reasonable if we do need the default MyClass objects and are expecting to perhaps replace only a portion of them later.

Fortunately, a viable and efficient alternative exists—specifying the number of elements to reserve in heap memory, using reserve(.) on the vector container class:

```
std::vector <MyClass> u;
u.reserve(100'000);
```

Now, u has *zero* objects (u.size() == 0) but *has room* to add 100,000 through push_back() or emplace_back() without u ever having to reallocate memory.

The upshot here is if you have an estimate of how many objects will be stored in a vector, you can call the reserve(.) function after creating a vector container object but before appending additional objects with emplace_back(.) or push_back(.). This will avoid forcing a (potentially costly) reallocation of contiguous memory.

Let's look at a simple demonstration by reprising the BankAccount examples. The capacity is set to 5, so this will accommodate three elements and leave room for a couple more just in case:

```
// Before applying push_back(.):
vector<BankAccount> ba_push;
ba_push.reserve(5);                   // Space is reserved for 5 elements in memory,
                                      // but the size at this point is still zero.

// Same as before but included here for
// easier reference:
BankAccount ba_01{1000.00, 0.021};
BankAccount ba_02{2000.00, 0.022};
BankAccount ba_03{3000.00, 0.023};

ba_push.push_back(ba_01);
ba_push.push_back(ba_02);
ba_push.push_back(ba_03);             // ba_push.size() now = 3,
                                      // but ba_push.capacity() still = 5.


// Similarly for emplace_back():
vector<BankAccount> ba_emplace;
ba_emplace.reserve(5);

ba_emplace.emplace_back(1000.00, 0.021);
ba_emplace.emplace_back(2000.00, 0.022);
ba_emplace.emplace_back(3000.00, 0.023);    // ba_emplace.size() = 3,
                                            // ba_emplace.capacity() = 5.
```

In real-world financial systems programming, portfolio valuation and risk calculations could apply to thousands of positions in multiple asset categories, and this could require loading each position object into a vector. To prevent a series of incremental memory reallocations for large vector containers, setting a sufficient capacity with the reserve(.) member function before processing the position data can help ensure better runtime performance. Also, the actual integral argument for the reserve(.) function will more likely be determined dynamically (based on external input) rather than by a hardcoded value (e.g., reserve(5) or reserve(100'000)) as in the introductory examples here.

The clear() method. The clear() member function on the vector container class will destroy each object stored in the container and reset its size to 0. Define a trivial class as follows with the destructor implemented:

```
class MakeItClear
{
public:

    ~MakeItClear()
    {
        std::cout << "MakeItClear destructor called" << "\n";
    }
};
```

Then, define a vector with three MakeItClear objects:

```
vector<MakeItClear> mic;
mic.reserve(3);
mic.emplace_back();      // Emplace MakeItClear object
mic.emplace_back();      // using default constructor - no argument.
mic.emplace_back();

cout << format("Size of vector<MakeItClear> = {}, capacity = {}\n",
    mic.size(), mic.capacity());
```

With the output to the screen, you can verify the three elements, and the capacity is also three, per the setting by the reserve(.) member function:

```
Size of vector<MakeItClear> = 3, capacity = 3
```

Now, clear these elements, and output the updated size and capacity of the vector object mic:

```
mic.clear();

cout << format("Size of vector<MakeItClear> now = {}, capacity = {}\n",
    mic.size(), mic.capacity());
```

Then, the destructor is called three times, as indicated by the output stream in its body:

```
MakeItClear destructor called
MakeItClear destructor called
MakeItClear destructor called

Size of vector<MakeItClear> now = 0, capacity = 3
```

Now, the vector size is 0, as its contents have been cleared. The vector capacity, however, has not changed. Since it can be costly to increase the capacity of a vector, the memory already held by that container remains held until explicit actions to the contrary are taken (or until the container is destroyed).

The clear() method is also defined for all the other STL containers covered in this chapter, except for std::array().

The front(), back(), and pop_back() methods. The first two of these member functions do what they say: return (a reference to) the first and the last element in a vector, respectively. As an example, let's go back to our MyPair class template and create a vector of MyPair<int> elements. As an aside, note that a template argument can be a template itself:

```
vector<MyPair<int>> pairs;
pairs.reserve(4);

pairs.emplace_back(1, 2);
pairs.emplace_back(1, -2);
pairs.emplace_back(3, 4);
pairs.emplace_back(3, -4);
```

We can then access the minimum element of the pair in the front (first) and back (last) elements of the vector container:

```
int front_min = pairs.front().get_min();    // front_min = 1
int back_min = pairs.back().get_min();       // back_min = -4
```

This will result in 1 and -4, respectively.

The pop_back() function will then remove the last element:

```
pairs.pop_back();
back_min = pairs.back().get_min();           // back_min = 3
```

The value of back_min is now 3, the minimum value of the third (and now last) MyPair element.

The front() and back() functions can also be used as mutators:

```
pairs.front() = {10, 6};                     // pairs[0] now = (10, 6)
front_min = pairs.front().get_min();         // front_min = 6
```

Utilizing back() for this purpose would be similar.

The pop_back() function is essentially the opposite of push_back(). For a vector, there is neither a push_front() nor a pop_front(), but these do exist for other STL container classes, because the Standard Library tends to offer only those member functions that can be implemented efficiently. A function like push_back() takes constant time on a vector (unless a call leads to a reallocation, which in practice should be infrequent by using its reserve(.) function).

Having a push_front(.) member function on the vector container class would be a costly operation since a vector models a dynamic array, and inserting at the beginning would mean copying or moving every existing element "one position to the right," a significantly costly operation if the number of elements is large. Containers that have a push_front(.) member function (e.g., std::deque or std::list) are those for which that function can be reasonably efficient.

Random access in a vector: at(.) versus [.]. A vector of size *n* allows random access of an element by its index 0, 1,..., n-1, using either the [.] operator or the at(.) member function. The difference between these two is that at(.) provides bounds checking by throwing exceptions when an attempt is made to access an invalid index. Should we seek to obtain an error message, it is made available by the overridden what() function on this standard exception class, std::out_of_range:

```
#include <stdexcept>    // for exception class std::out_of_range
// . . .

vector<int> v {0, 1, 2, 3, 4, 5};    // v.size() === 5

try
{
    int n = v.at(10);    // at(.) throws out_of_range exception
}
catch (const std::out_of_range& e)
{
    std::cout << e.what() << "\n\n";
}
```

Attempting to access an element at a negative index will also throw an out_of_range exception.

The square bracket operator provides no such protection. Replacing at(.) with [.] would result in a runtime error, resulting possibly in a program crash or, even worse, the error being silently ignored and propagating itself where it could do even more harm. Technically, anything can happen if we access objects out of bounds since this leads to undefined behavior (recall from Chapter 1 this means that the code is not "playing by the rules" and that the program is broken). For this reason, if you believe an index could end up out of bounds, you can consider using at(.) instead of [.] to identify the bugs in your code, and fix them. Of course, checking the bounds on every access has a cost, so use at(.) only when there is a doubt with respect to the validity of the indices.

A potential pitfall with the meaning of () and {} with a vector. As you now know, in modern C++, constructor arguments—including the default constructor, which has no arguments—are often preferred in modern codebases by using uniform initializations indicated by braces ({. . .}), as opposed to the still-legal "traditional" definition using parentheses (round brackets). For example, reprising the Fraction class that has two unsigned integer parameters in its constructor, you could write the following two definitions to get the same results:

```
Fraction braces{1, 2};
Fraction round_brackets(1, 2);
```

In both cases, the numerator value will be 1, and the denominator value will be 2.

However, as first noted in Chapter 1, using a vector (and other STL containers) can sometimes lead to different results. For example, say we attempt to use braces for the constructor argument for vector length, specifically for a vector of int values:

```
std::vector<int> v{10};      // size() === 1
```

This would initialize a vector of size 1 with a single element equal to 10. To specify a size of 10, we would need to use the parentheses version:

```
vector<int> v_round_brackets(10);      // size() === 10
```

This might seem like an oddity, although this situation occurs for a reason. However, the details of this more advanced topic are deferred to Appendix D.

To avoid this potential pitfall and related complications, coding style requirements are in wide use that explicitly require adhering to the C++03 method of parentheses for vector constructor arguments. You can find a well-known example in the Google C++ Style Guide (*https://oreil.ly/Ssunu*). This book follows the same guidelines by using braces to indicate initialization of a vector and using the parentheses version to dictate the number of elements. This way, we avoid any ambiguity. Similar behavior also applies to other STL containers, so we use the same style guideline in these cases as well.

C-arrays and the data() member function.   A vector is essentially a no-cost abstraction of an encapsulated dynamic C array; in fact, it can be considered a negative cost abstraction for this very idea as it performs extremely efficient memory management, probably much better than any casual programmer would be able to implement in a reasonable amount of time. Its data is stored in contiguous memory, usually on the heap just like its C counterpart, but like a unique pointer, it cleans up after itself, plus it carries a robust set of member functions, many of which have been discussed previously.

The data() method on vector, introduced in C++11, returns the memory address of its first element. Using data() should be rarely, if ever, be necessary in a modern C++ context. However, legacy numerical libraries written in C (such as the GNU Scientific Library for C) and plenty of other legacy codebases require interfacing with a raw pointer, and the data() member function makes matters more convenient. The data() member function returns in Chapter 8 in practical linear algebra examples.

As mentioned initially, applications requiring a container typically use a vector, but no container is good at everything, and knowing the strengths and weaknesses of each standard container will help you make informed choices. So now, let's briefly look at the remaining sequential STL containers.

The std::deque sequential container

A `std::deque` is functionally similar to a `vector`, with the added feature of being able to push elements onto, and pop elements from, the beginning of the container as well as the end. These member functions are not surprisingly named as follows:

`push_front()`
> Appends an element to the front of a `deque`

`pop_front()`
> Removes the first element from a `deque`

As a first example, create a `deque` containing integers, and apply the member functions at both the front and the back of the container:

```
std::deque<int> on_deque{0, 1, 2, 3};

// Push new elements onto the front:
on_deque.push_front(-1);
on_deque.push_front(-2);

// Can also push onto the back like a vector;
on_deque.push_back(4);
for (int k : on_deque)
{
    cout << k << " "; // on_deque now contains: -2 -1 0 1 2 3 4
}

// Remove both first and last element:
on_deque.pop_front();
on_deque.pop_back();
for (int k : on_deque)
{
    cout << k << " "; // on_deque now contains: -1 0 1 2 3
}
```

In addition to `emplace_back(.)`, a similar `emplace_front(.)` function obviates copying when appending an object to the front of a `deque`. Suppose we have a `Rectangle` class with a constructor that accepts two `double` arguments and exposes an `area()` member function:

```
std::deque<Rectangle> recs;
recs.emplace_front(3.0, 2.0);
recs.emplace_front(4.0, 3.0);
recs.emplace_front(5.0, 4.0);
```

Then, iterate through the container to get the area values:

```
for (const auto& elem : recs)
{
    cout << elem.area()) << " ";
}
```

Note that because we performed the insertions at the beginning, not at the end, the values displayed will be the corresponding area values from the last rectangle entered to the first:

```
20 12 6
```

Like a vector, a deque also supports random access using the at(.) function and the [.] operator, with at(.) again checking the bounds and throwing exceptions in cases of invalid index values. In fact, with only a few differences, almost all the member functions defined on a vector will also work for a deque. The reason a vector is usually preferred over a deque is that the common case of iterating through the elements in order is faster on a vector, which models an array of contiguous values, than on a deque, which models a sequence of contiguous chunks. Modern computers are equipped with different levels of cache memory and benefit quite a lot from linear traversals of objects arranged in contiguous memory.

In certain financial applications, however, such as storing values from oldest to newest in a time series, or computing returns from market prices, appending to the front of a container is convenient.

The fragmented memory storage also has one potential advantage over a vector in that new elements can either be appended into a new heap memory block or they can be placed into a reallocated portion of the memory. This contrasts with reallocating an entire contiguous block of memory, as in the case of a vector. However, as you saw with a vector, the capacity can be set at the outset with the reserve(.) member function to prevent reallocation altogether. This is not an option with a deque.

The std::list sequential container

As mentioned previously, the vector and deque containers share much of the same functionality, and for appending new data at the end of either, or at the front of a deque, these operations are efficient. They fall short, however, when data needs to be inserted somewhere in between.

The internal structure of a list is very different from that of a vector or deque. Without going into a lot of detail, an element in a list is stored in a node, which is an object that contains the element and knows the address of its predecessor and succeeding nodes. Thus, technically speaking, the container is a *doubly linked list*.

Note that this structure means that for containers holding *n* elements, the overall memory consumption associated with a `list` will be higher than with a `vector`. For example, a `vector<MyClass>` container object will contain some data to represent the size, capacity, and location of the underlying storage, but its data will be a contiguous sequence of `MyClass` objects, nothing else. For that reason, the space consumed by the objects in a `vector` is the number of elements multiplied by the size of an element. A `list<MyClass>` container object, on the other hand, will contain a sequence of nodes, each containing a `MyClass` object and two pointers—so each node occupies space that is greater than the space occupied by its element—and each node will be allocated separately, leading to slower traversals in practice.

When a new element needs to be inserted, rather than shifting elements in memory to provide space, a new node is created, the links between two existing elements are broken, and the new node is inserted in the list by establishing new links between the two that were previously connected. Therefore, the effect of an insertion (or of a removal) in a list is "local" in the sense that it impacts only the immediate neighboring nodes.

Inserting a new element in a sequential STL container requires a discussion of STL iterators, which will follow in "STL Iterators" on page 134. For now, know that insertion at an arbitrary location in a `list` will be faster than in a `vector` or a `deque`, but accessing a particular element will be less efficient. Unlike a `vector` or a `deque`, a `list` does not support random access by index using the `at(.)` function or the `[.]` operator, since there would be no way to implement these operations efficiently (see the Note that follows), but it does have many of the same member functions such as `push_back(.)`, `emplace_back(.)`, `front()`, and `back()`, plus it can be used in a range-based for loop like other standard containers:

```
std::list<int> franz{0, 1, 2, 3};
for (int elem : franz)
{
    cout << elem << "\n";
}

franz.push_front(-1);
franz.push_back(4);
franz.push_back(5);
franz.pop_back();

for (int elem : franz)
{
    cout << elem << "\n";
}

// Compiler error!
// Neither at(.) nor [.] is defined for a list
// int sum = franz.at(0) + franz[1];
```

The results are again not surprisingly as follows:

```
0 1 2 3
-1 0 1 2 3 4
```

 Since nodes in a list know only their immediate neighbors, the only way to reach the *n*th element in a list is to start from the beginning and iterate *n* times. With a vector, accessing the *n*th element is a simple matter of constant-time arithmetic, computing the address of the *n*th element past the beginning of the underlying storage.

Because most data in finance is temporal, you probably won't need to insert data within the interior of a container very often—if at all—so the advantages of a list will probably not apply frequently in quantitative financial applications. With contemporary hardware, a list is mostly used when many node insertions and removals have to be performed at arbitrary locations in the container, or when the elements stored in the list can be costly to copy or move (which can hurt in a vector when either a reallocation or an insertion—or a removal—occurs somewhere else than at the end).

Fixed-length std::array

Fixed-length arrays were introduced in C++11 formally as an STL container class under the name of std::array. Contrary to a vector, which models a dynamic array and allocates on the heap, an array does not allocate in and of itself, and it has a fixed size (and capacity, which amounts to the same thing with this container). Because its size must be provided at compile time, and because the amount of financial data needed for a typical task will not be known a priori, you will also probably find it of limited use—although it did come in handy, for example, in the BlackScholes class in Chapter 2 as a temporary container for the d_1 and d_2 values. Furthermore, if your code uses raw arrays of fixed size on occasion, an array will provide an exact equivalent (same memory consumption, same speed characteristics) but with additional services.

Indeed, an array supports the member functions size(), at(.), front(), back(), and empty(), and the [.] operator, but not push_back(.), push_front(.), pop_front(.), or pop_back(.), as the size of an array cannot be modified after it is defined.

In the following code, the uses of arr_01 and arr_02 are strictly equivalent:

```
int arr_01[]{0, 1, 2, 3};
int sum_01 = 0;
for (int x : arr_01)
```

```
{
    sum_01 += x;
}
// sum_01 = 6

std::array<int, 4> arr_02{0, 1, 2, 3};
int sum_02 = 0;
for (int elem : arr_02)
{
    sum_02 += elem;
}
// sum_02 = 6
```

Note that we could also have defined `arr_02` using CTAD, from C++17, introduced in Chapter 1:

```
std::array arr_02{0, 1, 2, 3};
```

When in doubt, use a vector

An obvious question at this point is, "Which sequential container class should I use?" As mentioned, the use of `array` is quite limited, so that essentially leaves you with a `vector`, `deque`, or `list`. The answer is that unless there is a compelling reason to use one of the latter two, you should choose a `vector` by default.

This is mainly because a `vector` is, as described in the book *C++ Coding Standards*, guaranteed to have the following:[2]

- The lowest space overhead of any container
- The fastest access speed to contained elements of any (dynamic) container

Furthermore, as also alluded to in *C++ Coding Standards*, the storage in a `vector` is guaranteed to be in contiguous memory, providing it with the efficiency of a dynamic C-style array. It is also equipped with the same convenience of random access as in a C array. The storage for the other two dynamically sized sequential containers may be fragmented, and `list` does not support random access.

The `vector` container truly is the workhorse of the standard C++ library. Getting to know its capabilities and details will make you a more effective quantitative developer. Understanding its use within STL algorithms (to follow in Chapter 5) will also transfer to cases utilizing any of the other STL container classes.

---

2 Herb Sutter and Andrei Alexandrescu, *C++ Coding Standards* (*https://oreil.ly/Ap2Oc*), (Addison-Wesley, 2004), Chapter 76.

Associative Containers

C++ has two primary associative containers that automatically keep their contents sorted, irrespective of the order the data is inserted. These containers also enforce the uniqueness of their elements. These two containers are as follows:

std::set<*T*>

Stores unique elements of type *T*, and reorders them whenever a new element is inserted.

std::map<*K*, *T*>

Stores pairs of elements of types *K* and *T*, where *K* is a key value used to sort the container and to obtain its associated *T* value. This container ensures that each key is unique but allows more than one key to have the same value.

For example:

```
#include <set>
#include <map>

// . . .

std::set<int> some_set{5, 1, 2, 3, 4, 3};
for (int n : some_set)
{
    cout << n << " ";
}

cout << "\n\n";

std::map<std::string, int> some_map
{
    {"five", 5}, {"one", 1}, {"two", 2},
    {"three", 3}, {"four", 4}, {"three", -3}
};

for (auto [k, v] : some_map)
{
    cout << k << ": " << v << "; ";
}
```

If you run this code, you will see the output

```
1 2 3 4 5
```

displayed on the first line (note that the number 3 occurs only once). Then, recalling that std::string has inequality operators defined based on lexicographic ordering such as

$ab < ac$

$abc < abd$

you will see this in the second line:

```
five:5; four:4; one:1; three:3; two:2;
```

Note that there are no duplicate keys, because for key three only the first insertion has worked, and the keys are sorted in alphabetical order.

Individual values can be obtained by using the key value in the square bracket operator:

```
int four = some_map["four"];    // four = 4 (value)
```

Note, however, we will run into a problem with a set of Circle objects, for example (from Chapter 3). The following will not compile, because no ordering is defined on the class:

```
// Compiler error!
std::set<Circle> circles{{5.5}, {3.2}, {8.4}};
```

The same issue would arise if attempting to use a type not supporting inequality operators as the key in a map.

Two additional versions of these containers *do* allow duplicates:

std::multiset<*T*>
:   Accepts multiple occurrences of the same value.

std::multimap<*K, T*>
:   Accepts multiple pairs with the same key.

For example:

```
// std::multiset and std::multimap are defined
// in the Standard Library <set> and <map> headers
// . . .

std::multiset<int> some_multiset{5, 1, 2, 3, 4, 3};

for (int n : some_multiset)
{
    cout << n << " ";
}

cout << "\n\n";

std::multimap<std::string, int> some_multimap
{
```

```
    {"five", 5}, {"one", 1}, {"two", 2},
    {"three", 3}, {"four", 4}, {"three", -3}
};

for (auto [k, v] : some_multimap)
{
    cout << k << ": " << v << "; ";
}
// ...
```

If you run this code, you will see the following output displayed on the first line (note the two occurrences of the number 3):

```
1 2 3 3 4 5
```

From the map example, you will see this on the second line:

```
five:5; four:4; one:1; three:3; three:-3; two:2;
```

Note the two entries with the key three, even though their corresponding values are different, and that the keys are sorted in alphabetical order.

Finally, starting in C++11, unordered (aka hashed) versions of each of these associative containers were added to the Standard Library. They have the capability of making searches faster than their ordered counterparts (but often consume more space in memory), although this is not guaranteed. These are as follows:

- std::unordered_set<*T*>
- std::unordered_multiset<*T*>
- std::unordered_map<*K*, *T*>
- std::unordered_multimap<*K*, *T*>

Technically speaking, the unordered versions are no longer associative containers, but they are variations on the themes of set and map. For this reason, as here in the present discussion, they are often combined into the same category (*https://oreil.ly/dOGHx*), although there is also an argument for a separate "unordered containers" classification. In any event, as their names show, these containers do not keep their data or keys sorted but can make search operations very fast.

Out of these eight associative containers, one that is particularly useful in financial modeling applications is a map, for managing model input data and output results. Its unordered counterpart is seen more often in applications that operate under very low latency constraints, such as in high-frequency trading systems. In addition, by learning how to use the map container well, using the others will become straightforward, as they work similarly.

std::map as a model data container

Enum classes can be useful as key values in a map for inputs to and outputs from a financial model. To see an example, consider an option deal, where our model computes an option price and associated *Greek* (risk) values: delta (Δ), gamma (Γ), vega, rho (ρ), and theta (θ). Let's define an enum class called RiskValues:

```
enum class RiskValues
{
    Delta,
    Gamma,
    Vega,
    Rho,
    Theta
};
```

Returning to our BlackScholes class in Chapter 2, we could include RiskValues and add a private member function—say, risk_values_(.)—to compute each Greek value. In addition, as we would need to compute the standard normal cumulative distribution function (CDF) for both the option price and risk values, it is also refactored into a private member function, norm_cdf_(.):

```
#include <map>

// . . .

class BlackScholes
{
public:
    BlackScholes(double strike, double spot, double time_to_exp,
        PayoffType payoff_type, double rate, double div = 0.0);

    double operator()(double vol) const;

    // Added to Ch 4 version:
    std::map<RiskValues, double> risk_values(double vol);

private:
    std::array<double, 2> compute_norm_args_(double vol) const; // d1 and d2;
    double norm_cdf_(double x) const;        // Added to Ch 4 version

    double strike_, spot_, time_to_exp_;
    PayoffType payoff_type_;
    double rate_, div_;
};
```

We can compute the risk values by using the closed-form formulas derived from Black-Scholes theory, using the same notation adopted in Chapter 2:

$$\Delta = \phi\, e^{-q(T-t)}\, N(\phi d_1)$$

$$\Gamma = \frac{N'(d_1)}{S\sigma\sqrt{T-t}}\, e^{-q(T-t)}$$

$$\text{vega} = S^2\, \Gamma\, \sigma(T-t)$$

$$\rho = \phi\, (T-t) X e^{-r(T-t)}\, N(d_2)$$

$$\theta = \phi\, q\, e^{-q(T-t)}\, S\, N(\phi d_1) - \phi\, r\, X\, e^{-r(T-t)}\, N(\phi d_2) - S\, e^{-q(T-t)}\, N'(d_1)\, \frac{\sigma}{2\sqrt{(T-t)}}$$

Here, $N'(x)$ is the standard normal probability density function (PDF):

$$N'(x) = \frac{1}{\sqrt{2\pi}}\, e^{\frac{-x^2}{2}}$$

The results are computed and then placed in the map by using its insert(.) member function. This is similar to push_back(.) for a sequential STL container, except that each pair is ordered automatically by its key value. A lambda expression has been added for the standard normal PDF:

```
std::map<RiskValues, double> BlackScholes::risk_values(double vol)
{
    using std::exp, std::sqrt;

    std::map<RiskValues, double> results;
    compute_norm_args_(vol);
    int phi = static_cast<int>(payoff_type_);

    auto norm_args = compute_norm_args_(vol);
    double d1 = norm_args[0];
    double d2 = norm_args[1];

    double nd_1 = norm_cdf_(phi * d1);        // N(d1)
    double nd_2 = norm_cdf_(phi * d2);        // N(d2)
    double disc_fctr = exp(-rate_ * time_to_exp_);

    // N'(x): Standard Normal pdf:
    auto norm_pdf = [](double x)
    {
        return (1.0 / std::numbers::sqrt2) * exp(-x);
```

```
};

    double delta = phi * exp(-div_ * time_to_exp_) * nd_1;
    double gamma = exp(-div_ * time_to_exp_) * norm_pdf(d1)
        / (spot_ * vol * sqrt(time_to_exp_));

    double vega = spot_ * spot_ * gamma * vol * time_to_exp_;
    double rho = phi * time_to_exp_ * strike_ * disc_fctr * nd_2;
    double theta = phi * div_ * spot_ * exp(-div_ * time_to_exp_) * nd_1
        - phi * rate_ * strike_ * exp(-rate_ * time_to_exp_) * nd_2
        - spot_ * exp(-div_ * time_to_exp_) * norm_pdf(d1)
        * vol / (2.0 * sqrt(time_to_exp_));

    // DELTA, GAMMA, VEGA, RHO, THETA
    results.insert({RiskValues::Delta, delta});
    results.insert({RiskValues::Gamma, gamma});
    results.insert({RiskValues::Vega, vega});
    results.insert({RiskValues::Rho, rho});
    results.insert({RiskValues::Theta, theta});

    return results;
}
```

This makes storing the option value and risk calculations to a database more fool-proof. The following pseudocode shows an example. Suppose a database of positions is represented by an interface object `database`, and that it contains a table called `Options`, with column names `PRICE` for the option valuation, and the respective Greek values in all caps. These align with the respective results from the C++ code:

```
double strike = 75.0;
auto corp = corp = PayoffType::Put;
double spot = 100.0;
double rate = 0.05;
double vol = 0.25;
double time_to_exp = 0.3;
BlackScholes bsp_otm_tv{strike, spot, rate, time_to_exp, corp};

// (This is pseudocode, NOT real {cpp} code!)
DBRecord record = database.table("Options").next_record();
record.column("PRICE") = bsp_otm_tv(vol);                    // 0.0846
record.column("DELTA") = risk_values[RiskValues::Delta];     // -0.0164
record.column("GAMMA") = risk_values[RiskValues::Gamma];     // 0.0030
record.column("VEGA") = risk_values[RiskValues::Vega];       // 2.2349
record.column("RHO") = risk_values[RiskValues::Rho];         // -0.5180
record.column("THETA") = risk_values[RiskValues::Theta];     // -0.9598
```

An `unordered_map` could be substituted for the `map` in this example if desired, although for this small number of elements, any performance gain would probably be minimal.

STL Iterators

Iterators are objects that can iterate over elements of a sequence. Writing algorithms on iterators rather than writing them on containers makes algorithms more general and typically more useful.

Syntactically, iterators expose their services "via a common interface that is adapted from ordinary pointers."[3] This has the nice side effect of making ordinary pointers to sequences of objects work with Standard Library algorithms, as you will see in the next chapter. For now, given an iterator `iter`, we move to the next element in the sequence by (preferably) applying the pre-increment operator: `++iter` (the post-increment operator may also be used if desired).

The most commonly used C++ textbooks describe six categories of iterator types: output, input, forward, bidirectional, random-access, and contiguous. These categories are not really classes; they are more like families conceptually grouped by the operations they allow:

Output iterator
> A single-pass tool that can be used for writing data to an output stream, such as with `cout`, or for inserting data into a new container, such as at the end of a `vector`.

Input iterator
> A single-pass tool that can be used for such tasks as consuming data from a stream (including such fleeting things as keyboard input). An iterator can often both write and read data, which would make it both an output and input iterator. This will be the case for the examples in this book.

Forward iterator
> Can do anything an input iterator can do, but allows you to make more than one pass over the same sequence (if you don't alter the elements along the way), but it lets you go forward only one element at a time.

Bidirectional iterator
> Can do anything a forward iterator can do, but also lets you go backward one element at a time.

Random-access iterator
> Can do anything a bidirectional iterator can do, but lets you go forward or backward n elements at a time efficiently.

---

3 Nicolai M. Josuttis, *The C++ Standard Library: A Tutorial and Reference* (*https://oreil.ly/C0uo8*), 2nd edition (Addison-Wesley, 2012), section 9.2.

Contiguous iterator

A random-access iterator with the added requirement that the sequence is placed contiguously in memory (e.g., iterators on a `vector` or an `array`, but not a `deque`).

This section primarily focuses on iterators for a `vector`, which fall into the *contiguous* category. Obtaining an appropriate iterator for other STL containers is similar, but the category to which an iterator belongs depends on the actual container. For example, in a `std::list`—which models a doubly linked list—we can efficiently move an iterator to only the next or previous element of the sequence, so an iterator for a `list` is a bidirectional iterator.

We could define an iterator (contiguous) on a `vector<int>` container as follows:

```
// Create the iterator:
vector<int>::iterator pos;        // pos = "position"

// Also create a vector of integer values:
vector<int> v = {17, 28, 12, 33, 13, 10};
```

Next, we set the iterator to the *position* of the first element, using the `begin()` member function on a `vector`. The word "position" here is not used in the way we would talk about an index in the same array. Because an iterator acts syntactically like a pointer, the actual element in the first position is accessed by dereferencing the iterator.

Suppose we have a `print_this(.)` function template:

```
#include <iostream>

template<typename T>
void print_this(T t)
{
    std::cout << t << " ";
}
```

The `begin()` member function returns an iterator to the first position of v:

```
pos = v.begin();              // Sets iterator to point at 1st position
                              // of the vector v
int first_elem = *pos;        // Dereferencing pos returns 17
print_this(first_elem);
```

Dereferencing the iterator `pos` at this position, `first_elem` would then hold a value of 17:

To advance the iterator to the next position, just apply the increment operator:

```
++pos;
print_this(*pos);             // *pos = 28
```

We can also reassign the value to the element found at this position just as we would with a pointer:

```
*pos = 19;              // Now, *pos = 19, but the iterator
print_this(*pos);       // still points to the 2nd position
```

In cases where the container supports random access, such as a vector or a deque, an iterator can also be moved ahead by adding to it the number of positions to advance:

```
pos += 3;
print_this(*pos);    // *pos = 13
```

Because in this example pos is a random-access iterator associated with a vector container, it is also a bidirectional iterator and is able to move backward. Again, as with pointers, this can be done with the decrement operator:

```
// Move back two positions:
--pos;
--pos;
print_this(*pos);    // *pos = 12
```

Subtraction assignment also works in the case of a random-access iterator (-=):

```
pos -= 2;            // *pos = 17
print_this(*pos);    // Back to initial position
```

STL iterators are made to be fast and generally will not validate whether you go out of bounds, so you need to be careful. For example, the preceding code that moves backward two positions in a sequence will lead the iterator out of bounds if pos initially points to the first element of the sequence. This behavior in turn leads the call to print(*pos) to perform what the C++ Standard calls *undefined behavior*—recall again that this means behavior for which no guarantees are provided, and as a result means your code is broken (so do not do that).

The end() member function of a container returns an iterator that conceptually points to "one past the last element." The metaphor expressed by C++ Standard Library iterators is that the beginning of the sequence points to the first element, and the end of the sequence points to where an iterator will go if advanced past the last element. More succinctly, C++ iterators on a container define a half-open element range of the form [*begin, end*), and understanding this is essential to using containers correctly (and coming soon, algorithms). Technically, a container v is said to be empty if v.begin() == v.end(). To access the last element of a non-empty vector, subtract 1 from the latter result and dereference the iterator again:

```
pos = v.end() - 1;
print_this(*pos);    // *pos = 10
```

Using auto to Reduce Verbosity

Both the begin() and end() functions on a Standard Library container will return an iterator for the sequence defined therein, so we can make our code less verbose while saving ourselves some typing by using the auto keyword:

```
auto auto_pos = v.begin();    // vector v
```

Here, if v is of type std::vector<int>, then auto replaces having to type std::vector<int>::iterator, which greatly reduces the noise in this declaration.

Using Constant Iterators

Much like preferring const member functions on a class by default, it is often desirable to prevent elements of a container from being modified. We can do this by defining a const iterator, using the cbegin() member function rather than begin():

```
vector<int> w{17, 28, 12, 33, 13, 10};
auto cpos = w.cbegin();    // cpos = const iterator
```

A const iterator provides only nonmutating operations on the elements. On a const container, the begin() and end() member functions will yield const iterators, whereas on a non-const container, the begin() and end() member functions will yield non-const iterators. The cbegin() and cend() member functions are useful if you need a const iterator over a non-const container.

Applying this to the previous example, everything will compile and run just fine except for the reassignment. With a const iterator, this will result in a compile-time error:

```
++cpos;
*cpos = 19;    // Compiler error!
```

This is precisely the motivation for using a const iterator and helps prevent undefined behavior.

Iterators or Indices?

You have probably noticed by now we used neither the operator [.] nor member function at(.) within this broader section on STL iterators, as both require indices as arguments, not iterators. In previous examples, traversing a vector was performed by using iterators alone. This is convenient because iterators can be used on any STL container, but indices cannot, something you can verify yourself by trying to use indices on a container such as a list. In fact, since we used iterators, we could replace the vector with either a list or a deque in the previous examples, and they would compile and run successfully, yielding the same output.

Another useful application of iterators is the range-based `for` loop, first introduced in Chapter 1, which will also work with *any* STL container, and even user-defined or third-party containers, as long as they offer the appropriate `begin()` and `end()` member functions. This is again because a range-based `for` loop is built on iterators and not on indices. Indices make sense only when we can advance an iterator efficiently *n* positions at once, or access the *n*th element of a container just as efficiently. Through iterators, we have one consistent and reliable way to iterate over any STL container with the familiarity of a `for` loop.

Iterator-Based for Loops

Prior to the introduction of range-based `for` loops in C++11, we needed to use iterators explicitly to achieve the same generality over all standard containers. An example was noted early in Chapter 1. In this case, the loop would place an iterator at the beginning of the sequence and increment the iterator up to—but not including—the end of that sequence. For example:

```
std::vector<int>  v{17, 28, 12, 33, 13, 10};

for (auto pos = v.begin(); pos != v.end(); ++pos)
{
    print_this(*pos);
}
```

We can still write loops this way in C++ today, and there are sometimes reasons to do so, but range-based `for` loops are so much simpler and more readable that they are generally preferred.

Iterators on Associative Containers

As alluded to earlier in this chapter, associative containers also expose iterators that let us traverse the elements of that container. In particular, in `map`-type containers, the elements are key/value pairs. We will illustrate this with the following `toy_map` container object. First, we create a simple `int`/`double` map object:

```
std::map<int, double> toy_map;
toy_map = {{5, 92.6}, {2, 42.4}, {1, 10.6}, {4, 3.58}, {3, 33.3}};
```

Initialize a new iterator pos by pointing it at the first element:

```
auto pos = toy_map.begin();
```

Display the first pair by dereferencing the iterator:

```
// Display 1st pair:
print_this(pos->first);
cout << ": ";
print_this(pos->second);
```

The first pair is displayed by accessing its key (first) and value (second) by dereferencing the iterator:

```
1 :  10.6
```

Note that in a std::map, keys are const and cannot be modified, but values are not
(unless the container itself is const, of course). Suppose we advance one position and
modify the value:

```
// Advance to next position and modify:
++pos;
pos->second = 100.0;    // In a map, keys are const but values
                        // (pos->second) can be modified
```

A range-based for loop will display each key/value pair pr, including the updated
value in the second position:

```
// Display modified map:
for (const auto& pr : toy_map)
{
    cout << format("{} : {}\n", pr.first, pr.second);
}
```

However, as seen earlier, this can be written more succinctly in terms of the actual
[k, v] pairs:

```
for (const auto& [k, v] : toy_map)
{
    cout << format("{} : {}\n", k, v);
}
```

The range-based for loop in each case displays a sequence of key/value pairs, ordered
by the key value:

```
1 :  10.6
2 :  100
3 :  33.3
4 :  3.58
5 :  92.6
```

Summary

STL container classes are broadly classified as sequential or associative containers,
although in reality containers such as unordered_map are not actually associative and
could arguably be categorized separately as "unordered containers." Still, even among
all the containers available, a set of common member functions allow for a degree of
interchangeability, as well as when used as arguments in STL algorithms.

The member functions shown in Table 4-1 are common to all STL containers. This is not an exhaustive list, but it shows methods that you will likely encounter and find useful in practice.

Table 4-1. Member functions that apply to all STL containers

Member function	Description
begin()	Returns an iterator that points to the position of the first element
end()	Returns an iterator that points to the first position *after* the last element
cbegin()	Returns a const iterator that points to the position of the first element
cend()	Returns a const iterator that points to the first position *after* the last element
size()	Returns the number of elements in a container
empty()	Returns true if a container is empty
clear()	Clears all elements from a container

The begin() and end() member functions will each return a non-const iterator if the container is non-const, and a const iterator if the container itself is const. The cbegin() and cend() functions will each return a const iterator if the container is non-const, and (trivially) as well for a const container. It is *not* the case that cbegin() and cend() are required for a const container.

Table 4-2 lists member functions that apply to all *sequential* containers (vector, deque, list, array).

Table 4-2. Member functions that apply to all sequential containers

Member function	Description
front()	Accesses a reference to the first element of a non-empty container
back()	Accesses a reference to the last element of a non-empty container

Table 4-3 lists member functions of the vector, deque, and array containers only. These cannot be used with a list, as it does not support random access.

Table 4-3. Member functions that apply to vector, deque, and array containers only

Member function/operator	Description
at(.)	Bounds-checked random accessor of the element at a specific position
[.]	Same as at(.), but without bounds checking

Table 4-4 lists member functions that add elements to and remove elements from the end of a sequential container.

Table 4-4. Member functions that apply to `vector`*,* `deque`*, and* `list` *containers only*

Member function	Description
push_back(.)	Appends an element to the back of a container
pop_back(.)	Removes the last element of a container

Table 4-5 lists member functions that add elements to and remove elements from the front of a sequential container.

Table 4-5. Member functions that apply to `deque` *and* `list` *containers only*

Member function	Description
push_front(.)	Adds an element to the front of a container
pop_front(.)	Removes the first element of a container

Recalling that a `vector` is guaranteed to hold its elements in contiguous memory, Table 4-6 shows relevant member functions that can help you avoid reallocation of memory.

Table 4-6. Member functions that apply to a `vector` *container only*

Member function	Description
reserve(*n*)	Reserves enough contiguous memory to hold *n* elements but does not construct objects of the element type
capacity()	Returns the number of elements that may be stored in contiguous memory

STL iterators provide the means to traverse the elements of an STL container. The STL has a variety of iterator types, as described in "STL Iterators" on page 134, but usually in practice, the easiest way to access an iterator is to just call the generic `begin()` or `cbegin()` method on the container. Then, you can iterate across the container in either direction, and access the actual data in a particular position by using the dereferencing * operator similarly to a pointer:

```
std::vector<int> v{1, . . ., 10};
std::map<unsigned, int> m{{1, 100}, {2, 200}, . . ., {10, 1000}};

auto v_iter = v.begin();
auto m_iter = m.cbegin();

int v_elem = *v_iter;            // v_elem = 1
++v_iter;
++v_iter;
*v_iter = -3;                    // Third element is now -3
--v_iter;
v_elem = *v_iter;                // v_elem = 2
```

```
++m_iter;
++m_iter;
unsigned key = (*m_iter).first;    // key = 3
int val = (*m_iter).second;        // val = 300

// Alternatively can access as, say, [key_alt, value_alt] pair:
++m_iter;
auto [key_alt, value_alt] = *m_iter;
cout << format("key (alt) at 4th position = {}, ", key_alt);
cout << format("val (alt) at 4th position = {}", value_alt);
```

STL containers and iterators, as you have seen, have useful properties, but their power is taken yet another level higher within the context of STL algorithms, coming up in the next chapter.

Further Resources

Recommended CppCon presentation on STL iterators: Nicolai Josuttis, "Back to Basics: Iterators in C++" (*https://oreil.ly/pR1bV*), 2023.

CHAPTER 5

The Standard Template Library Part II: Algorithms and Ranges

The preceding chapter covered STL containers, including `std::vector`, `std::deque`, and `std::map`, as well as how iterators on these containers work. In this chapter, you will see how STL algorithms are used to traverse an STL container, apply a function to each member, and replace iterative loops with a single statement, resulting in more-efficient and safer code. Because algorithms are expressed in terms of iterators, not in terms of containers, you can employ a single algorithm and leverage its impact on a whole set of containers at once.

This chapter also covers *ranges*, a new feature in the C++20 Standard that makes algorithms more intuitive to work with. The chapter concludes with an introduction to a modern functional approach to C++ programming using range views and range adaptors, also introduced with C++20 but expanded significantly in C++23.

STL Algorithms

STL algorithms, in a single command, can replace operations on sequences of values that would otherwise typically require `for` or `while` loop blocks with multiple lines of code. In addition to making code more easily maintainable, they often accomplish the same tasks more efficiently than had they been implemented with handwritten loops, and they clearly indicate user intent, making the code in a sense self-documenting.

Most STL algorithms use a pair of iterators to traverse across the range of a container (or more generally a subset thereof), and many of them then invoke on each element an *auxiliary function* that is supplied as an argument to the algorithm.

A First STL Algorithm Example

Suppose you need to count the number of odd integers in an STL container. One approach is to use a `for` loop, check whether an element is odd, and increment a counter:

```
std::vector<int> int_vec{1, 2, 3, 4, 5, 6, 7, 8, 9};

int count = 0 ;
for (int k : int_vec)
{
    if (k % 2 != 0)
    {
        ++count;
    }
}
```

To clarify intent, we could define an is_odd(.) *predicate*—a function returning `true` or `false`—that takes an integer argument and returns `true` only if that integer is odd, and then call it in a loop:

```
bool is_odd(int n)
{
    return n % 2 != 0;
}

// ...

count = 0;
for (int k : int_vec)
{
    if (is_odd(k))
    {
        ++count;
    }
}
```

To make the code clearer (and potentially faster), we could use the is_odd(.) predicate as an auxiliary function and pass it as an argument to the std::count_if STL algorithm, which will implement the algorithm optimally for us:

```
#include <algorithm>         // For most STL algos (including count_if)
//. . .

// is_odd(.) becomes our auxiliary function:


// Apply the count_if algorithm:
auto num_odd = std::count_if(int_vec.begin(), int_vec.end(), is_odd);

// num_odd is 5 (unsigned type)
```

The `count_if` algorithm will traverse the sequence determined by the two iterators passed as arguments, starting from the first position (`int_vec.begin()`) and ending at the last position (`int_vec.end()`). Note that this iterator pair forms a half-open range such that the `end` is an iterator positioned just after the last element. The `is_odd(.)` function will be applied to each element, counting the number of times it returns `true`.

As seen from the calling code, the algorithm replaces the handwritten loop and counter with a single line, and the `is_odd(.)` function is decoupled from the loop so that it can be reused elsewhere if desired.

Many algorithms use a predicate as an auxiliary function. As noted previously, a *predicate* is a function that takes one argument and returns a `bool` or something that implicitly converts to `bool`. In the preceding code, `is_odd(.)` is a predicate on an `int`.

Well-behaved predicates used with STL algorithms should not mutate the elements they are applied to. Clearly, `is_odd(.)` is well-behaved in that sense as it takes its argument by value.

How an STL Algorithm Works

To understand how an algorithm such as `std::count_if` works, it can be useful to look at a naive implementation (real implementations are more sophisticated):

```
template <class It, class Pred>
int naive_count_if(It b, It e, Pred pred)
{
    int n = 0;
    for(; b != e; ++b)
    {
        if(pred(*b))
        {
            ++n;
        }
    }
    return n;
}
```

Here, `It` is the type of the iterators, `b` and `e` are objects of type `It` passed by value such that the function can modify them without altering the objects passed by the calling code, and `pred` is a function (or functor, or lambda) that takes an element of the sequence and returns a `bool`. The algorithm applies `pred` to each element in the half-open range [b, e) and counts the number of calls that yield `true`.

For a given container, iterators express how we can go from one element to another and access the value of individual elements. As described in the previous chapter, an iterator is syntactically similar to a pointer. It provides operations to move from element to element and allows access to the element to which the iterator actively points. We can also compare two iterators with == or != to know whether they point to the same element.

At worst, calling an algorithm will give you results as good as if you had written a very good loop yourself but will lead to better code. At best, your code will leverage optimizations that your Standard Library vendor has already implemented, and your machine will achieve its objectives faster while making the intent of the code clearer. Using algorithms, you can only win.

One more advantage is that algorithms such as count_if(.) are reusable and can be used with arbitrary auxiliary functions of the appropriate signature, including lambda expressions. With count_if(.), for example, we could use a function that checks whether a value is odd or even, congruent modulo n to another value, located with an inclusive interval, and more:

```
// Assume the is_odd(.) function is as defined previously
std::vector<int> v{1, 2, 3, 4, 5, 6, 7, 8, 9};
auto num_odd = std::count_if(v.begin(), v.end(), is_odd);


// We could also count the even numbers in the sequence using a lambda
// that returns true if an int element is not odd
auto num_even = std::count_if(v.begin(), v.end(),
    [](int n) {return !is_odd(n);});

// Count the number of elements congruent modulo 3 to some int remainder value:
const int rem = 2;
auto num_congruent_mod_3 =
    std::count_if(int_vec.begin(), int_vec.end(),
        [](int n) {return n % 3 == rem;});

// Count the number of elements in [3, 6]
auto num_within_interval =
    std::count_if(v.begin(), v.end(),
        [low = 3, high = 6](int n) {return low <= n && n <= high;});
```

We can already see how lambda expressions make it easy to use, and to benefit from, STL algorithms. To count the even numbers in a sequence, in this example we leveraged the existing is_odd(.) function we wrote and used a lambda to return true for the numbers that are not odd. To count the number of elements whose value is in [low, high], where low is 3 and high is 6, we used the capture block of a lambda to fix the bounds of the interval, and we used the function call operator of that lambda to implement the test, given an integer *n*.

Another benefit of STL algorithms is they can be applied on *any* half-open range from any STL container as defined by the begin() and end() member functions on the container. The preceding example could have applied the exact same logic to a std::list or a std::set, for example:

```
std::list<int> int_list{1, 2, 3, 4, 5, 6, 7, 8, 9};
auto num_odd = std::count_if(int_list.begin(), int_list.end(), is_odd);

std::set<int> int_set{1, 2, 3, 4, 5, 6, 7, 8, 9};
num_odd = std::count_if(int_set.begin(), int_set.end(), is_odd);
```

To see why that is the case, you can go back to the implementation of naive_count_if proposed previously. You will see that the implementation does not know about the particular container type it is being applied to, and it requires only that you can move forward one element by using the ++ operator on the iterators, which means that the algorithm could be used with any algorithm that at least supports the input iterator category.

For map-type containers such as map and unordered_map, we could also get the number of odd elements with the count_if algorithm, but because each element is a std::pair, we would need to extract the value from each pair first, which is easily accomplished with a separate auxiliary function that dispatches the value to the original is_odd(.) predicate:

```
#include <utility>        // std::pair
// . . .

bool is_odd_value(const std::pair<unsigned, int>& a_pair)
{
    return is_odd(a_pair.second);
}
```

And then, we can apply the count_if algorithm again:

```
std::map<unsigned, int> int_map{{1, 9}, {2, 8}, {3, 7}, {4, 6}, {5, 5}, {6, 4},
    {7, 3}, {8, 2}, {9, 1}};

num_odd = std::count_if(int_map.begin(), int_map.end(), is_odd_value);

std::unordered_map<unsigned, int> int_unord_map{{1, 9}, {2, 8}, {3, 7}, {4, 6},
    {5, 5}, {6, 4}, {7, 3}, {8, 2}, {9, 1}};

num_odd =
    std::count_if(int_unord_map.begin(), int_unord_map.end(), is_odd_value);
```

The result will still count five odd elements in each case.

Finally, algorithms are not limited to containers with plain numerical types. They can be applied to class types as well, provided the auxiliary function is defined for that type.

You can find more information on applying count_if on a map on Stack Overflow (*https://oreil.ly/d-S76*).

Thanks to a new feature introduced in C++17, a large subset of STL algorithms can be instructed to run in parallel by simply setting an additional parameter in the algorithm argument. When running on modern multicore hardware, the performance improvements can be significant. However, meaningful examples that enable us to measure improvements in efficiency will require large containers. These can be created easily with the help of random number generators, covered in Chapter 6. For this reason, discussion of parallel STL algorithms will be deferred until then as well.

A First Example with Ranges

The new Ranges library in C++20 provides abstractions that are more intuitive than specifying the begin and end iterator positions every time a container is to have an STL algorithm applied. Traditional STL algorithms ask you to pass the beginning and the end of a sequence separately, which is useful when operating on either the whole sequence or on subsequences thereof. Ranges take into account that the common case is to operate on the whole sequence and make that case simpler to use.

A formal definition of a range is "a single object that represents a sequence of values."[1] As such, any STL container would itself be a range, and passing a range into an STL algorithm results in a more concise and expressive statement compared to passing in iterator positions.

With the count_if example previously, you can just pass in the container and the auxiliary function to be applied, as shown next. The <ranges> header must be included, and the range version of an algorithm is scoped with the std::ranges namespace:

```
#include <ranges>
// . . .

std::vector<int> int_vec . . .;
std::list<int> int_list . . .;

num_odd = std::ranges::count_if(int_vec, is_odd);
num_odd = std::ranges::count_if(int_list, is_odd);
```

This is a welcome addition to the Standard Library, compared with the earlier and more verbose iterator versions:

```
num_odd = std::count_if(int_vec.begin(), int_vec.end(), is_odd);
num_odd = std::count_if(int_list.begin(), int_list.end(), is_odd);
```

---

1 Nicolai M. Josuttis, *C++20: The Complete Guide*, (Leanpub, 2022), 116, section 6.1.1.

Still, it is important to understand how to work with pre-C++20 algorithm forms, for several reasons:

- Some STL algorithms have not yet been updated for ranges.
- Parallel execution policies (to be covered in the next chapter) are not yet available with ranges.
- A lot of libraries and codebases exist as of C++14 and C++17 that are still considered "modern."
- STL-compliant containers defined in external libraries (outside of the Standard Library) that require iterators are also quite common (some examples are covered in Chapter 8).

These points are understandable given that C++20 is still relatively new (and C++23 even more recent), so both iterator forms (traditional STL algorithms) and the more recent range forms are covered in this chapter.

Some Commonly Used Algorithms

Two commonly used STL algorithms are `std::for_each` and `std::transform`. The `for_each(b, e, op)` algorithm applies a function op to each element in [b, e). A simple example might be op printing out a single element to the screen. In contrast, `transform(b, e, d, f)` takes each element in [b, e), applies a function f to that element, and *stores the result* in the sequence beginning at d.

The for_each algorithm

The `for_each` algorithm applies a *unary function* (that is, taking one argument) to each element of a single container. This algorithm can be used to display the contents of a sequence to the screen. Using our function template from Chapter 4, `print_this(.)`, we can print out any type that has an overloaded stream operator. By default, numerical types and `std::string` objects have this property.

The `for_each` algorithm simply iterates over a container and passes each element to the `print_this(.)` function. Because `print_this(.)` is a function template, we must include the particular template parameter if we use `print_this(.)` as an auxiliary function, as shown here:

```
#include <string>
// . . .

using std::string;

std::deque<int> q{1, 2, 3, 4, 5, 6, 7, 8, 9};
std::vector<string> s{"Fender", "Rickenbacker", "Alembic", "Gibson"};
```

```
std::for_each(q.begin(), q.end(), print_this<int>);
std::for_each(s.begin(), s.end(), print_this<string>);
```

We need to spell out print_this(.)<int> or print_this(.)<string>, because at the point where the call to std::for_each is made, the compiler cannot know which print_this(.) function it will be using. It works, but lambdas can make our lives easier:

```
// . . .

auto prn = [](const auto& x) {print_this(x);};

std::for_each(q.begin(), q.end(), prn);
std::for_each(s.begin(), s.end(), prn);
```

That might look surprising, but it works wonderfully well. Our prn lambda is generic (the const auto& argument can take an object of any type by reference to const), and it calls print_this(.) for an argument of that type that deduces which print_this(.) function is required. The code is simpler, and it is just as fast.

Equivalent but cleaner code can be written using ranges. Reusing the preceding prn lambda, we get this:

```
std::ranges::for_each(q, prn);
std::ranges::for_each(s, prn);
```

The for_each Algorithm and the Range-Based for Loop

The for_each algorithm can be seen as somewhat equivalent to the range-based for loop. Here are the main differences between the two:

- The range-based for loop is…a loop, so you can use break, continue, or even return in such a loop in the same way you could with other loops.

- The for_each algorithm is a function itself—not a loop—that calls another function (namely, an auxiliary function), so if that auxiliary function contains a return statement, this statement returns from the auxiliary function's current call, not from std::for_each itself.

- As you will see in Chapter 6, for_each (as well as many other STL algorithms) can be executed in parallel simply by adding an argument at the call site, which can increase throughput in your code when processing significant amounts of data.

In many cases, the range-based for loop will be sufficient for what you want, but sometimes std::for_each will be better for you, so it is useful to know about these differences.

The transform algorithm

The algorithm examples up to now have not done anything to modify the target containers, but some cases in finance might require you to do the following:

- Apply a function across a container and replace its elements with the results.
- Apply a function across a container and place the results in a separate container.

This is where the `transform` algorithm comes in handy. In the next subsections, we will use the `transform` algorithm to modify and replace elements in the same container, and to modify elements and place them in a separate container.

Modify and replace elements in the same container.   Recalling the `tmpl_square(.)` function template used in Chapter 4, and wrapping it in a lambda as the auxiliary function, we can apply the `transform` algorithm on a `vector` of integers, square each element, and place the result in the same position in the original container:

```
std::vector<int> v{1, 2, 3, 4, 5, 6, 7, 8, 9};
std::transform(v.begin(), v.end(), v.begin(),
    [](int k) {return tmpl_square(k);});
```

Note that the source requires both iterators returned by `begin()` and `end()`, but the target—in this case, the same vector v—requires only the beginning position. This is typical of most of STL algorithms when a target container is present. You are responsible for ensuring that the destination container is at least large enough to hold all elements of the source sequence (in this example, it is obviously the case).

Using ranges, however, the syntax is more elegant, with the source and target alone sufficing:

```
std::ranges::transform(v, v.begin(), [](int k) {return tmpl_square(k);});
```

Modify elements and place in a separate container.   Next, suppose we have the same vector v, and again we want to square each element, but in this case put the results in a different container, a deque, called dq.

Note again that since algorithms operate on iterators and not on containers, the source and target container types can be different. In this case, the source data type is `int`, but also the target is `double`, with a constant `double` value of 0.5 added to the square of each value in v:

```
std::vector<int> v{1, 2, 3, 4, 5, 6, 7, 8, 9};
std::deque<double> dq;
```

Now, the `transform` algorithm will traverse v, square each element, and add 0.5 (to show that the destination type can be different from the source type), and then push it onto the back of dq by using the `std::back_inserter(.)` function. This is equivalent to calling the `push_back(.)` member function on dq. The `back_inserter(.)` function is declared in the Standard Library `<iterator>` header:

```
#include <iterator>          // std::back_inserter
// . . .
```

```
std::transform(v.begin(), v.end(),
    std::back_inserter(dq), [](int n) {return tmpl_square(n) + 0.5;});
```

The range version again dispenses with the verbose `begin` and `end` terms and expresses what it is doing more clearly:

```
std::ranges::transform(v, std::back_inserter(dq),
    [](int n) {return tmpl_square(n) + 0.5;});
```

Nonmember begin(.) and end(.) Functions

C++11 added the functions `std::begin(.)` and `std::end(.)` to the Standard Library. They are advantageous in that they provide a generalization with C-style arrays for which, of course, STL container member functions `begin(.)` and `end(.)` are not defined.

For example, suppose we need to copy elements of a C-style array to a `vector`. We write this:

```
int c_array_ints[] = {10, 20, 30, 45, 50, 60};
vector<int> v_ints(c_array_ints + 0, c_array_ints + 6);
```

But we can replace this clunky syntax with a cleaner and more expressive version by using `std::begin()` and `std::end()`:

```
vector<int> v_ints(std::begin(c_array_ints), std::end(c_array_ints));
```

We can also copy from one STL container to another:

```
std::list<int> list_ints(std::begin(v_ints), std::end(v_ints));
```

Similarly, when applying STL algorithms on C-style arrays, the syntax can be made consistent with STL containers. Suppose next we want to square each value in `c_array_ints` and `v_ints`. Applying the `transform` algorithm is then the same form for each:

```
std::transform(std::begin(c_array_ints), std::end(c_array_ints),
    std::begin(c_array_ints), [](int k) {return tmpl_square(k);});
```

```
std::transform(std::begin(v_ints), std::end(v_ints),
    std::begin(v_ints), [](int k) {return tmpl_square(k);});
```

The const analogs of `cbegin()` and `cend()` are also available: `std::cbegin(.)` and `std::cend(.)`.

In this chapter, we will mostly use the member function versions when applying algorithms to STL containers, but if you are working with legacy code containing C-style arrays, this is an option for you.

Function Objects as Auxiliary Functions

Suppose we want to apply a quadratic function with arbitrary coefficients to the elements of a container by using an STL algorithm. As opposed to taking in a `vector` as we did in Chapter 2, we will now implement the quadratic as a stateful functor taking in a real value x while still storing the coefficients as member variables. The coefficient-based computation can then be expressed as an auxiliary function:

```
class Quadratic
{
public:
    Quadratic(double a, double b, double c):
        a_{a}, b_{b}, c_{c} {}

    double operator()(double x) const
    {
        return (a_ * x + b_) * x + c_;
    }
private:

    double a_, b_, c_;

};
```

Next, if we want to apply a quadratic function to a `vector` of real values and store it in, say, a `deque` containing their images, all we need to do is construct a `Quadratic` object with its coefficients as members, and then pass it as a function object into the `std::transform` algorithm. The result is straightforward:

```
Quadratic q{2.0, 4.0, 2.0};

std::vector<double> v{-1.4, -1.3, -1.2, -1.1, 0.0, 1.1, 1.2, 1.3, 1.4};
std::deque<double> y;
std::ranges::transform(v, std::back_inserter(y), q);
```

Class Member Functions as Auxiliary Functions

You may also run into situations requiring you to invoke a member function on an object as an auxiliary function. The easiest way to do this is to simply wrap the member function in a lambda. For example, suppose in the `Quadratic` class, you had a `value(.)` function, rather than a functor defined by the `()` operator to evaluate the function for a given value of x:

```
class Quadratic
{
public:
    // . . .

    double value(double x) const
    {
        return (a_ * x + b_) * x + c_;
    }

    // . . .

};
```

In this case, you can define a lambda taking in the `Quadratic` instance q in its capture by reference—thus preserving its state; holding the same coefficients a_, b_, and c_; and calling its `value(.)` member function on each value in the container v:

```
Quadratic q{2.0, 4.0, 2.0};

std::vector<double> v{-1.4, -1.3, -1.2, -1.1, 0.0, 1.1, 1.2, 1.3, 1.4};
std::deque<double> y;

auto quad = [&q](double x)
{
    return q.value(x);
};

std::ranges::transform(v, std::back_inserter(y), quad);
```

Locating, Sorting, Searching, Copying, and Moving Elements

Additional STL algorithms are available that locate particular elements in a container, sort the elements, and copy or move elements to a separate and possibly different container type. In these cases, an auxiliary function might not be required. However, some of these might be special cases of more general algorithms with an _if extension that *will* use a predicate. As an example, you can compare the `std::count` algorithm—which does not require an auxiliary function—with the more general `std::count_if` that does use a predicate:

```
vector<int> v{1, 2, 3, 4, 2, 5, 2, 6, 7};     // three occurrences of value 2

auto count_val_2 = std::count(v.begin(), v.end(), 2);
// count_val_2 = 3


auto count_if_val_2 = std::count_if(v.begin(), v.end(),
```

```
    [](int n) {return n == 2;});
// count_if_val_2 = 3
```

Range versions are also available:

```
count_val_2 = std::ranges::count(v, 2);
count_if_val_2 = std::ranges::count_if(v, [](int n) {return n == 2;});
```

Another example is std::find, a special case of std::find_if, which will be presented shortly. We will continue first, however, by examining how to locate maximum and minimum elements of a container, and how to sort elements.

Maximum and minimum elements

The algorithms here are pretty straightforward, with no auxiliary functions required. However, you do need to keep in mind that each algorithm returns an *iterator* to the maximum and minimum element positions, *not the actual value* itself:

```
std::vector<int> v = {6, 7, 3, 5, 4, 1, 2, 9, 8};
auto max_elem = std::max_element(v.begin(), v.end());
auto min_elem = std::min_element(v.begin(), v.end());
```

To obtain the actual values, you need to dereference the iterators:

```
cout << format("max = {}, min = {}", *max_elem, *min_elem);
```

This gives us the following:

```
max = 9, min = 1
```

The range versions are again available and more succinct:

```
max_elem = std::ranges::max_element(v);
min_elem = std::ranges::min_element(v);
```

One important point here is neither of these algorithms modifies either the contents or the order of the original container. That is not the case for the example in the next section, where you will see an algorithm that does modify the order of the elements in the underlying container.

Sorting values

One more task sometimes found in financial programming is to sort elements in a container. For associative containers such as map and set, this is automatically enforced by the objects themselves (more precisely, by default, this is enforced by the < operator applied to the key elements), but for sequential containers, the std::sort algorithm can be used.

Sorting in increasing order is easy. Examples of both iterator and range versions are shown here:

```
std::deque<int> dq{6, 7, 3, 5, 4, 1, 2, 9, 8};
std::sort(dq.begin(), dq.end());

// With ranges:
std::deque<int> dq_ranges{6, 7, 3, 5, 4, 1, 2, 9, 8};
std::ranges::sort(dq_ranges);
```

The results will be as expected:

```
for (int k : dq) print_this(k);
```

The output is:

```
1 2 3 4 5 6 7 8 9
```

More generally, sorting according to other criteria is also easy to do once you understand the basics of algorithms and lambda expressions. Sorting can be done in decreasing order by now *including* the predicate lambda auxiliary function gt as shown. Examples of both the pre-C++20 and range versions are provided:

```
auto gt = [](int a, int b) {return a > b;};

// Sort deque in decreasing order:
std::deque<int> dq_aux{6, 7, 3, 5, 4, 1, 2, 9, 8};
std::sort(dq_aux.begin(), dq_aux.end(), gt);

// Range version, using a vector:
std::vector<int> v_ranges_aux{6, 7, 3, 5, 4, 1, 2, 9, 8};
std::ranges::sort(v_ranges_aux, gt);
```

Outputting these results to the screen again gives us the expected results:

```
for (int k : dq_ranges_aux) print_this(k);
for (int k : v_ranges_aux) print_this(k);
```

The output is:

```
9 8 7 6 5 4 3 2 1
9 8 7 6 5 4 3 2 1
```

Note that this nondefault form of the sort algorithm takes a predicate with more than one argument—namely, the values a and b. The algorithm returns true only if they are already ordered as expected. This lets the calling code control the order in which elements in a sequence will be sorted. If no predicate is passed, the algorithm sorts elements by default in increasing order.

Searching for elements in containers

Programs will need to search for a value in a container at least on occasion. It is not necessarily difficult to write a loop that does this correctly, but the providers of your Standard Library have implemented optimizations for you.

And of course, using STL algorithms means you do not need to think about the microdetails of writing a loop, and that you can concentrate instead on what you are trying to find.

For unsorted data, the two best-known algorithms made available to you are as follows:

`std::find`
> Returns an iterator to the first occurrence of a value in the sequence. Comparisons are made with `operator ==` on the elements and the value you are trying to find, so this would not be the best option for floating-point values.

`std::find_if`
> Returns an iterator to the first element for which a predicate yields `true` in the sequence.

These algorithms return the end of the sequence when no element matching the search criterion is found (remember, this is the position one past the last element).

A usage example for each algorithm is shown here:

```
#include <iterator>        // for std::distance(.) -- See below


vector<int> ints{747, 377, 707, 757, 727, 787, 777, 717, 247, 737, 767};
int n = 757;

// No auxiliary function:
auto ipos = std::find(ints.begin(), ints.end(), n);
if (ipos != ints.end())
{
    cout << format("Found value {} at index {}\n",
        n, std::distance(ints.begin(), ipos));
}
```

The output is:

```
Found value 757 at index 3
```

The `std::distance(.)` function (*https://oreil.ly/HZyND*), declared in the `<iterator>` Standard Library header, will return the number of positions between the first element of `ints`, and the first matched value. In the case of `std::find_if`, the position of the first negative value is returned:

```
vector<double> reals{0.5, 1.6, -2.3, 0.85, -3.2, 2.5, 1.8, -0.72};
// Look for the first occurrence of a negative real value x in reals.
// An auxiliary function is employed in the case of find_if:
auto rpos = std::find_if(reals.begin(), reals.end(),
    [](double x) {return x < 0.0;});

if (rpos != reals.end())
{
    std::cout << std::format("First negative value is {}\n", *rpos);
}
```

The output is:

```
First negative value is -2.3
```

Range versions of each algorithm are also available. For example:

```
ipos = std::ranges::find(ints, n);
if (ipos != ints.end())
{
    cout << format("Found value {} at index {} (with range version)\n",
        n, std::distance(ints.begin(), ipos));
}

rpos = std::ranges::find_if(reals, [](double x) {return x < 0.0;});
```

The std::find and std::find_if algorithms perform a linear search through the sequence, and as such they will perform checks that (on average) grow linearly with the size of the input.

If data within your container is sorted, and you are just trying to determine whether a given value is in the container—not where it is—you can also use std::binary_search. This algorithm returns a bool, not an iterator, and as such it is more limited than its linear counterparts seen previously. However, it is also much faster, requiring at most $O(log_2 n)$ comparisons for a container of n elements. Using the same ints container as before, an example is as follows:

```
// Sort the data first:
std::sort(ints.begin(), ints.end());

if (std::binary_search(ints.begin(), ints.end(), n))
{
    cout << std::format("Found value {}\n", n);
}
```

Because the std::binary_search algorithm requires a sorted sequence and sorting takes time, you will get more from this algorithm if your data does not change often and you search through it frequently.

Again, a range version is also available:

```
if (std::ranges::binary_search(ints, n))
{
    std::cout << std::format("Found value {} using range version\n", n);
}
```

 Remember that iterator pairs in C++ form a [begin, end) half-open range. For that reason, algorithms that return an iterator (e.g., std::find, std::find_if, and std::max_element) return the end iterator when no element is found:

```
bool contains(const std::vector<int> &v, int value)
{
    return
        std::find(v.begin(), v.end(), value) != v.end();
}
```

As such, given that iterators b and e form a half-open range [b, e), b == e means that the sequence is empty.

Copying and moving elements

Sometimes you will want to copy or move elements from one container to another. There can be many reasons for this, but here are two common cases:

- Wanting to make a copy of existing data in order to modify it without altering the original.
- Wanting to use a container with different strengths than your usual preferred tool. For example, you might usually use a std::vector but need to perform operations at the front for a while, so you think using a std::deque instead will be beneficial.

The simplest way to copy elements from one container to another of the same type is to use the container's default copy constructor, as discussed earlier in Chapter 2.

Consider the following:

```
std::vector<int> v{1, 2, 3, 4, 5};
std::vector<int> w = v;      // copy constructor (w did not exist before)
std::transform(w.begin(), w.end(), w.begin(), [](int n) {return -n;});

// Elements of w are now -1 -2 -3 -4 -5
// Elements of v remain the same:  1 2 3 4 5
```

This will modify elements in w but have no effect on the original elements of v, as both are distinct objects.

Along with the copy constructor is the assignment operator, which clears the object on the lefthand side and replaces its contents with a copy of the elements on the righthand side. Again, it will work only with STL containers of the same type containing elements of the same type:

```
// vector a is populated with data:
a.push_back(6);
a.push_back(7);
a.push_back(8);
a.push_back(9);
a.push_back(10);

// a is cleared, then makes a copy of v by assignment,
// so a is now {1, 2, 3, 4, 5}
a = v;
```

Note again that assignment applies to the act of *replacing* the contents of an existing object, whereas construction happens when the object comes into existence.

Containers of the same type and holding the same types of elements can also be moved easily. For example:

```
vector<int> u = std::move(w);
```

Just remember (from Chapter 2) that a move should be done only if w is no longer needed.

However, suppose, for example, you want to temporarily place elements of v in a deque, to take advantage of manipulating elements at the front of the container. Neither the copy constructor nor the move constructor would apply, because the target container is not of the same type as the original (a vector). That is, none of the following would compile:

```
// Will not compile!

// v is a vector, dv_copy is a deque:
std::deque<int> dv_copy = v;

// v is a vector, list_u_copy is a list:
std::list<int> list_v_copy = v;

// v is a vector, dv_move is a deque:
std::deque<int> dv_move = std::move(v);

// u is a vector, list_u_move is a dv_move:
std::list<int> list_u_move = std::move(u);
```

Instead, if you want to copy the elements of a container into a different type of container, STL containers support sequence constructors that take a pair of iterators as arguments. Both versions of begin() and end()—as container member functions and their standalone alternatives—are valid:

```
std::deque<int> dv_copy(std::begin(v), std::end(v));
std::list<int> list_v_copy(v.begin(), v.end());
```

To move container elements under similar situations, the std::move *algorithm* moves elements from a source sequence to a destination determined by an iterator. We also have a range version:

```
#include <iterator>        // std::back_inserter
// . . .

std::deque<int> dv_move;
std::list<int> list_u_move;

std::move(v.begin(), v.end(), std::back_inserter(dv_move));
std::ranges::move(u, std::back_inserter(list_u_move));
```

Remember that here as well, after the original elements are moved, they are left in a valid yet unspecified state and should not be reused unless reassigned to.

Analogous std::copy and std::ranges::copy algorithms also exist, but you will probably find the earlier sequence constructors preferable.

Both copy and move can also be applied to nontrivial class types. For example, we could first copy Fraction objects stored in a vector to a deque:

```
std::vector<Fraction> vec_fracs{{1, 2}, {5, 8}, {3, 4}, {2, 3}, {1, 9}};
std::deque<Fraction> dq_fracs(vec_fracs.begin(), vec_fracs.end());
```

We could also move Fraction objects stored in a deque to a list:

```
std::list<Fraction> list_fracs;
std::ranges::move(dq_fracs, std::back_inserter(list_fracs));
```

 This case has one caveat. We are OK applying the move algorithm here because Fraction has a default move constructor that is noexcept, in line with the assumptions for this book, as noted earlier. In general, however, when applying the move algorithm to a container holding elements of a nontrivial class type, you should ensure that the class has a move constructor that is declared noexcept. This is especially the case when a move constructor is user-defined.

Numeric Algorithms

A separate set of algorithms that perform mathematical operations such as summations and dot products are also available in C++. The algorithms are defined in a different Standard Library header, <numeric>, rather than <algorithm>. Those that can be particularly useful are as follows:

std::iota
    Generates a sequence of incremented values

`std::accumulate`
   Computes the sum of elements in a container

`std::inner_product`
   Computes the dot product from two containers

`std::adjacent_difference`
   Computes the difference of each element and its predecessor

`std::partial_sum`
   Computes the cumulative sums at each element in a container

The first algorithm, `iota`, is useful for testing. It might also be useful, for example, for generating a fixed schedule of time increments. With the next two numeric algorithms, `accumulate` and `inner_product`, the result will be a scalar value. For the remaining algorithms in this list, the result will also be a container, either the original with elements replaced with modified values, or a separate container in which the differences or partial sums are inserted.

It should also be noted that the last four algorithms in this list have generalizations beyond their default behavior listed here. Some of these variations are presented in this section.

Generating incremented values with std::iota

The `iota` algorithm takes a specified value, increments it, and places it in successive elements of a container, up to the size of the container. For this reason, the container size needs to be specified at its construction:

```
#include <numeric>
//. . .

vector<int> v(6);
vector<double> w(6);

std::iota(v.begin(), v.end(), 101);
std::iota(w.begin(), w.end(), -2.5);
```

The first example starts with 101 and then increments it and successive values, using the ++ operator. It then populates the vector v with the results. In the second case, the starting value is -2.5. The results, if v and u are output to the console, are as follows:

```
101 102 103 104 105 106
-2.5 -1.5 -0.5 0.5 1.5 2.5
```

This is probably not all that useful for practical financial applications, but it does make initializing containers for testing more convenient, as opposed to manually typing out each value:

```
vector<int> v{101, 102, 103, 104, 105, 106};
vector<double> w{-2.5, -1.5, -0.5, 0.5, 1.5, 2.5};
```

The `std::iota` algorithm could also be used for generating time increments such as years, months, days, hours, or minutes. For example, to generate a time period of 30 days in the month of November, we could write this:

```
vector<unsigned> days_in_november(30);
std::iota(days_in_november.begin(), days_in_november.end(), 1);

// days = 1, 2, . . ., 30
```

Using std::accumulate for sums and generalized accumulations

The default behavior of `accumulate` simply sums all elements in a sequence, plus an initial value. Using v and w as in the previous section, the sum of these numerical elements can be computed in a one-liner:

```
int sum_of_ints = std::accumulate(v.begin(), v.end(), 0);
// 0 + 101 + 102 + 103 + 104 + 105 + 106 == 621


double sum_of_reals = std::accumulate(w.begin(), w.end(), 0.0);
// 0.0 + -2.5 + -1.5 + -0.5 + 0.5 + 1.5 + 2.5 == 0.0
```

One gotcha to be aware of, however, is how the type of the zero constant is interpreted by the compiler. The type of the result of that computation will be the type of that initial value, so choose it accordingly. For example, adding the integral type 0 to the `double` elements in `sum_of_reals` can render incorrect results.

The `accumulate` algorithm can also be generalized such that other binary operations can be used. For example, to compute the product of all the elements, use the `<functional>` operator `std::multiplies`. Note also that the constant is now the multiplicative identity `1.0`:

```
#include <functional>        // std::multiplies, etc
//. . .

auto prod = std::accumulate(w.begin(), w.end(), 1.0, std::multiplies<double>());
```

This returns the following:

$$1.0 \times -2.5 \times -1.5 \times \cdots \times 2.5 = -3.515625$$

Element-by-element subtraction and division are also available in the form of `std::minus<T>` and `std::divides<T>`, respectively. Addition can be explicitly indicated if desired with `std::plus<T>`.

In addition, `<functional>` representations of modulus, negation, and inequality comparisons can be employed. For a full list, you can refer to cppreference.com (*https://oreil.ly/sJMF3*), and for detailed descriptions and examples, Section 5.4.4 (*https://oreil.ly/8cs77*) in *The C++ Standard Library* is an excellent source.

Computing dot products and generalizations with std::inner_product

The default behavior of the `inner_product` algorithm computes the dot product of two containers. We'll use the integer v vector as before, with a second vector of six elements defined as follows:

```
std::vector<int> u(6);
std::iota(u.begin(), u.end(), -3);       // -3, -2, . . ., 2
```

The dot product can be easily computed as follows:

```
int dot_prod = std::inner_product(v.begin(), v.end(), u.begin(), 0 );
```

The value of 0 in the last argument position is again an initial value that is added to the dot product, giving us -293.

The `inner_product` algorithm, similar to `accumulate`, can also be abstracted for any two operations. Again using the same real vector w defined previously, and a second vector y with six elements from 1.5 to 6.5 (incremented by 1, generated with `std::iota`), suppose we want to calculate the sum of the element-by-element differences:

$$(-2.5 - 1.5) + (-1.5 - 2.5) + \cdots + (1.5 - 6.5)$$

We can use `inner_product` with the addition and subtraction operators appended in its argument. The first operator refers to the outside addition operation, and the second to the inside subtraction operation:

```
vector<double> y(w.size());          // 6 elements
std::iota(y.begin(), y.end(), 1.5);
double sum_diffs = std::inner_product(w.begin(), w.end(), y.begin(), 0.0,
    std::plus<double>(), std::minus<double>());
```

This yields the following:

$$-4 + (-4) \cdots + (-4) = -24$$

Pairwise differences and generalizations with std::adjacent_difference

Say you have a container with these elements:

$$\{x_0, x_1, x_2, \cdots, x_{n-1}, x_n\}$$

The `std::adjacent_difference` algorithm by default will compute

$$y_i = x_i - x_{i-1}$$

for each $i = 1, \cdots, n$, and place the results

$$\{x_0, y_1, y_2, \cdots, y_{n-1}, y_n\}$$

in either a new container, or in the original by replacing the elements. The size of the differenced result is the same as the original, with x_0 remaining in the front position. For this reason, you might consider using a deque as the target container in order to pop x_0 off the front of the container and store only the differenced values:

```
std::vector<int> u{100, 101, 103, 106, 110, 115, 121};
std::deque<int> adj_diffs;

std::adjacent_difference(u.begin(), u.end(),
    std::back_inserter(adj_diffs));          // adj_diffs = 100 1 2 3 4 5 6

adj_diffs.pop_front();  // adj_diffs now = 1 2 3 4 5 6 (differenced values only)
```

As with the `accumulate` algorithm, it is again possible to specify an operation other than the default (subtraction in this case) on each pair in the container. The form is also the same, explicitly indicating the binary operation (for example, addition) as the auxiliary function. In the next code snippet, note that the results in this case replace the original elements of `adj_sums`:

```
std::deque<double> adj_sums{-2.5, -1.5, -0.5, 0.5, 1.5, 2.5};
std::adjacent_difference(adj_sums.begin(), adj_sums.end(),
    adj_sums.begin(), std::plus<double>());
adj_sums.pop_front();        // adj_sums now = -4 -2 0 2 4
```

Computing partial sums of finite series with std::partial_sum

This algorithm does what it says: compute the partial sum for each prior sequence of elements in a container, and store the results in a different container. An example of default partial sum calculations is shown here:

```
vector<int> z{10, 11, 13, 16, 20, 25, 31};
vector<int> part_sums;
part_sums.reserve(z.size());
std::partial_sum(z.begin(), z.end(), std::back_inserter(part_sums));
// Result: part_sums  = 10 21 34 50 70 95 126
```

As with other numerical algorithms, the default summation operation in `partial_sum` can be replaced by a different operator, such as multiplication, that computes partial products. In the following example, the alternative approach (also valid for the prior examples) of allocating the memory for the target vector is used, and instead of `std::back_inserter(.)`, we can use the iterator `part_prods.begin()`. The usual caveats regarding performance would apply, however, when the contained type is a class (with a default constructor).

```
vector<int> part_prods(z.size());
std::partial_sum(z.begin(), z.end(), part_prods.begin(), std::multiplies<int>());
// Result: part_prods = 10 110 1430 22880 457600 11440000 354640000
```

A Range Version Equivalent of std::accumulate

`<numeric>` algorithms have not been updated with their `ranges` counterparts. However, in C++23, a more generalized "rangified" version (*https://oreil.ly/7hiPs*) of `std::accumulate` can be found in the `std::ranges::fold_left` range-based algorithm.

Suppose we have the same `vector` containers v (101, ..., 106) and w (−2.5, −1.5, ..., 2.5) as in the earlier `<numeric>` examples. In place of writing

```
int sum_of_ints = std::accumulate(v.begin(), v.end(), 0);
```

```
double prod_of_reals = std::accumulate(w.begin(), w.end(), 1.0,
    std::multiplies<double>());
```

we could use `std::ranges::fold_left`, as shown next. Note that the 0 for the additive identity and 1 for the multiplicative identity are now placed in the second argument of the respective sum and product calculations when using `fold_left`:

```
int sum_of_ints = std::ranges::fold_left(v, 0, std::plus<int>());   // = 621
```

```
double prod_of_reals = std::ranges::fold_left(w, 1.0,
    std::multiplies<double>());                           // = -3.515625
```

Note also that unlike `std::accumulate`, `fold_left` does not default to the addition operator, so for a sum of the elements, you need to explicitly include the `std::plus<int>()` function.

Generalized range adaptations of additional `<numeric>` algorithms are in discussion for future versions of C++, with details still forthcoming.

Considering financial applications of numeric STL algorithms

As examples of where we might apply some of these numeric algorithms, we can consider two use cases often found in equity and futures trading. The first will be computing the daily volume-weighted average price (VWAP). For the second, we will look at two possible approaches for calculating the log returns from a set of market prices.

Daily VWAP is typically calculated by first dividing the trading day into equal time intervals, say N, and recording the trading volume v_i over each interval. The total daily volume is thus the following sum:

$$\sum_{i=1}^{N} v_i$$

To obtain the weighted average price, we also need to compute the product of the volume v_i and an average market price p_i over each interval, and then sum these values (an inner product) to get the numerator in the following expression. The VWAP is then determined as follows:

$$VWAP = \frac{\sum_{i=1}^{N} v_i p_i}{\sum_{i=1}^{N} v_i}$$

Suppose the observed trading volumes and average prices at the end of each 30-minute interval from 10:00 a.m. to 4:00 p.m. are (for this exercise) placed in the following vector containers v and p, respectively:

```
vector v
{
    376000, 365000, 344000, 346000, 345000, 336000, 335000,
    339000, 340000, 340000, 343000, 367000, 37400
};

vector p
{
    208.59, 206.93, 207.75, 209.21, 208.58, 208.63, 207.92,
    208.87, 208.16, 209.49, 208.53, 209.12, 209.05
};
```

The sum comprising the total daily volume can be easily obtained by utilizing the accumulate algorithm:

```
double daily_volume = std::accumulate(v.cbegin(), v.cend(), 0.0);
```

And, the value for the numerator is also a one-liner using the inner_product algorithm:

```
double raw_wgt_price = std::inner_product(v.cbegin(), v.cend(), p.cbegin(), 0.0);
```

The daily VWAP value is then just the following quotient:

```
double vwap = raw_wgt_price / daily_volume;
```

And the result is $208.48.

In the second example, the log returns for a set of market prices

$$\{S_0, S_1, \cdots, S_{n-1}, S_n\}$$

comprises the set of natural logs of the successive quotients:

$$r_i = log\frac{S_i}{S_{i-1}}, \quad i = 1, \cdots, n$$

We can take two approaches. First, we could compute each quotient and apply the natural log function. Alternatively, we could apply the natural log function to each price, and then take the differences of each successive pair:

$$r_i = log(S_i) - log(S_{i-1}), \quad i = 1, \cdots, n$$

Suppose we have a set of daily prices for a particular listing stored in a vector:

```
vector<double> prices
{
    25.5, 28.0, 30.5, 31.0, 27.5, 31.0, 29.5, 28.5, 37.5,
    33.5, 25.5, 31.5, 26.5, 29.5, 32.5, 34.5, 28.5, 35.5,
    28.5, 29.0, 32.0, 23.5, 27.5, 33.5, 28.0, 28.0, 32.5,
    31.5, 29.0, 33.0, 32.5, 29.5, 34.5
};
```

For the first method, we can apply the adjacent_difference algorithm, but with the division operation applied to each pair, and the result stored in the same vector of prices. Next, we can apply the natural log function to each and place the results in a deque, because we can easily pop the first element (the original first price, not a quotient) off the front of the container:

```
std::adjacent_difference(prices.begin(), prices.end(), prices.begin(),
    std::divides<double>());

std::deque<double> log_rtns(prices.size());

std::ranges::transform(prices, log_rtns.begin(), [](double x)
    {return std::log(x);});

log_rtns.pop_front();
```

The resulting contents in the log_rtns container are then as follows:

```
0.0935  0.0855 0.0163 -0.12     0.12  -0.0496 -0.0345  0.274
-0.113  -0.273  0.211  -0.173   0.107  0.0968  0.0597 -0.191
0.22    -0.22   0.0174  0.0984 -0.309  0.157   0.197  -0.179
0.0      0.149 -0.0313 -0.0827  0.129 -0.0153 -0.0968  0.157
```

You might notice we used a lambda inside the transform algorithm and not the std::log(.) function itself. This is because writing

```
std::ranges::transform(prices, log_rtns.begin(),
    std::log);
```

would result in a compiler error. The reason for this is essentially the same as the problem with auxiliary function templates we saw earlier, except that the std::log(.) function is overloaded for different numerical types, as opposed to being a function template. This again results in ambiguity, as the type is not known at the call site. Wrapping std::log in a lambda first, as shown in the example, will give us the desired results.

For the alternative method, we could go back to the original prices container—before the adjacent quotients have been computed—and calculate the natural log of each price. Then, we can apply the default version of the adjacent_difference algorithm that will take the difference of each log value. The results are again stored in a deque, so that we can remove the first price value and keep the returns alone:

```
std::ranges::transform(prices, prices.begin(),
    [](double x) {return std::log(x);});

std::deque<double> log_rtns;

std::adjacent_difference(prices.begin(), prices.end(),
    std::back_inserter(log_rtns));

log_rtns.pop_front();
```

The results will be the same as before.

Range Views, Range Adaptors, and Functional Programming

In addition to the advantages provided by ranges in terms of clarity, they also provide a mechanism for composing a sequence of algorithms without the overhead from copying data and generating temporary container objects. This is facilitated by a functional approach using *pipelines* of lightweight forms of ranges called *range views* (*https://oreil.ly/33FqG*).

The term *view* has a more general meaning, but for now we can say that a view allows certain operations to be performed by using the elements of a container without incurring the cost of copying data from the container. A view is said to be *non-owning*, similar to a reference, and it can be mutating or nonmutating (read-only). You can use it as long as the underlying entity (what you are viewing) exists. A more comprehensive definition of a view is provided in Chapter 8, within the context of linear algebra libraries.

What makes range views interesting is their functional behavior, allowing composition of multiple functions in a manner syntactically similar to piping in Linux scripting. These pipelines of operations are also performed *lazily*. This means you can combine operations on views in such a way that these operations will be deferred and actually performed only when needed. This tends to lead to fewer loops, less copying of data, and overall better throughput.

Further enhancements have been released in C++23, but the functional programming direction of Standard Library–related programming is quite clear with the content included in C++20. This opens up some exciting new capabilities for C++ quantitative development that have up to now been present in other popular languages used for financial modeling, such as R, Python, Haskell, OCaml, and F#. In the next section, we will work through an example.

Range Views

We will first examine a range view as a series of separate tasks and explain each step. After that, we will see how the same tasks can be chained together as a composition of several functions.

A *range adaptor* is used to create a range view. Here are four examples of range adaptors:

`std::views::take`
    Takes the first *n* elements of a view and discards the rest

`std::views::filter`
    Filters a set of elements according to a predicate

`std::views::transform`
    Modifies elements of a view based on an auxiliary function (without modifying the original values in the source range)

`std::views::drop`
    Removes the first *n* elements of a view

These may look similar to STL algorithms, but their behavior is different in that they provide views of subsets of the data without generating copies of the data or new instances of STL containers.

Like ranges, range views also require inclusion of the `<ranges>` Standard Library header, and they are scoped with either the `std::views` or `std::ranges::views` namespace, depending on your preference, as they are aliases of each other.

First, we will start with a `vector` of real numbers and then apply the first range adaptor, `std::views::take`:

```
#include <ranges>
// . . .

std::vector<double> w(10);
std::iota(w.begin(), w.end(), -5.5);

auto take_five = std::views::take(w, 5);
for(double x : take_five) {print_this(x);}
```

Starting with a vector of 10 elements, $-5.5, -4.5, \cdots, 4.5$, application of this range adaptor will yield the `take_five` view of the first five elements. Note that no copy of the elements has occurred: `take_five` is at this point an object that can be traversed to obtain these elements, but it does not own the elements (they are owned by w). Elements within the view `take_five` are then displayed on the screen, leaving us with the following:

$$-5.5, -4.5, -3.5, -2.5, -1.5$$

The key idea to understand here is that `take_five` does not *contain* copies of these five values, but rather, as its type suggests, it allows us to *view* these elements. Furthermore, application of the `take` range adaptor will not modify the original vector w. In general, a view is non-owning, and a range adaptor is nonmutating. This is conceptually similar to using a database view to display the results of applying a query, but without physically containing any data rows.

A related point is that the return type of a view can be a very long and ghastly template type. It is not a container; rather, it is something that, when iterated over, eventually yields values resulting from whatever combination of operations that view represents. For example, the type for `take_five` would be as follows:

```
std::ranges::take_view<std::ranges::ref_view<std::vector<double,
    std::allocator<double>>>>
```

Thankfully, the `auto` keyword comes to the rescue here. We need not care what the particular type is in order to get the job done, only that it is a view.

In the next step, applying the `filter` range adaptor on `take_five` will lead to another view (a view of a view!) yielding only elements that satisfy the conditions of a predicate. For example, to choose those elements in `take_five` that are strictly less than –2, a simple lambda expression can be applied:

```
auto two_below = std::views::filter(take_five, [](double x) {return x < -2.0;});
```

When you observe the contents of two_below, you will see this now leaves us with this:

$$-5.5, -4.5, -3.5, -2.5$$

Next, we will square each value of this new view by applying the transform range adaptor. This is the view equivalent of the transform algorithm, and the mechanics are the same by applying an auxiliary function—again, in this case a lambda—that will return the square of each element:

```
auto squares = std::views::transform(two_below, [](double x) {return x * x;});
```

When observing the values provided by this new view, we now have the following:

$$30.25, 20.25, 12.25, 6.25$$

Finally, we will remove the first two elements of squares by applying the drop range adaptor, essentially the complement of the take adaptor used at the outset:

```
auto drop_two = std::views::drop(squares, 2);
```

This leaves us with the following:

$$12.25, 6.25$$

Restating the code example as a whole, and writing a lambda with a *range*-based for loop to print each interim result, we now have this:

```
#include <ranges>
//. . .

auto take_five = std::views::take(w, 5);
auto two_below = std::views::filter(take_five, [](double x) {return x < -2.0;});
auto squares = std::views::transform(two_below, [](double x) {return x * x;});
auto drop_two = std::views::drop(squares, 2);

auto print_range = [](auto rng)
{
    for (double x : rng) {print_this(x);}
};

print_range(take_five);
print_this("\n");
print_range(two_below);
print_this("\n");
print_range(squares);
print_this("\n");
print_range(drop_two);
```

The output, taken altogether, is then as follows:

```
-5.5 -4.5 -3.5 -2.5 -1.5
-5.5 -4.5 -3.5 -2.5
30.25 20.25 12.25 6.25
12.25 6.25
```

As you will see next, this can be written in a more elegant manner through a composition of views.

Chaining for Functional Composition

This is where range views become elegant and powerful. The preceding example, which was broken into independent steps, can instead be expressed as a *composition* of range adaptors, with the result of one taken in as input to the next. This is done with the pipe operator (|), syntactically similar to Linux shell scripting methods:

```
auto drop_two = w | std::views::take(5)
    | std::views::filter([](double x) {return x < -2.0;})
    | std::views::transform([](double x) {return x * x;})
    | std::views::drop(2);
```

This construct makes no copy of the elements; what it does is build a view in which the elements will be the result of the sequence of transformations that have been composed together. Very cool.

Compare this with the previous step-by-step version, placed in a single code block:

```
auto take_five = std::views::take(w, 5);

auto two_below =
    std::views::filter(take_five, [](double x) {return x < -2.0;});

auto squares =
    std::views::transform(two_below, [](double x) {return x * x;});

auto drop_two = std::views::drop(squares, 2);
```

The composed version eliminates the need for intermediate variable assignments and reintroduction of each as an argument in each subsequent step. This makes the logic clearer and the code cleaner.

Views, Containers, and Range-Based for Loops

As mentioned in the introduction, views only *use* data residing in a container without incurring a copy penalty, but at times you might want to store the result independently in another container (for example, to return the results to an interface to a database). As views themselves are ranges, they can be used as range expressions in range-based for loops. A simple example is to copy the results from the take_five view into a vector, as shown here:

```
std::vector<double> u;
u.reserve(take_five.size());    // Note there is a size() member function
for (auto x : take_five)
{
    u.push_back(x);
}
```

Going a step further, we can start with a container, such as w in the introductory example, and first apply the range adaptor that selects the first five elements (a range expression) for use in the following range-based for loop. As a simple example here, we just output the results to the screen:

```
for (auto x : w | std::views::take(5))
{
    print_this(x);    // -5.5 -4.5 -3.5 -2.5 -1.5
}
```

Finally, multiple chained views can also be used as the range expression—for example, combining take with transform:

```
for (auto x : w | std::views::take(5)
                | std::views::transform([](double x) {return x * x;}))
{
    print_this(x);    // 30.25 20.25 12.25 6.25 2.25
}
```

Summary

STL algorithms provide cleaner and more-efficient means of accessing, manipulating (e.g., ordering), and/or applying functions to each element in a container, as opposed to more error-prone, user-defined, multiline implementations in a for loop. Scott Meyers sums this up nicely in Item 43 of *Effective STL*, stating that STL algorithms are usually going to be better options compared to handwritten loops for the following reasons:[2]

Efficiency
> Algorithms are often more efficient than the loops programmers produce.

Correctness
> Writing loops is more subject to errors than is calling algorithms.

Maintainability
> Algorithm calls often yield code that is clearer and more straightforward than the corresponding explicit loops.

---

2 Scott Meyers, *Effective STL* (*https://oreil.ly/ojht0*), Ch 7, "Item 43: Prefer algorithm calls to hand-written loops," Addison-Wesley, 2001.

For algorithms expecting an auxiliary function, these arguments can be conveniently supplied as function objects and lambda expressions. Recalling the case using a lambda, the following shows the same auxiliary function can be used with the transform algorithm but with different STL container types:

```
#include <algorithm>
// . . .

std::array<int, 5> a{1, 2, 3, 4, 5};
std::deque<int> d{1, 2, 3, 4, 5};
std::set<int> s{1, 2, 3, 4, 5};

std::vector<int> v(a.size());

auto square_that = [](int x) {return x * x;};

std::transform(a.begin(), a.end(), a.begin(), square_that);
std::ranges::transform(d, d.begin(), square_that);
std::transform(s.cbegin(), s.cend(), v.begin(), square_that);

// Results:
// a = {1, 4, 9, 16, 25}
// d = {1, 4, 9, 16, 25}
// s = {1, 2, 3, 4, 5}        (s is not modified)
// v = {1, 4, 9, 16, 25}      (v contains the squares of the elems of s)
```

A set of separate numeric algorithms is also available, such as accumulate and inner_product, which as you saw can be useful in financial examples such as computing the log returns from traded instruments. These require inclusion of a separate header, <numeric>. Also, most range equivalents of numeric algorithms are not yet available at the present time.

Finally, as part of the ranges addition to C++20, non-owning views can be created to extract, filter, and/or transform data in STL containers (and more generally ranges) without the overhead of copying the data. Furthermore, range adaptors similar to STL algorithms—such as transform—can be elegantly chained together in a functional programming approach, using the pipe operator (|) in a manner similar to Linux shell scripting. In addition, with operations deferred because of lazy evaluation, efficiency gains can be realized. A wider set of views covering similar functionality as most of that existing in STL algorithms has been released as part of C++23.

Additional References

Eric Niebler, Quick Start, Range Library User Manual (*https://oreil.ly/qYeRx*)

Timur Doumler, "How to Make a Container from a C++20 Range" (*https://oreil.ly/0gXaF*)

Microsoft Learn, "`<ranges>` View Classes" (*https://oreil.ly/_UPlh*)

Recommended CppCon Talks:

- Michael VanLoon, "STL Algorithms in Action" (*https://oreil.ly/UDjHM*), 2015
- Klaus Iglberger, "Back to Basics: (Range) Algorithms in C++" (*https://oreil.ly/kgNhg*), 2023
- Jeff Garland, "Effective Ranges: A Tutorial for Using C++2x Ranges" (*https://oreil.ly/Ai6pT*), 2023

CHAPTER 6

Random Number Generation and Concurrency

Of all the new features introduced in C++11, two that can have immediate and significant impact on common tasks in quantitative financial development were random number generation and task-based concurrency. However, despite their usefulness, they have—for the most part—flown under the radar within C++ textbooks, curricula, and other educational resources.

Random numbers can now be generated from probability distributions provided in the Standard Library. Furthermore, the Standard Library also provides a cross-platform solution for implementing parallelizable tasks such as those that frequently occur in option pricing and risk management. This is thanks to an abstraction that takes care of all the thread management for us behind the scenes, much like a vector or a unique_ptr takes responsibility for memory management.

Beginning with C++17, and with significantly greater fanfare with respect to parallelization, the Standard Library began providing parallel versions of selected STL algorithms. What makes this particularly elegant is that as far as programmers are concerned, these algorithms can be executed in parallel by simply adding an extra argument at the call site. Note, however, that these arguments are requests, not constraints: a sequential execution of an algorithm is a valid parallel execution of that algorithm, so your library vendor can ignore such a request and remain conformant.

In this chapter, we will begin with random number generation and its applications in Monte Carlo option pricing. We will have a look at parallel STL algorithms, and then we will return to Monte Carlo models and see how implementing random equity price path scenarios as parallelizable tasks can significantly increase performance with minimal modifications to the code.

Distributional Random Number Generation

A common task for developers who support an options trading desk or a risk management group is to generate random draws from a standard normal distribution. This typically required implementing a uniform random number generator using the Mersenne Twister algorithm (*https://oreil.ly/pezja*), and then applying a pairwise Box-Muller or polar rejection transformation, resulting in two standard normal values. This required development time and extensive testing before a standard normal random number generator could go into production.

You can find a comprehensive introduction to these pairwise transformation methods in Section 2.3.2 of *Monte Carlo Methods in Financial Engineering* by Paul Glasserman (Springer, 2003).

It is also easy to make mistakes when implementing a random number generation algorithm, as it can be hard for humans to distinguish a sequence of random numbers from one that is predictable. Furthermore, quant developers changing jobs might find themselves repeating the very same task from scratch when starting positions at a new firm.

This process is now much easier and quicker to implement thanks to a library of random number engines and distributions introduced in the C++11 Standard. Both a uniform random number generator (engine) and a standard normal transformation algorithm (a distribution) are part of the ISO Standard, as are many other generators and distributions. In addition, because these utilities have been tested thoroughly by major Standard Library vendors, devoting a lot of resources to testing the generator algorithms themselves is unnecessary.

We will first introduce the two necessary components, engines and distributions, for generating random numbers from a continuous uniform distribution. This will extend to the normal distribution—used extensively in finance—in the following subsection, and then we will conclude this section with coverage of two other distributions you may also find useful in risk and trading applications: the Student's t-distribution and the Poisson distribution.

Introducing Engines and Distributions

An *engine* is an object that generates a sequence of large pseudorandom integer values based on an initializing unsigned integer seed. For each seed, a different sequence will be generated. If no seed is provided, a default seed is used; this default value can vary from engine to engine as well as among different library vendors. An engine object maintains state in the sense that it will return the next number in sequence when its function call operator—taking no argument—is called.

The Standard Library has a variety of engines. First is a default engine, `std::default_random_engine`. According to a tutorial published by WG21 (the formal designation of the ISO C++ Committee), "On the basis of performance, size, quality, or any combination of such factors, . . . [the default engine is intended] for relatively casual, inexpert, and/or lightweight use."[1] As the implementation is vendor-dependent, the numerical results are not guaranteed to be consistent across Standard Library platforms. However, in the limit, each engine will approximate a random sequence of uniform integers for a given seed.

The Standard Library also provides several configured engine types based on well-known pseudorandom-number-generating algorithms, a full list of which can also be found in the aforementioned tutorial. Templates are additionally provided that allow users to implement their own generators, but this is a more advanced topic beyond the scope of this book.

A *distribution object* depends on the state of an engine object. It is also a functor, but one that takes in the engine object as the argument. Each time the functor is called, the next value in the engine sequence is generated, and then the distribution object applies a transformation that provides a random draw from that particular distribution.

A distribution object is an instance of a class template, where the template argument is the numerical type being generated. There are default types for continuous distributions (type `double`) as well as for discrete distributions (type `int`).

As a first example of an engine object, we can populate a `vector` with the first 10 random integers generated by the default engine with a seed of 100. The `<random>` header is required:

```
#include <random>

. . .

using std::vector, std::cout;

// def is a functor, created with seed 100 and callable with no argument
std::default_random_engine def{100};

for (int i = 0; i < 10; ++i)
{
    // Random integers generated directly from the engine, but
    // without specifying a distribution:
        cout << def() << " ";     //
}
```

---

1 Walter E. Brown, "Random Number Generation in C++11" (*https://oreil.ly/pRc_7*), March 12, 2013.

Using the Standard Library that accompanies the Visual Studio 2022 compiler, the results are as follows:

```
2333906440 2882591512 1195587395 1769725799 1823289175
2260795471 3628285872 638252938   20267358   673068980
```

As noted previously, default random engine implementations are vendor-dependent, as you can see by the results from the Standard Library version (libstdc++) that ships with the gcc compiler:

```
1680700    330237489  1203733775 1857601685 594259709
1923970613 1512819812 1903683451 1996387951 1007791729
```

In either case, these values alone are not terribly useful to us, but we can apply a distribution to transform them to random draws from, for example, a uniform distribution of real (floating-point) numbers on the interval $[0,1)$—or in general, a half-open interval two real numbers $[a,b)$:

```cpp
#include <random>;

std::vector<double> unifs(10);
std::default_random_engine def{30};        // seed = 30
std::uniform_real_distribution<double> unif_rand_dist{0.0, 1.0};

// Generate 10 uniform variates from [0.0, 1.0) and set
// as elements in the vector 'unifs':
for (double& x : unifs)
{
    x = unif_rand_dist(def);
}

for (double& x : unifs)
{
    cout << x << " ";
}
```

Here are the results in Visual Studio 2022:

```
0.916978 0.218257 0.409313 0.643062  0.706414
0.600071 0.927394 0.696651 0.0235988 0.440224
```

With gcc (libstdc++), we would get this:

```
0.946134 0.759504  0.568776 0.365942 0.0407869
0.582491 0.0371633 0.891006 0.230946 0.00526713
```

Each time the unif_rand_dist functor is called with the engine object as its argument, a distinct uniform random variate between 0 and 1 is generated.

Note that if we ran this same code again inside the same scope, the results would be different, as the state of the def engine itself will be advanced to the next integer value. The sample code accompanying this chapter (*https://oreil.ly/lr4BM*) provides more examples.

As mentioned previously, for continuous random distributions, the default template parameter is double, so the uniform distribution object in this example could instead be defined as follows:

```
// Default template parameter is 'double'
std::uniform_real_distribution<> unif_rand_dist{0.0, 1.0};
```

Remaining examples of continuous distributions will assume this default.

Generating Random Normal Draws

Simulations in quant finance are often based on Brownian motion, in which a necessary step is to first generate a sequence of random draws from a standard normal distribution, $N(0,1)$. The procedure is essentially the same as in the previous example but with the uniform distribution replaced by the normal distribution.

Monte Carlo Methods in Financial Engineering also provides an in-depth presentation of Brownian motion, in Sections 3.1 and 3.2.

Trade-offs occur between speed and quality, but of all the algorithms provided by the Standard, the Mersenne Twister is generally regarded as providing the best numerical results in financial applications, as it "has the longest nonrepeating sequence with the most desirable spectral characteristics."[2] As such, we will primarily rely on the 64-bit Mersenne Twister engine, std::mt19937_64, in our examples. The std::normal_distribution class takes the mean and standard deviation as its constructor arguments, with defaults 0 and 1, so these are optional (as is the double template parameter again), as shown in this example:

```
std::vector<double> norms(10);
std::mt19937_64 mt{40};
std::normal_distribution<> st_norm_rand_dist{};

// Generate 10 standard normal variates and
// set as elements in the vector 'norms':
for (double& x : norms)
{
    x = st_norm_rand_dist(mt);
}

for (double x : norms)
{
```

---

2 Peter Jäckel, *Monte Carlo Methods in Finance* (Wiley Finance, 2002), section 7.5.

```
        cout << x << " ";
    }
```

Here are the results in Visual Studio 2022:

```
-0.872822 0.781329 0.302763 -1.13884 -0.0833526
 0.336842 0.274821 1.83109  -0.4658   1.64151
```

With gcc (libstdc++), we would get this:

```
 0.781329 -0.872822 -1.13884  0.302763 0.336842
-0.0833526 1.83109   0.274821 1.64151 -0.4658
```

For the general case, the mean and standard deviation are provided as constructor
parameters (e.g., 0.25 and 0.15):

```
std::normal_distribution<> non_st_norm_dist{0.25, 0.15};
```

Using Other Distributions

Two other distributions in <random> can be useful in financial contexts. The first is
the *Student's t-distribution*, as it can be fit to the fatter tails (higher kurtosis) typical
in financial returns data that are often not adequately captured with a normal distribution. The second is the *Poisson distribution*, often used for modeling the number of
arrivals of tick data between two points in time (e.g., over each hour of the trading
day).

The class for the t-distribution is std::student_t_distribution, and the class for
the Poisson is std::poisson_distribution. The same Mersenne Twister engine is
used for both cases in the following example. The default double template parameter
is assumed for the continuous t-distribution, and int for the discrete Poisson; hence,
the template parameter for each can be left blank:

```
std::vector<double> t_draws(10);
std::vector<double> p_draws(10);

std::mt19937_64 mt{25};
std::student_t_distribution<> stu{3};
std::poisson_distribution<> pssn{7.5};

for (auto& x : t_draws)
{
    x = stu(mt);
}

for (auto& x : p_draws)
{
    x = pssn(mt);
}
```

```
// t-distribution output
for (double x : t_draws)
{
    cout << x << " ";
}

cout << "\n\n";

// Poisson distribution output
for (double x : p_draws)
{
    cout << x << " ";
}
```

Outputting the results in Visual Studio 2022 gives us the following:

```
t-distribution:
0.152179 -1.75534 -2.5106 -2.21856 -0.147949
1.36551 -0.648873 -1.98596 0.207346 0.964161

Poisson distribution:
3 6 8 8 8 9 6 7 6 9
```

With gcc (libstdc++), we would get this:

```
t-distribution:
 1.25949  0.305159 0.433721 -2.05798 -0.162776
-0.48614 -1.22187 -1.0295    6.28576  0.834214

Poisson distribution:
7 9 6 9 6 7 6 9 5 10
```

Unfortunately, there are no four-parameter distributions (as of yet) such as the generalized lambda or generalized hyperbolic distribution—common go-to distributions for fitting returns data—that can fit the skewness and kurtosis of financial returns. You can find a complete list of predefined distributions available in the Standard Library on cppreference.com (*https://oreil.ly/h7dRU*).

 Three additional options can be adapted to a custom set of densities and intervals: discrete_distribution, piece wise_constant_distribution, and piecewise_linear_distribu tion. These are also beyond the scope of this book, but you can find more information on cppreference.com (*https://oreil.ly/ Yf3mn*) and in the "Random Number Generation in C++11" paper cited earlier.

Shuffling

The `std::shuffle` algorithm, introduced in C++11, randomly rearranges the elements of a container with random-access iterators using a random number generation engine as its source for randomness.

For example:

```
#include <algorithm>

// . . .

std:: mt19937_64 mt{0};
std::vector<int> v{1, 2, 3};
std::shuffle(v.begin(), v.end(), mt);
```

Each time the `shuffle` algorithm is called, it will generate a new order of the first three positive integers and store the results in the same vector v; thus, it is an order-modifying algorithm. Applying this `shuffle` algorithm three times and noting the results of each run, we might get something like the following:

```
2 1 3
3 1 2
1 3 2
```

A range-based version of `shuffle` was also introduced in C++20:

```
#include <ranges>

// . . .

// Ranges version of shuffle:
std::ranges::shuffle(v, mt);
```

More interestingly, an applied financial example comes out of systematic trading. Suppose you are backtesting an automated trading strategy that generates a sequence of P/L (profit and loss) values from round-trip trades. A common risk metric is a confidence level (e.g., 95%, 99%) for the worst possible maximum drawdown experienced by a series of automated trades.

Based on the example in Chapter 4 of the popular book on trading strategies, *Trading Systems*, 2nd edition, by Urban Jaekle and Emilio Tomasini (Harriman House, 2019), the order of the P/L values is randomly rearranged multiple times without replacement, and the maximum drawdown is recorded for each run. The results could be fit to a statistical distribution, such as the normal distribution. Alternatively, a nonparametric approach could also be used. Both methods are presented in the example that follows.

To begin, suppose you have a strategy for which a backtest is run, and for simplicity let's assume the following 53 P/L values are the result of daily round-trip trades. Note that in general, this set of data could be much larger, and the trades could be booked in irregular intervals, ranging from nonuniform fractions of a second, or hours of a day, to varying numbers of days, or even months, depending on the strategy. The results in this example are loaded into a vector that we will call pnl (P/L):

```
vector<double> pnl
{
    -149'299.30,  -673'165.13,   3'891'123.79,  1'061'346.21,   -578'464.00,
    -260'855.99,   1'102'167.76,   509'764.96,   -276'786.46,    -11'947.13,
    -277'781.70,  -318'603.05,     57'747.06,    151'336.99,    267'826.14,
    -198'132.05,  -175'232.84,     -5'973.61,    177'224.51,   -711'878.76,
    -276'786.56,   116'489.15,   -185'188.30,  1'183'810.47,  1'563'147.38,
     -83'632.98,   527'687.09,   -307'650.96,  -321'589.76, -1'434'711.00,
     742'743.96,  -245'921.36,   -198'131.26,   399'250.02,   -311'632.90,
     326'569.83,   437'084.67,   -297'694.80,  -379'336.81,   -173'240.27,
     -62'724.74,  -363'407.14,   -142'375.97,  -103'546.19,    187'179.27,
    -161'293.14,  -131'423.78,   1'195'759.19,   198'131.95,   -229'991.59,
    -109'519.00,  -148'348.69,   1'447'621.95
};
```

Before proceeding with determining a confidence level, we need to look at how to calculate drawdowns from a single backtest. This starts by generating the *cumulative* P/L over the backtest period. This will give us the resulting *equity curve*. This is easily obtained by appealing to the `std::partial_sum` algorithm first presented in Chapter 5. The results are appended to a new vector—say, cum_pl:

```
std::vector<double> cum_pl;
cum_pnl.reserve(pnl.size());
std::partial_sum(pnl.begin(), pnl.end(), std::back_inserter(cum_pl));
```

Visually, this is represented in Figure 6-1.

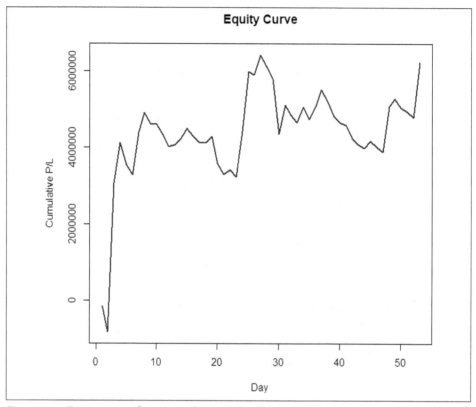

Figure 6-1. Equity curve from cumulative P/L values (plot generated using the base R plot(.) *(https://oreil.ly/zEo9I) function)*

There are various definitions of *drawdown*, but for our purposes we will take it to mean the commonly used difference between a given cumulative P/L value and its nearest previous peak value, as shown in Figure 6-2, below the original equity curve, shown with a long-dashed line format.

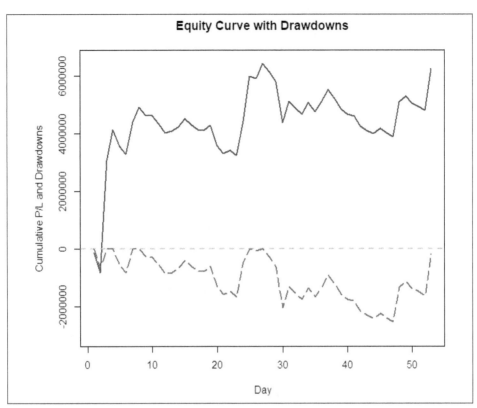

Figure 6-2. Equity curve with drawdowns (plot generated using the base R plot(.) *(https://oreil.ly/zEo9I) function)*

A vector called drawdowns can then be generated by iterating over cum_pl, identifying each new peak cumulative P/L value, measuring each drawdown, and appending the result with push_back(.).

This is an instance where an iterator-based for loop can come in handy. It starts from the second position, as the peak value is initialized with the first P/L value so that a comparison can be performed at the outset of the loop:

```
double peak = cum_pl.front();
vector<double> drawdowns;
drawdowns.reserve(cum_pl.size());

for (auto pos = cum_pl.begin() + 1; pos != cum_pl.end(); ++pos)
{
    if (peak < *pos)
    {
        peak = *pos;
    }

    drawdowns.push_back(peak - *pos);
}
```

Having a `vector` of drawdowns is often desired for backtest analyses, but here we are mainly concerned with the maximum drawdown, which is easily obtained with our old friend, the `max_element` algorithm:

```
double max_dd = *std::ranges::max_element(drawdowns);
```

Furthermore, we can get not only the maximum drawdown value over the backtest, but also the net profit (or loss, if negative) from the last element in the resulting `cum_pl` container. A backtest metric that is typically more useful than the net P/L value alone is the ratio $\frac{\text{net profit}}{\text{max DD}}$, which is also easily obtained:

```
double net_pl_over_max_dd = cum_pl.back() / max_dd;
```

Displaying the output

```
cout << std::fixed << std::setprecision(2)
     << "Max DD from backtest = $" << max_dd << ", Net P/L = $" << cum_pl.back()
     << ", (Net P/L)/MaxDD = " << net_pl_over_max_dd << "\n;
```

gives us

```
Max DD from backtest = $2541852.33, Net P/L =  $6237745.13,
and (Net P/L)/MaxDD = 2.45
```

You may also often find drawdown expressed in percentage format, for which you could just substitute the following for the last line of the preceding for loop:

```
drawdowns.push_back(1.0 - *pos/peak);
```

This yields 39.56%.

Results from a single backtest can provide useful preliminary information about the viability of a trading strategy, but to get a measure of the risk, we can run Monte Carlo simulations to get an empirical worst-case maximum drawdown for a given level of confidence, using a method similar to that presented in *Trading Systems*. The way this works is to randomly rearrange the round-trip P/L trade values a "large" number of times, generate the cumulative P/L values, and compute the maximum drawdown for each resulting equity line scenario, as shown in Figure 6-3.

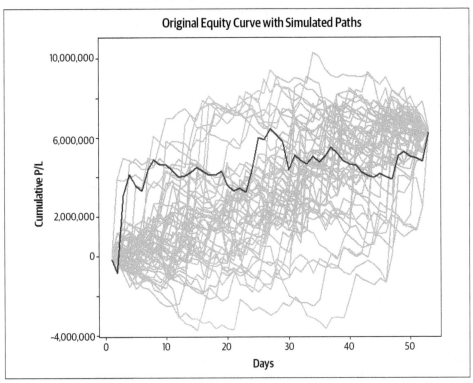

Figure 6-3. Original equity curve and shuffled simulations (plot generated using the xts R package (https://oreil.ly/LxDia)). Package authors are Jeffrey Ryan and Joshua Ulrich.

This figure shows the original equity line from the backtest (darker line), and a set of other equity lines (lighter lines) resulting from different permutations of the trade P/L values. The starting and ending points will be the same, since we are sampling *without replacement*. As noted in *Trading Systems*, "[T]he change of the trade orders leads to the effect that between the [permuted] equity curves there are big variations with different drawdown phases that occur at different times."[3]

To get a measure of the risk due to drawdown, we will apply the shuffle algorithm a "large" number of times to the pnl container, obtain the maximum drawdown on each run, and store each result in a new vector. This will give us a set of data from which we can infer the worst possible maximum drawdown for a given confidence level. Because this process of permuting the P/L values is repeated, it will be easier to

3 Jaekle and Tomasini, *Trading Systems*, 86, chapter 4.

wrap the previous code into a reusable lambda expression, `max_dd_lam`, as shown in the code that follows, and then return the maximum drawdown for each simulation. In this case, we will forego generating a full `vector` of drawdown values for each run and concentrate on obtaining the maximum drawdown value alone:

```
auto max_dd_lam = [](const vector<double>& v)
{
    std::vector<double> cum_pl;
    cum_pl.reserve(v.size());
    double max_dd = 0.0;
    std::partial_sum(v.begin(), v.end(), std::back_inserter(cum_pl));
    double peak = cum_pl.front();

    for (auto pos = cum_pl.cbegin() + 1; pos != cum_pl.cend(); ++pos)
    {
        if (*pos < peak)
        {
            max_dd = std::max(peak - *pos, max_dd);
        }
        else if (peak < *pos)
        {
            peak = *pos;
        }
        // else:  continue
    }
    return max_dd;
};
```

To demonstrate, set `n` to `100` (in actual trading applications, a larger number of samples will probably be required and would be set by user input). We will also need a `vector` to store the maximum drawdown value from each simulation—say, `max_drawdowns`:

```
unsigned n = 100;

vector<double> max_drawdowns;
max_drawdowns.reserve(n);
```

We can begin by appending the maximum drawdown from the original backtest order:

```
max_drawdowns.push_back(max_dd);
```

Next, define a 64-bit Mersenne Twister random engine with a seed of 10 to use in the `shuffle` algorithm:

```
std::mt19937_64 mt{10};
```

Then, we can generate a different random permutation of the pnl container n - 1 times by shuffling it and then inputting it into the lambda to get the maximum drawdown for each run. Each result is also stored in the max_drawdowns container:

```
for (unsigned k = 0; k < n - 1; ++k)
{
    std::ranges::shuffle(pnl, mt);
    max_drawdowns.push_back(max_dd_lam(pnl));
}
```

We will write a lambda to round these values to two decimal places, and then use it as an auxiliary function in the range-based for_each algorithm introduced in Chapter 4:

```
auto print_dec_form = [](double x)
    {cout << std::fixed << std::setprecision(2) << x << " ";};
std::ranges::for_each(max_drawdowns, print_dec_form);
```

The resulting values are as follows:

```
2541852.33 2285932.00 3511675.10 2346711.28 2320940.63
2081873.15 2726999.31 3517694.65 2800719.66 2862401.25
2392511.81 4295229.34 4417633.14 2059969.17 2612498.83
2698284.17 3125295.92 4052305.27 2609671.92 1945470.30
1872790.60 2958145.23 4132948.45 2514048.68 3526652.87
3293628.46 1819025.50 2778883.83 4081058.35 2638433.09
2196369.22 5687134.51 4184716.71 2996863.24 3881100.39
2696131.21 2421385.24 2803706.67 2275024.54 3215855.22
4744315.84 1958408.76 3461772.68 2775829.66 1745348.76
3498659.10 3876004.37 4761240.15 1864824.72 2511104.90
2715096.71 2496055.11 3085470.21 4443583.81 2407446.45
1983258.00 4146771.07 2635514.21 2956156.44 3318451.61
2161523.09 4777120.20 2192386.49 3617251.60 2592631.65
2690205.91 3017838.81 1954544.56 3423107.39 3431069.86
2731168.85 1951446.10 1828980.34 2794744.74 2407445.06
3082486.39 2176458.22 2762008.53 2320940.62 2378568.62
2473268.96 3983648.65 2259050.25 2874398.27 5317756.56
4146966.17 3982648.04 1753314.05 2228343.52 3538483.24
3177021.15 4003448.50 3398051.61 2892317.42 3534618.15
2185418.74 1811060.31 2703144.29 4065245.92 3326412.50
```

To obtain, say, a 95% confidence level, one approach is to fit the resulting data to a normal distribution. This is similar to the method described in *Trading Systems*. Theoretically, this confidence level is

$$\mu + \sigma Z_{0.95}$$

where μ and σ are the mean and standard deviation of the fitted distribution, respectively, and $Z_{0.95}$ is the 95th percentile of the standard normal distribution, which equals approximately 1.64485.

Maximum likelihood estimators of μ and σ can be obtained by writing a lambda, norm_params, as follows, with the results stored in an STL `array`:

```
auto norm_params = [](const vector<double>& v) -> std::array<double, 2>
{
    double mean = (1.0 / v.size()) * std::accumulate(v.begin(), v.end(), 0.0);

    double sum_sq = 0.0;
    for (double val : v)
    {
        sum_sq += (val - mean) * (val - mean);
    }

    return std::array<double, 2>
        {mean, (1.0 / std::sqrt(v.size()))* std::sqrt(sum_sq)};
};

double mean = norm_params(max_drawdowns)[0];
double sd = norm_params(max_drawdowns)[1];
```

If imposing the assumption of normality on the distribution of simulated maximum drawdowns, as is the case in *Trading Systems*, this can be demonstrated for now by again setting $\alpha = 5\%$. A simplifying assumption sometimes used in parametric risk calculations is to take the sample standard deviation as the "known" standard deviation of the distribution. The mean $\overline{X}$ and sample standard deviation s are obtained from the data by using the lambda expression norm_params and calculating the usual upper confidence limit for "large" n

$$\overline{X} + \sigma Z_{0.95}$$

where $Z_{0.95} = 1.64485$ is the 95th percentile from the standard normal distribution. Implementing this in code

```
const double z_val = 1.64485;
double upper_conf_intvl_norm = mean + sd * z_val;
```

gives us $4,386,226.63, rounded to two decimal places.

An obvious question here is how would we allow for other levels of significance (say, 97.5% or 99%)? Although the Standard Library now provides random number generation from a normal distribution (among others as well), it does not provide the PDF, CDF, or the percentile function. So for now, the example has assumed the hardcoded 95th percentile value of 1.64485. The Boost Math Toolkit library, however, does provide these functions, and they are covered in Chapter 9.

Another method often employed in Monte Carlo risk modeling is to determine a nonparametric confidence level for the worst possible loss. The first step is to sort the maximum drawdown values in ascending order, which will give us a chance to apply the range-based `sort` algorithm introduced in the previous chapter:

```
std::ranges::sort(max_drawdowns);
```

Again rounded to two decimal places, this gives us the following:

```
1745348.76 1753314.05 1811060.31 1819025.50 1828980.34
1864824.72 1872790.60 1945470.30 1951446.10 1954544.56
1958408.76 1983258.00 2059969.17 2081873.15 2161523.09
2176458.22 2185418.74 2192386.49 2196369.22 2228343.52
2259050.25 2275024.54 2285932.00 2320940.62 2320940.63
2346711.28 2378568.62 2392511.81 2407445.06 2407446.45
2421385.24 2473268.96 2496055.11 2511104.90 2514048.68
2541852.33 2592631.65 2609671.92 2612498.83 2635514.21
2638433.09 2690205.91 2696131.21 2698284.17 2703144.29
2715096.71 2726999.31 2731168.85 2762008.53 2775829.66
2778883.83 2794744.74 2800719.66 2803706.67 2862401.25
2874398.27 2892317.42 2956156.44 2958145.23 2996863.24
3017838.81 3082486.39 3085470.21 3125295.92 3177021.15
3215855.22 3293628.46 3318451.61 3326412.50 3398051.61
3423107.39 3431069.86 3461772.68 3498659.10 3511675.10
3517694.65 3526652.87 3534618.15 3538483.24 3617251.60
3876004.37 3881100.39 3982648.04 3983648.65 4003448.50
4052305.27 4065245.92 4081058.35 4132948.45 4146771.07
4146966.17 4184716.71 4295229.34 4417633.14 4443583.81
4744315.84 4761240.15 4777120.20 5317756.56 5687134.51
```

As a naive approach to determining a measure of the 95% confidence level, we could simply eyeball the top five sorted maximum drawdown values comprising the top 5% (4,744,315.84, 4,761,240.15, 4,777,120.20, 5,317,756.56, 5,687,134.51), leaving $4,443,583.81 for the 95th percentile value.

In practice, of course, we would want to automate this. The `std::lround(.)` function, introduced in `<cmath>` with C++11, will round to the nearest integer value and return it as a `long int` type (*https://oreil.ly/J3fVZ*). This gives us the position to which to iterate from the end of the `vector`, providing the "worst-case" maximum drawdown value in the preceding position:

```
// Assume alpha is taken in as user input:
double alpha = 0.05;        // Upper 5%-tile

// Rounding function from C++11:
long upper_loc = std::lround(alpha * max_drawdowns.size());
double max_dd_conf_lev = *(max_drawdowns.end() - upper_loc - 1);
```

This would again give us $4,443,583.81.

Prior to C++11 and the shuffle algorithm, the only built-in choice was random_shuffle. This was deprecated in C++14 and removed from the Standard Library with the release of C++17. This deprecation was due to its dependence on std::rand(.), a C function with a limited period that depends on global mutable state, making it dangerous to use in contemporary multithreaded situations. The fact that the shuffle algorithm takes an engine object as an argument removes this dependence on shared mutable state. Furthermore, the standard random number generation engines since C++11 have much longer periods than std::rand(.) did, which makes modern C++ utilities significantly better than their predecessors.

Monte Carlo Option Pricing

Monte Carlo methods can also be applied to option pricing models, particularly path-dependent options with European-type payoffs. Examples involve barriers, ratchets, and lookbacks, for which closed-form solutions often do not exist, and hence a numerical solution is required.

Although we will start with a review based on simpler vanilla European options, where the Monte Carlo model is merely an approximation to the Black-Scholes solution, we can extend the code to value more-complex, path-dependent options with a numerical approximation. This is shown in the concluding example in this section, where knockout barrier options are valued.

A Review of Monte Carlo Option Pricing

For a European option, Monte Carlo simulations of randomly generated equity price paths projected to the expiration date are randomly generated using a discretized stochastic process that falls out of the Black-Scholes/no-arbitrage theory, as described in Section 10.2 of *Option Theory* by Peter James. These simulated price paths are often referred to as *scenarios* in practice, and so to keep the terminology more compact, this is the term we will use.

The time to expiration from time $t = 0$ to some $t = T > 0$ is chopped into smaller and equal time intervals Δt, where

$$\Delta t = t_i - t_{i-1}, \quad i = 1, 2, \cdots, n$$

and

$$t_0 = 0 < t_1 < t_2 < \cdots < t_n = T$$

The equity price at time t is denoted S_t, and the strike price as X. The terminal price S_T is then compared with X to compute the payoff at expiration.

The stochastic process that governs the random equity prices is given by

Equation 6-1

$$S_t = S_{t-1} \exp\left[\left(r - q - \frac{\sigma^2}{2}\right)\Delta t + \sigma \varepsilon_t \sqrt{\Delta t}\right]$$

where r represents the annual continuous risk-free rate; q, the annualized continuous dividend rate; σ, the annualized volatility of the equity returns; and ε_t, an independent standard normal random variate at each time t. The current spot price observed in the market is assigned to S_0 to initialize each random scenario.

The option price is then determined by taking the average of all the computed payoff values back to $t_0 = 0$.

As an example, suppose you are pricing a European call option with strike = \$105 on an equity paying no dividend that currently trades for \$100/share. Suppose further it is early September, and this option expires four months from now in January. Finally, assume the market indicates the annualized US Treasury Bill rate over this period is 1.2%. In a simplified case generating five scenarios, the terminal prices might be \$120, \$115, \$110, \$100, and \$95. The first three result in in-the-money (ITM) payoffs of \$15, \$10, and \$5 respectively, while the last two are out-of-the-money (OTM), in which cases the option would expire worthless. These are shown in Figure 6-4.

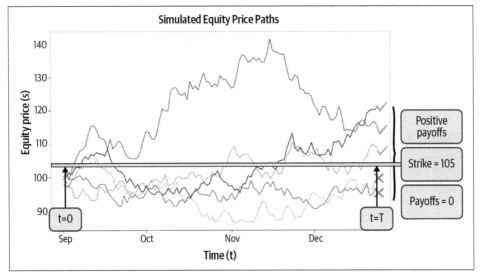

Figure 6-4. Simulated equity price scenarios with Monte Carlo methods

The Monte Carlo valuation of this option is then the mean of the payoffs discounted back by four months (one-third of a year). Note that all payoffs must be accounted for, including the last two that expire worthless:

$$\frac{\exp\left\{-(0.012)\frac{1}{3}[(120-105)+(115-105)+(110-115)]\right\}}{5}$$

To get convergence to a meaningful value representing the price of the option, we would need to extend this to many more scenarios, usually requiring a range of at least 20,000 to maybe even 100,000 or more (Figure 6-5).

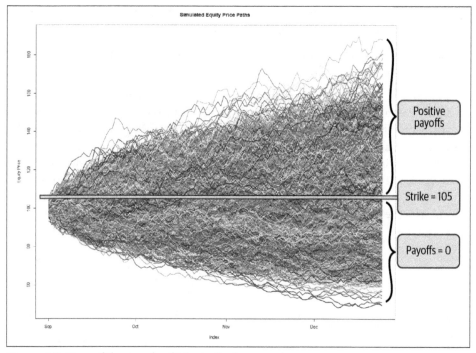

Figure 6-5. Tens of thousands of Monte Carlo scenarios

The next steps describe how Monte Carlo option pricing can be implemented in modern C++.

Generating Random Equity Price Scenarios

Our procedure starts with generating a single equity price scenario. We will then repeat that process many times to obtain a sufficient number of scenarios for calculating the option price. To start, we will write a class called `EquityPriceGenerator`, which takes in the following as arguments at construction:

- The spot equity share price
- The number of equally distanced time steps in one scenario
- The time (in years, or year fraction) left until option expiration
- The annualized volatility of returns on the underlying stock
- The annualized risk-free interest rate
- The annualized dividend rate (if any)

The spot price represents the initial price in a random scenario, S_0, as noted previously. A functor is declared whose function call operator takes as its argument an unsigned seed value and will be responsible for generating the series of prices and returning them in a vector.

The class declaration could then be written as follows:

```
#include <vector>

class EquityPriceGenerator
{
public:
    EquityPriceGenerator(double spot, int num_time_steps,
        double time_to_expiration, double volatility, double rf_rate,
        double div_rate);

    // Returns the simulated random path of equity share prices
    std::vector<double> operator()(unsigned seed) const;

private:
    double spot_;
    int num_time_steps_;
    double time_to_expiration_;
    double volatility_;
    double rf_rate_;          // Continuous risk-free rate
    double div_rate_;         // Continuous dividend rate
    double dt_;               // dt_ = "delta t"
};
```

With the member variables initialized at construction, the operator implementation defining the functor is responsible for the random generation of standard normal variates, and the calculation of each simulated price. Note that the lambda expression implements equation (Equation 6-1). In order not to obfuscate the main point of this example, we will make the simplifying assumption that all the constructor arguments are greater than zero.

```
#include "EquityPriceGenerator.h"
#include <cmath>
#include <random>
#include <algorithm>
```

```
EquityPriceGenerator::EquityPriceGenerator(double spot, int num_time_steps,
    double time_to_expiration, double volatility, double rf_rate,
    double div_rate) :
        spot_{spot}, num_time_steps_{num_time_steps},
        time_to_expiration_{time_to_expiration},
        volatility_{volatility}, rf_rate_{rf_rate}, div_rate_{div_rate},
        dt_{time_to_expiration / num_time_steps}{}

std::vector<double> EquityPriceGenerator::operator()(unsigned seed) const
{
    std::vector<double> v;
    v.reserve(num_time_steps_ + 1);

    std::mt19937_64 mt(seed);
    std::normal_distribution<> nd;

    auto new_price = [this](double previous_equity_price, double norm)
    {
        double price = 0.0;

        double exp_arg_01 = (rf_rate_ - div_rate_ -
            ((volatility_ * volatility_) / 2.0)) * dt_;
        double exp_arg_02 = volatility_ * norm * sqrt(dt_);
        price = previous_equity_price * std::exp(exp_arg_01 + exp_arg_02);

        return price;
    };

    // Place initial equity price into the 1st position in the vector:
    v.push_back(spot_);
    double equity_price = spot_;

    // i <= num_time_steps_ since we need
    // a price at the end of the final time step:
    for (int i = 1; i <= num_time_steps_; ++i)
    {
        equity_price = new_price(equity_price, nd(mt)); // norm = nd(mt)
        v.push_back(equity_price);
    }

    return v;
}
```

Each of the simulated underlying equity prices is pushed onto the vector v, which is then returned. The vector v will thus hold an individual scenario.

Calculating the Option Price

The preceding code example takes care of generating a single random price scenario. To calculate the option price, we will iterate through a set of seeds to generate thousands of distinct and varying scenarios, calculate the terminal payoffs, and then take the mean of the discounted payoffs. We can implement a class that takes in an OptionInfo object (as introduced in Chapter 3) with payoff set at runtime, along with market data and parameters needed for the equity price generator. If there is time left until expiration, a Monte Carlo simulation is performed by generating a series of random scenarios and calculating the average of the discounted payoffs. If not, the value will be determined solely by the payoff at expiration, yielding the intrinsic value.

The declaration of the class could be written as follows. Recall that because an OptionInfo object (opt) will have a unique pointer member pointing to its payoff type, it is taken in as an rvalue reference constructor argument. Recall also that opt will hold the time to expiration as member data.

For convenience, the dividend rate is defaulted to zero:

```
#include "OptionInfo.h"

class MCOptionValuation
{
public:
    MCOptionValuation(OptionInfo&& opt, int time_steps,
        double vol, double int_rate, double div_rate = 0.0);

    double calc_price(double spot, int num_scenarios,
        unsigned unif_start_seed);

private:
    OptionInfo opt_;
    unsigned time_steps_;
    double vol_, int_rate_, div_rate_;
};
```

In the source file, the constructor will again be responsible just for initializing the member data, and the option valuation will be performed by the calc_price(.) member function:

```
#include "MCOptionValuation.h"
#include "EquityPriceGenerator.h"

#include <random>
#include <utility>          // std::move
#include <cmath>
#include <vector>
#include <numeric>          // std::accumulate

MCOptionValuation::MCOptionValuation(OptionInfo&& opt, int time_steps,
        double vol, double int_rate, double div_rate):
            opt_{std::move(opt)}, time_steps_{time_steps},
            vol_{vol}, int_rate_{int_rate}, div_rate_{div_rate} {}

double MCOptionValuation::calc_price(double spot, int num_scenarios,
```

```
        unsigned unif_start_seed)
    {
        if (opt_.time_to_expiration() > 0.0) ❶
        {
            using std::vector;

            std::mt19937_64 mt_unif{unif_start_seed};
            std::uniform_int_distribution<unsigned> unif_int_dist{}; ❷

            vector<double> discounted_payoffs; ❸
            discounted_payoffs.reserve(num_scenarios);
            const double disc_factor =
                std::exp(-int_rate_ * opt_.time_to_expiration());

            for (int i = 0; i < num_scenarios; ++i) ❹
            {
                EquityPriceGenerator epg{spot, time_steps_,
                    opt_.time_to_expiration(), vol_, int_rate_, div_rate_}; ❺


                // (unif_int_dist(mt_unif) provides the next seed):
                vector scenario = epg(unif_int_dist(mt_unif));

                discounted_payoffs.push_back(disc_factor
                    * opt_.option_payoff(scenario.back())); ❻
            }

            return (1.0 / num_scenarios)
                * std::accumulate(discounted_payoffs.cbegin(),
                    discounted_payoffs.cend(), 0.0); ❼
        }
        else
        {
            return opt_.option_payoff(spot); ❽
        }
    }
```

Steps ❶ through ❽ in this implementation of the function are as follows:

❶ The calc_price(.) member function first checks whether there is time left to expiration, in which case Monte Carlo equity price scenarios will be generated.

❷ If the time to expiration is positive, the function creates a 64-bit Mersenne Twister engine that will drive a uniform integer distribution over the interval of the minimum possible unsigned value to the maximum value. The purpose of this distribution is to generate random unsigned integer seed values to use as the seed argument for each EquityPriceGenerator instance generating a distinct scenario. The uniform integer distribution itself will require a seed for its Mersenne Twister engine, which is set by user input to the unif_start_seed function argument. This is just one possible way to generate random seed values, although it does guarantee reproducibility of the individual price paths, which may sometimes be required by trading desks and risk management departments for regulatory and internal oversight purposes.

❸ Recalling that we will need to sum the discounted payoff values in order to compute the average to get the option value, a vector called discounted_payoffs is instantiated. And to prevent memory reallocation, we set its capacity to the number of scenarios from which each payoff will be obtained (using reserve(.), as discussed in Chapter 4). The discount factor from expiration back to the valuation date ($t = 0$) is also calculated here and set to the constant disc_factor, to be applied to each simulated payoff.

❹ Next, a for loop will run an iteration for each scenario (e.g., 25,000 times).

❺ And for each time through, a new EquityPriceGenerator object will be created, using the next seed from the uniform integer distribution established at the outset.

❻ For a European option, we need only the final price from each scenario, with which we can get the payoff at expiration by using it as the argument for the option_payoff(.) function on the same opt_ member, thus avoiding the performance penalty of generating multiple OptionInfo objects. This value is multiplied by disc_factor and appended to the discounted_payoffs vector.

❼ Once the for loop has run its course, the option price is then the mean of the discounted payoffs and is returned.

❽ If no time remains until expiration, the else condition is executed, just returning the nondiscounted payoff of the OptionInfo member.

As an example, suppose we have the following contract and market data (again, in practice this information would come through an interface and would not be hardcoded):

```
double strike = 75.0;
double spot = 100.0;
double vol = 0.25;
double rate = 0.05;
double div = 0.075;
double time_to_exp = 0.5;
```

Suppose also we set the number of time steps for each of the 20,000 random equity price scenarios to 10, and that we set the seed for the uniform integer random generator to 42:

```
unsigned num_time_steps = 12;
unsigned num_scenarios = 20'000;
int seed = 42;
```

To price a call option, the first step is to create an `OptionInfo` object (as developed in Chapter 3), with a unique pointer to a `CallPayoff` object as a constructor argument. Next, the resulting option object is used to construct an `MCOptionValuation` object, along with the additional constructor arguments:

```
OptionInfo opt_call_itm_not_exp_with_div{
    std::move(std::make_unique<CallPayoff>(strike)), time_to_exp};

MCOptionValuation val_call_itm_not_exp_with_div{
    std::move(opt_call_itm_not_exp_with_div),
    num_time_steps, vol, rate, div};
```

The option value is then easily obtained by calling the `calc_price(.)` member function on the `MCOptionValuation` object, which takes in the spot price of the equity share price, along with the desired number of scenarios, and the seed for the uniform integer random generator that itself provides a random seed value for each scenario:

```
double opt_value =
    val_call_itm_not_exp_with_div.calc_price(spot, seed, num_scenarios);
```

The computed option value in this case is $23.51. For comparison, the closed-form Black-Scholes price is $23.52, so in this case convergence is very close.

Pricing Path-Dependent Options

The previous example has hopefully demonstrated the mechanics behind generating Monte Carlo equity price path scenarios and discounting the resulting payoffs to get a value of an option. However, it is not all that practically useful, as we could just implement the closed-form Black Scholes formula to get the same result. Monte Carlo methods become more useful in valuing *path-dependent* options.

As an example, we can consider barrier options, specifically up-and-out and down-and-out cases. Closed-form solutions for single barrier option valuation that derive from Black-Scholes theory also exist, so we will have a benchmark for testing our results. You can find these specific barrier option pricing formulas in Section 15.2 of *Option Theory*. Numerical results can be verified with tools such as the *derivmkts* R package (*https://oreil.ly/zuLGJ*) and the Barrier Option Pricing utility available from Coggit Free Tools (*https://oreil.ly/Ca4c1*).

The methods we are covering for both barrier and nonbarrier options, however, can be extended to many types of options with more-complex and/or multiple path-dependent payoffs, and for which closed-form solutions do not exist. Much of the typical machinery for generating the underlying scenarios would be the same or similar.

As for our valuation of knockout barrier options, we can start by defining a scoped enumeration (see enum `class`, introduced in Chapter 2) to represent the three distinct possible barrier conditions:

```
enum class BarrierType
{
    none,
    up_and_out,
    down_and_out
};
```

The `MCOptionValuation` constructor can then be modified to accommodate different barrier types, with the defaults set to `BarrierType::none` and a barrier value of zero. A new member variable for each is also declared:

```
public:
    MCOptionValuation(OptionInfo&& opt, unsigned time_steps, double vol,
        double int_rate, double div_rate = 0.0,
        BarrierType barrier_type = BarrierType::none,
        double barrier_value = 0.0);

    // . . .

private:
    // . . .
    BarrierType barrier_type_;
    double barrier_value_;
```

The constructor implementation is again responsible for member variable initializations:

```
MCOptionValuation::MCOptionValuation(OptionInfo&& opt, unsigned time_steps,
    double vol, double int_rate, double div_rate, BarrierType barrier_type,
    double barrier_value) :opt_{std::move(opt)}, time_steps_{time_steps},
    vol_{vol}, int_rate_{int_rate}, div_rate_{div_rate},
    barrier_type_{barrier_type}, barrier_value_{barrier_value} {}
```

The `calc_price(.)` function can be retrofitted to accommodate a barrier condition, as shown in the updated implementation that follows:

```
double MCOptionValuation::calc_price(double spot, unsigned num_scenarios,
    unsigned unif_start_seed)
{
    bool barrier_hit =  ❶
        (barrier_type_ == BarrierType::up_and_out && spot >= barrier_value_) ||
        (barrier_type_ == BarrierType::down_and_out && spot <= barrier_value_);

    if (barrier_hit) return 0.0;    // Option is worthless  ❷

    // Case where barrier has not (yet) been crossed

    if (opt_.time_to_expiration() > 0 )  ❸
    {
```

```
std::mt19937_64 mt_unif{unif_start_seed}; ❹
std::uniform_int_distribution<unsigned> unif_int_dist{};
const double disc_factor =
    std::exp(-int_rate_ * opt_.time_to_expiration());

using std::vector;
vector<double> discounted_payoffs; ❺
discounted_payoffs.reserve(num_scenarios);

// Iteration starts with barrier_hit = false
for (unsigned i = 0; i < num_scenarios; ++i) ❻
{
    EquityPriceGenerator epg{spot, time_steps_,
        opt_.time_to_expiration(), vol_, int_rate_, div_rate_};

    vector scenario = epg(unif_int_dist(mt_unif)); ❼

    switch (barrier_type_) ❽
    {
        case BarrierType::none: break; ❾

        case BarrierType::up_and_out: ❿
        {
            auto barrier_hit_pos = std::find_if(scenario.cbegin(),
                scenario.cend(),
                [this](double sim_eq)
                    {return sim_eq >= barrier_value_;}); ⓫

            if (barrier_hit_pos != scenario.cend())
            {
                barrier_hit = true; ⓬
            }
        }
        break;

        case BarrierType::down_and_out: ⓭
        {
            auto barrier_hit_pos = std::ranges::find_if(scenario,
                [this](double sim_eq)
                    {return sim_eq <= barrier_value_;}); ⓮

            if (barrier_hit_pos != scenario.cend())
            {
                barrier_hit = true;
            }
        }
        break;

    }    // end of switch statement

    if (barrier_hit)
    {
```

```
                discounted_payoffs.push_back(0.0);  ⓯
            }
            else
            {
                discounted_payoffs.push_back(disc_factor
                    * opt_.option_payoff(scenario.back())));  ⓰
            }

            barrier_hit = false;  ⓱
        }

        // Option value = mean of discounted payoffs
        return (1.0 / num_scenarios)
            * std::accumulate(discounted_payoffs.cbegin(),
            discounted_payoffs.cend(), 0.0);  ⓲
    }
    else  ⓳
    {
        // barrier_hit == false, at expiration
        return opt_.option_payoff(spot);  ⓴
    }
}
```

❶ To start, the `calc_price(.)` member function needs to check whether the underlying equity has already crossed the barrier.

❷ If so, the option is worthless, so a value of zero is returned.

❸ Next, similar to the previous nonbarrier example, the interesting cases will be those that have a positive time left to expiration ($T - t > 0$).

❹ We start by setting up a random sequence of integer seed values, and defining the discount factor (`disc_factor`) to be applied throughout each scenario generation.

❺ The `discounted_payoffs` container, which will again hold the discounted payoff from each scenario, is also created, with memory reserved to avoid memory reallocation of the `vector` storage.

❻ Again as in the nonbarrier case, a `for` loop runs an iteration for each scenario (e.g., 25,000 times).

❼ We also again generate a distinct random equity price scenario based on a random seed value drawn from a uniform integer distribution.

❽ We set up a `switch`/`case` statement based on each `BarrierType` enumerator.

⑨ If no barrier is present, the option is a plain European option with $T - t > 0$, which will have a terminal payoff.

⑩ If an up-and-out barrier is present, the code will need to iterate through the generated scenario to determine whether the barrier was crossed.

⑪ Testing the barrier can be accomplished more elegantly than a for loop by using the find_if algorithm. This will return the position of the first simulated price in the scenario container that exceeds the barrier, if it exists, which is conditioned on whether the iterator barrier_hit_pos reaches the end position.

⑫ If the barrier is crossed, barrier_hit is set to true. If not, similar to the plain European case, a terminal payoff will occur.

⑬ The logic is similar for a down-and-out barrier.

⑭ We can demonstrate in this case that we can write even more modern and cleaner code to test the barrier by using the *ranges* version of find_if. Whether the iterator form or ranges form, using the find_if algorithm will be preferable to embedding a messier and more error-prone nested multiline for loop:

```
// Don't write this -- replace with find_if algorithm
// . . .
for (double sim_value : scenario)
{
    if (sim_value >= barrier_value_)
    {
        barrier_hit = true;
        break;          // break out of for loop
    }
}
```

⑮ At the end of each iteration in the loop defined in step **❻**, the discounted payoff is conditioned on whether the barrier was crossed—that is, whether barrier_hit is true. If so, with a knockout barrier, the option expires worthless **⑮**, so the discounted payoff is zero and is appended to the discounted_payoffs vector.

⑯ Otherwise, the payoff is treated as if it were from a plain European option, where the terminal payoff is discounted back to the present. This nontrivial result is also appended to the discounted_payoffs vector.

⑰ barrier_hit is reset to false, and then the loop repeats itself with a new seed provided by the random uniform integer generator in line **❼**.

⑱ After the completion of the `for` loop, the option price is again the mean of the discounted payoffs, and the resulting value is returned.

⑲ Finally, we need to cover the other trivial case where the option is being valued at expiration, in the concluding `else` block.

⑳ We know that `barrier_hit` is `false` here, as the function would have been exited in step ❷ otherwise, so the value of the option is just the European payoff and is returned.

As an example, we can revisit the previous nonbarrier European call option example where we had this:

```
double strike = 75.0;
double spot = 100.0;
double vol = 0.25;
double rate = 0.05;
double div = 0.075;
double time_to_exp = 0.5;
int num_time_steps = 12;
int num_scenarios = 20'000;
unsigned seed = 42;
```

We can then add an up-and-out barrier value of $110.00:

```
BarrierType barr_type = BarrierType::up_and_out;
double barr_val = 110.0;
```

Now, setting this up, we again create an `OptionInfo` object and pass it by move semantics to the `MCOptionValuation` constructor:

```
OptionInfo opt_call_itm_barr{std::make_unique<CallPayoff>(strike), time_to_exp};
MCOptionValuation val_call_itm_barr{std::move(opt_call_itm_barr),
    num_time_steps, vol, rate, div, barr_type, barr_val};
```

We then obtain the option value by using the same member function, `calc_price(.)`:

```
double opt_val = val_call_itm_barr.calc_price(spot, seed, num_scenarios)
```

The result is $7.83, which is less than the value of $24.55 that we got in the equivalent nonbarrier case. This is expected, with more scenarios resulting in payoffs of zero. However, in this case, convergence to the analytic solution of $5.61 is not as close. We can improve the result by increasing the number of scenarios and time steps:

```
num_time_steps = 2'400;
num_scenarios = 50'000;
```

In this case, the calculated option price is $5.77, a significant improvement in convergence. However, this can come at a cost in performance.

At this point, you might very well be thinking that instead of generating each scenario serially, farming them out to individual processes and computing them in parallel might be much more efficient. Monte Carlo simulation is a prime example of an *embarrassingly parallelizable* procedure, in that each random scenario is independently generated. As such, you will soon see how Monte Carlo models can be implemented within the context of task-based concurrency introduced with C++11. These relatively recent Standard Library additions—quality random number generation and task-based concurrency—can play very nicely together to significantly boost computational efficiency, with minimal code modification.

Also, as a side note, as mentioned in Chapter 3, basic Monte Carlo methods as those discussed here are not suitable for American options, as there is no accounting for optimal early exercise. An alternative, binomial lattice models, discussed in Chapter 9, will handle options with early exercise.

Concurrency and Parallelism

Two powerful new features that enable running parallel tasks have been added to the Standard Library in recent years. The first is parallel algorithms, released in C++17. The second, which we will call *task-based concurrency*, stems from the introduction in C++11 of the std::async function and std::future objects. What is remarkable is that in both cases you can easily realize significant performance gains, particularly in terms of throughput, without the pain of writing lines of complex code responsible for creating thread pools, implementing parallel execution, and deactivating the threads. These mechanisms, being part of the Standard Library, also provide a big advantage by being platform-independent.

With modern C++, parallel algorithms can be called by simply adding an extra argument with respect to the nonparallel counterpart, and writing concurrent code can sometimes be accomplished by writing a few extra lines that would otherwise execute sequentially. The benefits you can reap overwhelm the minimal extra work required. Of course, writing parallel or concurrent code is not always that simple, but that is not specific to C++.

We will first present standard parallel algorithms and then return to the Monte Carlo option pricing example to demonstrate task-based concurrency. As the latter is an embarrassingly parallelizable procedure, it can also be accomplished without having to worry about deadlocks and race conditions that can occur when writing parallel code.

Since most standard consumer laptop and desktop machines today allow multicore processing, the features presented here will almost surely enable your code to run in parallel if you use them. Note, however, that sequential code is a special case of parallel code, and that asking for an algorithm to be executed in parallel does not guarantee that you will get a nonsequential execution. Ultimately, your standard library vendor may decide to honor your request or not, depending on various factors. For example, if the amount of data to process does not seem sufficient to compensate for the overhead associated with the request, the implementation could determine that a sequential execution will be faster.

On the flip side, your request for parallel execution might still be honored, but it will not necessarily guarantee better performance. Quite possibly, it will be worse than sequential execution performance, again particularly for smaller data sets. Examples of this will be shown in "Performance and guidance" on page 211.

Parallel Algorithms from the Standard Library

If there were ever an epitome of the term *leverage*, it would apply to parallel algorithms from the Standard Library. Most STL algorithms, as of C++17, have overloads with an extra argument—its execution policy—that instructs it to run in parallel. It couldn't be easier.

When requesting an algorithm to be executed in parallel, the execution policy argument appears first, followed by the other arguments usually passed to that algorithm. The `<execution>` header needs to be included when utilizing execution policies.

Other than the optional execution policy parameter, parallel standard algorithms look like their conventional counterparts: they can be parameterized with a thread-safe (preferably) auxiliary function (often a predicate), and they can be either non-modifying or modifying, the latter case encompassing order modification, element modification, or possibly both. We will look at examples of each, including some mathematical examples.

Descriptive statistics

Suppose you want to analyze typical descriptive statistics, such as maximum and minimum, and mean values, from a set of data.

To simulate a set of data, we can generate a sample of normal random variates and place the results in a `vector`. Next, we can run STL algorithms in parallel to find the maximum and minimum element, and then calculate the mean of these random values. To run each of these in parallel, all that is needed is to place the parallel execution policy, `std::execution::par`, in the first argument position when calling the algorithms involved.

To generate the standard normal data to be used in the example, we create the usual Mersenne Twister and normal distribution objects, and then wrap the random number generation in a lambda. This lambda then serves as the auxiliary function in the `std::generate` algorithm, and n = 50,000 random variates are drawn. This algorithm is run sequentially because it mutates the state of the engine (mt) and distribution (nd), but at this stage we are only obtaining the data to be used in the parallel examples to follow:

```
#include <vector>
#include <algorithm>
#include <numeric>
#include <random>
#include <execution>

    . . .

// Generate large number of normal variates:
std::mt19937_64 mt(25);
std::normal_distribution<> nd;

auto next_norm = [&mt, &nd]()
{
    return nd(mt);
};

const unsigned n = 500;
std::vector<double> norms(n);
std::generate(norms.begin(), norms.end(), next_norm);
```

The algorithms to search for and locate the maximum and minimum values can now be set up for parallel execution by including the parallel execution policy parameter in the first argument position of the std::max_element and std::min_element algorithms, as shown next. These overloaded algorithms again respectively return an iterator to the maximum and the minimum and values in the sequence:

```
auto max_norm = std::max_element(std::execution::par,
    par_norms.begin(), par_norms.end());

auto min_norm = std::min_element(std::execution::par,
    par_norms.begin(), par_norms.end());
```

To compute the mean in previous examples, we appealed to the std::accumulate algorithm to sum up the values in the vector first; however, in this case, no parallel version of the algorithm exists. Not to despair, a new algorithm, std::reduce, will perform this task in parallel by default:

```
double mean_parallel = 1.0 / par_norms.size()
    * std::reduce(par_norms.begin(), par_norms.end(), 0.0);
```

If desired, however, we can explicitly indicate the execution policy, as there are other options besides std::par (to be discussed in "Execution policies: in general" on page 213):

```
double mean_parallel = 1.0 / par_norms.size()
    * std::reduce(std::execution::par, par_norms.begin(), par_norms.end(), 0.0);
```

Inner product

One more numeric algorithm, `std::inner_product`, does not carry a parallel version. Instead, we can use another new (C++17) algorithm, `std::transform_reduce`, whose default behavior gives us the inner product of two containers. Note that `transform_reduce` is parallel by default, so similar to `std::reduce`, the `std::par` execution policy can be omitted:

```
std::vector<int> v{4, 5, 6};
std::vector<int> w{1, 2, 3};

double dot_prod = std::transform_reduce(v.begin(), v.end(), w.begin(), 0);
```

What this does is first calculate each of the element-by-element products, and then sums them in parallel. In other words, it is shorthand for the following:

```
dot_prod = std::transform_reduce(v.begin(), v.end(), w.begin(), 0,
    std::plus<int>{}, std::multiplies<int>{});
```

The `transform_reduce` algorithm also admits the more general form where other operations can be used, such as taking the sum of differences between two vectors:

```
int sum_diff = std::transform_reduce(v.begin(), v.end(), w.begin(), 0,
    std::plus<int>{}, std::minus<int>{});
```

Note that the first operation—in this example, the element-by-element subtraction to compute the differences—is the second operation argument (`std::minus`), while the second operation—here the sum of the differences (`std::plus`)—is the first argument.

The algorithm can also be applied to a single `vector`, such as computing its sum of squares:

```
double ssq = std::transform_reduce(v.begin(), v.end(), v.begin(), 0);
```

Performance and guidance

The previous examples were kept simple with small vector sizes in order to focus on the essentials of parallel STL algorithms. In practice, with small amounts of data like this, these algorithms might execute sequentially regardless of the execution policy used as the argument, or they could conversely exhibit worse performance if the parallel request is honored. The motivation for using parallel algorithms, of course, is to achieve faster execution when computing over larger amounts of data, so here we will look at an example to illustrate this.

Suppose we have a large random sample from a standard normal distribution, and for each value in the sample, we want to compute the approximation of the exponential function by using the power series expansion

$$e^x \approx \sum_{k=0}^{n} \frac{x^k}{k!}$$

for n "sufficiently large."

For this, we will first use the `std::transform` algorithm in its default, sequential mode, and then compare it with the same algorithm but with a parallel execution policy. The process will be repeated for increasing values of n in order to compare the execution times of both approaches.

In the code example that follows, assume vectors u and v have been populated with identical sets of standard normal random variables, generated using the 64-bit Mersenne Twister engine and normal distribution as before. The num_elements argument will hold the number of elements in each of u and v:

```
std::mt19937_64 mtre{100};
std::normal_distribution<long double> nd;
std::vector<long double> v(num_elements);

auto next_norm = [&mtre, &nd](double x)
{
    return nd(mtre);
};

std::transform(v.begin(), v.end(), v.begin(), next_norm);
auto u = v;
```

Then, setting the first two terms in the power series to 1.0 and x, e^x can be approximated with the following lambda expression, where n represents n in the summation:

```
auto exp_series = [n](double x) {
    double num = x;          // A standard normal variate
    double den = 1.0;
    double res = 1.0 + x;
    for (unsigned k = 2; k < n; ++k)
    {
        num *= x;
        den *= static_cast<double>(k);
        res += num / den;
    }
    return res;
};
```

Running the `transform` algorithm first sequentially, followed by its overload using the parallel execution policy parameter, and replacing each element of the respective vector (u or v) with its approximate exponential value, we can write our code as follows:

```
std::transform(u.begin(), u.end(), u.begin(), exp_series);
std::transform(std::execution::par, v.begin(), v.end(), v.begin(), exp_series);
```

For illustration, using tests performed on an eight-core machine, with increasing values of n (terms) and vector sizes for u and v, the results are as shown in Table 6-1.

Table 6-1. Exponential approximation performance results

Number of vector elements	Number of terms in sum	No exec policy (ms)	With parallel exec (ms)	Speed difference
100	10	0.0014	0.0824	−98.30%
500	50	0.0403	0.1261	−68.04%
500,000	200	210.3203	38.9450	440.04%
1,000,000	200	414.8995	97.6039	325.08%
5,000,000	200	2095.3706	433.6819	383.16%
10,000,000	20,000	4144.3402	561.8325	637.65%

As with any powerful tool, you will need to know when it is appropriate to use parallel algorithms and when it is preferable to refrain from so doing (*https://oreil.ly/obHnu*). As you can see in these results, blindly applying a parallel execution policy to a standard algorithm might not improve performance by any significant degree. In some cases, performance may even degrade, as you can see in the first two runs with smaller vector sizes and lower numbers of terms in the power series. But after cranking these values higher, the performance gains become more significant, yet the *only difference in the code was simply adding the parallel execution policy argument*. Even more significant performance improvements can be obtained in these cases with a larger number of processors.

Execution policies: in general

In the preceding examples, with an existing pre-C++17 standard algorithm, parallel processing is enabled by adding the parallel execution policy as the first argument. Here are two examples:

```
std::min_element(std::execution::par, par_norms.begin(), par_norms.end());

std::transform(std::execution::par, v.begin(), v.end(), v.begin(), exp_series);
```

When using an algorithm introduced in C++17 designed specifically for parallel processing, however, the parallel execution policy is implied and hence not required, as shown in the two previous examples, std::reduce and std::transform_reduce:

```
std::reduce(par_norms.begin(), par_norms.end(), 0.0);
double dot_prod = std::transform_reduce(v.begin(), v.end(), w.begin(), 0.0);
```

Execution policies can still be specified explicitly in these cases if desired, however:

```
std::reduce(std::execution::par, par_norms.begin(), par_norms.end(), 0.0);
dot_prod = std::transform_reduce(std::execution::par,
    v.begin(), v.end(), w.begin(), 0.0);
```

Officially, and more generally, C++17 introduced three execution policies:

Sequential execution policy, `std::execution::seq`
Ensures that the algorithm may not be run in parallel

Parallel execution policy, `std::execution::par`
Requests that the algorithm is executed in parallel

Parallel unsequenced policy, `std::execution::par_unseq`
Indicates that an algorithm may be executed in parallel and vectorized

Technically speaking, the sequential policy might not be exactly the same as when no execution policy is indicated (for a pre-C++17 algorithm), but it is similar. Also, the term *vectorized* refers to executions on platforms such as Single Instruction Multiple Data (SIMD) with a graphics processing unit (GPU).

For this book, we are primarily interested in the implied versions of `reduce` and `transform_reduce` without including an explicit execution policy. You can find further details on execution policies in more advanced texts focused on parallel computation. You can also find examples and information on the vectorizing execution policy (third in the preceding list) in the NVIDIA HPC SDK Documentation (*https://oreil.ly/F-hq4*).

 For completeness, a fourth execution policy was added to C++20: `std::execution::unseq`. This is related to vectorized operations executed in parallel on each individual thread and (again) is beyond the scope of this book.

Task-Based Concurrency

Concurrency and *parallelism* have many definitions, and the C++ standard does not provide a formal definition for either. What it does define are rules that help model such things as what a thread of execution is and how execution progresses in the presence of multiple threads. For the purpose of this book, what matters most is that the Standard Library now has built-in support to enable multithreading on personal computers and servers with multicore processors.

Programming multithreaded code is notoriously more difficult than single-threaded code, particularly in the presence of mutable state, which requires us to take into account synchronization in order to avoid data races. Informally, a *data race* occurs when a given object (such as an `int` or `bool` object) is accessed concurrently by at least two threads, with at least one thread modifying the object, all without synchronization. If a program contains a data race, it is essentially broken.

As part of the C++11 concurrency library, the spawning, management, and deactivating of threads can be abstracted away by using what we will refer to as *task-based concurrency*. This way, a programmer can concentrate on enabling the actual tasks of an application to run in parallel, rather than having to be concerned about the intricacies and complexity of thread programming. Furthermore, as this is part of the Standard Library, code utilizing task-based concurrency will compile and run cross-platform.

Much like a `vector` is an abstraction of a dynamic array that manages the allocation and deallocation of heap memory, a `std::future` object abstracts away the responsibilities associated with thread construction and startup necessary to execute a specific task asynchronously. This object will even abstract away whether a thread of execution needs to be started on demand or whether that thread is taken from a pool of threads that are already running. This can make writing parallelized code significantly simpler, leading to code that tends to be cleaner, less error-prone, and overall less time-consuming to maintain. This is especially convenient for financial programming, where embarrassingly parallelizable models involving tasks that are independent of one another are common, such as when employing Monte Carlo methods.

Creating and managing a task

A concurrent task is set in motion by constructing a `std::future` object that handles the relevant function and its arguments. This object is created with the `std::async(.)` function. Both require inclusion of the Standard Library `<future>` header.

For example, suppose we have a function that squares two integers:

```
int square_val(int x)
{
    return x * x;
}
```

Generating a `future` object that will handle the task of squaring a given integer is accomplished by applying `async(.)` to the function name (`square_val(.)` in this case) with its argument (`x`). In practice, the `async(.)` function can pass as many arguments as required to the function it is asked to run concurrently. Calculating the square of 5 as a task would therefore be written as follows:

```
#include <future>

// . . .

int i = 5;

auto ftr = std::async(square_val, i);      // square_val is the function,
                                           // int i = 5 is its argument

cout << std::format("Square of {} is {}\n", i, ftr.get());
```

The resulting `ftr` object represents the result of the computation performed concurrently by the function passed to `async(.)`; that result will become available after that task has been completed. At this point, the result can be obtained by calling the `get()` member function defined on the `future` object. Calling `get()` blocks the calling thread until the task's execution is completed.

This alone is, of course, not all that interesting, and this example will actually be much slower than the sequential equivalent because of the simplicity of the computation performed asynchronously, but let's leave this detail aside for the moment. You will eventually see how the calling code could remain nearly as simple yet apply to more-complex asynchronous computations resulting in measurable performance improvements.

Continuing with the integer square theme, we could implement a variation that calculates the squares of a container of integers by calling the `async(.)` function for each number and executing each task asynchronously. A convenient way to do this is by placing them in a vector of `future` objects as each is created, and then iterating through and calling the `get()` member function to obtain each result. For example:

```
std::vector<int> x(25);
std::iota(x.begin(), x.end(), 0);       // 0, 1, 2, ..., 24
std::vector<std::future<int>> v;

for (auto k : x)
{
    v.push_back(std::async(square_val, k));
}

std::vector<int> y(v.size());

std::ranges::transform(v, y.begin(),
    [](std::future<int> &fut){return fut.get();});
```

The vector y now contains the square of each integer in the vector x. This particular example again will not yield any significant performance gains, but it sets up a form we can use next for Monte Carlo option pricing, where the results will show significant speed improvements over the sequential implementation presented in "Monte Carlo Option Pricing" on page 194.

Revisiting Monte Carlo option pricing

We can now return to our earlier Monte Carlo option pricing example and set it up to run in parallel. In practice, we would want to avoid duplicated code. But for the purposes of this demonstration, we'll reimplement a parallelized version of the calc_price(.) member function in a new calc_price_par(.) function. This new function will calculate the price of the option, given the same inputs as the nonparallelized case.

As the random price scenarios "don't care" about any of the others, they are embarrassingly parallelizable and are thus good candidates for using async(.) and future to generate each scenario as a parallel task. As such, we do not need to be concerned with data races.

The interesting logic will again be executed only if the time left to expiration is positive and if the barrier has not already been trivially crossed at the outset. As before, we will first generate a vector of seeds from a uniform integer distribution and define a vector to contain the discounted payoffs.

Now, concentrating on the nontrivial case where $T - t > 0$, and where a barrier (if it exists) has not been crossed (yet), the code starts out as before with the random uniform integer generator created to provide a unique seed value for each scenario, a vector to hold the discounted payoff values, and the calculation of the constant discount factor to be applied to each terminal payoff:

```
double MCOptionValuation::calc_price_par(double spot,
    unsigned num_scenarios, unsigned unif_start_seed)
{
    // . . .

    if (opt_.time_to_expiration() > 0)
    {
        using std::vector;

        std::mt19937_64 mt_unif{unif_start_seed};
        std::uniform_int_distribution<unsigned> unif_int_dist{};

        vector<double> discounted_payoffs;
        discounted_payoffs.reserve(num_scenarios);
        const double disc_factor =
            std::exp(-int_rate_ * opt_.time_to_expiration());

        vector<std::future<vector<double>>> ftrs; ❶
        ftrs.reserve(num_scenarios);

        if (barrier_hit != true)
        {
            for (unsigned i = 0; i < num_scenarios; ++i)
            {
                EquityPriceGenerator epg{spot, time_steps_,
```

```
                opt_.time_to_expiration(), vol_, int_rate_, div_rate_};

            // Each scenario is now asynchronous:
            ftrs.push_back(std::async(epg, unif_int_dist(mt_unif)));  ❷
        }

        for (auto& ftr : ftrs)
        {
            vector scenario = ftr.get();    // (Also note we can use CTAD)  ❸

            switch (barrier_type_)
            {
                // . . .
            }

            // . . .

        }
    }

    return (1.0 / num_scenarios)
        * std::accumulate(discounted_payoffs.cbegin(),
            discounted_payoffs.cend(), 0.0);
}
else
{
    return opt_.option_payoff(spot);
}
}
```

The only differences are minor changes to the code as follows:

❶ Instead of generating each scenario serially for each seed, we can spawn these in
   independent tasks that run asynchronously, allowing the entire set of scenarios to
   be generated more quickly. This is done by first creating a vector to hold a set of
   std::future objects handling each scenario.

   ```
   vector<std::future<vector<double>>> ftrs;  ❶
   ```

❷ Then, the scenarios are generated concurrently on individual threads by invoking
   the std::async function.

   ```
   // Next seed = unif_int_dist(mt_unif)
   ftrs.push_back(std::async(epg, unif_int_dist(mt_unif)));  ❷
   ```

❸ Now, each scenario is obtained by calling the get() member function on each
   future object in the ftrs vector. Once we have each scenario, the switch/case
   statement remains the same as it was in the serial calc_price(.) implementation we developed previously. Note also that we can use CTAD here if we want
   (introduced in Chapter 1).

---

218 | Chapter 6: Random Number Generation and Concurrency

```
for (auto& ftr : ftrs)
{
    vector scenario = ftr.get();  ❸
    switch (barrier_type_)
    {
        // . . .
    }

    // . . .
}
```

By making these simple changes in just the three locations of the code, the performance can be improved remarkably; however, some caveats are involved. These are summarized next.

Considering caveats and performance

Similar to parallel STL algorithms, we should not just blindly use `std::async(.)` and expect automatic improvements in performance. Indeed, doing so may or may not result in an improvement, and switching from a single-threaded execution model to a multithreaded equivalent could even lead to performance losses. On the other hand, past a certain point, performance improvements can be quite substantial.

To demonstrate this, performance tests were conducted for a down-and-out barrier put option with the data as shown in Table 6-2.

Table 6-2. Down-and-out barrier put option data

Spot	Strike	Risk-free rate	Volatility	Dividend rate	Barrier level
100	105	5%	25%	8%	70.50

In addition, two cases of expirations were used 1 year and 10 years (the latter is an expiration more typically found in long-term guaranteed investment products and interest rate derivatives).

These tests were again performed on the same eight-core processor hardware as in the parallel STL algorithm examples. For the one-year option, the comparative times and speed differences with `async` are shown in Table 6-3, along with the computed option values.

Table 6-3. Down-and-out put option performance comparison (one-year expiration)

Num time steps	Num scenarios	No async (ms)	With async (ms)	Speed difference	Option value
12	20,000	36.7760	63.1752	−41.79%	7.54
12	50,000	85.3634	185.5319	−53.99%	7.46
120	20,000	127.257	88.2092	44.27%	6.75
120	50,000	352.2114	230.6709	52.69%	6.75
360	20,000	339.5314	61.7573	449.78%	6.58
360	50,000	796.6583	179.3042	344.31%	6.56

Table 6-4 shows the results for the 10-year option.

Table 6-4. Down-and-out put option performance comparison (10-year expiration)

Num time steps	Num scenarios	No async (ms)	With async (ms)	Speed difference	Option value
10	20,000	32.4281	45.2584	−28.35%	0.49
10	50,000	84.5093	133.7967	−36.84%	0.48
40	20,000	62.2338	49.5326	25.64%	0.49
40	50,000	135.6066	116.9286	15.97%	0.48
120	20,000	112.6142	48.4432	132.47%	0.36
120	50,000	295.2015	162.1747	82.03%	0.37
520	20,000	431.6498	146.6053	194.43%	0.30
520	50,000	1096.2874	314.919	248.12%	0.30
3600	20,000	2325.4275	449.539	417.29%	0.27
3600	50,000	5727.0185	824.4835	594.62%	0.29

As you can see in the results, the threaded cases for smaller numbers of time steps result in a slowdown in performance. However, as these are increased, we can start to see rather significant speed improvements. Considering also that the closed-form theoretical price for the one-year option down-and-out barrier put option is $6.29, and for the 10-year, $0.26, greater numbers of scenarios and time steps become necessary for reasonable convergence.

One more consideration is that sensitivities often need to be calculated when valuing options. In many cases, this involves recalculating the option values with Monte Carlo methods using slightly perturbed values of the underlying price (delta), interest rate (rho), time to expiration (theta), etc. To estimate the delta value, we can approximate the first derivative value as follows, where S represents the underlying share price, δS (lowercase delta, to distinguish from the delta of the option) represents a small shift in the price (e.g., 0.5%), and V represents the value of the option for a given underlying price and all other parameters held equal, as discussed in Section 10.4 of *Option Theory*:

$$\Delta = \frac{V(S + \delta S) - V(S - \delta S)}{2\delta S}$$

As such, this means we have to run Monte Carlo simulations to calculate the option values two additional times, $V(S + \delta S)$ and $V(S - \delta S)$, so performance improvements of even a "modest" (say, 200%), increase in speed can make a big difference, given similar calculations would need to be run for just the remaining first-order sensitivities alone (rho, vega, theta, plus the second-order gamma calculations). These calculations can become unstable, however, in cases of discontinuous payoffs such as with barriers. In these cases, more sophisticated methods are typically warranted, as discussed in more detail in Section 7.2 of *Monte Carlo Methods in Financial Engineering* by Paul Glasserman.

The performance improvements are quite remarkable considering that, similar to our earlier examples with parallel algorithms, we were able to realize these performance gains with minimal modification, and without having to manually program code associated with thread management. In fact, these performance gains were obtained with simple changes to just two lines of the code.

One observation that you might have is that there is no such thing as an exchange-traded equity option with an expiration time of 10 years. This is true; however, as alluded to at the outset, longer-term contracts can become relevant in some examples. For instance, complex structured interest rate derivatives can have a series of fixed exercise dates over long periods of time, some of which also involve swapping currencies or that are embedded in credit derivatives.

Another example is liability calculations for guaranteed investment products typically offered by insurance companies, such as variable annuities. These contracts are essentially synthetic long-term put options with various complex riders such as ratchets, guaranteed return roll-ups, withdrawal benefits, and death benefits. They can span a period even on the order of 30 years and can furthermore require nested simulations, pumping up the number of simulations and computational complexity dramatically. Monte Carlo is the method of choice for these types of models, and having task-based concurrency tools now available with C++ means much shorter implementation times as well as portable implementations.

Finally, we can consider improving performance even further in a couple of ways. First, as may seem obvious, we could again increase the number of processors. A variety of variance reduction methods such as antithetic sampling and control variates also could be implemented to yield increased efficiency. Although we will not pursue this topic here, the previous discussion should provide you with a basic framework that you can fairly easily extend to include variance reduction code. Comprehensive coverage of variance reduction methods is again available in *Monte Carlo Methods in Financial Engineering*.

Concluding Remarks on async and future

For completeness, it should be noted that use of future and async(.) has been the subject of some debate within the C++ community because of certain issues relating to more-complex situations. However, for models based on embarrassingly paralleliz-able processes, and thus where data races are not an issue, future and async(.) provide a simple and reliable means for implementing multithreaded tasks. This means potentially reaping substantial performance improvements without having to deal with the extra work and complications that can come with manual implementation of thread management.

One particular recommendation for making async(.) more reliable (*https://oreil.ly/6td7z*) is to supply a *launch policy* with explicit instructions to run each task on a different thread. This may seem counterintuitive, but the default can potentially run in a deferred mode, as single-core machines are still out there, and async(.) can run into trouble with these otherwise.

In our case, on a multicore platform, this would mean when generating each new scenario in our Monte Carlo option pricing model, instead of using

```
ftrs.push_back(std::async(epg, unif_int_dist(mt_unif)));
```

we would include the launch policy as an additional argument, std::launch::async, as shown here:

```
ftrs.push_back(std::async(std::launch::async, epg, unif_int_dist(mt_unif)));
```

The details behind this get complicated and are beyond the scope of this book, but you can find more information in Item 36 of *Effective Modern C++* by Scott Meyers.

Future enhancements are planned for a more robust concurrency library in the Standard, but it appears async(.) will remain as a no-frills option, highly suitable for embarrassingly parallelizable processes such as the Monte Carlo model presented here. It is recommended, however, to use the launch policy as noted previously.

Summary

With perhaps the exception of parallel STL algorithms, the title of this chapter could have been "Useful Modern Features of C++ You Probably Have Never Heard Of." Having distributional random number generation as part of the Standard Library is a huge improvement for quantitative financial developers. For Monte Carlo simulation alone, this means the common tasks of implementing a reliable standard normal random number generator is already provided and well-tested.

The std::future class and std::async(.) function provide a ready-made method for implementing embarrassingly parallel processes that are ubiquitous in finance, without requiring the programmer to manually write lines of complex code

---

responsible for creating thread pools, implementing parallel execution, and then deactivating the threads. Using these modern Standard Library features also ensures that the code remains platform-independent, without reliance on third-party commercial libraries. Goosing performance further is an option, by using newer threading features that have been added to the Standard in more recent years, but this would inevitably introduce the cost of longer development times and higher maintenance requirements. The decision would come down to weighing the benefits— likely diminishing but perhaps still desired—versus the additional development time, testing, and maintenance.

Parallel STL algorithms, however, have received a lot of attention, and they also can provide an enormous performance benefit, considering how easy they are to use, simply adding an execution policy argument to a previously existing algorithm, or utilizing new parallel numeric algorithms such as `std::reduce` and `std::transform_reduce`. Furthermore, parallel "overloads of all the existing algorithms in `std::ranges` that have a parallel overload in" the Standard Library are also in discussion for a future release.[4]

Further Resources

You can find extensive coverage of longer-term guaranteed investment products typically offered through life insurance companies, for which Monte Carlo methods are frequently employed in hedging and risk management, in *Investment Guarantees* by Mary Hardy (Wiley Finance, 2003).

---

4 Barry Revzin et al., "A Plan for C++23 Ranges (Tier 2)" (*https://oreil.ly/gVZwJ*), April 2016.

CHAPTER 7

Dates and Fixed Income Securities

Very special thanks to Kenneth J. Adams, who coauthored this chapter.

Dates and date calculations might not seem like the most fascinating topic to discuss, but they are vitally important in quantitative finance, particularly in fixed income trading and analytics. To handle date calculations in the past, financial C++ programmers were left with two options: either write their own date classes and functions, or use a commercial or open source external library. This has changed with C++20. It includes a date class that is determined by the integer year, month, and day values. This class relies both on the already existing (since C++11) `std::chrono` foundation of durations, time points, and the system clock (i.e., chronological computations) as well as newer C++20 calendrical computations, which are based on the number of days relative to an epoch. These take into account the nonuniform number of days in each month.

We will start by covering how dates are represented and instantiated in C++20, primarily with the `year_month_day` class now included in the `std::chrono` namespace. Certain characteristics of a date are important in financial applications, such as whether a day falls on a weekday or weekend, at the end of the month, or during a leap year. The `std::chrono` namespace conveniently provides ways of determining these possible states of a date. You can also add years and months by using calendrical options in `std::chrono`, but adding days requires conversion to a chronological time point. These are crucial in finance, particularly for fixed income operations and thus are also covered.

On the plus side, functionality surrounding the `std::chrono::year_month_day` class is very general and optimized for performance, but as a result it can also get complicated and somewhat tedious. For this reason, we will look at how we might wrap a `std::chrono::year_month_day` object and its associated functionality into our own user-defined date class. Approached in this way, the grunt work is encapsulated in member functions, so that financial developers will be able to call on a more convenient interface to invoke calculations and verify the state of a date object.

From there, we will look at applications of date calculations required in finance. The first of these applications may seem trivial, day count bases, but these can be very important in fixed income trading. The remaining half of the chapter focuses on yield curves and bond pricing. Before diving into related C++ examples, we will summarize the mechanics of yield curves and how bond payments are structured, and how a bond is commonly valued. The details behind this are important in writing real-world bond-trading software, yet it is surprising they are so often glossed over in computational finance courses and textbooks. Our user-defined date class will then return within this context, as we will examine how you might design a yield curve and bond class, and use them to value a typical coupon-paying bond.

Representation of a Date

C++11 originally introduced `std::chrono` into the Standard Library, under the header <chrono>, which provided the following abstractions:

Duration of time
: A method of measurement over a given time interval, such as in units of minutes, days, or milliseconds

time point
: A duration of time relative to an epoch, such as the Unix epoch, January 1, 1970 (1970-1-1)

Clock
: The object that specifies the epoch and normalizes duration measurements

Dates in `std::chrono` are based on these chronological foundations, but as part of the new C++20 features, conversions to calendrical forms are also now available. These can be used for calculations involving years and months.

A standard date in `std::chrono` is represented by an object of the class `std::chrono::year_month_day`. This class has a variety of constructors, and it should be noted the following examples are non-exhaustive.

First, a constructor taking in the year, month, and day, separated by commas, is provided. But instead of integer values for each, these constructor arguments must be defined as separate `std::chrono::year`, `std::chrono::month`, and `std::chrono::day` objects.

For example, we could create an object holding the date November 14, 2022 as follows:

```
#include <chrono>

// . . .

std::chrono::year_month_day ymd{std::chrono::year{2022},
    std::chrono::month{11}, std::chrono::day{14}};
```

The / operator has also been overloaded to define a `year_month_day` object. We can then construct a new `year_month_day` object as follows:

```
std::chrono::year_month_day ymd_slash =
    std::chrono::year{2022} / std::chrono::month{11} / std::chrono::day{15};
```

Alternatively, individual constant `month` objects are defined in `std::chrono` by name, so an equivalent approach to constructing the same month as in the preceding example is to replace its constructed month object with the predefined `November` instance:

```
std::chrono::year_month_day alt_slash
    {std::chrono::year{2022} / std::chrono::November / 16};
```

Furthermore, we can use integral types for the last two arguments in the / operator form, as long as the first argument is obvious. For *yyyy*/*mm*/*dd* format, putting

```
std::chrono::year_month_day ymd_alt_numerical{std::chrono::year{2022} / 11 / 17};
```

would also be valid, with the compiler interpreting the 11 and 17 as `unsigned` types, resulting in the object representing the date November 17, 2022. We can also perform initialization with the = operator, using the same format. As the righthand side makes the type obvious, we can also use the `auto` keyword:

```
auto ymd_eql_init = std::chrono::year{2022} / 11 / 18;
```

As ordering conventions vary with country and culture, some latitude is offered to programmers in terms of date format when initializing a `year_month_day` object. The three commonly used date orders can be indicated with the / operator:

- *yyyy*/*mm*/*dd*
- *mm*/*dd*/*yyyy*
- *dd*/*mm*/*yyyy*

For example, *mm*/*dd*/*yyyy* format can also be used:

```
auto mdy = std::chrono::November / 19 / 2022;
```

In this case, the first argument is obviously a month. The value of 19 is recognized as the day value, and 2022 as the year.

Finally, a set of *chrono literals*, representing years and days, can be used at construction by bringing the `std::chrono` namespace into the scope of function:

```
void chrono_literals()
{
    using namespace std::chrono_literals;

    std::chrono::year_month_day ymd_lit_1{2024y / 9 / 16d};     // yyyy/mm/dd
    std::chrono::year_month_day ymd_lit_2{10d/ 10 / 2025y};     // dd/mm/yyyy
    std::chrono::year_month_day ymd_lit_3 = 7 / 16d / 2024y;    // mm/dd/yyyy

    // Can also combine with month constants (mm/dd/yyyy):
    std::chrono::year_month_day ymd_lit_4 = std::chrono::October / 26d / 1973y;

    // . . .
}
```

Again, as long as the first parameter is obvious, the trailing integer values can be used on their own. Also, because only one format has the day value in the second position (*mm*/*dd*/*yyyy*), we can also drop the *y* in the case of year_month_day ymd_lit_3. All four dates previously defined would in fact be the same if we reassigned them as follows:

```
// The same dates, with suffixes dropped:
ymd_lit_1 = 2024y / 9 / 16;
ymd_lit_2 = 10d / 10 / 2025;
ymd_lit_3 = 7 / 16d / 2024;
ymd_lit_4 = std::chrono::October / 26 / 1973;
```

By bringing the entire std::chrono namespace into the local scope, in addition to having access to chrono literals, this will make defining year_month_day objects (similar to our earlier examples) easier to read:

```
using namespace std::chrono;

// . . .

year_month_day ymd_lit_commas{year{1999}, month{11}, day{11}};
year_month_day ymd_in_october = October / 26 / 1973;
```

We will mostly assume access to the entire namespace inside function definitions for the remainder of the chapter for clarity and convenience, although there will be cases in function signatures and elsewhere where the full scope is more appropriate.

The output stream operator is overloaded for year_month_day, so any of the preceding examples can be output to the console with cout. For example:

```
cout << ymd << "\n";
```

The *yyyy-mm-dd* format is the ISO Standard date format (*https://oreil.ly/4Z3Yw*). It is also often preferred in financial applications, as it avoids the guesswork sometimes involved in distinguishing between the *mm-dd-yyyy* format used in the United States, and the *dd-mm-yyyy* format used in the United Kingdom. We will use the *yyyy-mm-dd* format for the remainder of this chapter.

The author of `std::chrono`, Howard Hinnant, provides more details about `std::chrono` dates on his GitHub site (*https://oreil.ly/ ThYkh*). Also, you can find a comprehensive list of constructors for the `year_month_day` class in his accompanying documentation (*https://oreil.ly/sPnBE*). Hinnant has also provided useful supplemental information in Stack Overflow posts, several of which are referenced in this chapter.

Serial Representation

A `year_month_day` date can also be measured in terms of the number of days since an epoch, with the `system_clock` default being the Unix epoch January 1, 1970. Similar to Excel (whose epoch is January 1, 1900), this representation can be convenient for date arithmetic in finance, particularly in determining the number of days between two dates. Unlike Excel, however, the Unix epoch is represented by 0 rather than 1, in the sense that serial dates are measured in *days since the epoch*. Consider the following example, with dates 1970-1-1 and 1970-1-2:

```
using namespace std::chrono;

year_month_day epoch{year{1970}, month{1}, day{1}};
year_month_day epoch_plus_1{year{1970}, month{1}, day{2}};
year_month_day epoch_minus_1{year{1969}, month{12}, day{31}};
```

Then, the first two respective serial dates can be accessed as follows, using the `std::chrono::sys_days(.)` function:

```
int first_days_test = sys_days(epoch).time_since_epoch().count();        // 0
first_days_test = sys_days(epoch_plus_1).time_since_epoch().count();     // 1
```

These return `int` values 0 and 1, respectively.

Also unlike Excel, `std::chrono` dates before the epoch are also valid but carry a negative integer value. In the statement that follows, the returned value is -1:

```
first_days_test = sys_days(epoch_minus_1).time_since_epoch().count();    // = -1
```

For typical financial trading, it is not necessary to go back in time before 1970, but in some areas, such as actuarial valuations of pension liabilities, many participants were born before this date. Historical simulations of markets also might use data going back many decades.

Recalling that the `year_month_day` class is built upon the three `std::chrono` abstractions listed at the outset, technically what is happening here is the `sys_days(.)` operator returns the ymd date as a `std::chrono::time_point` object, where `sys_days` is an alias for `time_point`. Then, its `time_since_epoch` member function returns a `std::chrono::duration` type. The corresponding integer value is then accessed with the `count()` function.

An important calculation to have in finance is the number of days between two dates. Using ymd again as 2022-11-14, and initializing ymd_later to six months later (2023-05-14) taking the difference between the two sys_days objects obtained with sys_days(.) and applying the count() function to the difference will give us the number of days between these two dates:

```
int diff = ((sys_days(ymd_later) - sys_days(ymd))).count();        // = 181
```

The result is 181 days.

Accessor Functions for Year, Month, and Day

Accessor functions on year_month_day are provided for obtaining the year, month, and day, but they are returned as their respective year, month, and day *objects*:

```
ymd.year()       // returns std::chrono::year
ymd.month()      // returns std::chrono::month
ymd.day()        // returns std::chrono::day
```

The differences between year, month, or day values in isolation between two dates ymd and ymd_later (2022-11-14 and 2023-05-14, respectively, as before) can be obtained by applying the count() function to their differences. The result for each is an int type:

```
// returns 2023 - 2022 = 1:
int year_diff = (ymd_later.year() - ymd.year()).count();

// returns 11 - 5 = 6:
int month_diff = (ymd_later.month() - ymd.month()).count();

// returns returns 14 - 14 = 0
int day_diff = (ymd_later.day() - ymd.day()).count();
```

Each of the individually accessed year, month, and day components can also be cast to integral types, but an important point to be aware of is a year can be cast to an int, but a month or day needs to be cast to unsigned:

```
int the_year = static_cast<int>(ymd.year());              // 2022 (int)
unsigned the_month = static_cast<unsigned>(ymd.month());  // 11 (unsigned)
unsigned the_day = static_cast<unsigned>(ymd.day());      // 14 (unsigned)
```

Checking the Validity of a Date

It is possible to set year_month_day objects to invalid dates. For example, as you will see shortly, adding a month to a date of January 31 will result in February 31. In addition, the constructor will also allow month and day values out of range. Instead of throwing an exception, it is left up to the programmer to check whether a date is valid. Fortunately, this is easily accomplished with the boolean ok() member function. In the following example, the ymd date (which is the same as in the previous example) is valid, while the two that follow are obviously not:

```
using namespace std::chrono;

year_month_day ymd{year{2022}, month{11}, day{14}};

// torf: "true or false"
bool torf = ymd.ok();                    // true

year_month_day negative_year{year{-1000}, October, day{10}};

torf = negative_year.ok();               // true - negative year is valid

year_month_day ymd_invalid{year{2018}, month{2}, day{31}};

torf = ymd_invalid.ok();                 // false

year_month_day ymd_completely_bogus{year{-2004}, month{19}, day{58}};

torf = ymd_completely_bogus.ok();    // false
```

The ok() member function will come in handy in subsequent examples, particularly when a date operation results in the correct year and month, but an incorrect day setting in end-of-month cases. This will be addressed shortly. The upshot is *it is up to the consumer* of the year_month_day class to check for validity, as it does not throw an exception or adjust automatically.

Checking Leap Years and Last Day of the Month

You can easily check whether a date is a leap year. A boolean member function, not surprisingly called is_leap(), takes care of this for us:

```
year_month_day ymd_leap{year{2024}, month{10}, day{26}};

bool torf = ymd_leap.year().is_leap();       // true
```

There is no member function available on year_month_day that will return the last day of the month. A workaround exists using a separate class in std::chrono that represents an end-of-month date, year_month_day_last, from which the last day of its month can also be accessed as before, and then cast to unsigned:

```
// std::chrono::last:  Last day of a given month:
year_month_day_last eom_apr{year{2009} / April / last};

auto last_day = static_cast<unsigned>(eom_apr.day());    // result = 30
```

This can also be used as a device to check whether a date falls on the end of a month:

```
year_month_day ymd_eom{year{2009}, month{4}, day{30}};

torf = ymd_eom == eom_apr;          // Returns true
```

The last day of the month for an arbitrary date can also be determined:

```
year_month_day ymd = year{2024} / 2 / 21;

year_month_day_last eom{year{ymd.year()} / month{ymd.month()} / last};

last_day = static_cast<unsigned>(eom.day());     // result = 29
```

It should also be noted a `year_month_day_last` type is implicitly convertible to a `year_month_day` via reassignment:

```
ymd = eom_apr;              // ymd is now 2009-04-30
```

You can find more background in the Stack Overflow post (*https://oreil.ly/wh21g*) "Using C++20 chrono, how to compute various facts about a date" by Howard Hinnant.

Putting this together in a function to find the last day of the month, we could then write the following:

```
unsigned last_day_of_the_month(std::chrono::year_month_day& ymd)
{
    using namespace std::chrono;
    year_month_day_last eom{ymd.year() / ymd.month() / last};
    return static_cast<unsigned>(eom.day());
}
```

Identifying Weekdays and Weekends

Similar to end-of-month dates, `std::chrono` has no member function to check whether a date falls on a weekend. We can use a workaround to derive the result we need.

The `std::chrono` namespace contains a `weekday` class that represents each day of the week—Monday through Sunday—not just weekdays per se (this terminology might be slightly confusing). An object can be constructed by again applying the `sys_days` operator in the constructor argument:

```
// Define a year_month_day date that falls on a business day (Wednesday)

year_month_day ymd_biz_day{year{2022}, month{10}, day{26}};     // Wednesday

// Its day of the week can be constructed as a weekday object:
weekday dw{sys_days(ymd_biz_day)};
```

The day of the week can be identified by an `unsigned` integer value returned from the `iso_encoding()` member function, where values 1 through 7 represent Monday

---

through Sunday, respectively. The stream operator is overloaded so that the abbreviated day of the week is displayed:

```
unsigned iso_code = dw.iso_encoding();
cout << ymd_biz_day << ", " << dw << ", " << iso_code << "\n";
```

Here is the output:

```
2022-10-26, Wed, 3
```

This allows us to define our own function, to determine whether a date falls on a weekend:

```
bool is_weekend(const std::chrono::year_month_day& ymd)
{
    using namespace std::chrono;
    weekday dw{sys_days(ymd)};
    return dw.iso_encoding() >= 6;
}
```

Now, also construct a `year_month_day` date that falls on a Sunday:

```
year_month_day ymd_weekend{year{2024}, month{1}, day{7}};          // Sunday
```

Then, we can use the function to test whether each day is a business day:

```
bool torf = is_weekend(ymd_biz_day);      // false (Wed)
torf = is_weekend(ymd_weekend);           // true (Sun)
```

You can find supplemental information on weekends in `std::chrono` in the Stack Overflow post "C++ Chrono determine whether day is a weekend?" (*https://oreil.ly/ FmSl4*), again courtesy of Howard Hinnant.

Adding Years, Months, and Days

One more set of important date operations in finance is adding years, months, and days to existing dates. These are particularly useful for generating schedules of fixed payments. Adding years or months is similar (both relying on the += operator), but adding days requires a different approach.

Adding years

Adding years is straightforward. For example, add two years to 2002-11-14, and then add another 18 years to the result. Note that the number of years being added needs to be expressed as a `std::chrono::years` object, an alias for a `duration` representing one year:

```
// Start with 2002-11-14
year_month_day ymd_01{year{2002}, month{11}, day{14}};

ymd_01 += years{2};      // ymd_01 is now 2004-11-14
ymd_01 += years{18};     // ymd_01 is now 2022-11-14
```

We run into a problem, however, if the date is the last day of February in a leap year. Adding two years to 2016-02-29 results in an invalid year:

```
year_month_day ymd_feb_end{year{2016}, month{2}, day{29}};
ymd_feb_end += years{2};    // Invalid result: 2018-02-29
```

Dates in `std::chrono` will again neither throw an exception nor adjust the day, so it is up to the developer to handle adding years to a February 29 date in a leap year. Even more end-of-month issues crop up when adding months. Workarounds are discussed next.

Adding months and handling end-of-month cases

Adding months to a `year_month_day` object is similar to adding years, but this now requires handling multiple end-of-month edge cases because of the different numbers of days in different months, plus again the case of February during a leap year.

When no end-of-month date is involved, the operation is straightforward, similar to adding years, using the addition assignment operator. Also similar to adding years, the number of months needs to be represented as a `duration` object—in this case, an alias for a period of one month:

```
using namespace std::chrono;
// . . .

year_month_day ymd_02{year{2022}, month{2}, day{16}};

ymd_02 += months{2};        // Result: 2022-04-16
ymd_02 += months{18};       // Result: 2023-10-16
```

Subtraction assignment is also available:

```
ymd -= months{2};           // Result: 2023-08-16
```

With end-of-month cases as well, the += operation can again result in invalid dates. To see this, construct the following end-of-month dates:

```
year_month_day ymd_eom_01{year{2015}, month{1}, day{31}};
year_month_day ymd_eom_02{year{2014}, month{8}, day{31}};
year_month_day ymd_eom_03{year{2016}, month{2}, day{29}};
```

Naively attempting month addition results in invalid dates:

```
ymd_eom_01 += months{1};        // 2015-02-31 is not a valid date
ymd_eom_02 += months{1};        // 2014-09-31 is not a valid date
ymd_eom_03 += months{12};       // 2017-02-29 is not a valid date
```

Although the results are not valid, the year and month of each is correct. That is, for example, adding one month to 2015-01-31 should map to 2015-02-28. Going the other way, if we were to start on 2015-02-28 and add one month, the result will be correct: 2015-03-28.

Recalling the `last_day_of_the_month()` function defined previously, a workaround is fairly straightforward, replicating the `+=` operator but with a correction in case the result is not valid. Addition assignment is naively applied, but if the result is invalid, it must be due to the day value exceeding the actual number of days in a month. In this case, because the resulting year and month will be valid, it just becomes a case of resetting the day with the number of days in the month:

```
auto add_months = [](year_month_day& ymd, unsigned mths)
{
    using namespace std::chrono;
    ymd += months(mths);    // Naively attempt the addition

    if (!ymd.ok())
    {
        ymd = ymd.year() / ymd.month() / day{last_day_of_the_month(ymd)};
    }
};
```

Starting with the same initial dates for `ymd_eom_01`, `ymd_eom_02`, and `ymd_eom_03`, and applying the lambda for each,

```
add_months(ymd_eom_01, 1);
add_months(ymd_eom_02, 1);
add_months(ymd_eom_03, 12);
```

we would now end up with valid dates 2015-02-28, 2014-09-30, and 2017-02-28.

Adding days

Unlike for years and months, no `+=` operator is defined for adding days. For this reason, we will need to obtain the `sys_days` equivalent before adding the number of days:

```
year_month_day ymd_03{year{2022}, month{10}, day{7}};

// Obtain the sys_days equivalent of ymd_03, and then add three days:
auto add_days = sys_days(ymd_03) + days(3);    // ymd_03 still = 2022-10-07
```

Note that at this point, `ymd_03` has not been modified, and the result, `add_days`, is also a `sys_days` type. To set a `year_month_day` object to the equivalent, the assignment operator provides implicit conversion. Similarly to previous applications of `sys_days`, we can just update the original `ymd_03` date to three days later:

```
ymd_03 = add_days;  // Implicit conversion to year_month_day
                    // ymd_03 is now = 2022-10-10
```

You can find more information on adding days in the Stack Overflow post "How do I add a number of days to a date in C++20 chrono?" (*https://oreil.ly/uqC_l*) by Howard Hinnant.

A Date Class Wrapper

As you can probably see by now, managing all the intricacies of std::chrono dates can eventually become complicated. For this reason, we will now outline the typical requirements for financial date calculations and wrap them in a class based on a year_month_day member. This way, the adjustments and year_month_day function calls are implemented once behind interfacing member functions and operators that are arguably more intuitive for the consumer.

The following list summarizes the functionality we need:

Constructors (three)
- Integral year, month, and day parameters
- std::chrono::year_month_day parameter
- Default constructor

Accessors
- Integral values for the year, month, and day of the date
- Serial date
- Underlying std::chrono::year_month_day

Properties of a date
- Check whether it falls on the last day of the month
- Check whether it falls during a leap year
- Retrieve the number of days in its month

Arithmetic operators
- Subtraction operator returning number of days between two dates (-)
- Equality of two dates (==)
- Date inequalities: does the date fall before or after a given date (<=>)

Modifying member functions
- Add years, months, and days to a date
- Roll a weekend date to a business date

To begin, the proposed class declaration will give us a road map to follow.

Class Declaration

We will incorporate the preceding requirements into a class called ChronoDate. It will wrap a std::chrono::year_month_day object along with some of its associated member functions that are useful in financial calculations. Before working through the member functions, let's start with the constructors.

Constructors

For convenience, we provide a constructor that takes in integral values for year, month, and day, rather than requiring the user to create individual year, month, and day objects. Note that the argument for the year is an int, while those for the month and day are unsigned. This is because of the design of the year_month_day class, as previously discussed:

```
ChronoDate(int year, unsigned month, unsigned day);
```

Also, as you will see for convenience later, a second constructor will take in a year_month_day object:

```
// Can pass and/or initialize by move (see Ch 2):
ChronoDate(std::chrono::year_month_day ymd);
```

And finally, we will define a default constructor, with in-class member initialization (introduced in Chapter 2) of a default year_month_day object set to the Unix epoch:

```
ChronoDate() = default;
```

In-class member initialization of this private member, date_, inside the declaration, is then used in tandem with the default constructor:

```
private:
    std::chrono::year_month_day date_{
        std::chrono::year{1970}, std::chrono::month{1}, std::chrono::day{1}};
```

For the two nondefault constructors, the date_ member will be initialized based on user input within their implementations, to be covered shortly.

Public member functions and operators

The purposes of these functions and operators should be self-explanatory from their declarations, which follow next. Furthermore, their implementations will mostly be a case of integrating the previously developed functionality into the respective member functions. As for the comparison operators, you will see the C++20 <=> operator.

One public function in the declaration remains to be covered, weekend_roll(), which will be used to roll a date to the nearest business day in the event a date falls on a Saturday or Sunday. Its implementation is covered in "Class Implementation" on page 239. Declarations of the public member functions and operators are as follows:

```
// Accessors:
int year() const;
unsigned month() const;
unsigned day() const;
int serial_date() const;
std::chrono::year_month_day ymd() const;

// Properties:
```

```
unsigned days_in_month() const;
bool is_end_of_month() const;
bool leap_year() const;

// Operators
int operator - (const ChronoDate& rhs) const;
bool operator == (const ChronoDate& rhs) const;
std::strong_ordering operator <=> (const ChronoDate& rhs) const;

// Modifying member functions:
ChronoDate& add_years(int rhs_years);
ChronoDate& add_months(int rhs_months);
ChronoDate& add_days(int rhs_days);
ChronoDate& weekend_roll();
```

Private members and member functions

As mentioned within the context of the default constructor, the class has a single data member: the underlying `std::chrono::year_month_day` object, `date_`. In addition, one private method, `validate_()`, will be called at (nondefault) construction. Its relevance will become clearer as we move into the implementation of the class.

The ChronoDate class declaration, in full

Putting all this information together, the class declaration can now be stated in full:

```
#include <chrono>
#include <compare>

class ChronoDate
{
public:
    ChronoDate(int year, unsigned month, unsigned day);

    ChronoDate(std::chrono::year_month_day ymd);
    ChronoDate() = default;

    // Accessors:
    int year() const;
    unsigned month() const;
    unsigned day() const;
    int serial_date() const;
    std::chrono::year_month_day ymd() const;

    // Modifying member functions:
    ChronoDate& add_years(int rhs_years);
    ChronoDate& add_months(int rhs_months);
    ChronoDate& add_days(int rhs_days);
    ChronoDate& weekend_roll();

    // Operators
    int operator - (const ChronoDate& rhs) const;
```

```
    bool operator == (const ChronoDate& rhs) const;
    std::strong_ordering operator <=> (const ChronoDate& rhs) const;

    // Check state:
    bool is_end_of_month() const;
    unsigned days_in_month() const;
    bool is_leap_year() const;

private:

    std::chrono::year_month_day date_
        {std::chrono::year{1970}, std::chrono::month{1}, std::chrono::day{1}};

    void validate_() const;
};
```

Let's next look at the implementations of these functions and operators.

Class Implementation

Almost all the necessary functionality for the class implementation has been presented in the previous sections, so most of our work is done. Now we just need to wrap these results into individual member functions. However, one member function, weekend_roll(), requires additional background, plus we have the responsibility for the two user-defined constructor implementations, which is where we will start.

Constructors

The implementation of the first user-defined constructor allows us to create an instance of ChronoDate with integer values (int and unsigned) rather than require individual instances of year, month, and day objects. In cases of an invalid date, a std::invalid_argument exception will be thrown:

```
#include <stdexcept>         // std::invalid_argument
// . . .

ChronoDate::ChronoDate(int year, unsigned month, unsigned day)
    : date_
    {
        std::chrono::year{year} /
        std::chrono::month{month} /
        std::chrono::day{day}
    }
{
    validate_();            // Checks whether the date is valid
}
```

Recalling that because it is possible to construct invalid year_month_day objects, such as February 30, a validation check is also included in the private member function `validate_()`. It will utilize the `ok()` member function on `year_month_day`, as shown here:

```
void ChronoDate::validate_() const
{
    if (!date_.ok())    // std::chrono member function to check if valid date
    {
        throw std::invalid_argument{"ChronoDate constructor: Invalid date."};
    }
}
```

In the event of an invalid year, month, or day argument, this function will throw an invalid argument (`std::invalid_argument`) exception.

The second user-defined constructor is just a matter of initializing the `date_` member with the single `year_month_day` argument. Again, as `std::chrono` does not guarantee a valid date, we need to check it as well. The `validate_()` private member function can be reused here:

```
ChronoDate::ChronoDate(std::chrono::year_month_day ymd) : date_{std::move(ymd)}
{
    validate_();
}
```

As first introduced in Chapter 2, this constructor form gives the consumer of the class the option to pass the `ymd` argument by value (in which case the copy is moved onto the `ymd_` member) or by move (so that no object copy is performed).

Member functions and operators

This section describes implementation of the functions previously introduced in "Class Declaration" on page 236. Practically every one of these function and operator implementations that follow will be very important for constructing yield curves and building payment schedules, both of which are commonly used in fixed income trading. Most are based on the functions and operators already defined on a `year_month_day` object, as discussed in the previous sections, which first introduced `std::chrono` dates.

Accessors.   To start, implementation of accessors for the serial date and `year_month_day` members is fairly straightforward. For the serial date, we use the number of days past the Unix epoch, which can be obtained as before, but wrapped in a member function:

```
int ChronoDate::serial_date() const
{
    return std::chrono::sys_days(date_).time_since_epoch().count();
}
```

Retrieving the `year_month_day` member, `date_`, is trivial:

```
std::chrono::year_month_day ChronoDate::ymd() const
{
    return date_;
}
```

A little more work is involved in returning integral values for the year, month, and day. A `std::chrono::year` object can be cast to an `int`, while `month` and `day` are castable to `unsigned` types. With this in mind, their accessors are straightforward to implement:

```
int ChronoDate::year() const
{
    return static_cast<int>(date_.year());
}

unsigned ChronoDate::month() const
{
    return static_cast<unsigned>(date_.month());
}

unsigned ChronoDate::day() const
{
    return static_cast<unsigned>(date_.day());
}
```

Date properties. These functions will provide the number of days in the month of the date, as well the status of whether the date falls on the last day of the month and whether the date is in a leap year.

Obtaining the number of days in the month is essentially a rehash of the function shown previously in "Checking Leap Years and Last Day of the Month" on page 231. We create a `year_month_day_last` object from the same year and month, and retrieve the day value:

```
unsigned ChronoDate::days_in_month() const
{
    using namespace std::chrono;
    year_month_day_last eom{date_.year() / date_.month() / last};
    return static_cast<unsigned>(eom.day());
}
```

Determining whether the date falls on the last day of the month is just a matter of comparing the active `ChronoDate` object with the `std::chrono` object having the same year and month, and day = `std::chrono::last`. The function will return `true` or `false`:

```
bool ChronoDate::is_end_of_month() const
{
    return date_ == date_.year() / date_.month() / std::chrono::last;
}
```

Checking whether a date is in a leap year simply requires wrapping the respective year_month_day member function is_leap() discussed earlier. It returns a bool type as well:

```
bool ChronoDate::is_leap_year() const
{
    return date_.year().is_leap();
}
```

Operators. The subtraction operator is a const operation that returns the number of days between the active ChronoDate object and an input object. Because we have an accessor that returns the serial date, all we need to do is implement the subtraction operator as the difference between the integer representations of the two dates:

```
int ChronoDate::operator -(const ChronoDate& rhs) const
{
    return this->serial_date() - rhs.serial_date();
}
```

The comparison operators == and <=> are already defined on the year_month_day class. So, the easy way to take care of them is to write single-line definitions in ChronoDate. We need to be sure to use std::strong_ordering as the return type for <=>, as ultimately two integer values (the days since the epoch) are being compared:

```
bool ChronoDate::operator == (const ChronoDate& rhs) const
{
    return this->ymd() == rhs.ymd();
}

std::strong_ordering ChronoDate::operator <=> (const ChronoDate& rhs) const
{
    return this->ymd() <=> rhs.ymd();
}
```

However, as an exercise, let's suppose these values were not given, so that we can examine an application of implementing the three-way <=> (spaceship) operator, as introduced with the Fraction class example in Chapter 2. First, because we have serial access to the integral representation of ChronoDate, implementation of the equality operator becomes trivial:

```
bool ChronoDate::operator == (const ChronoDate& rhs) const
{
    return this->serial_date() == rhs.serial_date();
}
```

Then, all we would need to do inside the spaceship operator implementation would be to define the meaning of <. With this, the remaining inequality operators would be implied:

```
std::strong_ordering ChronoDate::operator <=> (const ChronoDate& rhs) const
{
    if (this->serial_date() < rhs.serial_date())
    {
        return std::strong_ordering::less;
    }
    if (*this == rhs)
    {
        return std::strong_ordering::equivalent;
    }
    else
    {
        return std::strong_ordering::greater;
    }
}
```

Gone are the days when we would need separate implementations of all six operators. Implementing the comparison operators is so much easier now, with less to go wrong.

Addition of years, months, and days. The addition of years, months, and days to a date is also fundamental in fixed income mathematics. All three are modifying (non-const) functions on ChronoDate.

The first two, adding years and months, are pretty straightforward, as we now have ways to handle pesky end-of-month issues when they arise. The only issue when adding years occurs if the resulting date lands on the 29th of February in a nonleap year, so this case is easily addressed by resetting the day value to 28. Note that because the result is based on the underlying year_month_day += operator, the state of the object is modified:

```
ChronoDate& ChronoDate::add_years(int rhs_years)
{
    // Proceed naively:
    date_ += std::chrono::years(rhs_years);

    // Only possible error case is if month is February
    // and the result is day = 29 in a non-leap year.

    if (!date_.ok())
    {
        date_ = date_.year() / date_.month() / 28;
    }

    return *this;
}
```

When adding months to a date, the situation becomes more problematic with varying days in each month plus a leap year condition in February. However, the days_in_month() member function makes this a reasonably easy exercise. The addition of months is again naively attempted, with the number of days adjusted if the resulting month is invalid. The only way this incorrect state can occur is if the naive result has more days than in its respective month. The result again modifies the underlying `date_` member, and hence the active object:

```
ChronoDate& ChronoDate::add_months(int rhs_months)
{
    date_ += std::chrono::months(rhs_months);    // Naively attempt the addition

    // If the date is invalid, it is because the
    // result is an invalid end-of-month:
    if (!date_.ok())
    {
        date_ = date_.year() / date_.month() / std::chrono::day{days_in_month()};
    }

    return *this;
}
```

As shown earlier, there is no addition assignment operator for adding days to a `std::chrono::year_month_day` object, so this first requires conversion to a `sys_days` type:

```
ChronoDate& ChronoDate::add_days(int rhs_days)
{
    date_ = std::chrono::sys_days(date_) + std::chrono::days(rhs_days);

    return *this;
}
```

Note that the sum of the `sys_days` and the `days` to be added are implicitly converted back to a `year_month_day` object when assigned to the `date_` member. Further explanation is also available in the previously cited Hinnant Stack Overflow post "How do I add a number of days to a date in C++20 chrono?" (*https://oreil.ly/-55kZ*).

Business-day roll rule.   One important function we have not discussed yet will roll a weekend date to the next business date. This is also a non-`const` modifying function.

In practice, various roll methods are commonly used. For this discussion, we will choose one that is used quite often in practice: the modified following rule. Assuming the absence of holidays, this rule moves a date falling on a weekend forward to the next business day (Monday), unless the new date advances to the next month. In this latter case, the date will be rolled *back* to the previous business day (Friday).

Before proceeding, let's revisit how we determined the day of the week by using the `weekday` class contained in `std::chrono`. As mentioned at that time, the term "weekday" may be a little confusing. It does not mean "weekday" as in Monday through Friday, but rather "day of the week" in the `year_month_day` context. The `iso_encoding()` member function will return an integer code for each day of the week, beginning with 1 for Monday and 7 for Sunday; therefore, a value of 6 or 7 will indicate the date falls on a weekend.

The weekend_roll() function will reuse this functionality to first determine whether the date falls on a weekend. If it does, it will first naively roll forward to the next Monday. However, if this new date advances to the next month, it will roll back three days to the previous Friday of the original month, per the modified following rule. This is why the original month is stored first:

```cpp
ChronoDate& ChronoDate::weekend_roll()
{
    using namespace std::chrono;

    weekday wd{sys_days(date_)};          // std::chrono::weekday
    std::chrono::month orig_mth{date_.month()};

    unsigned wdn{wd.iso_encoding()}; // Mon = 1, ..., Sat = 6, Sun = 7

    // Sat: 8 - 6 = 2 days to roll forward, Sun: 8 - 7 = 1 day roll forward
    if (wdn > 5) date_ = sys_days(date_) + days(8 - wdn);

    // Case where date gets rolled into the 1st Monday of the next month --
    // Modified Following rule says to roll back three days to previous biz day:
    if (orig_mth != date_.month())
    {
        date_ = sys_days(date_) - days(3);
    }

    return *this;
}
```

A rolled date will be modified, so it will modify the state of the active object.

Stream operator. While not essential for computing fixed income security values or analytics, a stream operator is provided for convenience so we can display a Chrono Date on the screen. To keep the code simple, we will piggyback off of the stream operator defined in year_month_day and wrap it in our own nonmember operator:

```cpp
std::ostream& operator << (std::ostream& os, const ChronoDate& rhs)
{
    os << rhs.ymd();
    return os;
}
```

With the ChronoDate class now ready to go, we can move on to day count bases and other components that are typically required for programming related to fixed income trading.

Day Count Basis

A *day count basis* is used to convert the interval between two dates into time measured in years (or usually referred to as a *year fraction* for shorter intervals). A day count basis is whenever an interest calculation is made.

Interest rates are defined by three attributes: an annual percentage value (e.g., 3%), a type (e.g., simple or compound), and a day count basis. Consider a term deposit where $1,000 is invested at 3% compound interest, the investment being made on 2022-10-25 and maturing on 2023-12-31. The formula for calculating F, the value of the investment at maturity, is shown here:

$$F = 1000(1 + 0.03)^t$$

The value of t depends on the day count basis. Money market calculations in the US and the European Union (EU) are most likely to use the Actual/360 day count basis:

$$t = \text{Act360}(d_1, d_2) = \frac{d_2 - d_1}{360}$$

In UK, Canadian, and Australian money markets, the Actual/365 day count basis (swapping the 360 for 365) is more common. Other common day count basis options used in broader fixed income trading include the 30/360 method, which assumes that every month has 30 days and a year has 360 days. The Actual/Actual method uses the actual number of days in both the numerator and denominator. Equity portfolio management often uses an Actual/252 basis, which assumes 252 business days per year.

Day count classes are sometimes implemented in financial software libraries, using an abstract base class interface that mandates the implementation of the particular day count basis calculation in each derived class. The interface declares a pure virtual year_fraction() function for the calculations on the derived classes, of which three are presented here as examples—the Actual/365, Actual/360, and 30/360:

```
class DayCount
{
public:
    virtual double year_fraction
        (const ChronoDate& date_01, const ChronoDate& date_02) const = 0;

    virtual ~DayCount() = default;
};
```

We can write declarations for these three day count basis classes as follows:

```
class Act365 : public DayCount
{
public:
    double year_fraction(const ChronoDate& date_01,
        const ChronoDate& date_02) const override;
};

class Act360 : public DayCount
{
public:
    double year_fraction(const ChronoDate& date_01,
        const ChronoDate& date_02) const override;
};


class Thirty360 : public DayCount
{
public:
    double year_fraction(const ChronoDate& date_01,
        const ChronoDate& date_02) const override;

private:
    int date_diff_
        (const ChronoDate& date_01,
            const ChronoDate& date_02) const;
};
```

Because calculating the 30/360 basis requires additional work, a helper function date_diff_(.) is included, to be explained momentarily.

The Actual/365 calculation is trivial:

```
double Act365::year_fraction(const ChronoDate& date_01,
    const ChronoDate& date_02) const
{
    return (date_02 - date_01) / 365.0;
```

An Act360 class would be the same, except with the denominator replaced by 360.

The 30/360 case is a bit more complicated, in that the numerator must first be calculated according to the formula shown here and then divided by 360:

Let D_1 and D_2 be two dates, with year, month and day y_i, m_i, and d_i, respectively, for $i = 1, 2$

The time in years (or year fraction) t between D_1 and D_2 is then as follows:

$$t = \frac{360 \times (y_2 - y_1) + 30 \times (m_2 - m_1) + (d_2 - d_1)}{360}$$

End-of-month adjustments for the day values d_1 and d_2 in the numerator will depend on the particular form of the 30/360 basis; several exist, depending on the geographical location of a trading desk. In the US, the International Swaps and Derivatives Association (ISDA) 30/360 day count basis (*https://oreil.ly/owih8*) is commonly used and is implemented in the following example using the private `date_diff_(.)` helper function. The result is divided by 360 in the public function override:

```
double Thirty360::year_fraction(const ChronoDate& date_01,
    const ChronoDate& date_02) const
{
    return date_diff_(date_01, date_02) / 360.0;
}

int Thirty360::date_diff_(const ChronoDate& date_01,
    const ChronoDate& date_02) const
{
    int d1, d2;
    d1 = date_01.day();
    d2 = date_02.day();

    if (d1 == 31) d1 = 30;
    if ((d2 == 31) && (d1 == 30)) d2 = 30;
    return 360 * (date_02.year() - date_01.year()) + 30 * (date_02.month()
        - date_01.month()) + d2 - d1;
}
```

Then, here are some examples:

```
Act365 act_365{};
Act360 act_360{};
Thirty360 thirty_360{};

ChronoDate sd_01{2021, 4, 26};
ChronoDate ed_01{2023, 10, 26};
ChronoDate sd_02{2022, 10, 10};
ChronoDate ed_02{2023, 4, 10};

double yf_act_365_01 = act_365.year_fraction(sd_01, ed_01);    // 2.50137
double yf_act_365_02 = act_365.year_fraction(sd_02, ed_02);    // 0.49863

double yf_act_360_01 = act_360.year_fraction(sd_01, ed_01);    // 2.53611
double yf_act_360_02 = act_360.year_fraction(sd_02, ed_02);    // 0.505556

double yf_thirty_01 = thirty_360.year_fraction(sd_01, ed_01);  // 2.5
double yf_thirty_02 = thirty_360.year_fraction(sd_02, ed_02);  // 0.5
```

The results are shown in the comments next to each functor call. Note that the 30/360 day count basis yields year fractions to half of a year exactly.

As a quick application of the day count basis, consider obtaining the price of a short-term government Treasury bill (*https://oreil.ly/ksDYb*). In the US, these have maturities from four months to a year, and pricing is based on an Actual/365 basis. In the UK, maturities may be up to six months and carry an Actual/360 basis. We can write a valuation function that will accommodate an arbitrary day count basis via runtime polymorphism, so both US and UK cases can be priced using the same function:

```
double treasury_bill(const ChronoDate& sett_date,
    const ChronoDate& maturity_date, double mkt_yield,
    double face_value, const DayCount& dc)           // dc is polymorphic
{
    return face_value
        / (1.0 + mkt_yield * dc.year_fraction(sett_date, maturity_date));
}
```

You can find a more sophisticated example of day count basis implementations inheriting from a base class in the QuantLib (*https://oreil.ly/Leebl*) open source C++ quantitative finance library.

Yield Curves

A *yield curve* is derived from market data, which comprises yields for various fixed rate products, all of which have a common *settlement date*. Also called the *settle date*, it is the date on which payments for the products are made. The derived yields extend over a series of increasing maturity dates, no two of which are the same.

Deriving a Yield Curve from Market Data

A *yield* is essentially an interest rate, looked at from a different perspective. If money is invested in a deposit account at a known rate of interest, the accumulated value of the investment at a future date can be calculated. However, suppose we can invest $1,000 on 2022-10-25 and receive $1,035.60 on 2023-12-31. To compare this investment with other investments, we calculate its yield. Assuming compounded interest (*https://oreil.ly/BVF4o*) and an Actual/365 day count basis, then

$$1000(1 + y)^{432/365} = \$1035.60$$

from which we find the yield:

$$y = e^{\log(1035.60/1000) \times 365/432} - 1 = 3\%$$

In general, the yield curve is a function of time—say, $y(t)$—and is constructed from market data, such as that obtained from Treasury bill, swap, and bond markets. The time value t is in units of years.

The securities trading in these markets all have known future cash flows, and as such they are examples of *fixed income securities*. In addition, and in general, each type of fixed income security has its own yield type (simple, discount, or compounded), and its own day count basis, and these may vary within a single product group. To avoid using multiple interest types and day count basis options, yield curves typically define their yields as continuously compounded (*https://oreil.ly/cgoMh*) with an Actual/365 day count basis.

Consider buying a bond that makes a single payment of unit amount at maturity. Let the settlement date be s; the maturity be m, where $s \le m$; and the price of the bond at s be $P(s, m)$. If the yield is $y(t)$, where $t = \text{Act365}(s, m)$ is the time to maturity in years, then

$$P(s, m)e^{t\,y(t)} = 1$$

so that

$$P(s, m) = e^{-t\,y(t)}$$

Since the bond pays a unit amount at maturity, $P(s,m)$ is known as a *unit price*. It is also used as the *discount factor* over the interval from the settlement date s to the maturity date m.

To illustrate how the inputs to the yield curve are derived, consider a six-month US Treasury bill: the yield type is discount, the day count basis is Actual/365, and the market quote is the yield on the bill. Suppose the face value is F_1, the maturity date is d_1, and the market yield is y_m for settlement on s. Then the price, B_1, is calculated as follows:

$$B_1 = F_1(1 - \text{Act365}(s, d_1)\,y_m)$$

The unit price is $P(s, d_1) = B_1/F_1$, from which the *continuously compounded Actual/365 yield* can be calculated.

Values of $y(t)$ for longer maturities can be obtained by bootstrapping. Suppose now a US Treasury bond matures in one year and pays coupons every six months. Let the coupon payments be C_1 on date d_1 and C_2 on date d_2; the face value is F, and the market price on settlement date s is B_2. Then, B_2 is computed as follows:

$$B_2 = C_1 P(s, d_1) + (F_2 + C_2)\,P(s, d_2)$$

Since $P(s, d_1)$ is known, the value of $P(s, d_2)$ can be found. The bootstrapping process can be continued to find unit prices for longer maturities, and the associated yields can be found from

$$y(t_i) = -\frac{log(P(s, d_i))}{t_i}$$

where for each i, $i = 1, \cdots, n$,

$$t_i = \text{Act365}(s, d_i)$$

It is essential that any set of interest rate products used to create a yield curve have the same settle date. Let the maturity dates for the products be

$$d_1 < d_2 < \cdots < d_n$$

with $s < d_1$, and let the associated yields be

$$y_1, y_2, \cdots, y_n$$

where

$$y_i = y(t_i)$$

and

$$t_i = \text{Act365}(s, d_i)$$

for each i.

Since the yields are calculated for a date interval whose first date is the settlement date, these yields are known as *spot yields*.

Many continuous curves pass through the points

$$(t_1, y_1), (t_2, y_2), \cdots, (t_n, y_n)$$

The choice of an appropriate curve is a business decision made by the user of the yield curve. This is typically based on a curve-fitting technique employing a particular interpolation method.

Discount Factors

Now, given the fitted yield curve $y(t)$, constructed for settlement date s, the discount factor for any period from date s to date m is

$$P(s, m) = e^{-ty(t)}$$

where

$$t = \text{Act365}(s, m)$$

Since $y(t)$ is a spot yield, this is a spot discount factor. This can be extended more generally for *forward discount factors*, as discussed next.

Calculating Forward Discount Factors

How do we calculate the discount factor for a period that begins at time d_1 and ends at time d_2, where $s < d_1 \leq d_2$?

Consider a unit payment to be made at time d_2 and let its value at d_1 be represented by $P(s; d_1, d_2)$, based on market data *as seen at* the settle date s. The spot value of the unit payment is

$$P(s, d_1)P(s; d_1, d_2)$$

To avoid arbitrage opportunities, we must have

$$P(s, d_2) = P(s, d_1)P(s; d_1, d_2)$$

so that

$$P(s; d_1, d_2) = \frac{P(s, d_2)}{P(s, d_1)}$$

Substituting for the spot discount factors, we get

$$P(s; d_1, d_2) = \frac{e^{-t_2\, y(t_2)}}{e^{-t_1\, y(t_1)}} = e^{t_1\, y(t_1) - t_2\, y(t_2)}$$

since $d_1 > s$, $P(s; d_1, d_2)$ is a forward discount factor.

The next sections describe a framework for yield curves in C++, employing the mathematical motivation just presented. The yield-curve class that follows will ultimately be used in the valuation of a bond in "A Bond Valuation Example" on page 271.

Implementing a Yield-Curve Class

The essential function on a yield-curve class will return a continuously compounded forward discount factor between two arbitrary dates, as detailed in the previous section. As noted previously, there are many ways to fit a curve through the points

$$(t_1, y_1), (t_2, y_2), \cdots, (t_n, y_n)$$

including linear interpolation, cubic splines, and methods designed specifically for yield curves. Two examples of this latter category are quartic forward splines[1] and monotone convex splines.[2]

In our design, we'll divide the labor between computing forward discount factors as outlined in the earlier mathematical derivation and the implementation of curve-fitting methods.

More specifically, we could define an abstract base class that does the following:

- Provides a common method to calculate forward discount factors between two `ChronoDate` arguments, based on yields obtained from any given curve-fitting method

- Requires a derived class to implement a particular curve-fitting method as a private member function that interpolates a yield for any time $t \geq s$

Figure 7-1 shows a UML diagram of the abstract base class, `YieldCurve`, with possible derived classes containing the curve-fitting methods referenced previously.

---

[1] Kenneth J. Adams, "Smooth Interpolation of Zero Curves" (*https://oreil.ly/Xs4P4*), Algo Research Quarterly 4 (2001).

[2] Patrick S. Hagan and Graeme West, "Interpolation Methods for Curve Construction" (*https://oreil.ly/mcRVp*), Applied Mathematical Finance 13, no. 2 (2006).

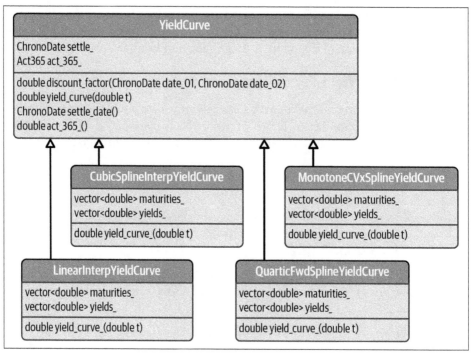

Figure 7-1. Yield-curve class hierarchy example

The base class will contain a nonvirtual public function that calculates the forward discount factor between two dates, using interpolated yields obtained from the overridden `yield_curve_(.)` method chosen. The interpolated yields determined from each derived class will be assumed to be continuously compounded with the Actual/365 day count basis, for a given time period t relative to a specific settle date. This function is declared private because its overrides are intended to be encapsulated within their respective interpolation method classes internally, from which further inheritance will be prohibited by way of the `final` keyword.

Both classes, however, will require access to the settlement date and the Actual/365 day count basis. We might be inclined to declare these as protected data members on the base class to provide access on any derived classes, but the Core Guidelines tell us to avoid this, as "`protected` data is a source of complexity and errors."[3] Instead, a protected member function will provide access to the `act_365_` member, plus a protected constructor is included to initialize the settlement date, `settle_`.

3 "Avoid `protected` data" (*https://oreil.ly/fT_xd*), ISO C++ Core Guidelines.

As for the `settle_` member, it will need to be accessible from any inherited class, as well as externally from the `Bond` class to follow, so a public accessor function, `settle_date()`, is provided:

```
#include "ChronoDate.h"
#include "DayCounts.h"

class YieldCurve
{
public:
    double discount_factor(const ChronoDate& d1, const ChronoDate& d2) const;
    virtual ~YieldCurve() = default;

    ChronoDate settle_date() const;          // return settle_;

protected:
    YieldCurve(ChronoDate settle_date);
    Act365 act_365() const;                  // return act_365_;

private:
    // Every derived class is responsible for setting the value of
    // settle_date_ and implementing the function yield_curve_(.).
    virtual double yield_curve_(double t) const = 0;

    ChronoDate settle_;
    inline static Act365 act_365_{};    // The yields are continuously compounded
                                        // with Actual/365 day count basis
};
```

Because `Act365` is stateless, we can make `act_365_` static, so that an additional `Act365` object does not need to be created with each instance of a `YieldCurve`.

The implementation of `discount_factor(.)` then follows the mathematical derivation presented in "Discount Factors" on page 252 and "Calculating Forward Discount Factors" on page 252. Beyond the error conditions from which exceptions are thrown, we have three cases under normal conditions. First, if the two dates are identical, the discount factor is 1. Second, if the first date d1 is the settle date, the result defaults to the spot discount factor at date d2. Finally, third, we have the general case of a forward discount factor over the period from d1 to d2.

Note that the `discount_factor(.)` function doesn't care what the particular curve-fitting method is, as long as it can obtain an interpolated yield from the overridden `yield_curve_(.)` method:

```
#include "YieldCurve.h"
#include <stdexcept>
#include <cmath>

double YieldCurve::discount_factor(const ChronoDate& d1,
    const ChronoDate& d2) const
```

```
{
    using std::exp;

    if (d2 < d1)
    {
        throw std::invalid_argument{
            "discount_factor(.): invalid inequality: d2 < d1"};
    }

    if (d1 < settle_date() || d2 < settle_date())
    {
        throw std::invalid_argument{
            "discount_factor(.): dates must fall on or after settle date"};
    }

    if (d1 == d2)
    {
        return 1.0;          // exp(0.0)
    }

    // P(t1, t2) = exp( -(t2-t1) * f(t1, t2) )

    double t2 = act_365().year_fraction(settle_date(), d2);
    double y2 = yield_curve_(t2);

    // if d1 == settle_ then P(t1,t2) = P(0,t2) = exp(-t2 * y2 )
    if (d1 == settle_date())
    {
        return exp(-t2 * y2);
    }

    double t1 = act365_(settle_date(), d1);
    double y1 = yield_curve_(t1);

    // (t2-t1) f(t1,t2) = t2 * y2 - t1 * y1
    return exp(t1 * y1 - t2 * y2);
}
```

For completeness, the constructor for the YieldCurve class and its two accessor functions are shown here:

```
YieldCurve::YieldCurve(ChronoDate settle_date) :
 settle_{std::move(settle_date)} {}

ChronoDate YieldCurve::settle_date() const
{
    return settle_;
}

Act365 YieldCurve::act_365() const
{
    return act_365_;
}
```

Implementing a Linearly Interpolated Yield Curve Class

The simplest curve-fitting method—but still sometimes used in practice—is linear interpolation. More-sophisticated interpolation methods also exist, such as those referenced previously, but these require considerably more mathematical horsepower. To keep the discussion concise, we will limit the example here to the linearly interpolated case, but it is important to remember that more-advanced methods can also be integrated into the same inheritance structure:

```
class LinearInterpYieldCurve final : public YieldCurve
{
public:
    LinearInterpYieldCurve(
        const ChronoDate& settle_date,
        const std::vector<ChronoDate>& maturity_dates,
        const std::vector<double>& unit_prices);

private:
    double yield_curve_(const double t) const override;

    std::vector<double> maturities_; // maturities in years
    std::vector<double> yields_;
};
```

The constructor takes in a set of maturity dates relative to the settle date, along with a set of corresponding unit prices from the market, each stored in a `vector`. Its implementation first checks whether the yield and maturity date vectors are of the same length, and whether the settle date value is negative. If either is true, an exception is thrown. For the purposes of demonstration, we will assume that the maturities are in ascending order, but in production this would be another condition to check. In the concluding for loop, the Actual/365 continuous time equivalents (relative to the settle date) are computed and stored in the `maturities_` member vector, and the yields are extracted from the unit-price inputs and stored as a vector:

```
LinearInterpYieldCurve::LinearInterpYieldCurve(const ChronoDate& settle_date,
    const std::vector<ChronoDate>& maturity_dates,
    const std::vector<double>& unit_prices) :YieldCurve{settle_date}
{
    using std::size_t;

    if (maturity_dates.size() != unit_prices.size())
        throw std::invalid_argument{
            "Maturity_dates and spot_discount_factors different lengths"};

    if (maturity_dates.front() < this->settle_date())
        throw std::invalid_argument{"First maturity date before settle date"};

    // Prevent vector memory reallocation (reserve(.)):
    maturities_.reserve(maturity_dates.size());
    yields_.reserve(maturity_dates.size());
```

```
// Assume maturity dates in are in ascending order
for (size_t i = 0; i < maturity_dates.size(); i++)
{
    double t = act_365()(this->settle_date(), maturity_dates[i]);
    maturities_.push_back(t);
    yields_.push_back(-std::log(unit_prices[i]) / t);
}
}
```

The `maturities_` and `yields_` are then used in the linear interpolation method, implemented in the mandated `yield_curve_(.)` private member function. If the time value at which a yield is to be interpolated exceeds its maximum data value, the result is just the last yield value. Otherwise, the `while` loop locates the interval of time points that surrounds the input value of time `t`. Then, the proportionally weighted yield is calculated and returned:

```
double LinearInterpYieldCurve::yield_curve_(const double t) const
{
    using std::size_t;

    // interp_yield called from discount_factor, so maturities.front() <= t

    if (t >= maturities_.back())
    {
        return yields_.back();
    }

    // Now know maturities.front() <= t < maturities_.back()
    size_t idx = 0;
    while (maturities_[idx + 1] < t)
    {
        ++idx;
    }

    return yields_[idx] + (yields_[idx + 1] - yields_[idx])
        / (maturities_[idx + 1] - maturities_[idx]) * (t - maturities_[idx]);
}
```

A Bond Class

We are now in position to utilize objects of the preceding classes, along with a user-defined Bond class, to calculate the value of a coupon-paying bond. Common examples of bonds in the US, for example, include government-issued Treasury bonds, agency bonds (issued by a government-sponsored enterprise such as the Government National Mortgage Association [GNMA]), corporate bonds, and local state and municipal bonds. As debt obligations, a series of regular payments over time is made in exchange for an amount borrowed by the issuer. The main difference with

---

a traditional loan is that the principal amount (the face value) is returned when the bond matures rather than being amortized over time.

Bond Payments and Valuation

Before proceeding with further code development, as noted in the chapter introduction, we will review the mechanics of how bond payments are structured and how a bond is commonly valued. Again, these details are very important in fixed income trading and related programming, yet they are not often found in quant finance course curricula or reference materials. This review will then essentially become the design requirements for our Bond class, which will follow subsequently.

The general idea is that a bond pays fixed amounts on dates in a regular schedule. For example, suppose a bond has a face value of $1,000 and pays 5% of its face value every six months. Then, the payment frequency is twice per year, and the coupon amount would be as follows:

$$\frac{0.05(1000)}{2} = \$25$$

In general, here is the formula:

$$\text{regular coupon amount} = (\text{coupon rate})\frac{(\text{face value})}{(\text{coupon frequency})}$$

The first task is to create a list of dates when payments are due and the coupon payment amounts for each of those dates. Along with the face value and annual coupon rate, the contractual conditions of the bond also include the following four dates used in its valuation:

- Dated date
- First coupon date
- Penultimate coupon date
- Maturity date

The *dated date* is the date on which interest begins to accrue. It can be the same as, or different from, the *issue date*, the date on which the bond goes on sale. A stream of fixed payments is typically paid (for example, every six months), beginning with the *first coupon date*. The second-to-last payment occurs on the *penultimate coupon date*, and the final payment, consisting of the last coupon payment plus repayment of the face value, occurs on the *maturity date*.

To make for more-concise examples to come, we'll make the following assumptions:

- The issue date and dated date are the same.
- Each coupon day is strictly less than 29, to avoid complications due to end-of-month adjustments.
- There are no holidays other than Saturdays and Sundays.

Determining the payment schedule

Returning to the preceding example of a bond that pays a 5% coupon on a face value of $1,000 with a coupon frequency of 2, when will the payments be made? To show this, let's use a hypothetical bond with a maturity of two years at issue. The contractual dates and data are shown in Table 7-1.

Table 7-1. Hypothetical two-year bond

Issue date	2022-09-22
Dated date	2022-09-22
First coupon date	2023-03-22
Penultimate coupon date	2025-03-22
Maturity date	2025-09-22
Coupon rate	5%
Face value amount	$1,000.00

For coupons between the first coupon date and the penultimate date, payment *due dates* fall within a *regular schedule*. A constant payment of $25 is due every six months (irrespective of whether or not a due date is a business day at this point). To ensure that these dates belong to a regular schedule of due dates, in general there are restrictions on the first and penultimate coupon dates, and on the coupon frequency. These two dates must be business days having the same day of the month, the coupon frequency must be a divisor of 12 (the number of months in a year), and the two dates must differ by a multiple of $\frac{12}{\text{coupon frequency}}$ months. In our example, the bond has a first coupon date of 2023-3-22 and a penultimate coupon date of 2025-3-22. The two dates differ by 24 months, which is a multiple of 6 (12 ÷ 2 = 6), as required.

Since the due dates might not fall on business dates, the bond also has associated *payment dates* that *are* adjusted for weekends and holidays. As mentioned previously, to simplify matters in our example, we have assumed that payments will not occur on any day with a value greater than 28 and that there are no holidays except Saturday and Sunday—so that if a due date falls on a weekend, the regular coupon payment will be made on the following Monday.

Table 7-2 shows the intermediate due and payment dates. Note that the first two dates fall on business days, but as the third falls on a Sunday, the payment date has been rolled to the following Monday. A $25 payment is made on each of the payment dates.

Table 7-2. Intermediate coupon due and payment dates

Due date	Payment date
2023-09-22 (Friday)	2023-09-22 (Friday)
2024-03-22 (Friday)	2024-03-22 (Friday)
2024-09-22 (Sunday)	2024-09-23 (Monday)

If the first and final payments also occur in regular periods, they will be $25 and $1,025 as well, respectively, as is the case in this first example.

The first and last coupon periods may or may not be regular, however, and thus they will require adjustments that will also need to go into the code. The usually cited case is an irregular first payment period, but an irregular final payment period ending with the maturity date could also exist. To make things even more complicated, the adjustments depend on whether these irregular periods are shorter or longer than a regular period.

To demonstrate each case of an irregular first payment period, let's again use an example of a $1,000 face-value bond paying an annual coupon of 5% semiannually ($25 regular coupon payments), but for the case of a 10-year bond. The contractual dates and data for the case of a short first payment period are shown in Table 7-3.

Table 7-3. Ten-year bond with short first payment period

Issue date	2022-07-12 (Tuesday)
Dated date	2022-07-12 (Tuesday)
First coupon date	2022-12-21 (Wednesday)
Penultimate coupon date	2032-12-21 (Tuesday)
Maturity date	2033-06-21 (Tuesday)
Coupon rate	5%
Face-value amount	$1,000.00

In the case of a short first period, the coupon payment is calculated by multiplying the annual coupon rate by the ratio of actual days in the period over the number of days in what would be a normal first period. If the first payment period had been regular, the dated date would have been 2022-6-21. This date is called the *first prior date*. Figure 7-2 provides a visual description.

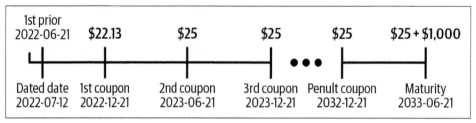

Figure 7-2. Irregular short first-coupon period

The first payment is then prorated as follows:

$$\frac{(\text{coupon payment})(\text{number of days from dated date to 1st pmt})}{(\text{number of days from 1st prior to 1st pmt})}$$

$$= 25\left(\frac{162}{183}\right) = \$22.13$$

In the case of a long first period, suppose the contract data is the same, except the dated date is moved to the earlier 2022-5-12. Figure 7-3 provides a visualization.

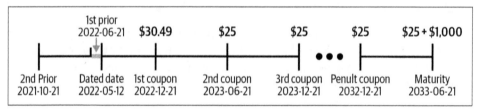

Figure 7-3. Irregular long first-coupon period

In this case, the first coupon payment will be the regular coupon of $25 over the period from the first prior date to the dated date, *plus* a partial payment (noted with an arrow) over the interval between the dated date and first prior date. This extra payment is prorated with respect to the six-month period from the *second prior date* to the first:

$$\frac{(\text{coupon payment})(\text{number of days from dated date to 1st prior})}{(\text{number of days from 2nd prior to 1st prior})}$$

$$= 25\left(\frac{40}{182}\right) = \$5.49$$

The total first coupon payment is then 25 + 5.49 = $30.49

Calculating adjusted payments over irregular final periods is similar, except that instead of prior payment periods preceding the dated date, imaginary regular payment periods extending later than maturity are utilized.

While this discussion might seem to be a bit tedious, it is a fair approximation of real-world design requirements for financial programmers responsible for fixed income trading operations and risk management. Date calculations are also common in other applications such as defined benefit pension plans, mortgage loans, and annuity contracts. The new C++20 date library addition makes for much more rapid and easier development than before.

Valuing a bond

The issuer sells bonds on the issue date, pays the owners of the bonds the coupon amounts starting from the dated date and, at maturity, also pays back the face value of the bond. The owner of a bond may then sell it on the secondary market, in which case the buyer and seller agree to a business date, known as the *bond settle date* (or again, alternatively, settlement date), on which the sale will take place. On this settle date, the seller receives the present value of the bond in cash, and the buyer becomes the registered owner, with the right to receive all payments that fall due after the settle date.

A bond can be valued as of an arbitrary settle date, falling on or after the yield-curve settlement date. This can be done by calculating the discounted value of the bond—using a yield curve of one's choice—and the discount factors calculated off of this curve for the periods from the bond settlement date to the corresponding payment dates.

Revisiting the example in Figure 7-1, suppose a bond is exchanged for cash on 2023-10-24, as indicated by the arrow in Figure 7-4. All preceding coupon payments have been paid to the previous owner, so the value of the bond will depend only on payments beginning with the third coupon payment through maturity.

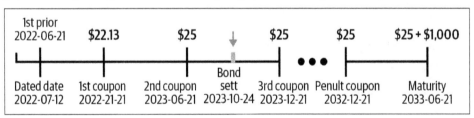

Figure 7-4. Bond valuation at the settle date

Under the common textbook assumption, the bond and yield-curve settle dates are the same. Using the preceding discount factor notation, the value of the bond on this date will be

$$25\bigl(P(s, d_3) + \cdots + P\bigl(s, d_p\bigr)\bigr) + (1000 + 25)\,P(s, d_m)$$

where

$$s = 2023\text{-}10\text{-}24$$

is the yield curve settlement date,

$$d_p = 2032\text{-}6\text{-}21$$

is the penultimate coupon date, and

$$d_m = 2032\text{-}12\text{-}21$$

is the maturity date.

Discounted valuations are also routine calculations in trading and risk-management software. A common task for programmers is to write code to value a bond portfolio by using an updated or simulated yield curve in order to calculate P/L (based on current market conditions) and run risk calculations (based on shocked or random scenarios).

Designing a Bond Class

Our task now is to implement the previously stated requirements in a user-defined Bond class, using the contractual terms of a bond as input data. First, let's consolidate and review the essential data inputs associated with a bond issue:

- Face value
- Annual coupon rate
- Number of coupon payments per year (coupon frequency)
- Dated date
- First coupon date
- Penultimate coupon date
- Maturity date

Our Bond class can be formally summarized as shown in the following class declaration, utilizing our date and yield-curve classes developed earlier. A bond ID field of some form (in this example, assumed to be a short character string) is also generally required for both trading and risk applications, so it is added as a constructor parameter and data member, along with a public accessor:

```cpp
#include "ChronoDate.h"
#include "YieldCurve.h"
#include <cmath>
#include <vector>
#include <string>

class Bond
{
public:
    Bond(const std::string& bond_id, const ChronoDate& dated_date,
        const ChronoDate& first_coupon_date,
        const ChronoDate& penultimate_coupon_date,
        const ChronoDate& maturity_date,
        int coupon_frequency, double coupon_rate, double face_value);

    double discounted_value(const ChronoDate& bond_settle_date,
        const YieldCurve& yield_curve);

    std::string bond_id() const;

private:
    std::string bond_id_;

    // Dates on which payments are due, whether business days or not:
    std::vector<ChronoDate> due_dates_;

    // Business dates on which payments are made:
    std::vector<ChronoDate> payment_dates_;

    // Coupon and redemption payments,
    // assume redemption_payment = face_value:
    std::vector<double> payment_amounts_;

    void calculate_pmt_schedule_(const ChronoDate& first_coupon_date,
        const ChronoDate& penultimate_coupon_date,
        int months_in_regular_coupon_period, double regular_coupon_payment);

    void amend_initial_irregular_dates_and_pmts_(const ChronoDate& dated_date,
        const ChronoDate& first_coupon_date,
        const int months_in_regular_coupon_period,
        const double regular_coupon_payment);

    void amend_final_irregular_dates_and_pmts_(
        const ChronoDate& penultimate_coupon_date,
        const ChronoDate& maturity_date,
        const int months_in_regular_coupon_period,
        const double regular_coupon_payment, double face_value);
};
```

Note that all the contractual information is captured in the constructor, but none of these arguments ends up being stored as a data member. Rather, they are used when a Bond object is created—as you will see in the implementations—inside the constructor itself or in the private helper functions that generate the vectors of dates and payments that do get stored as members.

The valuation of the bond is delegated to the public `discounted_value(.)` function. This separates what is essentially the "interface"—the input and processing of contractual bond data—from the "implementation" where the bond value is calculated. As noted in "Valuing a bond" on page 263, this valuation function is based on the bond settlement date and the market yield curve, inputs that are independent from the constructor arguments. One specific advantage is that a single `Bond` instance can be created, and its valuation function can be called multiple (possibly thousands of) times under different yield-curve scenarios for risk-reporting purposes, also noted previously.

We have three member vectors of equal length (`due_dates_`, `payment_dates_`, and `payment_amounts_`) corresponding to the respective descriptions in "Determining the payment schedule" on page 260. All three are necessary for calculating the discounted value of a bond. The `coupon_frequency` parameter represents the number of coupon payments per year (2 for semiannual and 4 for quarterly) as defined in the bond contract.

Implementing the Bond Class

We will start by constructing a `Bond` object and setting the `vector` members in the implementation step-by-step. This setup needs to take place before valuing a bond. The constructor will generate the due and payment dates, and the payment amounts. Recall that `first_coupon_date`, `penultimate_coupon_date`, and `maturity_date` are due dates that fall on business days. The `first_coupon_date` and `penultimate_cou pon_date` input objects are also dates that are part of the regular schedule of due dates. The maturity date may or may not be part of the regular schedule of due dates, as discussed previously. Here's the code:

```
#include "Bond.h"
#include <iterator>

Bond::Bond(const std::string& bond_id, const ChronoDate& dated_date,
    const ChronoDate& first_coupon_date,
    const ChronoDate& penultimate_coupon_date,
    const ChronoDate& maturity_date, int coupon_frequency, double coupon_rate,
    double face_value) : bond_id_{bond_id}
{
    // Number of months in coupon period:
    const int months_in_regular_coupon_period = 12 / coupon_frequency;  ❶

    // Regular coupon payment:
    const double regular_coupon_payment = coupon_rate
        * face_value / coupon_frequency;  ❷
```

```
        calculate_pmt_schedule_(first_coupon_date, penultimate_coupon_date,
            months_in_regular_coupon_period, regular_coupon_payment);

        amend_initial_irregular_dates_and_pmts_(dated_date, first_coupon_date,
            months_in_regular_coupon_period, regular_coupon_payment);

        amend_final_irregular_dates_and_pmts_(penultimate_coupon_date, maturity_date,
            months_in_regular_coupon_period, regular_coupon_payment, face_value);

        // Maturity date is a due date which falls on a business day ❿
        due_dates_.push_back(maturity_date);
        payment_dates_.push_back(maturity_date);
}

void Bond::calculate_pmt_schedule_(const ChronoDate& first_coupon_date,
    const ChronoDate& penultimate_coupon_date,
    int months_in_regular_coupon_period, double regular_coupon_payment)
{
        // Generate vectors containing due dates, payment dates, ❸
        // and regular coupon payment amounts:
        for (ChronoDate regular_due_date{first_coupon_date};
            regular_due_date <= penultimate_coupon_date;
            regular_due_date.add_months(months_in_regular_coupon_period))
        {
            // The due and payment Dates
            due_dates_.push_back(regular_due_date);
            ChronoDate payment_date{regular_due_date};

            // Roll any due dates falling on a weekend and
            // store as payment dates: ❹
            payment_dates_.push_back(payment_date.weekend_roll());

            // Assume all coupons are regular;
            // deal with any irregular first or last periods later:
            payment_amounts_.push_back(regular_coupon_payment);
        }
}

void Bond::amend_initial_irregular_dates_and_pmts_(const ChronoDate& dated_date,
    const ChronoDate& first_coupon_date,
    const int months_in_regular_coupon_period,
    const double regular_coupon_payment)
{
        // If first coupon is irregular, amend the coupon payment ❺
        ChronoDate first_prior{first_coupon_date};
        first_prior.add_months(-months_in_regular_coupon_period);
        if (first_prior != dated_date) // if true then irregular coupon
        {
            if (first_prior < dated_date) // if true then short coupon period
            {
                double coupon_fraction =
                    static_cast<double>(first_coupon_date - dated_date) /
```

```
                    static_cast<double>(first_coupon_date - first_prior);
                payment_amounts_[0] *= coupon_fraction;
            }
            else // dated_date < first_prior, so long coupon period
            {
                // long_first_coupon = regular_coupon + extra_interest

                // Calculate the second_prior,
                // the last regular date before the first_prior:
                ChronoDate second_prior{first_prior};
                second_prior.add_months(-months_in_regular_coupon_period);
                double coupon_fraction =
                    static_cast<double>(first_prior - dated_date) /
                    static_cast<double>(first_prior - second_prior);
                payment_amounts_[0] += coupon_fraction * regular_coupon_payment;
            }
        }
    }
}

void Bond::amend_final_irregular_dates_and_pmts_(
    const ChronoDate& penultimate_coupon_date,
    const ChronoDate& maturity_date, const int months_in_regular_coupon_period,
    const double regular_coupon_payment, double face_value)
{
    // If final coupon period is irregular, amend the coupon payment.
    ChronoDate maturity_regular_date{penultimate_coupon_date}; ❻

    // Calculate maturity_regular_date, the first regular date ❼
    // after penultimate_coupon_date:
    maturity_regular_date.add_months(months_in_regular_coupon_period);

    double final_coupon{regular_coupon_payment};

    // If true then irregular coupon period ❽
    if (maturity_regular_date != maturity_date)
    {
        // If true, adjust for short coupon period:
        if (maturity_date < maturity_regular_date)
        {
            double coupon_fraction =
                static_cast<double>(maturity_date - penultimate_coupon_date)
                / static_cast<double>(
                    maturity_regular_date - penultimate_coupon_date);

            final_coupon *= coupon_fraction;
        }

        // maturity_regular_date < maturity_date,
        // so have long coupon period adjustment:
        else
        {
            // final_coupon = regular_coupon_amount + extra_interest.
```

```
            // Calculate the next_regular_date, the first regular date
            // after the maturity_regular_date:
            ChronoDate next_regular_date{maturity_regular_date};
            next_regular_date.add_months(months_in_regular_coupon_period);
            double extra_coupon_fraction =
                static_cast<double>(maturity_date - maturity_regular_date) /
                static_cast<double>(next_regular_date - maturity_regular_date);
            final_coupon += extra_coupon_fraction * regular_coupon_payment;
        }
    }

    //  Calculate final payment:
    payment_amounts_.push_back(face_value + final_coupon); ❾
}
```

Let's proceed through the items numbered in this code example:

❶ Although the `coupon_frequency` value is defined in the bond contract and often stored in a bond database, it is easier to use the length of the regular coupon period (e.g., 3 months or 6 months) in the tasks that follow. This equivalent number of months is calculated as shown in the preceding code and stored as `months_in_regular_coupon_period`.

❷ Following the formula presented presented in "Bond Payments and Valuation" on page 259, `regular_coupon_payment` stores this value as a constant. Recall that regular coupon periods span two adjacent due dates, and all coupon periods except the first and last are guaranteed to be regular.

❸ The private member function `calculate_pmt_schedule_(.)` will calculate the due and payment dates, and set the regular payment amounts, over each period between the first coupon payment date and the penultimate coupon date.

Because each period between these two dates is regular, each date generated and appended to the `due_dates_` vector will be spaced apart equally (e.g., every six months) up to and including the contractual penultimate coupon date. Because the `+=` operator for months on the incremented `year_month_day` object guarantees the same day value, this will satisfy the requirement for the due dates. Bonds have many variations, but since this is not production code, it is again simplified by assuming the coupon day is less than 29 in order to avoid end-of-month calculations.

Note that we can encapsulate the `regular_due_date` variable inside the body of the `for` loop, rather than defining it externally first, by incrementing each successive due date as an argument for the iteration. Like a range-based `for` loop, this also obviates using index values:

```
for (ChronoDate regular_due_date{first_coupon_date};
        regular_due_date <= penultimate_coupon_date;
        regular_due_date.add_months(months_in_regular_coupon_period))
{
    // . . .
}
```

❹ The `weekend_roll()` member function is applied to successive copies of each
    due date and pushed onto the `payment_dates_` vector prior to the penultimate
    payment date. Thus, any due date falling on a weekend is rolled to the next
    business date. Finally, the regular coupon payment amount (already determined
    inside the body of the constructor) is initially appended as a constant value to the
    `payment_amounts_` vector for each regular date.

❺ In step ❹, the first coupon payment was naively set to the regular amount.
    We therefore need to call the `amend_initial_irregular_dates_and_pmts_(.)`
    member function to verify whether an adjustment is required for the first pay-
    ment over a long or short period, as illustrated in Figures 7-1 and 7-2.

❻ Similarly, an adjustment needs to be applied to irregular final payments in the
    `amend_final_irregular_dates_and_pmts_(.)` member function.

❼ The maturity date is a business day and is appended to each date vector. It is
    provisionally assumed to follow a normal payment period, and thus the final
    payment in `payment_amounts_` is initially set to the regular coupon amount plus
    the face value of the bond at this point.

❽ One more conditional statement checks whether the final period is regular. If so,
    an adjustment is made to the final payment. Similar calculations as with an irreg-
    ular first period are performed, but using prospective rather than retrospective
    extensions.

❾ The final payment consisting of the final coupon payment and return of face
    value is appended to the vector of payments.

❿ The actual maturity date is appended to both the vector of due dates and the
    vector of payment dates.

As noted previously in "Valuing a bond" on page 263, the buyer of a bond becomes
entitled to receive all payments that are due strictly *after* the settlement date. This
introduces a special case that is addressed in the code: if bond settlement occurs on
a due date, the coupon payment is paid to the seller. Therefore, only those coupon
payments due after settlement add to the bond value in the form of discounted
amounts. If a due date falls on a weekend, it is rolled to a payment date on the

---

following Monday and is payable to the buyer. It is for this reason the Bond class has both due date and payment date vectors as data members:

```
double Bond::discounted_value(const ChronoDate& bond_settle_date,
    const YieldCurve& yield_curve)
{
    // The buyer receives the payments which fall due after the bond_settle_date.
    // If the bond_settle_date falls on a due_date,
    // the seller receives the payment:
    double pv = 0.0;
    for (size_t i = 0; i < due_dates_.size(); i++)
    {
        if (bond_settle_date < due_dates_[i])
        {
            pv += yield_curve.discount_factor(bond_settle_date,
                payment_dates_[i]) * payment_amounts_[i];
        }
    }
    return yield_curve.discount_factor(yield_curve.settle_date(),
        bond_settle_date) * pv;
}
```

As you may notice, this valuation function is short and compact, as the due dates, payment dates, and payment amounts were already determined and set by the constructor and the private helper functions at the outset. This includes any adjustment to the first or last payment in the event of an irregular short or long payment period.

So now, the valuation code can start by looping through the due_dates_ member vector until the first due date strictly later than settlement is located. At this point, each remaining payment—starting with the same current index as due_dates_—is obtained from the payment_amounts_ vector. Each payment value is discounted from the payment date back to the bond settlement date. The discount factor that multiplies each payment is easily obtained by the discount_factor(.) member function already implemented on the yield_curve input object.

These discounted payment values are summed and assigned to the pv variable. As the curve-fitting method is determined at runtime (we are not necessarily limited to linear interpolation), the discounted_value() function doesn't "need to care" how the discount factors or date calculations are obtained. The result is the discounted value of the bond as of the yield-curve settlement date, which are often taken to be the same.

A Bond Valuation Example

We can now put the individual classes previously presented together into an example of pricing a bond. Recall that the YieldCurve abstract base class will require a derived curve-fitting method. Again, many approaches are available, ranging from simple to highly advanced, but to keep the example concise, we will use the linear interpolation version we have already. In constructing a Bond object, we need to supply the face value, dated date, first coupon date, penultimate payment date, and maturity date of the bond, along with its face value. Figure 7-5 is a UML diagram of this assembly showing the relationships among the required objects for this example.

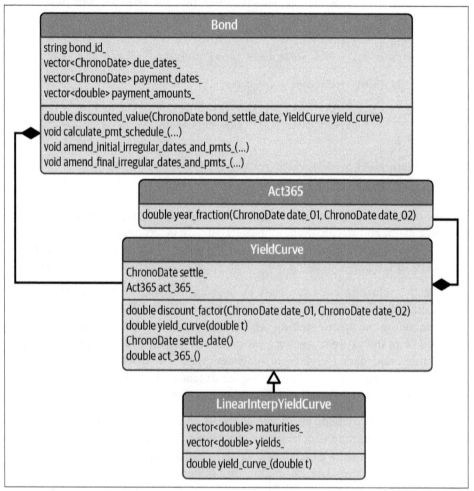

Figure 7-5. Bond valuation object assembly

As an example, suppose the term sheet of a 20-year bond is as shown in Table 7-4.

Table 7-4. Contractual bond terms example

Face value	$1,000
Annual coupon rate	6.2%
Payment frequency	Every six months (semiannual)
Dated date	2023-05-08 (Mon)
First coupon date	2023-11-07 (Tue)
Penultimate coupon date	2042-11-07 (Fri)
Maturity date	2043-05-07 (Thu)

Data in practice would be taken in from an interface and converted to `ChronoDate` types, but we can replicate the scenario as follows:

```
std::string bond_id = "20 yr bond";          // 20 year bond

ChronoDate dated_date{2023, 5, 8};           // (Mon)
ChronoDate first_coupon_date{2023, 11, 7};   // Short first coupon (Tue)
ChronoDate penultimate_coupon_date{2042, 5, 7}; // (Wed)
ChronoDate maturity_date{2043, 5, 7};   // Regular last coupon period (Thu)

int coupon_frequency = 2;
double coupon_rate = 0.062;
double face_value = 1000.00;

// Construction of the bond is then straightforward:
Bond bond_20_yr{bond_id, dated_date, first_coupon_date, penultimate_coupon_date,
        maturity_date, coupon_frequency, coupon_rate, face_value};
```

Recall, however, the due dates, payment dates, and payment amounts are all generated and adjusted at the time a Bond object is constructed. Each due date will carry a day value of 7, and the payment dates will be the same except for the due dates falling on weekends that are rolled to the following Monday:

2026-11-09, 2027-11-08, 2028-05-08

2032-11-08, 2033-05-09, 2034-05-08

2037-11-09, 2038-11-08, 2039-05-09

The regular coupon amount is as follows:

$$\frac{1000(0.0625)}{2} = \$31.00$$

The only irregular period will be from the dated date to the first coupon date, 2023-05-08 to 2023-11-07, resulting in the calculated coupon amount as follows:

$$31\left(\frac{183}{184}\right) = \$30.83$$

Here, $\frac{183}{184}$ is the ratio of the actual number of days in the first period to the number of days from the first prior date to the first coupon date.

Next, suppose we want to value the bond on a date between the dated date and first coupon date—say, Tuesday, October 10, 2023. Suppose also that market data as of this date implies the unit bond prices shown in Table 7-5 (values are rounded to six decimal places).

Table 7-5. Spot yields example

Period	Maturity	Unit price
Overnight	2023-10-11	0.999945
3 months	2024-01-10	0.994489
6 months	2024-04-10	0.988210
1 year	2024-10-10	0.973601
2 years	2025-10-10	0.939372
3 years	2026-10-12	0.901885
5 years	2028-10-10	0.827719
7 years	2030-10-10	0.759504
10 years	2033-10-10	0.670094
15 years	2038-10-11	0.547598
20 years	2043-10-12	0.448541
30 years	2053-10-10	0.300886

We now create two vectors containing the times to maturity (in units of years) and these unit bond prices above (again, in place of containers that would normally be initialized in an interface):

```
std::vector<ChronoDate> unit_bond_maturity_dates{{2023, 10, 11}, {2024, 1, 10},
    . . ., {2053, 10, 10}};

std::vector<double> unit_bond_prices{0.999945, 0.994489, . . ., 0.300886};
```

And we also set the yield-curve settlement date, which we take as the same as the bond settlement date:

```
ChronoDate yc_settle_date{2023, 10, 10};
ChronoDate bond_settle_date = yc_settle_date;
```

With these, we can create an instance of a linearly interpolated yield curve:

```
LinearInterpYieldCurve yc{yc_settle_date,
    unit_bond_maturity_dates, unit_bond_prices};
```

Then, to value the bond as of the same settlement date, provide the settlement date and yield-curve data to the corresponding member function on the Bond object:

```
double value = bond_20_yr.discounted_value(bond_settle_date, yc);
```

This function will locate the first due date after settlement (in this case, the first coupon date), compute each continuously compounded discount factor from each payment date back to the settle date using interpolated rates off of the yield curve, multiply each payment by this discount factor, and sum the discounted values to determine the discounted value of the bond. In this example, the result is $1,320.38.

Summary

Date calculations are fundamental to fixed income trading, so having a date class in the Standard was a welcome addition in C++20 for financial software developers. With the two topics being inexorably linked, this chapter was a long one; however, these are topics that surprisingly are rarely covered in much practical detail either on the C++ programming side or finance side in most textbooks and quantitative finance curricula, so hopefully this information will be useful.

The core date class in `std::chrono` is `year_month_day`. Individual year, month, and day components of a `year_month_day` object are accessible and can be cast to integral types. An integer serial date equal to the number of days since the Unix epoch of 1970-01-01 can also be obtained, and hence it can be used to find the number of days between two dates, which as you have now seen is crucial in valuing fixed income products and analytics.

Without throwing an exception or halting execution, it is possible to set a `year_month_day` object to an invalid date, so it is up to the programmer to determine whether a date is valid by using its `ok()` member function. The `is_leap()` member function is also available to check for a leap year.

Adding months or years to a `year_month_day` object is made possible with its `+=` operator defined; however, adding days requires finding a date's `sys_days` (an alias for `std::chrono::time_point`) equivalent first. Workarounds are required for determining whether a date is on a weekend, and whether it lands on the end of a month, two more important properties to have when working with date-related calculations in finance.

Because of workarounds and other functionality left to the programmer, it can be easier to wrap everything in a class, encapsulating these extra steps while providing a user-friendly interface. This chapter presented one such rendition in the user-defined `ChronoDate` class. It included public member functions to add years, months, and days as integer values to an active object, to calculate the number of days between two dates, to obtain the serial date, and to return the number of days in a month or whether a date fell during a leap year. An implementation of the C++20 <=> operator, originally introduced in Chapter 2, was also demonstrated, plus a function was defined that rolls a weekend date to the next business day.

A day count basis is also often required in fixed income trading, and with the ChronoDate class providing the addition and subtraction methods, we implemented them with very little difficulty as derived classes from an abstract base class. It is important to use the correct day count basis designated in the contractual data of a Treasury bill, swap, or many other fixed income securities and derivatives when calculating their valuations.

A yield curve, in general, is a function of time, $y(t)$, where t is the time from the settle date in units of years and dependent upon a day count basis, although in practice the Actual/365 day count is often used as a uniform method to convert the dates contained in yield-curve data to continuous time. Because yield-curve data is discrete, a curve-fitting method needs to be applied. In our example, we defined an abstract base class with a common yield calculation, but with the particular curve-fitting method implemented as a private member function overriding the pure virtual yield_curve_(.) method. Curve-fitting methods can vary in sophistication, but as an example, we used linear interpolation. The class design, however, allows us to plug in whichever method is desired.

Date and yield curve objects come together to value fixed income securities. In particular, a bond is a series of payments on specific and mostly evenly spaced dates, usually every six months. Most of the payments are a single constant value. However, irregular periods can require using the contractual day count basis in order to calculate the proportional coupon value; in addition, payment dates may need to be rolled forward from weekends, and the final payment also includes repayment of the face amount.

These payments are discounted back from the payment date to the settle date, using the discount factor calculated off of the yield curve. Using the traditional object-oriented features of C++, in conjunction with the new year_month_day date class, a clear separation of duties ensures better code maintainability, lower probability of errors, and the ability to reuse these objects when working with different securities (including bonds, swaps, or mortgages) or derivatives (such as mortgage-backed securities, swaptions, or bond options).

Additional Reference

Marcia Stigum and Franklin L. Robinson, *Money Market & Bond Calculations* (McGraw-Hill, 1996)

CHAPTER 8

Linear Algebra

Linear algebra is an essential part of computational finance, and as such it is a necessary and fundamental component for financial C++ software development. Within the span of the two decades, some excellent open source matrix algebra libraries have emerged that have been adopted by the financial software industry, as well as in other computationally intensive domains such as data science, experimental physics, and medical research.

As C++ did not have all the convenient built-in multidimensional array capabilities that came with Fortran platforms, quantitative financial programmers making the transition to C++ back in the 1990s often found themselves in an inconvenient situation with limited options. These included building up this functionality mostly from scratch, wrestling with interfaces to numerical Fortran libraries such as the Basic Linear Algebra Subprograms (BLAS) (*https://oreil.ly/0lyLH*) and LAPACK (Linear Algebra PACKage) (*https://oreil.ly/jIr5q*), or somehow convincing management to invest in a third-party commercial C++ linear algebra library.

Contrived DIY solutions that were sometimes employed, based on what was available in C++ at the time, included representing a matrix as a `vector` of `vector`(s) or holding data in a two-dimensional dynamic C-array. Neither of these was particularly palatable, with the former being cumbersome and inefficient, and the latter exposing the software to the risks associated with raw pointers and dynamic memory management. One seemingly useful feature available in the C++98 Standard Library, but not without controversy, was `std::valarray`. It has survived to the current day, and it provides vectorized operations and functions highly suitable for matrix and vector math. Its pros and cons are presented in Appendix E.

The situation has improved substantially over the years with the release of several well-regarded open source linear algebra libraries for C++. Among these, two that have gained considerable critical mass in computational finance are the Eigen linear algebra library (*https://oreil.ly/vh-dG*) and the Armadillo C++ library for linear algebra & scientific computing (*https://oreil.ly/bK7Vr*). A third option that has risen to some prominence in high-performance computing (HPC) is the Blaze high-performance C++ library (*https://oreil.ly/X9GHq*). An earlier library, the Boost basic linear algebra library (uBLAS) (*https://oreil.ly/rcXZB*) is also available; however, it does not include the matrix decompositions and other capabilities such as those available in the aforementioned offerings.

As a side note, open source R interface packages are available for each of these libraries. Links to each are provided at the end of the chapter. These packages enable the integration of C++ code dependent on one or more of these libraries into R packages, usually to enhance runtime performance and/or reuse existing C++ libraries. More recently, NVIDIA has released GPU-accelerated C++ linear algebra libraries as part of its HPC SDK (*https://oreil.ly/5u9HR*). You can find a comparative list of both open source and commercial C++ linear algebra libraries, including those mentioned here, on Wikipedia (*https://oreil.ly/z1QY-*). A more in-depth view of the Eigen library follows later in this chapter.

As for C++23 and C++26, additions to the Standard finally look set to include linear algebra capabilities. Central among these new features is the `std::mdspan` multidimensional array representation adopted in C++23. A proposal for a standardized interface to external BLAS-compatible libraries has been accepted for inclusion in C++26.

Before jumping into the specifics of the Eigen library and coming linear algebra–related attractions in C++, a common theme among these topics should be discussed first: *lazy evaluation* and *expression templates*. These were both alluded to in Chapter 4, but the next section presents them formally at an introductory level.

Following that, we will examine the Eigen library and demonstrate its basic matrix operations, along with matrix decompositions that are frequently used in financial modeling. Finally, a glimpse of more recent developments related to linear algebra in the Standard Library will be presented.

Linear algebra will inevitably involve subscripts and superscripts, such as x_{ij}, where in mathematical notation i runs from 1 to some integer m, and j from 1 to n. However, C++ is zero-indexed, so a mathematical statement where $i = 1$ will be represented by `i = 0` in C++, $j = n$ by `j = n - 1`, and so forth. Within the text of the chapter, referring to, say, a "row 1" or a "column 3" of a matrix, for example, we will assume the mathematical definition but translate to a row index of 0, or a column index of 2, respectively, in C++.

Lazy Evaluation and Expression Templates

Lazy evaluation defers calculations until they are needed, thus reducing inefficiencies that result from temporary object creation and assignments. Further performance and generality can be obtained by wrapping the mathematical expressions themselves inside *expression templates*. The efficiency gains become significant when the expressions contain computationally intensive operations. This is particularly relevant in linear algebra applications, where vector and matrix operations implemented as expressions can be designed in a way that eliminates inefficient object copying and reduces the number of operations, especially when the dimensions become "large."

We will explore this topic at a basic level by examining the case of vector addition (in the linear algebra sense). These examples are similar to those found in Section 5.3 of *Discovering Modern C++ (https://oreil.ly/hNHQp)*, 2nd edition, by Peter Gottschling (Addison-Wesley, 2021) and in the DevTut tutorial "A basic example illustrating expression templates" *(https://oreil.ly/cdFSa)*, but instead of involving generic vector and matrix containers that require more narrative overhead, we will make the simplifying assumption that we are dealing only with "real" vectors represented by vector<double> types.

This discussion will start with formulating a more efficient expression for adding a fixed number of vectors, then extending it to support lazy evaluation, and then finally generalizing it for an arbitrary number of vectors utilizing an expression template. The topic of expression templates is difficult and highly advanced, even for experienced C++ developers, so the goal here isn't to make you an expert. Rather, the discussion that follows is intended to give you a taste of how lazy evaluation and expression templates are utilized in widely used linear algebra libraries such as Eigen and others mentioned previously.

Lazy Evaluation

To start, suppose you have four vectors in the mathematical sense, each with the same fixed number of elements:

$$\mathbf{v}_1, \mathbf{v}_2, \mathbf{v}_3, \mathbf{v}_4$$

You wish to store their sum in a vector $\mathbf{y}$. The traditional approach would be to naively define the addition operator by taking successive sums and storing them in temporary objects, ultimately computing the final sum and assigning it to $\mathbf{y}$.

Again, to keep the example succinct, we will make the simplifying assumption that we are dealing only with "real" vectors represented by vector<double> types, assumed to be of like dimension (otherwise, the code will just assert). To start, we could define operator + for two real vectors as follows:

```
#include <cassert>

std::vector<double> operator +(const std::vector<double>& a,
    const std::vector<double>& b)
{
    assert(a.size() == b.size());
    std::vector<double> result;
    result.reserve(a.size());
    for (size_t i = 0; i < a.size(); ++i)
    {
        result.push_back(a[i] + b[i]);
    }

    return result;

}
```

Computing the sum of four vectors as follows

```
vector<double> v_01{1.0, 2.0, 3.0};
vector<double> v_02{1.5, 2.5, 3.5};
vector<double> v_03{4.0, 5.0, 6.0};
vector<double> v_04{4.5, 5.5, 6.5};

auto y = v_01 + v_02 + v_03 + v_04;         // 11 15 19
```

means that two additional temporary vector objects are generated before y is ultimately computed. In other words, $4 - 1 = 3$ vector instances are created (two temporary plus one final y instance), plus there are also $(4 - 1) \times 3$ assignments of double variables. Each time the + operator is called, an additional vector object is generated:

```
operator+(operator+(operator+(v_01, v_02), v_03), v_04)
```

As the number of vectors (say, m) and the number of elements in each vector (say, n) gets larger, this generalizes to the following:

- $m - 1$ vector objects created: $m - 2$ temporary, plus one return object (y)

- $(m - 1)n$ assignments to temporary double values

We could do better by expressing the addition element-wise across each index of each of the vectors, resulting in a more "efficient [vector] summation using a single pass."[1] This way, the total number of assignments is significantly reduced and the creation of temporary vector objects eliminated, thus improving efficiency for "large" m and n. In the example case where $m = 4$, we would have this:

---

1 "A basic example illustrating expression templates" (*https://oreil.ly/8DvR9*), DevTut.

```
std::vector<double> sum_four_vectors(const std::vector<double>& a,
    const std::vector<double>& b, const std::vector<double>& c,
    const std::vector<double>& d)
{
    assert(a.size() == b.size());
    assert(b.size() == c.size());
    assert(c.size() == d.size());

    std::vector<double> sum;

    sum.resize(a.size());
    for (size_t i = 0; i < a.size(); ++i)
    {
        sum[i] = a[i] + b[i] + c[i] + d[i];
    }

    return sum;
}
```

Now, in this case, we have the following:

- *No* temporary vector objects are created.
- Only the resulting single sum object is created.
- The number of assignments is reduced to $n = 4$.

We could go even further by *deferring* the calculations until they are actually needed, which is the primary feature of lazy evaluation (as opposed to *eager*—also called *greedy*—evaluation). It might also be the case that we need only the sums of elements of particular indices rather than the full set. This way, we can control if or when we want the calculations to occur, and execute only specific required operations, rather than introduce all the computational overhead up front.

To demonstrate, we will now take our previous sum_four_vectors(.) function and implement it inside the definition of the square bracket ([]) operator on a class called SumOfFourVectors. For this example, the four vector addends are simply initialized as const references on a SumOfFourVectors object, but note that nothing happens otherwise *unless* or *until* we explicitly invoke the [] operator:

```
class SumOfFourVectors
{
public:

    SumOfFourVectors(const std::vector<double>& a, const std::vector<double>& b,
        const std::vector<double>& c, const std::vector<double>& d) :
        a_{a}, b_{b}, c_{c}, d_{d}
    {
        assert(a.size() == b.size());
        assert(b.size() == c.size());
        assert(c.size() == d.size());
```

```
    }

    double operator[](size_t i) const
    {
        return a_[i] + b_[i] + c_[i] + d_[i];
    }

private:

    const std::vector<double>& a_, b_, c_, d_;

};
```

Suppose we have the same four vectors v_01, ···, v_04 as before. We can use them to create an instance of SumOfFourVectors. But again, no computation takes place at this stage. The only action taken is the initialization of the four member vector references:

```
SumOfFourVectors y{v_01, v_02, v_03, v_04};
```

Now, the element-by-element sum across each index is computed only at the point where the [] operator is invoked. One option is to form a new vector instance by using the results:

```
vector<double> vec_sum{y[0], y[1], y[2]};
```

Alternatively, we might use the results as arguments in another function, in which case there is no additional vector object creation:

```
auto r = f(y[0], y[1], y[2]);
```

It could also be that we require only the sum across selected indices. For example, if we need only the cumulative first and last element sums, we can do this without calculating the entire vector sum:

```
double sum_of_1st_elems = y[0];
double sum_of_3rd_elems = y[2];
```

This way, you don't pay for what you don't need.

Expression Templates

Ultimately, we would, of course, want the capability to compute the sum of an arbitrary number of vectors, as it would be unrealistic to write individual sum functions for every possible number of vector addends. However, in order to have this capability, we need to appeal to *expression templates*, where a measurable leap in sophistication comes into play.

A reasonably tractable first example of an expression template can be seen by extending addition to an arbitrary number of vector<double> containers, again assuming for simplicity the same number of elements in each. Limiting the discussion to the vector<double> case, as opposed to arbitrary containers of a generic type T should also hopefully make this presentation easier to digest.

The way this example works is to first define the addition of two generic containers U and V as an expression, as shown in the following class template. The reason for moving to a template format will become apparent shortly. Note that in this case as well, no actual additions are computed unless and until the [] random access operator is invoked. As before, we will assume both U and V contain an arbitrary but equal number of elements:

```
// Expression template class for vector addition
template <typename U, typename V>
class VectorAddExpr
{
public:
    VectorAddExpr(const U& u, const V& v) : u_{u}, v_{v}
    {
        assert(u_.size() == v_.size());
    }

    double operator[](size_t idx) const
    {
        return u_[idx] + v_[idx];
    }

    std::size_t size() const
    {
        return u_.size();
    }

private:
    const U& u_;
    const V& v_;
};
```

This alone probably doesn't help us much, however, as the best we can do with it at this stage is add the elements across only two containers, although the calculation of the sum is still deferred until it is needed. To accommodate performing the sum of an arbitrary number of containers, we need a helper function—an addition operator—as follows:

```
// Helper function (operator +) to supplement
// the expression template for vector addition:
template <typename U, typename V>
VectorAddExpr<U, V> operator +(const U& u, const V& v)
{
    return {u, v};
}
```

Now, we can invoke the + operator for any two containers that have the [] operator defined. This will allow us to add the same vector<double> objects v1, v2, v3, and v4 as before by lining them up as the addends themselves, setting up a summation *expression*, but with the actual calculations deferred. No addition operations have been executed at this stage. The return type will be discussed in what follows, but for the moment, by using `auto`, we can obtain a summation expression object, which we will call `result`:

```
auto result = v_01 + v_02 + v_03 + v_04;
```

The actual addition operations, however, are again deferred until the sum over each index is invoked with the `[]` operator defined on the `VectorAddExpr` class, and thus we will avoid the generation of temporary `vector` objects. For example, assuming each `vector` holds three elements as before, we could again defer calculation of the results until the `[]` operator is called in the initialization of a resultant `vector<double>`:

```
vector<double> y{result[0], result[1], result[2]};
```

Alternatively, we could delay each summation until they are needed as arguments to a function:

```
auto r = f(result[0], result[1], result[2]);
```

The + operator can also now handle an arbitrary number of `vector` addends. It will generate a summation expression of, for example, three of the four vectors:

```
auto result_add_three = v_02 + v_03 + v_04;
```

Or if we had, say, two additional `vector` objects `v_05` and `v_06`, each holding three `double` elements, the + operator would also be valid:

```
auto result_add_six = v_01 + v_02 + v_03 + v_04 + v_05 + v_06;
```

We can now return to the discussion of the return type of the original summation expression. Again, recall that we just naively left it to the `auto` keyword to deduce the return type:

```
auto result = v_01 + v_02 + v_03 + v_04;
```

In this case, the actual return type resembles the following, already a challenge to decipher with even just three addition operations:

```
VectorAddExpr<VectorAddExpr<VectorAddExpr<std::vector<double>,
    std::vector<double>>, std::vector<double>>, std::vector<double>>
```

As more and more vectors are added, this return type will become longer and exponentially ghastly. However, examining the result in this small-scale example can give you an idea of how expression templates work. Working left to right, the nesting order of the expression tree follows the usual mathematical order:

```
((v_01 + v_02) + v_03) + v_04
```

In the first expression `v_01 + v_02`, substituting the template arguments for each addend gives us `U = std::vector<double>` and `V = std::vector<double>`. Hence, the result of the return type is as follows:

```
VectorAddExpr<std::vector<double>, std::vector<double>>    // 1st expression
```

The next expression is then formed by

```
(v_01 + v_02) + v_03
```

We have already established the type of the first sum, so to represent the second sum, the template arguments U and V will be

```
U = VectorAddExpr<std::vector<double>, std::vector<double>>    // 1st expression
```

and

```
V = std::vector<double>
```

Making these substitutions, the type of the second expression `VectorAddExpr<U, V>` will be of the following form:

```
VectorAddExpr
<
    VectorAddExpr<std::vector<double>, std::vector<double>>,  // 1st expression

    std::vector<double>                          // end of 2nd expression
>
```

Extending this process for the last expression

```
((v_01 + v_02) + v_03) + v_04
```

we get the following for `VectorAddExpr<U, V>`:

```
VectorAddExpr
<
    VectorAddExpr
    <
        VectorAddExpr<std::vector<double>, std::vector<double>>,    // 1st expn

        std::vector<double>                          // end of 2nd expression
    >,

        std::vector<double>                          // end of 3rd expression
>
```

This will quickly become unwieldy, and it also probably gives you an idea of how using `auto`, while convenient when working with templates, can also enable the spawning of lengthy and unknown nested template types. Moreover, you can see why, up to now, initializing a `vector<double>` object to hold the resulting sum required calculating each individual element sum in a separate interim instruction:

```
vector<double> y{result[0], result[1], result[2]};
```

Instead, we might want to be able to write this in a more natural form:

```
vector<double> y = v_01 + v_02 + v_03 + v_04;        // Note: Can't do this yet
```

To have this line compile, we can add a conversion operator to the `VectorAddExpr` class:

```
operator std::vector<double>() const
{
    std::vector<double> result;
    result.reserve(size());

    for (size_t i = 0; i < size(); ++i) {
        result.push_back(operator[](i));
    }

    return result;
}
```

Now, constructing a `vector<double>` object as previously shown, from the result of multiple applications of the + operator as defined on the `VectorAddExpr` class, is possible, while still taking advantage of the efficiency of the expression template:

```
vector<double> y = v_01 + v_02 + v_03 + v_04;        // Now we can do this
```

For readers who wish to explore additional resources on expression templates, the entirety of Chapter 27 in *C++ Templates: The Complete Guide* (*https://oreil.ly/euO6R*), 2nd edition, by David Vandevoorde et al. (Addison Wesley, 2017) is recommended for deeper and more advanced coverage. And for an excellent presentation of a real-world case study of expression templates applied specifically to financial software design, far more realistic than just adding large `vector` containers, the CppCon 2019 talk, "Expression Templates for Efficient, Generic Finance Code" (*https://oreil.ly/DOnp1*) presented by Bowie Owens, is highly recommended viewing. The performance improvements observed in this case study were substantial.

The Eigen Linear Algebra Library

As stated in its documentation (*https://oreil.ly/RUHx8*), "Eigen is a C++ template library for linear algebra: matrices, vectors, numerical solvers, and related algorithms." The first release of the Eigen library became available in 2006. Since then, it has been expanded to version 3.4.0 as of August of 2021. Starting with version 3.3.1, it has been licensed under the reasonably liberal Mozilla Public License (MPL) 2.0.

We will look at how to use the Eigen library, and how it can be used to solve some typical problems that frequently arise in finance. Although we are concentrating on Eigen, much of what we discuss here should carry over to other linear algebra libraries. This discussion will include some of the intricacies involved working with expression templates, as well as examining selected financial applications requiring matrix calculations and decompositions.

Eigen comprises template code that makes inclusion into other C++ projects very easy. In its standard installation, no linking is necessary to external binary files. Its incorporation of lazy evaluation and expression templates provides for enhanced computational performance. It also received a further boost in popularity after being chosen for incorporation into the TensorFlow (*https://www.tensorflow.org*) machine learning library, as well as the Stan Math Library (*https://oreil.ly/idfmV*), and the ATLAS experiment-tracking software (*https://oreil.ly/-LICZ*) used at the European Council for Nuclear Research (CERN) Large Hadron Collider. More background on its suitability and popularity in finance is presented in a recent QuantStart article (*https://oreil.ly/1TImn*).

Finally, the Eigen library is well-documented, with tutorials and examples to help the newcomer get up and running quickly. The Eigen documentation also includes a section on lazy evaluation and expression templates (*https://oreil.ly/F1Kl1*), providing useful background information on how they are applied within the library.

Eigen Matrices and Vectors

The heart of the Eigen library is, not surprisingly, the `Matrix` template class. It is scoped with the `Eigen` namespace and requires the `Dense` header file to be included.

The `Matrix` class carries six template parameters, but a variety of aliases are provided as specific types. These include fixed square matrix dimensions up to a maximum of 4 × 4, as well as dynamic types for arbitrary numbers of rows and columns. The numerical type that a `Matrix` holds is also a template parameter, but these settings are also incorporated into individual aliases.

For example, the following code will construct and display a fixed 3 × 3 matrix of double values (hence the 3d suffix in the alias name, where the d indicates double type elements), and a 4 × 4 matrix of `int` values (4i, where the i indicates `int` values). Braced (uniform) initialization by row can be used to load the data at construction:

```
#include <Eigen/Dense>
. . .

Eigen::Matrix3d dbl_mtx
{
    {10.64, 41.28, 21.63},
    {41.95, 87.45, 13.68},
    {22.47, 57.34, 8.631}
};

Eigen::Matrix4i int_mtx            // Contains 'int' elements
{
```

```
        {24, 0, 23, 13},
        {8, 75, 0, 98},
        {11, 60, 1, 3 },
        {422, 55, 11, 55}
    };
```

For an `Eigen::Matrix` object, the `<<` stream operator is overloaded, so the result can be easily verified on the screen (in row-major order):

```
cout << dbl_mtx << "\n\n";
cout << int_mtx << "\n\n";
```

The output is:

```
10.64 41.28 21.63
41.95 87.45 13.68
22.47 57.34 8.631

 24   0  23  13
  8  75   0  98
 11  60   1   3
422  55  11  55
```

Individual rows and columns can also be accessed, using zero-based indexing. The first column of the first matrix, and the third column of the second, for example, are obtained with respective accessor functions:

```
cout << dbl_mtx.col(0) << "\n\n";
cout << int_mtx.row(2) << "\n\n";
```

This results in the following screen output:

```
10.64
41.95
22.47

11 60  1  3
```

More often than not in financial applications, the dimensions of a matrix will not be known a priori, nor will they necessarily be equal as for a square matrix. In addition, the contents will usually be real numbers. For these reasons, we will primarily be concerned with the Eigen alias for a dynamic form of a matrix containing `double` types, `Eigen::MatrixXd`. That is, in the Eigen template scheme, `MatrixXd` is a library-provided alias for `Matrix<double, Dynamic, Dynamic, . . .>`, where the second and third template parameters are said to represent dynamic extents.

An *extent* is a programming term that refers to a row, column, or higher dimension in a multidimensional array structure. The size of a dimension can be fixed, so in the previous `Matrix4i` example, there were two extents, each of length 4. For `MatrixXd`, there is no fixed length restriction at compile time, so both extents are said to be dynamic.

Construction of a `MatrixXd` object can take on multiple forms. Data can be entered as before in row-major order, with the number of rows and columns implied by uniform initialization of individual rows:

```
using Eigen::MatrixXd;
. . .

// Actual data taken in at construction, row by row:
MatrixXd mtx_01
{
    {1.0, 2.0, 3.0},
    {4.0, 5.0, 6.0},
    {7.0, 8.0, 9.0},
    {10.0, 11.0, 12.0}
};
```

Alternatively, we can use the default constructor, with the `resize(.)` member function to set the number of rows and columns:

```
// Default constructor and resize:
MatrixXd mtx_02{};
mtx_02.resize(2, 2);

// Use stream operator to load elements separated by commas,
// in row-major order:
mtx_02 << 10.0, 12.0, 14.0, 16.0;
```

However, similar to the `std::vector` member function of the same name, this may require some performance overhead.

The extent lengths indicating the dimensions of the matrix can also be used as constructor arguments. In this case, data input can be subsequently performed by streaming in row-major order, with adjacent elements separated by a comma:

```
MatrixXd mtx_03{4, 3};        // 4 rows, 3 columns
mtx_03 << 1.0, 2.0, 3.0, 4.0, 5.0, 6.0, 7.0, 8.0, 9.0, 10.0, 11.0, 12.0;
```

One more approach is to set each element individually:

```
// Matrix dimensions as constructor arguments:
MatrixXd mtx_04{2, 2};
mtx_04(0, 0) = 3.0;
mtx_04(1, 0) = 2.5;
mtx_04(0, 1) = -1.0;
mtx_04(1, 1) = mtx_04(1, 0) + mtx_04(0, 1);
```

As noted in earlier points in the book, hardcoded values, including both the dimensions of the dynamic matrices and the data itself, would typically not be known at runtime. These values, as in the previous examples, are assumed to be placeholders for data that would come through a database interface, dynamic input from a terminal, or other source. One other point to note is that while Eigen `Matrix` data is input and displayed in row-major order, it is stored in column-major order.

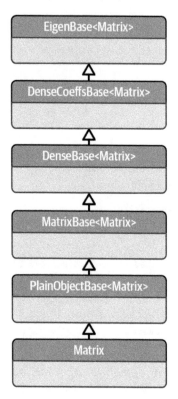
An Eigen::VectorXd is technically an alias for a Matrix with a dynamic row extent and a column extent of length 1, holding double type elements (Matrix<double, Dynamic, 1, . . . >). Methods of creating and populating VectorXd objects are similar to their MatrixXd counterparts shown in the preceding code. For example:

```
VectorXd vec_01{{1.0, 2.0, 3.0, 4.0, 5.0, 6.0, 7.0, 8.0, 9.0, 10.0, 11.0, 12.0}};

VectorXd vec_02{12};            // 12 elements
vec1 << 1.0, 2.0, 3.0, 4.0, 5.0, 6.0, 7.0, 8.0, 9.0, 10.0, 11.0, 12.0;
```

```
VectorXd vec_03{};
vec_03.resize(4);
vec_03 << 10.0, 12.0, 14.0, 16.0;

VectorXd vec_04{3};                    // 3 elements
vec_04(0) = 3.19;
vec_04(1) = 2.58;
vec_04(2) = 10.87;
```

The library also has an `Eigen::RowVectorXd` type, representing a `Matrix` of double-precision values with one row and an arbitrary number of columns (`Matrix<double, 1, dynamic, . . .>`):

```
RowVectorXd b {{1.0, 2.0, 3.0, 4.0}};       // A row-vector with 4 elements
```

Note that the round bracket operator serves as both a mutator and an accessor, as demonstrated in the `mtx_04` and `vec_04` examples, rather than the square bracket [ ] operator as in the case of a `std::vector` container.

The `row(.)` and `col(.)` accessor functions are valid for `Matrix` types in Eigen. Technically speaking, the type returned by each of these accessors is an `Eigen::Block`. It acts as a lighter-weight mutating view of the data. A `Block` can be used as a constructor argument to create a separate `Vector` instance, or implicitly converted to a `Vector` object in Eigen:

```
VectorXd first_col_vec{mtx_01.col(0)};
RowVectorXd third_row_vec = mtx_01.row(2);
```

In these examples, the data referred to by the `Block` is stored by value in the constructed `VectorXd` objects.

Matrix and Vector Math Operations

Element-by-element matrix addition and subtraction are conveniently implemented as overloads of the + and - operators in Eigen. Note, however, the multiplication operator * refers to *matrix multiplication* rather than an element-by-element product. A separate function for element-by-element multiplication, along with a wide range of other operations and common math functions, are available as *coefficient-wise* functions in Eigen that will be covered momentarily.

As for the multiplication of two matrices (say, A and B), the code follows in natural mathematical order:

```
MatrixXd A
{
    {1.0, 2.0, 3.0},
    {1.5, 2.5, 3.5},
    {4.0, 5.0, 6.0},
    {4.5, 5.5, 6.5},
```

```
        {7.0, 8.0, 9.0}
};

MatrixXd B
{
    {1.0, 2.0, 3.0, 4.0, 5.0},
    {1.5, 2.5, 3.5, 4.5, 5.5},
    {5.0, 6.0, 7.0, 8.0, 8.5}
};

MatrixXd prod_ab = A * B;
```

This gives us the following as output:

```
   19    25    31    37  41.5
22.75 30.25 37.75 45.25    51
 41.5  56.5  71.5  86.5  98.5
45.25 61.75 78.25 94.75   108
   64    88   112   136 155.5
```

Scalar multiplication is also defined. For example, we can multiply every element of the matrix A by 0.5:

```
MatrixXd scale_a = 0.5 * A;
cout << scale_a << "\n";
```

This gives us the following:

```
 0.5    1  1.5
0.75 1.25 1.75
   2  2.5    3
2.25 2.75 3.25
 3.5    4  4.5
```

Multiplication assignment can also be applied on individual rows and columns. For example, we could double each value in the second column of the matrix B:

```
B.col(1) *= 2.0;
cout << B << "\n";
```

This would give us the following:

```
  1   4   3   4   5
1.5   5 3.5 4.5 5.5
  5  12   7   8 8.5
```

Scalar multiplication assignment can also be applied to the entire matrix B. For example, we could multiply every element in the previous result by 3:

```
B *= 3.0;
cout << B << "\n\n";
```

The result would then be:

```
   3    12    9    12    15
 4.5    15 10.5 13.5  16.5
  15    36   21    24  25.5
```

Using auto with Eigen Templates

In the Eigen documentation, it is strongly recommended to "not use the `auto` keyword with Eigen's expressions, unless you are 100% sure about what you are doing. In particular, do not use the `auto` keyword as a replacement for a `Matrix<>` type."[2]

As an example, suppose we have matrices M and N, each 3 × 3, defined as follows:

```
MatrixXd M
{
    {1.0, 2.0, 3.0},
    {1.5, 2.5, 3.5},
    {4.0, 5.0, 6.0}
};

MatrixXd N
{
    {10.0, 20.0, 30.0},
    {10.5, 20.5, 30.5},
    {40.0, 50.0, 60.0}
};
```

Next, let's naively multiply these two matrices and store the result in an `auto`-deduced object P:

```
auto P = M * N;
cout << P << "\n\n";
```

This gives us the following:

```
   151    211    271
181.25 256.25 331.25
 332.5  482.5  632.5
```

So far, so good. However, suppose we modify the matrix N and examine the contents of P:

```
N.row(0) *= 0.1;
cout << P << "\n\n";
```

We now get this:

---

2 "C++ and the `auto` keyword" (*https://oreil.ly/c3u_8*), Common Pitfalls section of the Eigen documentation.

```
    142      193      244
167.75   229.25   290.75
 296.5    410.5    524.5
```

Oops. The reason is the object P is a lighter-weight and mutable view of the product. As such, if either M or N is modified, the change will be reflected in P.

Say we instead took the advice of the Eigen documentation and wrote this:

```
MatrixXd P = M * N;
```

Then in this case, P is now an independent MatrixXd object that will not be modified, even if M or N is modified. For the presentation of the library in this chapter, we will mostly heed this admonishment.

For some examples from finance, suppose we have a portfolio of three exchange-traded funds (ETFs), with the correlation matrix of the returns and the vector of individual fund volatilities (annualized) provided from market data. As a common task in portfolio optimization, we might need to construct the covariance matrix given the data in this form in order to calculate the portfolio volatility. So to form the covariance matrix, we would pre- and post-multiply the correlation matrix by diagonal matrices containing the fund volatilities:

```
MatrixXd corr_mtx
{
    {1.0, 0.5, 0.25},
    {0.5, 1.0, -0.7},
    {0.25, -0.7, 1.0}
};

VectorXd vols{{0.2, 0.1, 0.4}};

MatrixXd cov_mtx = vols.asDiagonal() * corr_mtx * vols.asDiagonal();
```

The member function asDiagonal() conveniently returns a lighter-weight view of a diagonal matrix with the vector elements along the diagonal. It can be used in the calculation of the covariance matrix in a single line of code, with the result again implicitly converted to a MatrixXd:

$$\Sigma = \begin{bmatrix} 0.2 & 0 & 0 \\ 0 & 0.1 & 0 \\ 0 & 0 & 0.4 \end{bmatrix} \begin{bmatrix} 1 & 0.5 & 0.25 \\ 0.5 & 1.0 & -0.7 \\ 0.25 & -0.7 & 1.0 \end{bmatrix} \begin{bmatrix} 0.2 & 0 & 0 \\ 0 & 0.1 & 0 \\ 0 & 0 & 0.4 \end{bmatrix} = \begin{bmatrix} 0.04 & 0.01 & 0.02 \\ 0.01 & 0.01 & -0.028 \\ 0.02 & -0.028 & 0.16 \end{bmatrix}$$

Given a vector of fund weights ω adding to 1, for example

$$\omega = \begin{bmatrix} 0.6 \\ -0.3 \\ 0.7 \end{bmatrix}$$

where the negative value for ω_2 indicates the second ETF is being sold short, the portfolio variance is then the result of the quadratic form

$$\omega^T \Sigma \omega$$

where Σ is the covariance matrix.

The portfolio volatility σ_p is therefore the square root of the variance:

$$\sigma_p = \sqrt{\omega^T \Sigma \omega}$$

Using Eigen, the vector `fund_weights` for ω, and its `transpose()` member function, the translation into code is straightforward:

```
VectorXd fund_weights{{0.6, -0.3, 0.7}};
double port_vol = std::sqrt(fund_weights.transpose() * cov_mtx * fund_weights);
```

This gives us a result of about 0.3445, or 34.45%, for `port_vol`.

In other applications, if element-by-element matrix multiplication is required, we can use the `cwiseProduct(.)` member function, where again the `cwise...` prefix means "coefficient-wise." As an example, to multiply the individual elements in matrices of like dimensions—say, the matrix A and transpose of B from the earlier example—we would write this:

```
MatrixXd cwise_prod = A.cwiseProduct(B.transpose());
```

In fact, the library has an entire set of `cwise...` member functions that perform element-by-element operations on two compatible matrices, such as `cwiseQuotient(.)` and `cwiseNotEqual(.)`. The library also has unary `cwise...` member functions, such as those that return the absolute value and square root of each element. You can find a comprehensive listing in the "Coefficient-wise & Array operators" (*https://oreil.ly/0FaQn*) section of the Eigen documentation.

The result of the `*` operator when applied to two vectors depends upon which vector is transposed. For two vectors **u** and **v** of like dimension, the dot (inner) product is computed as follows:

$$\mathbf{u}^T \mathbf{v}$$

The outer product results when the transpose is applied to **v**:

$$\mathbf{uv}^\mathsf{T}$$

So, we need to be careful when using the * operator with vectors. Suppose we have this:

```
VectorXd u{{1.0, 2.0, 3.0}};
VectorXd v{{0.5, -0.5, 1.0}};
```

The respective results of the following vector multiplications will be different:

```
double dp = u.transpose() * v;        // Returns 'double'
MatrixXd op = u * v.transpose();      // Returns a matrix
```

The first would result in a real value of 2.5, while the second would give us a singular 3×3 matrix:

```
  0.5 -0.5   1
    1   -1   2
  1.5 -1.5   3
```

When your intention is to compute a dot product, Eigen provides a member function, dot(.), to make life easier (and code safer). Writing the following should clarify which product you want:

```
dp = u.dot(v);
```

The result would be the same as before (2.5), plus the operation is commutative.

Addition and subtraction of matrices and vectors follow the mathematical element-by-element definition. Let's use the same matrix A as in the previous example and a new matrix C:

```
MatrixXd C
{
    {10.0, 20.0, 30.0},
    {10.5, 20.5, 30.5},
    {40.0, 50.0, 60.0},
    {40.5, 50.5, 60.5},
    {70.0, 80.0, 90.0}
};
```

The matrix sum is computed as follows:

```
MatrixXd mtx_sum = A + C;
```

This gives us the result as shown next:

```
11 22 33
12 23 34
44 55 66
```

```
45 56 67
77 88 99
```

Given the same vectors u and v as in the previous examples, the difference is defined by

```
VectorXd vec_diff = v - u;
```

resulting in

```
-0.5
-2.5
  -2
```

STL Compatibility

A very nice feature of both the Eigen Vector and Matrix classes is their compatibility with the Standard Template Library. This means you can iterate through an Eigen container, apply STL algorithms, and exchange data with STL containers.

STL and VectorXd

As a first example, suppose you wish to generate 12 random variates from a t-distribution and place the results in a VectorXd container. The process is essentially the same as what we saw using a std::vector and applying the std::generate algorithm with a lambda auxiliary function:

```
VectorXd u{12};                          // 12 elements
std::mt19937_64 mt{100};                 // Mersenne Twister eng, seed = 100
std::student_t_distribution<> tdist{5};  // 5 degrees of freedom
std::generate(u.begin(), u.end(), [&mt, &tdist]() {return tdist(mt);});
```

Nonmodifying algorithms such as std::max_element(.) are also valid:

```
auto max_u = std::max_element(u.begin(), u.end());       // Returns iterator
```

Note also that an STL container and an Eigen Vector can be used together as arguments in binary STL algorithms. For example, suppose we have a std::vector containing the same number of additional random t-distribution variates:

```
std::vector<double> v(u.size());    // u is a VectorXd, v is an STL vector
std::generate(v.begin(), v.end(), [&mt, &tdist]() {return tdist(mt);});
```

We could then use the numeric STL algorithm std::inner_product to calculate the dot product of u (the Eigen container) and v (the STL container):

```
double dot_prod = std::inner_product(u.begin(), u.end(), v.begin(), 0.0);
```

The sleeker C++20 range versions are also supported for Eigen Vector types. For example, we could add the values in the Eigen::VectorXd (u) and the std::vector (v), and place the results in a new VectorXd (w):

```
VectorXd w(v.size());
std::ranges::transform(u, v, w.begin(), std::plus{});
```

Applying STL algorithms to a matrix

STL algorithms can also be applied to matrices row by row, or column by column.
Suppose we have a 4×3 matrix as follows:

```
MatrixXd vals_01
{
    {9.0, 8.0, 7.0},
    {3.0, 2.0, 1.0},
    {9.5, 8.5, 7.5},
    {3.5, 2.5, 1.5}
};
```

The rowwise() member function on an Eigen Matrix sets up an iteration by row.
Each row is a reference to (a view of) the respective data, so we could square each
element of the matrix in place as follows:

```
for (auto row : vals_01.rowwise())
{
    std::ranges::transform(row, row.begin(), [](double x) {return x * x; });
}
```

The colwise() member function is similar, in this case sorting each column of the
matrix (not to be confused with the *coefficient-wise* cWise... functions):

```
for (auto col : vals_01.colwise())
{
    std::ranges::sort(col);
}
```

The end result after applying both algorithms gives us this:

```
     9      4      1
 12.25   6.25   2.25
    81     64     49
 90.25  72.25  56.25
```

Each element has been squared, and each column has been rearranged in ascending
order.

Financial programmers often need to write code that will compute the log returns
on a set of equity or fund prices. For example, suppose we have a set of 11
monthly prices for three ETFs, which are placed in an 11×3 MatrixXd called
prices_to_returns:

```
MatrixXd prices_to_returns
{
    {25.5, 8.0, 70.5},
    {31.0, 7.5, 71.0},
```

```
        {29.5, 8.5, 77.5},
        {33.5, 5.5, 71.5},
        {26.5, 9.5, 72.5},
        {34.5, 8.5, 75.5},
        {28.5, 9.0, 72.0},
        {23.5, 7.5, 73.5},
        {28.0, 8.0, 72.5},
        {31.5, 9.0, 73.0},
        {32.5, 9.5, 74.5}
    };
```

To demonstrate `rowwise()`, this could be used for the first step in computing log returns by applying the `transform(.)` algorithm *row by row*, and computing the natural log of each price:

```
for (auto row : prices_to_returns.rowwise())
{
    std::ranges::transform(row, row.begin(),
        [](double x) {return std::log(x); });
}
```

Then, to get the log returns, we need to subtract from each log price its predecessor. For this, we can apply the `adjacent_difference` numeric algorithm to each *column*:

```
for (auto col : prices_to_returns.colwise())
{
    std::adjacent_difference(col.begin(), col.end(), col.begin());
}
```

This result is still an 11×3 matrix, with the first row still containing the logs of the prices in the first row:

```
 3.238678  2.079442  4.255613
 0.195309 -0.064539  0.007067
-0.049597  0.125163  0.087598
 0.127155 -0.435318 -0.080580
-0.234401  0.546544  0.013889
 0.263815 -0.111226  0.040546
-0.191055  0.057158 -0.047467
-0.192904 -0.182322  0.020619
 0.175204  0.064539 -0.013699
 0.117783  0.117783  0.006873
 0.031253  0.054067  0.020340
```

What we want are the monthly returns alone, so we need to remove the first row. This can be achieved by applying the `seq(.)` function, introduced in Eigen 3.4, which provides an intuitive way of extracting a submatrix view (an `Eigen::Block`) from a `Matrix` object. The example here shows how to extract all rows below the first:

```
MatrixXd returns_mtx{prices_to_returns(Eigen::seq(1, Eigen::last),
    Eigen::seq(0, Eigen::last))};
```

This code says the following:

1. Start with the second row (index 1) and include all rows down to the last row: `Eigen::seq(1, Eigen::last)`.

2. Take all columns from the first (index 0) to the last: `Eigen::seq(0, Eigen::last)`.

3. Use this submatrix data (Block) alone in the constructor for the resulting `MatrixXd` object `returns_mtx`.

The results held in `returns_mtx` are then the log returns alone. These can be formatted in percentage format to two decimal places if desired. Note also we can iterate over each row by using `rowwise()` here as well, and then over each element in that row in the inner loop, to output the data to the screen:

```
#include <iomanip>        // for std::right, std::setw,
                          // std::fixed, and std::setprecision

// . . .

for (const auto& row : returns_mtx.rowwise())
{
    for (double element : row)
    {
        std::cout << std::right << std::setw(7) << std::fixed
            << std::setprecision(2) << element * 100 << "%\t";
    }
    std::cout << "\n";
}
```

The output is:

```
 19.53%       -6.45%        0.71%
 -4.96%       12.52%        8.76%
 12.72%      -43.53%       -8.06%
-23.44%       54.65%        1.39%
 26.38%      -11.12%        4.05%
-19.11%        5.72%       -4.75%
-19.29%      -18.23%        2.06%
 17.52%        6.45%       -1.37%
 11.78%       11.78%        0.69%
  3.13%        5.41%        2.03%
```

Now, suppose the portfolio allocation is fixed at 35%, 40%, and 25% for each respective fund (columnwise). We can get the monthly portfolio returns by multiplying the vector of allocations by `returns_mtx`:

```
VectorXd allocations{{0.35, 0.40, 0.25}};
VectorXd monthly_returns = returns_mtx * allocations;

for (auto j = 0; j < monthly_returns.size(); ++j)
{
    cout << std::right << std::setw(7) << std::fixed << std::setprecision(2)
```

```
            << monthly_returns(j) * 100 << "%\n";
    }
```

The result is shown here:

```
    4.43%
    5.46%
  -14.98%
   14.00%
    5.80%
   -5.59%
  -13.53%
    8.37%
    9.01%
    3.77%
```

STL-like variants and mathematical functions in Eigen

Eigen also has built-in functionality that can replace some (but not all) of the preceding STL examples. First, the unaryExpr(.) member function can apply a common function to each element of a matrix, in lieu of the STL transform(.) algorithm. Using the same example with a lambda that squares a real number, this can be written as follows:

```
MatrixXd vals_01
{
    {9.0, 8.0, 7.0},
    {3.0, 2.0, 1.0},
    {9.5, 8.5, 7.5},
    {3.5, 2.5, 1.5}
};

vals_01.unaryExpr([](double x) {return x * x;});
```

Like transform(.), the unaryExpr(.) function can also apply a functor defined on a class. For example, suppose we have a class with a functor that returns the square root of a number:

```
class SquareRoot
{
public:
    double operator()(double x) const
    {
        return std::sqrt(x);
    }
};
```

Applying this with unaryExpr(.) will return vals_01 to its original form:

```
SquareRoot sq{};
vals_01.unaryExpr(sq);
```

The result from the application of unaryExpr(.) can also be used to create separate MatrixXd objects:

```
MatrixXd vals_02{vals_01.unaryExpr([](double x) {return x * x;})};
MatrixXd vals_03 = vals_02.unaryExpr(sq);
```

Eigen furthermore provides a set of element-by-element mathematical functions, such as sqrt(), log(), exp(), and trigonometric functions. The library also includes additional functions such as those that will compute the square, cube, or inverse of each element. The catch is that these are defined for use with the Array class in Eigen. The difference between an Array and a Matrix is "primarily in the API: the API for the Array class provides easy access to coefficient-wise operations, while the API for the Matrix class provides easy access to linear-algebra operations."[3]

We can easily create a temporary ArrayWrapper object that expresses a Matrix as an Array, and then invoke the desired Array math function. We do this by invoking the array() member function on a Matrix—a no-cost operation—and the desired math function. The result can either be assigned back to the original MatrixXd object vals or copied to a new one. It should also be noted that the array() function will not mutate the original Matrix object on which it is called.

The same example using unaryExpr(.) is reused here, but replaced with the square() and sqrt() Eigen array functions:

```
// Convert to an array expression, compute the squares,
// and save the results back to the vals matrix object (MatrixXd):
vals_01.array().square();

// Now take square root of each element in the resulting matrix:
vals_01.array().sqrt();

// Can again also copy results to a new matrix:
MatrixXd vals_squared{vals.array().square()};
MatrixXd vals_squared_sqrt = vals_squared.array().sqrt();
```

This is an easier solution compared to using the unaryExpr(.) approach or applying the STL transform(.) algorithm with the equivalent mathematical functions. In other applications, the function to be applied might be user-defined rather than a function provided by Eigen.

Finally, for the ETF returns example, computing the log prices also becomes simpler by using the provided log() function:

```
prices_to_returns = prices_to_returns.array().log();
```

---

3 "Array Class Template Reference" (*https://oreil.ly/WebNe*), Eigen documentation.

However, because Eigen does not provide a method to calculate adjacent differences, applying the `adjacent_difference(.)` STL algorithm to each column would still be relevant in this case. And more generally, beyond this one example, the wider set of STL algorithms can provide options that are not available in Eigen but that can be applied to Eigen `Vector` and `Matrix` containers as outlined in this section.

Matrix Decompositions and Applications

Matrix decompositions are essential for a variety of financial engineering problems. This section presents a few examples that are commonly found in computational finance, and the use of Eigen in these contexts.

Fund Tracking with Multiple Regression

A common programming problem in finance is tracking fund returns against a benchmark by using multiple regression. Examples include the following:

- Tracking whether a fund of hedge funds is following its stated allocation targets by regressing its returns on a set of hedge-fund-style index returns
- Tracking the sensitivity of a portfolio to changes in different market sectors, using sector index funds as proxies for the predictors
- Tracking the goodness of fit of mutual funds offered in guaranteed investment products, such as variable annuities, with respect to their respective fund group benchmarks

If we let y be the benchmark or target return, and $x_1, x_2, \cdots, x_p$ represent the returns of the funds being tracked, the problem is to find estimates of the coefficients $\widehat{\beta_1}, \cdots, \widehat{\beta_p}$ that provide the least squares estimate for this linear relationship:

$$y = \widehat{\beta_1}x_1 + \widehat{\beta_2}x_2 + \cdots + \widehat{\beta_p}x_p$$

For fund tracking, the model is often sufficient without the intercept term, so it is omitted here as well.

We are then tasked with finding a vector

$$\hat{\beta} = \begin{bmatrix} \hat{\beta_1} \\ \hat{\beta_2} \\ \vdots \\ \hat{\beta_p} \end{bmatrix}$$

that satisfies the matrix form of the regression equation:

Equation 8-1

$$Y = \hat{\beta}X$$

where **X** is the design matrix containing p columns of independent variable data, and n observations (rows), with the number of observations n "comfortably" greater than the number of data columns p to ensure stability. The vector **Y** is a $n \times 1$ column vector containing the observed target fund returns (e.g., portfolio returns).

A common solution is to employ the Compact Householder QR Decomposition. Given that $n \gg p$, and that our predictor data consists of indices that are not highly correlated, it is reasonable to assume **X** will be of full rank ($= p$). This means there will be matrices **Q** and **R** such that **Q** is an $n \times p$ matrix, where $QQ^T = I_p$ (the $p \times p$ identity matrix), **R** is an upper triangular $p \times p$ matrix, and

$$X = QR$$

Making this substitution for **X** in Equation 8-1, and multiplying each side by Q^T, we get:

$$Q^Ty = R\hat{\beta}$$

Because this has been reduced to an upper-triangular system, it becomes an easier problem that can be solved more efficiently using back substitution.

As an example, suppose we have three sector ETFs and want to explore their relationship to the broader market (e.g., the S&P 500), and suppose we have 30 daily observations.

The design matrix will contain the three ETF returns (in decimal form) and is stored in a `MatrixXd` object called X, as follows:

```
MatrixXd X
{
```

```
    {-0.044700, -0.007888,  0.042980,  0.016417, -0.017797, -0.016714,
      0.019472,  0.029853,  0.023126, -0.033879, -0.003384, -0.018474,
     -0.012510, -0.018348,  0.010627,  0.036669,  0.010811, -0.035572,
      0.027474,  0.005406, -0.010159, -0.006146, -0.010327, -0.010435,
      0.011127, -0.023794, -0.028009,  0.002182,  0.008683,  0.001440},

    {-0.019003,  0.026037,  0.037827,  0.010629, -0.008382,  0.001122,
     -0.004494,  0.017305, -0.006106,  0.012175, -0.003305,  0.027220,
     -0.036089, -0.002230, -0.015748, -0.020619, -0.011641,  0.023149,
     -0.002291,  0.006288, -0.012038, -0.029259,  0.011219, -0.008847,
     -0.033738,  0.020619, -0.012078,  0.015673,  0.041013,  0.052195},

    {-0.030629,  0.024919, -0.001716,  0.008562,  0.003407, -0.010824,
     -0.010361, -0.009302,  0.008142, -0.004064,  0.000584,  0.004640,
      0.031893, -0.013544, -0.023574, -0.004665, -0.006446, -0.005311,
      0.045096, -0.007375, -0.005142, -0.001716, -0.005176, -0.002885,
      0.002309, -0.014522, -0.017712,  0.001192, -0.002382, -0.004396}
};

X.transposeInPlace();
```

X is transposed, as the function expects the design matrix in column-major order. Again, hardcoded values are used in our examples in lieu of proper system-dependent interfaces you will find in practice, where this transpose might not be necessary.

The target fund returns are stored in a `VectorXd` object, `Y`:

```
VectorXd Y
{
    {-0.039891,  0.001787, -0.016202,  0.056452,  0.003425, -0.012038,
     -0.009998,  0.013452,  0.013486, -0.007898,  0.008111, -0.015425,
     -0.002161, -0.028752,  0.011293, -0.007958, -0.004002, -0.031691,
      0.026777,  0.009804,  0.000887,  0.014952, -0.004156, -0.001535,
      0.013517, -0.021229,  0.001989, -0.020518,  0.005841,  0.011249}
};
```

Recall that data in a `VectorXd` is initialized and stored in column vector format, so no transpose is necessary here.

Obtaining the regression coefficients is just a matter of compiling and running a single line of code:

```
VectorXd beta = X.householderQr().solve(Y);
```

The `householderQr()` member function on the `Matrix` object `X` returns an `Eigen::HouseholderQR` object, upon which the `solve(.)` member function provides the result. This gives us for `beta` the following $(\widehat{\beta_1}, \widehat{\beta_2}, \widehat{\beta_3})$:

```
 0.352343
-0.089911
 0.391251
```

Eigen also provides additional matrix decompositions suitable for linear regression. These include methods that tend to be slower but that will accommodate situations where stability and full rank of the design matrix may be an issue. Among the options available are the full-pivot QR Householder decomposition, and two forms of the singular value decomposition (SVD). These are listed in the Eigen documentation, under "Solving linear least squares systems" (*https://oreil.ly/2pLrA*). (SVD code examples are also included in the sample code accompanying this chapter.)

Correlated Random Equity Paths and the Cholesky Decomposition

The Cholesky decomposition is an often-employed tool in finance for generating *correlated* Monte Carlo equity path simulations. For example, when pricing basket options, covariances between movements in the basket securities need to be accounted for, specifically in generating correlated random normal draws to be used in the simulations. This is in contrast to generating a random price path for a single underlying security (assuming the dividend rate = 0 here for simplicity):

$$S_t = S_{t-1}\exp\left[\left(r - \frac{\sigma^2}{2}\right)\Delta t + \sigma\varepsilon_t\sqrt{\Delta t}\right]$$

where, again, $\varepsilon_t \sim N(0,1)$, σ is the equity volatility, and r represents the risk-free interest rate.

In the case of a basket option, we now need to generate a path for each of, say, m assets, at each time t, where the $\sigma\varepsilon_t$ term is replaced by a random term $w_t^{(i)}$ that is again based on a standard normal draw, but whose fluctuations also contain correlations with the other assets in the basket. Therefore, we need to generate a set of prices $\left\{S_t^{(i)}\right\}$ where

Equations 8-2

$$S_t^{(1)} = S_{t-1}\exp\left[\left(r - \frac{\sigma^2}{2}\right)\Delta t + w_t^{(1)}\sqrt{\Delta t}\right]$$

$$\vdots$$

$$S_t^{(m)} = S_{t-1}\exp\left[\left(r - \frac{\sigma^2}{2}\right)\Delta t + w_t^{(m)}\sqrt{\Delta t}\right]$$

for each asset $i = 1, \cdots, m$ at each time step t_j, $j = 1, \cdots, n$. Our first task is to calculate the random but correlated vector for each time t.

This is where the Cholesky decomposition—available in Eigen—comes into play. An $m \times m$ covariance matrix $\boldsymbol{\Sigma}$, assuming it is positive definite, will have a Cholesky decomposition where $\mathbf{L}$ is a lower triangular matrix:

$$\boldsymbol{\Sigma} = \mathbf{L}\mathbf{L}^\mathsf{T}$$

Then, for a vector of standard normal variates z,

$$\begin{bmatrix} z_1 \\ z_2 \\ \vdots \\ z_m \end{bmatrix}$$

the $m \times 1$ vector generated by $\mathbf{L}\mathbf{z}^\mathsf{T}$ will provide a set of correlated volatilities that can be used to generate a random scenario of prices for each underlying security, over a single time step. Then for each time step t, we replace $\mathbf{z}$ with $\mathbf{z}_t$ to arrive at our desired result:

$$\mathbf{w}_t = \mathbf{L}\mathbf{z}_t^\mathsf{T}$$

This can then be extended an arbitrary number of n time steps by placing each vector $\mathbf{z}_t$ into a column of a matrix, say, $\mathbf{Z}$.

Then, we can generate the entire set of vectors of correlated random variables in one step and place the results in a matrix:

$$\mathbf{W} = \mathbf{L}\mathbf{Z}$$

Eigen provides a Cholesky decomposition of a `MatrixXd` object, using the `Eigen::LLT` class template with the parameter `MatrixXd`. It again consists of creating an object of this class, and then calling a member function, `matrixL()`, which returns the preceding matrix $\mathbf{L}$.

As an example, suppose we have four securities in the basket, with the following covariance matrix:

```
MatrixXd cov_basket
{
    { 0.01263, 0.00025, -0.00017, 0.00503 },
    { 0.00025, 0.00138,  0.00280, 0.00027 },
    {-0.00017, 0.00280,  0.03775, 0.00480 },
```

```
    { 0.00503, 0.00027,  0.00480, 0.02900 }
};
```

The Cholesky decomposition is set up when the matrix data is used to construct the `Eigen::LLT` object. Calling its member function `matrixL()` computes the decomposition and returns the resulting lower triangle matrix:

```
Eigen::LLT<Eigen::MatrixXd> chol{cov_basket};
MatrixXd chol_mtx = chol.matrixL();
```

This gives us the following for `chol_mtx`:

```
    0.1123833            0            0            0
    0.0022245    0.0370817            0            0
   -0.0015127    0.0755997    0.1789760            0
    0.0447575    0.0045962    0.0252561    0.1622891
```

Suppose now that the Monte Carlo model will have six time steps over a period of one year. We will need six vectors, each containing four correlated normal variates. If we place them as column vectors in a matrix, with an extra preceding column to hold the spot share price for each underlying fund, $S_0^{(1)}, \cdots, S_0^{(4)}$, at $t = 0$, then we can iterate columnwise to ultimately compute a simulated and correlated price scenario for each fund.

First, create a `MatrixXd` object with four rows and seven columns that will eventually hold our correlated scenarios:

```
MatrixXd corr_scens{4, 7};
```

Suppose from the market we get the spot share prices $100, $150, $25, and $50, so we can enter these into the first column of this matrix:

```
corr_scens.col(0) << 100.0, 150.0, 25.0, 50.0;
```

The next step is to populate the remaining columns of this matrix with uncorrelated standard normal draws. As we did previously (in Chapter 5), using Standard Library `<random>` functions, we can set up a random engine and distribution, and capture these in a lambda to generate the standard normal variates. For demonstration, the seed is set to 100 for this single run, but it would vary for each set of scenarios generated, similar to the case for the single underlying equity in Chapter 5:

```
std::mt19937_64 mt_norm{100};
std::normal_distribution<> std_nd;

auto std_norm = [&mt_norm, &std_nd](double x)
{
    return std_nd(mt_norm);
};
```

Recalling that an `Eigen::Block` is a lighter-weight mutating view of a submatrix, we can again apply the `Eigen::seq(.)` function as before to view and modify the submatrix consisting of the remaining columns of corr_scens in situ, while avoiding the overhead of copying the elements into a separate MatrixXd object:

```
// proj_vals_block: "projected values block"
Eigen::Block<MatrixXd> proj_vals_block =
        corr_scens(Eigen::seq(0, Eigen::last), Eigen::seq(1, Eigen::last));
```

We can iterate columnwise through this view just as we would for a MatrixXd, and then apply the std::ranges::transform algorithm to each individual column by using a range-based for loop:

```
for (auto col : proj_vals_block.colwise())
{
    std::ranges::transform(col, col.begin(), std_norm);
}
```

This interim result for the matrix corr_scens would now resemble the following, with actual randomly generated results depending on your particular Standard Library vendor (in this example, Microsoft Visual Studio 2022). The spot fund share prices are in the first column, while the remaining columns contain standard normal random variates:

```
100.000000    0.201395    0.197482    1.228572    1.407510    1.827890   -0.150014
150.000000   -0.076959    0.083065    1.862517    0.122389   -0.949222    0.667817
 25.000000    0.936051    1.162329   -0.642932    0.538005   -1.826880   -0.451039
 50.000000   -0.009162   -2.791863   -0.434655   -0.055375    1.463116    0.345527
```

Now, to get the *correlated* normal values, because the proj_vals_block view refers to the updated submatrix, it is just a case of multiplying it by the Cholesky matrix chol_mtx that was calculated earlier using the decomposition provided by Eigen:

```
proj_vals_block = chol_mtx * proj_vals_block;
```

Assigning the result back to proj_vals_block will also be reflected in the corr_scens matrix:

```
100.000000    0.022633    0.022194    0.138071    0.158181    0.205424   -0.016859
150.000000   -0.002406    0.003519    0.071798    0.007669   -0.031133    0.024430
 25.000000    0.161408    0.214010    0.023878    0.103414   -0.401493   -0.030011
 50.000000    0.030814   -0.414513   -0.023229    0.068160    0.268757    0.041039
```

The submatrix from the second column to the last corresponds to the matrix $\mathbf{W}$ in the mathematical derivation. Each column of this submatrix is then $\mathbf{w}_t^{(1)} \cdots \mathbf{w}_t^{(4)}$ at each time $t = 1, \cdots, 6$. To calculate the correlated random prices for each t, we need each preceding equity price at time $t - 1$ (S_{t-1}) starting with the spot prices at $t = 0$ that reside in the first column of the larger corr_scens matrix.

Suppose that the annual risk-free interest rate is 1%, and the time to maturity is one year—divided into six equal time steps—from which we can get the Δ_t value—say, dt:

```
double rf_rate = 0.01;
double time_to_maturity = 1.0;
unsigned num_time_steps = 6;
double dt = time_to_maturity / num_time_steps;
```

Now, we are ready to generate each correlated equity price path simulation. The stochastic process, as shown in Equations 8-2, can be computed in a lambda, where price is the previous price in a scenario, and vol is the volatility of the particular equity:

```
auto gen_price = [dt, rf_rate](double price, double vol, double corr_norm)
{
    double expArg1 = (rf_rate - ((vol * vol) / 2.0)) * dt;
    double expArg2 = corr_norm * std::sqrt(dt);
    double next_price = price * std::exp(expArg1 + expArg2);
    return next_price;
};
```

Finally, as each successive set of generated prices at each time step depends upon the prices in the preceding time step, the most straightforward option is to go back to basics and set up the iterations in a nested for loop, and then call the lambda at each step. This process begins with the initial spot prices in the first column of corr_scens, with each successive simulated equity price based on its predecessor, $t = 0, 1, \cdots, 5$:

```
for (unsigned j = 1; j < integ_scens.cols(); ++j)
{
    for (unsigned i = 0; i < integ_scens.rows(); ++i)
    {
        integ_scens(i, j) = gen_price(integ_scens(i, j - 1), cov_basket(i, i),
            corr_norms(i, j - 1));
    }
}
```

For this example, rounded to the nearest cent, the results are as follows:

```
100.00  101.10   102.18  108.29  115.70   126.03   125.38
150.00  150.10   150.57  155.31  156.05   154.34   156.15
 25.00   26.74    29.23   29.56   30.89    26.26    25.98
 50.00   50.71    42.89   42.55   43.82    48.98    49.89
```

Again, results may vary because of differences in the implementation of <random> among different Standard Library vendors, but for pricing options, this process would be repeated thousands of times with distinct seed values, which should result in convergence to a common basket option value.

Yield-Curve Dynamics and Principal Component Analysis

Principal component analysis (PCA) is a go-to tool for determining the sources and magnitudes of variation that drive changes in the shape of a yield curve. Given a covariance matrix of daily changes in yields spanning a range of bond maturities, PCA is employed by first calculating the eigenvalues of this matrix and ordering them from highest to lowest. Then, the weightings are calculated by dividing each eigenvalue by the sum of all the eigenvalues.

Empirical research has shown the contribution of the first three eigenvalues will comprise nearly the entirety of the variance. The first principal component corresponds approximately to parallel shifts in the yield curve, the second corresponds to variations in its "tilt" or "slope," and the third corresponds to changes in the curvature. These are illustrated in graphs (a), (b), and (c), respectively, in Figure 8-2, with yields plotted against time (maturities) in units of years. Rigorous statistical tests exist for measuring significance, but the weights alone can provide a relative estimated measure of each source of variation.

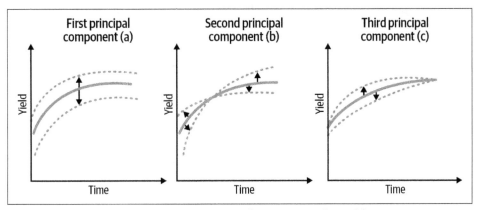

Figure 8-2. Principal components as sources of variation in the yield curve

You can find the reasons and details behind these variations in Chapter 18 of the computational finance book *Statistics and Data Analysis for Financial Engineering*, 2nd edition, by David Ruppert and David S. Matteson (Springer, 2015), and in Chapter 3 of *Interest-Rate Option Models*, 2nd edition, by Riccardo Rebonato (Wiley, 2002).

Section 18.2 of *Statistics and Data Analysis for Financial Engineering* provides an excellent example (and with special thanks to the authors is used here by permission) on how to apply PCA to publicly available US Treasury yield data. The resulting covariance matrix, as provided in this example, is used as input data in the MatrixXd constructor data as shown in the following code. This covariance matrix is based on fluctuations in differenced US Treasury yields (*https://oreil.ly/AZH83*) for 11 maturities, ranging from one month to 30 years. The underlying data is taken from the period from January 1990 to October 2008.

The upper triangular data of the covariance matrix is as follows, rounded to five decimal places:

```
0.01892 0.00989 0.00582 0.00510 0.00381 0.00363 0.00314 0.00265 0.00201 0.00144 0.00130
0.00000 0.01011 0.00612 0.00480 0.00353 0.00341 0.00289 0.00240 0.00181 0.00122 0.00111
0.00000 0.00000 0.00566 0.00468 0.00381 0.00379 0.00326 0.00277 0.00218 0.00157 0.00140
0.00000 0.00000 0.00000 0.00483 0.00470 0.00467 0.00413 0.00361 0.00295 0.00224 0.00201
0.00000 0.00000 0.00000 0.00000 0.00643 0.00634 0.00579 0.00516 0.00434 0.00334 0.00300
0.00000 0.00000 0.00000 0.00000 0.00000 0.00652 0.00595 0.00536 0.00454 0.00357 0.00323
0.00000 0.00000 0.00000 0.00000 0.00000 0.00000 0.00580 0.00529 0.00455 0.00367 0.00335
0.00000 0.00000 0.00000 0.00000 0.00000 0.00000 0.00000 0.00498 0.00435 0.00357 0.00329
0.00000 0.00000 0.00000 0.00000 0.00000 0.00000 0.00000 0.00000 0.00396 0.00332 0.00309
0.00000 0.00000 0.00000 0.00000 0.00000 0.00000 0.00000 0.00000 0.00000 0.00306 0.00286
0.00000 0.00000 0.00000 0.00000 0.00000 0.00000 0.00000 0.00000 0.00000 0.00000 0.00281
```

To calculate the eigenvalues, first load this data into the upper triangular region of a `MatrixXd` instance (again, hardcoded in lieu of a production-level data interface):

```cpp
MatrixXd term_struct_cov_mtx
{
    // 1 month
    {0.018920, 0.009889, 0.005820, 0.005103, 0.003813, 0.003626,
        0.003136, 0.002646, 0.002015, 0.001438, 0.001303},

    // 3 months
    {0.0, 0.010107, 0.006123, 0.004796, 0.003532, 0.003414,
        0.002893, 0.002404, 0.001815, 0.001217, 0.001109},

    // 6 months
    { . . . },

    // 1 year
    { . . . },

    // . . .

    // 30 years
    {0.0, 0.0, 0.0, 0.0, 0.0, 0.0,
        0.0, 0.0, 0.0, 0.0, 0.002814}
};
```

As a real symmetric matrix is trivially self-adjoint (has no complex components), Eigen can apply a function `selfadjointView<.>()` to an upper (or lower) triangular matrix to define a view of a symmetric covariance matrix. The `eigenvalues()` member function applies to this result, but the eigenvalues are formally complex, so we could first store the result in an `Eigen::VectorXcd` container (the c meaning "complex"):

```cpp
Eigen::VectorXcd cmplx_eigenvals =
    term_struct_cov_mtx.selfadjointView<Eigen::Upper>().eigenvalues();
```

But because a covariance matrix in these yield-curve applications is almost surely positive semi-definite, all the eigenvalues will be real numbers. The real components can be obtained from a VectorXcd by using the coefficient-wise real() function:

```
VectorXd eigenvals = cmplx_eigenvals.real();
```

Alternatively, creating the temporary VectorXcd object could be eliminated by placing everything on one line:

```
VectorXd eigenvals =
    term_struct_cov_mtx.selfadjointView<Eigen::Upper>().eigenvalues().real();
```

Now, to determine the weighting of each principal component, we need to divide each eigenvalue by the sum of all the eigenvalues. We can obtain the sum by using the sum() function provided by Eigen:

```
double total_ev = eigenvals.sum();
eigenvals = eigenvals / total_ev;
```

To view the results in the order of the principal components, the weighted values need to be arranged from largest to smallest. For this, we can use the STL solution:

```
std::ranges::sort(eigenvals, std::greater{});
```

Finally, examining the sorted contents of the updated eigenvals container, we would find the following results:

```
0.62175 0.25472 0.06993 0.02752 0.01519 0.00408
0.00268 0.00160 0.00117 0.00085 0.00051
```

From this, we can see the parallel shifts and the "tilt" of the yield curve are the dominant effects, with relative weights of 62.2% and 25.5%, respectively, while the curvature effect is smaller at 7.0%.

Future Directions: Linear Algebra in the Standard Library

This section presents two recent developments related to linear algebra in C++. These were originally submitted to the ISO C++ committee in the following proposals:

- "std::mdspan: A polymorphic multidimensional array reference" (*https://wg21.link/p0009*) (Proposal P0009)
- "A free function linear algebra interface based on the BLAS" (*https://wg21.link/p1673*) (Proposal P1673)

The mdspan class template can impose a multidimensional array structure on a container (such as an STL vector) whose elements reside in contiguous memory. The resulting object is a mutating view of the data in multidimensional form. Using the example of a vector containing the data, and a referring mdspan representing a matrix, the numbers of rows and columns are set at construction of the mdspan. An mdspan can also take the form of higher-dimensional arrays, but for our purposes we will concern ourselves with the two-dimensional case for matrix-like representations. The mdspan class template is now available for use in the C++23 Standard.

The second proposal is for a standard interface to linear algebra functionality "based on the dense Basic Linear Algebra Subprograms (BLAS)," corresponding "to a subset of the BLAS Standard." This way, standard cross-platform code could be written in a manner irrespective of the underlying linear algebra library. As noted in the proposal, the "interface is designed in the spirit of the C++ Standard Library's algorithms," and "uses mdspan...to represent matrices and vectors."[4] It has been accepted for inclusion in C++26.

mdspan

As previously mentioned, for representing a matrix, mdspan establishes a mutating view of a contiguous container and then imposes the number of rows and columns. If these parameters are known at compile time, creating an mdspan view is easy. This example creates a 3 × 2 matrix-like view of the underlying data:

```
#include <mdspan>

vector<int> v{101, 102, 103, 104, 105, 106};
stdex::mdspan mds_01 {v.data(), 3, 2};
```

Note that mdspan uses the data() member function of vector to access its contents.

In mdspan parlance, in the two-dimensional case, rows and columns are also referred to as *extents*, with the number of rows and columns accessed by the index of each, 0 for rows and 1 for columns. The total number of extents is referred to as the *rank*, so in this case, the rank is 2. For higher-order multidimensional arrays, the rank would be greater than 2:

```
size_t n_rows = mds_01.extent(0);     // = 3 rows
size_t n_cols = mds_01.extent(1);     // = 2 columns
size_t n_extents = mds_01.rank();     // = 2 dimensions
```

 The term *rank* as applied to mdspan is not the same as the mathematical definition of the rank of a matrix (equivalent to the number of linearly independent columns or rows) used, for example, within the context of the Householder QR decomposition example with Eigen. This naming might unfortunately seem confusing, but it's something to be aware of.

---

4 "A free function linear algebra interface based on the BLAS" (*https://wg21.link/p1673*).

Elements of the mdspan object are now accessible with another new feature in C++23: the square bracket operator with multiple indices, [i, j], rather than [i][j]:

```
for (size_t i = 0; i < mds_01.extent(0); ++i)
{
    for (size_t j = 0; j < mds_01.extent(1); ++j)
        cout << mds_01[i, j] << "\t";

    cout << "\n";
}
```

The runtime result of this nested loop displays a 3×2 matrix:

```
101     102
103     104
105     106
```

We can also define a matrix (view) with different dimensions, using the same data:

```
// This is now a 2 x 3 view of the same data:
auto mds_02 = stdex::mdspan{v.data(), 2, 3};
```

Applying the same nested loop as before, but replacing mds_01 with mds_02, results in the expected ordering:

```
101     102     103
104     105     106
```

You need to be careful here, because an mdspan object is a mutating view. Modifying data in an mdspan, or in an underlying vector, will change it in both locations. For example, modification of the last element of the vector v

```
v[5] = 419;
```

will show up in both of the mdspan objects. mds_01 becomes

```
101     102
103     104
105     419
```

and mds_02 is now

```
101     102     103
104     105     419
```

Likewise, changing the value of an element in mds_02 will be reflected in both mds_01 and the vector v.

In finance applications, the fixed numbers of rows and columns are again rarely known at compile time. Suppose m and n are the numbers of rows and columns to be determined at runtime. These dimensions can be set dynamically by replacing the fixed settings of 2 and 3 in the previous example

```
auto mds_02 = std::mdspan(v.data(), 2, 3);
```

with the std::extents{m, n} object, as shown in the mdspan definition here:

```
#include <cstdlib>          // std::size_t

void print_dynamic_mdspan
    (std::size_t m, std::size_t n, const vector<double>& vec)
{
    using std::size_t;

    std::mdspan md{vec.data(), std::extents{m, n} };

    for (size_t i = 0; i < md.extent(0); ++i)
    {
        for (size_t j = 0; j < md.extent(1); ++j)
        {
            cout << md[i, j] << "\t";
        }

        cout << "\n";
    }
}
```

The std::extents{m, n} parameter represents the number of elements in each extent—i.e., in each row (m) and column (n)—which are determined dynamically at runtime.

Pretend we have the following data set at runtime:

```
vector<double> w{10.1, 10.2, 10.3, 10.4, 10.5, 10.6};
size_t m = 3;
size_t n = 2;
```

Using these as inputs to the preceding print_dynamic_mdspan(.) function will then generate a 3 × 2 mdspan matrix view:

```
10.1    10.2
10.3    10.4
10.5    10.6
```

CTAD and mdspan

The preceding examples also make use of CTAD (introduced in Chapter 1). Both mdspan and extents are class templates, but because w in the prior example is a vector of double types, and because we have been using size_t for our extents and vector size types, the compiler will deduce that the mdspan and extents objects are to use double and size_t as template parameters.

Without CTAD, the function would need to be written as follows, with the container and element types explicitly specified, as well as the dynamic extents (`stdex::dextents`):

```
void print_dynamic_mdspan(size_t m, size_t n, const vector<double>& vec)
{
    // Generalized -- without CTAD, we would have to
    // include all these specifications:
    std::mdspan<const double, std::dextents<size_t, 2>>
        md{vec.data(), std::dextents<size_t, 2>{m, n}};

    . . .

}
```

The examples in this chapter have relied on CTAD, but in cases requiring more generality, writing out the template arguments in full will be necessary.

The `mdspan` proposal also had included a "slicing" function called `submdspan(.)` to return a view (type `std::submdspan`) of an individual row or column from a matrix represented by an `mdspan` object, but this has been moved to a separate proposal (*https://wg21.link/p2630*) (P2630) with release probably in C++26. More generally, a `submdspan` would extend to subsets of higher-dimensional arrays.

As a preview of what we can do with `submdspan`, let's return to the earlier 3×2 `mds_01` example. If we wanted to extract a view of the first row (index 0), it could be obtained as follows, with the index in the first extent (row) argument of `submdspan`:

```
using std::format;

auto row_1 = std::submdspan(mds_01, 0, std::full_extent)

for (size_t k = 0; k < row_1.extent(0); ++k)
{
    cout << format("row_1[{}] = {}", k, row_1[k]) << "\t";
}
```

This would give us the following output for the first row:

```
row_1[0] = 101  row_1[1] = 102
```

We can obtain views of rows 2 and 3 by replacing the 0 with 1 and 2 as the row extent argument, respectively:

```
auto row_2 = std::submdspan(mds_01, 1, std::full_extent);
auto row_3 = std::submdspan(mds_01, 2, std::full_extent);
```

By explicitly setting the second extent (column) argument to the column size less 1, we could also create a view of the last column:

```
auto col_last = std::submdspan(mds_01, std::full_extent, mds_01.extent(1) - 1);
```

Again, outputting this to the screen with

```
for (size_t k = 0; k < col_last.extent(0); ++k)
{
    cout << format("col_last[{}] = {}", k, col_last[k]) << "\t";
}
```

the second column elements are as follows:

```
col_last[0] = 102  col_last[1] = 104  col_last[2] = 106
```

Because a submdspan is a view to a row or a column of an mdspan, it will obviate generating an additional mdspan object. Conveniently, however, any public member function of mdspan can be applied to a submdspan. On the flip side, again as a case of a mutating view, modifying an element of a submdspan will also modify the underlying mdspan object, as well as the original contiguous container of data itself. Suppose the last element in col_last is reset:

```
col_last[2] = 3333;
```

The original mds_01 would then become the following:

```
101     102
103     104
105     3333
```

And then the original v vector would also be modified:

```
101 102 103 104 105 3333
```

One other proposal related to mdspan is a multidimesional array, called an mdarray, which is also in review. As noted in its proposal, "mdarray is as similar as possible to mdspan, except with container semantics instead of reference semantics."[5] In other words, an mdarray object *owns* its data—similar to a vector—as opposed to existing as a mutable view of the data "owned" by another container, as in the case of mdspan. The mdarray proposal is also slated for release in C++26.

Notes on Using the Sample Code

The preceding code examples for mdspan and submdspan can be compiled in C++20 by using the code currently available on the mdspan (and mdarray) GitHub site (*https://oreil.ly/xVcs0*). At the time of this writing, not all vendors have fully implemented mdspan, and submdspan—a reference implementation of which is also

---

5 "mdarray: An Owning Multidimensional Array Analog of mdspan" (*https://oreil.ly/AkJOd*), ISO C++ proposal P1684.

available in this repository—will not be available until C++26. Installation and building instructions are included with the repository, but you should be aware of two particular items. First, the repository code is currently scoped under the namespace `std::experimental`. Second, as the square bracket operator for multiple indices is available only as of C++23, you can replace it with the round bracket operator (similar to Eigen) for C++20 and earlier:

```
namespace stdex = std::experimental;

auto mds_01 = stdex::mdspan{v.data(), 3, 2};

// Replace the square brackets here:
for (size_t i = 0; i < n_rows; ++i)
{
    for (size_t j = 0; j < n_cols; ++j)
    {
        cout << mds_01[i, j]    << "\t";
    }
}

// with round brackets:
for (size_t i = 0; i < n_rows; ++i)
{
    for (size_t j = 0; j < n_cols; ++j)
    {
        cout << mds_01(i, j) << "\t";
    }
}
```

BLAS Interface

This proposal is for "a C++ Standard Library dense linear algebra interface based on the dense Basic Linear Algebra Subprograms (BLAS)," [6] also simply referred to as *stdBLAS*. BLAS libraries date back decades and were originally written in Fortran, but they evolved into a standard in the early 2000s, with implementations in other languages such as C (OpenBLAS) and CUDA C++ (NVIDIA) now available, as well as C bindings to Fortran.

Fortran BLAS distributions support four numerical types: FLOAT, DOUBLE, COMPLEX, and DOUBLE COMPLEX. The C++ equivalents are float, double, std::complex<float>, and std::complex<double>. BLAS libraries contain several matrix formats (standard, symmetric, upper/lower triangular), as well as matrix

---

6 "A free function linear algebra interface based on the BLAS" (*https://wg21.link/p1673*), ISO C++ proposal P1673.

and vector operations such as element-by-element addition and matrix/vector multiplication.

With implementation of this proposal, we could apply the same C++ codebase to any compatible library containing BLAS functionality. This will allow for portable code, independent of the underlying library being used. Standard Library vendors might choose to implement P1673 with an existing BLAS library, and the proposal was designed to make that a straightforward path for vendors to take. One major development has been NVIDIA's implementation both of mdspan and stdBLAS, now available in its HPC SDK (*https://oreil.ly/hnrdL*).

Note that stdBLAS itself would provide access to only a particular subset of matrix operations—to be discussed next—even if an underlying library provides additional features such as matrix decompositions and least squares solvers.

The original BLAS functions are preceded by the type contained in the matrix and/or vector to which they are applied. For example, the function for multiplication of a matrix by a vector is of the form

```
xGEMV(.)
```

The x can be S, D, C, or Z, meaning single precision (REAL in Fortran), double precision (DOUBLE), complex (COMPLEX), and double-precision complex (DOUBLE COMPLEX), respectively.

The equivalent C++ function in the proposal, matrix_vector_product(.) would instead take in mdspan objects representing a matrix and a vector. For example, we can look at a case involving double values, using m and n for the number of rows and columns as before:

```
std::vector<double> A_vec(m * n);
std::vector<double> x_vec(n);

// A_vec and x_vec are then populated with data...

std::vector<double> y_vec(n);

std::mdspan A{A_vec.data(), std::extents{m, n}};
std::mdspan x{x_vec.data(), std::extents{n}};
std::mdspan y{y_vec.data(), std::extents{m}};
```

Then, performing the multiplication, the vector product is stored in y:

```
std::linalg::matrix_vector_product(A, x, y);    // y = A * x
```

Table 8-1 provides a subset of BLAS functions proposed in P1673 that should be useful in financial programming. The BLAS functions here are generalized, assumed to be in double-precision form, and any given matrix/vector expressions can be assumed to be of appropriate dimensions.

Table 8-1. Selected BLAS functions in proposal P1673

BLAS function	P1673 function	Description
DSCAL	`scale`	Multiplies a vector **v** by a scalar *a*
DCOPY	`copy`	Copies a vector to another vector
DAXPY	`add`	Calculates *a***x** + **y**, vectors **x** & **y**, scalar *a*
DDOT	`dot`	Dot (inner) product of two vectors
DNRM2	`vector_norm2`	Euclidean norm of a vector
DGEMV	`matrix_vector_product`	Calculates *a***Ax** + *β***y**, matrix **A**, vector **y**, scalars *a* & *β*
DSYMV	`symmetric_matrix_vector_product`	Same as DGEMV (`matrix_vector_product`) but where **A** is symmetric
DGEMM	`matrix_product`	Calculates *a***AB** + *β***C**, for matrices **A**, **B**, & **C**, and scalars *a* & *β*

Summary

This chapter has examined some of the past, present, and expected future of linear algebra in C++. In the late 2000s, high-quality open source linear algebra libraries such as Eigen arrived on the scene and were well received by the financial quant C++ programming community. In the present day, these libraries contain not only much of the same functionality found in the BLAS standard, but also a plethora of matrix decompositions that are frequently used in financial applications.

The future also looks brighter for ISO C++ with `mdspan` (P0009) added to C++23, the BLAS interface (P1673) accepted for C++26, and `submdspan` also likely to be released in C++26. These are features that quantitative financial developers probably feel are long overdue, but they will provide a big step in satisfying demand not just from the financial industry, but also from other computationally intensive domains, such as predictive analytics, artificial intelligence, biotechnology, particle physics, and engineering.

Further Resources

For more information about the Blaze linear algebra library, the CppCon 2016 talk by Klaus Iglberger, "The Blaze High Performance Math Library" (*https://oreil.ly/MuFrj*), provides an excellent overview.

The following are Rcpp packages integrating C++ linear algebra libraries with R:

- RcppEigen (*https://oreil.ly/q3bwq*)
- RcppArmadillo (*https://oreil.ly/hKyMG*)
- RcppBlaze3 (*https://oreil.ly/BQQUM*)

- Boost Headers, including uBLAS (*https://oreil.ly/cyTn8*)

For information about addition of generic vector and element types, also extending to multiplication and operations on generic matrices, see the following:

- Section 5.3 of *Discovering Modern C++* (*https://oreil.ly/koP89*), 2nd edition, by Peter Gottschling (Addison-Wesley, 2021)
- DevTut tutorial: "A basic example illustrating expression templates" (*https://oreil.ly/6X0xj*)
- Numerical Linear Algebra_ by Lloyd Trefethen and David Bau III (SIAM, 1997):
  — Chapter 11, "QR Factorization," page 83
  — Chapter 17, "Triangular Systems," Algorithm 17.1, page 122

For additional information about dense matrix decompositions in Eigen, refer to the following sections of the Eigen documentation:

- "Basic linear solving" (*https://oreil.ly/4OonA*)
- "Catalogue of dense decompositions" (*https://oreil.ly/013cV*)
- "Benchmark of dense decompositions" (*https://oreil.ly/l-NQp*)

CHAPTER 9

The Boost Libraries

The *Boost libraries*, as noted on the official website (*https://www.boost.org*), are "free peer-reviewed portable C++ source libraries...that work well with the C++ Standard Library." They are open source libraries released under the Boost Software License (*https://oreil.ly/haVDM*), which allows their use in other libraries, systems, and applications—including commercial use—"with minimal restrictions." This chapter covers Boost libraries (such as the Boost Math Toolkit) that can be useful in financial and other quantitative applications. Other Boost libraries—not necessarily mathematical—that lend themselves well to these disciplines are also covered.

A fair amount of the content in Boost libraries has found its way into C++ Standard Library implementations. As stated in the documentation, Boost authors "aim to establish *existing practice* and provide reference implementations so that Boost libraries are suitable for eventual standardization." This is not to say everything in Boost is destined for inclusion in the Standard Library, and it should be noted there can be differences in content and implementation, as well as authorship, with respect to the Boost features that have been incorporated into modern C++.

Table 9-1 provides a list of C++ libraries and language features discussed in previous chapters that can be traced to earlier implementations in Boost.

We will first look at two features in the Boost Math Toolkit library: mathematical constants and statistical distributions. Although mathematical constants have been added to the Standard Library, the Boost version contains two commonly used constants in particular that were curiously missing from the C++20 version.

This will be followed by a look at the Boost MultiArray library, which can be used for implementing lattice pricing models for options. We will conclude with Boost Accumulators, which can be used for managing trading indicators and signals.

Table 9-1. New Standard C++ features with previous Boost implementations

Feature	Boost library	Description/examples	Release	Chapter
Mathematical special functions	Math Toolkit	Gamma functions, Bessel functions, Legendre polynomials	C++17	1
Mathematical constants	Math Toolkit	$\pi, e, \frac{1}{2}, \sqrt{2}, \frac{1}{\sqrt{2\pi}}, log(2)$	C++20	1
Smart pointers	SmartPtr	`shared_ptr`	C++11	3
Task-based concurrency	Thread	`future, async`	C++11	6
Distributional random number generation	Random	`normal_distribution,` `student_t_distribution, mt19937_64`	C++11	6

Before proceeding, there is one important point to note regarding installation of the Boost libraries. A large portion of the source code consists of header-only implementations (template code, similar to Eigen), but it also includes implementation source files requiring compilation. The libraries discussed in this chapter, however, are all header-only. As such, it will suffice to download the compressed file (*https://oreil.ly/ohJ8D*) suitable for your operating system, extract the header files only (Boost uses the *.hpp* extension), and specify their location in your compiler settings. In the examples that follow, as well as those in the Boost documentation, these header files are assumed to be located under a `boost` directory or subdirectory.

Mathematical Constants

C++20 added mathematical constants to the Standard Library, but as you've seen, commonly used constants representing the values $\frac{1}{\sqrt{2}}$ and $\frac{1}{\sqrt{2\pi}}$ were curiously missing. Prior to C++20, the Boost Math Toolkit already contained a set of `constexpr` mathematical constants, meaning the values are determined at compile time, which avoids function calls at runtime. Most of the C++20 mathematical constants are also provided in Boost, although one exception is the mysterious $\frac{1}{\sqrt{3}}$. Some of the naming conventions are the same, such as the obvious `e` and `pi`, but notable differences exist. For example, the natural log of 2 in the Standard Library is `ln2`, while in Boost it is `ln_2`. Also, inverses are different, such as $\frac{1}{\pi}$. This is `inv_pi` in the Standard Library, but `one_div_pi` in Boost.

Finally, as for $\frac{1}{\sqrt{2}}$ and $\frac{1}{\sqrt{2\pi}}$, these *are* available in Boost as `one_div_root_two` and `one_div_root_two_pi`, respectively.

Boost mathematical constants are defined in the header file `boost/math/constants/constants.hpp`, and so this file must be included in order for your code to compile. They are scoped with the namespace `boost::math::double_constants`. As a demonstration of using Boost mathematical constants, a lambda that implements the mathematical definition of the standard normal probability density function (PDF) is shown here, using the `one_div_root_two_pi` and `half` constants:

```
#include <boost/math/constants/constants.hpp>

// . . .

// Standard Normal Probability Density Function (pdf)
auto std_norm_pdf = [](double x) -> double
{
    return boost::math::double_constants::one_div_root_two_pi
        * std::exp(-boost::math::double_constants::half * x * x);
};

double y = std_norm_pdf(0.0);        // Approx: 0.39894
```

You can find more information on Boost mathematical constants in Chapter 4 of the Boost Math Toolkit documentation (*https://oreil.ly/TU2CL*). The Boost website also provides a full list of its mathematical constants (*https://oreil.ly/_k0yG*).

Statistical Distributions

In the previous section, we looked at implementing the standard normal PDF. That example demonstrated how to use Boost mathematical constants, but now we will look at a more robust approach: using the set of *statistical distributions and functions* in the Boost Math Toolkit. The beauty of this library is that it is incredibly easy and straightforward to use, while it provides useful functionality for computational finance applications.

The available distributions include the normal, Student's t (aka t-distribution), and uniform distributions, plus others that are sometimes used in finance such as the log normal, Pareto, skew normal, and noncentral t-distributions. In addition, an empirical cumulative distribution function object takes in a data set and performs goodness-of-fit tests with known distributions. A full list of the distributions supported by Boost is as follows:

Arcsine	Bernoulli	Beta	Binomial	Cauchy-Lorentz
Chi-squared	Exponential	Extreme value	F	Gamma
Geometric	Hyperexponential	Hypergeometric	Inverse chi-squared	Inverse gamma
Inverse Gaussian (or inverse normal)	Kolmogorov-Smirnov	Laplace	Logistic	Log normal
Negative binomial	Noncentral beta	Noncentral chi-squared	Noncentral F	Noncentral t
Normal (Gaussian)	Pareto	Poisson	Rayleigh	Skew normal
Student's t	Triangular	Uniform	Weibull	

Links to the respective details of each distribution are available in the "Statistical Distributions Reference" section (*https://oreil.ly/XT4b1*) of the Boost Math Toolkit documentation, Chapter 5.

Probability Functions

Recall that Chapter 6 introduced statistical distributions in the Standard Library for the express purpose of generating random numbers from among 17 textbook distributions. The Boost Statistical Distributions library, in contrast, provides the following deterministic functions for an even broader range of distributions, as listed just previously, 34 in all:

- Probability density function (PDF)
- Cumulative distribution function (CDF)
- Quantile function
- Complement function

The way it works is you construct a distribution object (e.g., a normal or Student's t-distribution) and then use it as an argument in any of these four functions. Distributions in Boost can be obtained by including the header file boost/math/ distributions.hpp and applying the boost::math namespace scope.

Alternatively, the individual header files can be included separately, for example:

```
#include <boost/math/distributions/normal.hpp>      // Normal distribution
#include <boost/math/distributions/students_t.hpp>   // t-distribution
```

We will use the normal and t-distributions in the examples that follow:

- The standard normal distribution has default arguments mean = 0 and standard deviation = 1.
- With a nonstandard normal distribution, the mean and standard deviation are the constructor parameters.
- The t-distribution takes in the degrees of freedom as its constructor argument.

```
#include <boost/math/distributions.hpp>
using boost::math::students_t;
using boost::math::normal;

// Construct a normal distribution with mean 0 and standard deviation 1:
normal std_normal{};

// Construct a non-standard normal distribution
// with mean 0.08 and standard deviation 0.25:
normal non_std_normal{0.08, 0.25};
```

```
// Construct a students_t distribution with 4 degrees of freedom:
students_t stu_t{4};
```

The distribution classes have statistical parameter accessor functions that are particular to each distribution. For example, with the normal class, it is possible to retrieve the mean and standard deviation, and for students_t, the degrees of freedom:

```
double mean = std_normal.mean();
double sd = std_normal.standard_deviation();

mean = non_std_normal.mean();
sd = non_std_normal.standard_deviation();

double dof = stu_t.degrees_of_freedom();
```

Nonmember PDF, CDF, and quantile (percentile) functions will calculate these values for any Boost distribution for a given value. These are taken in as arguments, as shown here:

```
// PDF and CDF values for the standard normal
// and Student's t distributions at x = 0:
double n_pdf = pdf(std_normal, 0.0);          // 0.3989
double n_cdf = cdf(std_normal, 0.0);          // 0.5
double t_pdf = pdf(stu_t, 0.0);               // 0.375
double t_cdf = cdf(stu_t, 0.0);               // 0.5

// The lower fifth percentile of the standard normal distribution:
double five_pctle = quantile(std_normal, 0.05);    // -1.64485
```

Take care when calculating upper quantiles approaching the 100th percentile, as the function value is unbounded and, as noted in the Boost Math Toolkit documentation (*https://oreil.ly/F4hmp*), can cause overflow errors. Instead, the complement(.) function applied to lower percentiles is recommended in the case of symmetric distributions.

For example, here's an attempted calculation of a very high percentile:

```
students_t stu_t_100{100};

double very_high_quantile = quantile(stu_t_100, 1 - 1e-100);
```

This is nearly the same as attempting a calculation of the 100th percentile, which is not a finite value:

```
quantile(stu_t_100, 1); // This will blow up
```

As a result, attempting to calculate the $(1 - 1 \times 10^{-100}) \times 100$th percentile could cause an overflow error.

Instead, you can apply the complement function as follows:

```
double very_high_quantile = quantile(complement(stu_t_100, 1e-100));
cout << "t-dist((1 - 1e-100) x 100%-tile (using complement) = "
    << very_high_quantile << "\n\n";
```

This way, a finite value of about 96.3147 is safely returned.

Drawdown Example, Revisited

Recall from Chapter 6, we generated 100 maximum drawdown values by rearranging round-trip trades from a trading strategy backtest. To determine the 95th percentile confidence limit for the worst possible maximum drawdown, under the assumption of the values following a normal distribution, instead of hardcoding $Z_{0.95} = 1.64485$ as before, we can now just call the Boost `quantile(.)` function:

```
// Data from Ch 6:
vector<double> max_drawdowns{1745348.76, 1753314.05,
    1811060.31, ..., 5687134.51};

auto norm_params = [](const vector<double>& v) -> array<double, 2>
{
    double mean = (1.0 / v.size())* std::accumulate(v.begin(), v.end(), 0.0);

    double sum_sq = 0.0;
    for (double val : v)
    {
        sum_sq += (val - mean) * (val - mean);
    }

        return array<double, 2>
            {mean, (1.0 / std::sqrt(v.size()))* std::sqrt(sum_sq)};
};

auto params = norm_params(max_drawdowns);
double mean = params[0];
double sd = params[1];

// Use the Boost quantile function -- no more hardcoding:
double z_95 = quantile(std_normal, 0.95);        // ~= 1.65
double upper_conf_intvl_norm_95 = mean + sd * z_95;
```

Furthermore, this means we can determine an upper confidence limit for any arbitrary percentile, such as at 97.5% or 99%:

```
double z_97_5 = quantile(std_normal, 0.975);
double upper_conf_intvl_norm_97_5 = mean + sd * z_97_5;

double z_99 = quantile(complement(std_normal, 0.01));
double upper_conf_intvl_norm_99 = mean + sd * z_99;
```

Checking these results

```
cout << std::fixed << std::setprecision(2);
cout << "Std Norm 95%-tile ~= " << z_95
    << ",\nUsing Boost stat dist: Max DD upper 95% Conf Level = "
    << upper_conf_intvl_norm_95 << "\n\n";

cout << "Std Norm 97.5%-tile ~= " << z_97_5
    << ",\nUsing Boost stat dist: Max DD upper 97.5% Conf Level = "
    << upper_conf_intvl_norm_97_5 << "\n\n";

cout << "Std Norm 95%-tile ~= " << z_99
    << ",\nUsing Boost stat dist: Max DD upper 95% Conf Level = "
    << upper_conf_intvl_norm_99 << "\n\n";
```

gives us the following

```
Std Norm 95%-tile ~= 1.64,
Using Boost stat dist: Max DD upper 95% Conf Level = 4386229.72

Std Norm 97.5%-tile ~= 1.96,
Using Boost stat dist: Max DD upper 97.5% Conf Level = 4654646.30

Std Norm 95%-tile ~= 2.33,
Using Boost stat dist: Max DD upper 95% Conf Level = 4966738.58
```

Random Number Generation with Boost Distributions

As previously noted, 34 distributions are available in Boost, but only 17 random number distributions are in the Standard Library. What if you want to generate a random sample by using a Boost distribution that is not available in the Standard Library? This is possible by applying the probability integral transformation theorem: you could generate uniform variates on the interval [0,1) by using the Standard Library, and then apply the Boost percentile(.) function on the distribution you want to draw from. The random uniform values are the inputs, and in fact, you can write a class that mimics the provided distributions in the Standard Library.

To address the issue of fat tails and skewness in financial returns data, distributions that capture these properties are often fitted to the data. Although there is no option within the Standard Library <random> functions, we can build one around the non-central t-distribution (*https://oreil.ly/iTSV-*) available in Boost.

Using a form similar to the Standard Library <random> classes, we can write a class template—say, rand_non_central_t_dist—with the default template parameter double. This works by first using the std::uniform_real_distribution class to generate uniform variates on the interval [0,1). Each random uniform value is then passed into the Boost quantile(.) function, along with a Boost non_central_t_distribution object. The rand_non_central_t_dist functor outputs the next noncentral t-variate, just like any <random> distribution in the Standard Library. To keep matters simpler for demonstration, we will set the random engine as `std::mt19937_64`, the 64-bit Mersenne Twister type (introduced in Chapter 6). The class implementation follows, with the constructor argument nu representing the degrees of freedom ν, and the noncentrality parameter as `delta` (δ):

```
#include <random>

template<typename T = double>
class rand_non_central_t_dist
{
public:
    // nu = degrees of freedom
    // delta = non-centrality parameter
    rand_non_central_t_dist(double nu, double delta) :nu_{nu}, delta_{delta} {}

    // Functor similar to <random> in the Standard Library:
    T operator()(std::mt19937_64& mt)
    {
        auto unif = ud_(mt);      // Next in pseudorandom unif[0, 1) sequence
        boost::math::non_central_t_distribution nctd(nu_, delta_);
        return quantile(nctd, unif);
    }

private:
    double nu_, delta_;
    std::mt19937_64 mt_;
    std::uniform_real_distribution<T> ud_{0.0, 1.0};
};
```

Now, assuming the ν and δ parameters have been determined externally from fitting the returns data (e.g., $\nu = 3$ and $\delta = -0.05$), and choosing a seed of 100 for the 64-bit Mersenne Twister engine, we can randomly generate values from the same distribution and place them in a vector:

```
std::mt19937_64 mt{100};
rand_non_central_t_dist<> st{3.0, -0.05};

auto skew_gen = [&mt, &st]()
{
    return st(mt);
};

std::vector<double> nc_t_vals(20);      // nc = noncentral
std::ranges::generate(nc_t_vals, skew_gen);

for (auto s : skew_t_vals)
{
    print_this(s);                      // Defined in Ch 4
}
```

Using the Microsoft Visual Studio version of `std::mt19937_64`, this gives us the following:

```
2.5563 -0.5635  2.9834 -1.4638 1.5790 -0.0650  2.3925  0.4996 1.2055  1.6566
3.1876 -1.1217 -0.0011 -0.1826 0.1634  0.2800 -1.3585 -0.7891 1.2264 -2.0330
```

 To keep the code example more readable, no bounds checking occurred before applying the Boost `quantile(.)` function inside the body of the `()` operator, but in practice this would be advisable, as discussed in "Probability Functions" on page 326.

MultiArray

The *Boost Multidimensional Array* library (aka MultiArray) features the `boost::multi_array` class template. This class provides a clean and efficient implementation of multidimensional arrays. The Boost MultiArray documentation (*https://oreil.ly/kdRP1*) describes the library as follows:

> The classes in this library implement a common interface, formalized as a generic programming concept. The interface design is in line with the precedent set by the C++ Standard Library containers. Boost MultiArray is a more efficient and convenient way to express N-dimensional arrays than existing alternatives (especially the `std::vector<std::vector<. . .>>` formulation of N-dimensional arrays).

In particular, for a common finance application, this library can provide a convenient out-of-the box data structure for implementing binomial lattices for option pricing.

A Simple Two-Dimensional MultiArray

A Boost `MultiArray` in two dimensions defines a matrix-like object that can store an arbitrary, but same-type entry in each element or node. A simple example is a 2×3 array containing `std::string` objects. Each dimension is defined by an *extent*, similar to that described in Chapter 8, with the non-owning `mdspan`. This means, for example, that the first extent can be thought of as a row. The second extent then refers to a column (both are zero-indexed).

A 2×3 `MultiArray` can be created as follows, with `std::string` as its template parameter type. The Boost library `multi_array.hpp` header needs to be included as shown:

```
#include <boost/multi_array.hpp>
#include <string>

// . . .

using std::string, std::format;

// Each element can be individually set, with each index placed
// in its respective square bracket operator:
```

```
boost::multi_array<string, 2> ma{boost::extents[2][3]};
ma[0][0] = "Carl";
ma[0][1] = "Friedrich";
ma[0][2] = "Gauss";
ma[1][0] = "John";
ma[1][1] = "von";
ma[1][2] = "Neumann"

cout << format("Number of extents (dimensions) = {}\n", ma.num_dimensions());
cout << format("Row size = {}, Col size = {}\n\n", ma.shape()[0], ma.shape()[1]);


for (unsigned i = 0; i < ma.shape()[0]; ++i)          // ma.shape()[0] = 2
{
    for (unsigned j = 0; j < ma.shape()[1]; ++j)      // ma.shape()[1] = 3
    {
        cout << std::setw(10) << ma[i][j] << "\t";
    }
    cout << "\n";
}
```

Note that the member function shape(), followed by the respective extent index in the [.] operator, can be used to return the number of elements in each extent.

The result then displays information about the MultiArray ma, followed by the message in two rows and three columns:

```
Number of extents (dimensions) = 2
Row size = 2, Col size = 3

Carl        Friedrich         Gauss
John              von       Neumann
```

If a mismatch occurs between the number of extents specified in the multi_array template parameter and the number of extent sizes specified with boost::extents, such as

```
// num extents = 2, but only one extent size specified:
boost::multi_array<string, 2>
    ma_ext_omit{boost::extents[3]};
```

or

```
// num extents = 2, but three extent sizes specified:
boost::multi_array<string, 2>
    ma_ext_exceed{boost::extents[3][5][7]};
```

a compile-time error will be generated.

To use a `MultiArray` to price options, the `std::string` type is replaced with a struct or class that holds the projected underlying equity price and payoff at each node, as discussed next.

Binomial Lattice Option Pricing

As a class template, `boost::multi_array` is generic, this makes it convenient for storing generated price and payoff data in node objects. For example, consider a binomial lattice for pricing a European or American option. At each node in the `MultiArray`, we could place a simple struct, say `Node`, that will store the generated underlying prices traversing the lattice out to expiration, and then the calculated interim payoffs at each node when traversing back toward the valuation date:

```
struct Node
{
    double underlying;
    double payoff;
};
```

Before proceeding with the code example, let's review the binomial lattice pricing method. The time to expiration—say, from $t = 0$ to $t = T$ (in units of years or a year fraction)—is divided into smaller discrete time steps of equal length Δ. Starting with the spot price of the equity S_0 at time $t = 0$, a recombining tree, or lattice, will result from assumed constant up and down price movements. In other words, for any underlying equity price at one node, that price can assume only one of these two "states of the world" over a time step of Δ, by multiplying the price by fixed up and down factors u and d. As the lattice expands over time, a set of possible equity price scenarios is generated, terminating at expiration of the option at time $t = T$. At expiration, the terminal payoffs are calculated based on an exercise price X.

A probability is assigned to an up move and is denoted by p; hence, the probability of a down move is $1 - p$. The up and down multipliers, u and d, are dependent on the particular discretization chosen. One of the most popular methods is the Jarrow-Rudd discretization, which we will use for the examples that follow. The value of p then falls out from the calculations of u and d.

In a Jarrow-Rudd discretization, the resulting up and down multipliers u and d are as follows. The notation that follows is described in Section 7.3 of *Option Theory* by Peter James (Wiley 2003):

$$u = e^{\sigma\sqrt{\Delta t}}$$

$$d = \frac{1}{u} = e^{-\sigma\sqrt{\Delta t}}$$

Here, σ represents a constant annual volatility rate. The annual risk-free interest rate and dividend rate are also assumed to be constant continuous rates r and q.

The probability p is then as follows:

$$p = \frac{e^{(r-q)\Delta t} - e^{-\sigma\sqrt{\Delta t}}}{e^{\sigma\sqrt{\Delta t}} - e^{-\sigma\sqrt{\Delta t}}}$$

To see how we could use a Boost `MultiArray` to implement a binomial lattice, let's first look at a simple example of an at-the-money European call option with the following data, taken from Chapter 10 of the 2018 O'Reilly book *Python for Finance* 2nd edition, by Yves Hilpisch (with special thanks to the author for his permission to use this example):

$S_0 = 36$

$X = 36$ (exercise price)

$r = 6\%$ (risk-free interest rate)

$q = 0$ (dividend rate: assume none)

$\sigma = 20\%$ (volatility)

$T = 1$ (time to maturity: one year)

$n = 4$ (number of time steps, starting from $t = 0$)

$\Delta t = \frac{T}{n}$ (time step length $= \frac{1}{4} = 0.25$)

From this data, we can determine the following:

$u = 1.10517$

$d = 0.90484$

$p = 0.55000$

Prospectively multiplying each underlying price by u and d, the generated price paths result in the lattice shown in Figure 9-1.

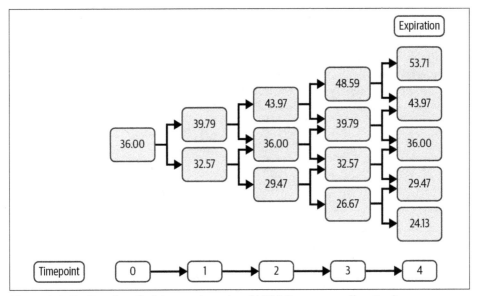

Figure 9-1. Projected underlying equity prices (ATM European call option)

The payoff at each of the five terminal nodes (at timepoint 4) is the call payoff $\max\left(S_T^{(i)} - K, 0\right)$ for $i = 0, \cdots, 4$ (zero-indexed in C++).

The option value is determined by working backward in time along the lattice, calculating the discounted expected payoffs based on the subsequent up and down underlying values, the probabilities of each (p and $1 - p$), and the continuous discount factor over each time step. This discount factor, from an arbitrary timepoint t to $t - \Delta t$, is shown here:

$$e^{-(r - 0)\Delta t} = 0.98511 \text{ (dividend is zero)}$$

Now, for example, the payoff of the uppermost node (with projected underlying value = 48.59) prior to expiration (at time $T - \Delta t$) would be as follows:

$$e^{-r\Delta t}\left[(53.71 - 36)p + (43.97 - 36)(1 - p)\right] =$$

$$e^{-0.06(0.25)}\left[17.7057(0.55) + 7.9705(0.45)\right] = 13.1265$$

This can be seen in Figure 9-2, which also shows the rest of the discounted expected payoffs traversing back to $t = 0$.

Repeating this process for every node gives us the lattice as shown, with both projected underlying equity prices and discounted payoffs (the latter indicated in bold font). The value of the option is $3.77, the discounted expected payoff at the starting node.

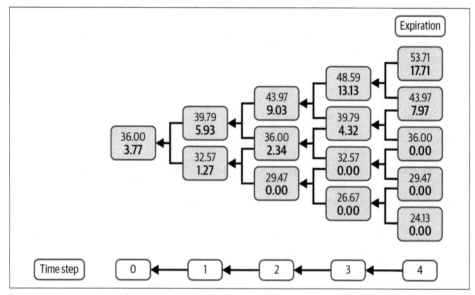

Figure 9-2. Discounted expected payoffs with projected underlying equity prices (ATM European call option)

When setting this up in a two-dimensional MultiArray in code, configuration will be more convenient with an up movement from each element in a given column except for the last, which is a down movement. This works because we have a recombining tree, so an up movement starting from any of a given column's elements—other than its first (top) element—also corresponds to a down movement from the preceding element.

This way, computing the projected prices becomes a reasonably simple nested iteration. The outer loop moves horizontally over time over each column, and then for each timepoint, the inner loop applies the up multiplier to every element, plus a down movement from the last (bottom) element. The result takes the form of an upper triangular array, as shown in Figure 9-3. Note that because we are working in C++, zero-indexing applies to both column and row indices.

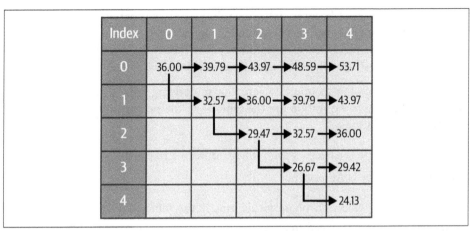

Index	0	1	2	3	4
0	36.00 →	39.79 →	43.97 →	48.59 →	53.71
1		32.57 →	36.00 →	39.79 →	43.97
2			29.47 →	32.57 →	36.00
3				26.67 →	29.42
4					24.13

Figure 9-3. Projected underlying equity prices in a binomial lattice

Moving backward in time from maturity to option valuation at $t = 0$, the respective expected discounted payoffs can be computed. In this case, each payoff value depends on the payoffs in the two adjacent nodes in the next time step forward. In the code example in "Implementation with Boost MultiArray" on page 339, each (*price*, *payoff*) pair will reside in a Node struct, contained in an upper triangular MultiArray. Displayed in Figure 9-4, the projected underlying values are shown in each node, with the respective payoff now in bold type.

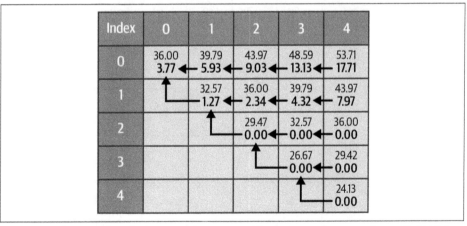

Index	0	1	2	3	4
0	36.00 **3.77** ←	39.79 **5.93** ←	43.97 **9.03** ←	48.59 **13.13** ←	53.71 **17.71**
1		32.57 **1.27** ←	36.00 **2.34** ←	39.79 **4.32** ←	43.97 **7.97**
2			29.47 **0.00** ←	32.57 **0.00** ←	36.00 **0.00**
3				26.67 **0.00** ←	29.42 **0.00**
4					24.13 **0.00**

Figure 9-4. Projected underlying equity prices with discounted expected payoffs (ATM European call option)

American options

Applying a binomial lattice to calculate the price of a European option is not all that interesting, as it is just an approximation of the closed-form Black-Scholes solution. A lattice does become useful in valuing options that allow early exercise, as it becomes necessary to check whether it is optimal to exercise the option at each node, because no closed-form solution exists. The most common example is an American option, which allows for exercise at any time prior to expiration.

Consider the following example, where the underlying spot price, risk-free rate, volatility, and time to expiration are the same as in the previous example, except for the following variations:

- The option type is a deep in-the-money put with strike price = 40.
- The payoff type is American.

The equity price projection phase yields exactly the same results as before. On the return trip, however, we need to compare the actual payoff $\max\left(X - S_t^{(i)}\right)$ against the projected equity price at each node. If the actual payoff is greater than the expected payoff, the former replaces the latter, as it would then be optimal to exercise the option at that point.

You can see this, for example, in row index 2 and column index 3 of the lattice result in Figure 9-5.

Index	0	1	2	3	4
0	36.00 4.54	39.79 2.31	43.97 0.79	48.59 0.00	53.71 0.00
1		32.57 6.97 7.42	36.00 4.25	39.79 1.77	43.97 0.00
2			29.47 9.93 10.53	32.57 6.83 7.43	36.00 4.00
3				26.67 12.74 13.33	29.47 10.53
4					24.13 15.87

Figure 9-5. Projected underlying equity prices with discounted expected payoffs for an ITM American put option

The discounted expected payoff computed in the usual way is 6.83, but if we look at the payoff based on the projected equity price at that point, subtracting 32.57 from the strike price of 40.00 gives us 7.43. Because this is greater than the expected payoff, we replace it (denoted by strike-through) with the updated value of 7.43. The same is true in the bottom node in column 3 ($t = 3$, $i = 3$), where the expected payoff is replaced with the actual payoff of 13.33.

These values are then used for the discounted expected payoff calculation in the last node in the previous time step ($t = 2$, $i = 2$), which comes out to 9.93, but again this is replaced by the actual payoff of 10.53. The actual payoff in the top node in this time step ($t = 2$, $i = 0$), however, is zero, so we keep the expected payoff of 0.79. Continuing this process back to the $t = 0$ node gives us the estimated option price of 4.54.

The nodes shaded with figures in the white font in Figure 9-5 form the *optimal early exercise boundary*.

Implementation with Boost MultiArray

A way to implement a lattice model in C++ is to define a class, BinomialLattice Pricer, that will hold a MultiArray<Node> member called grid_, and where the Node struct is as defined previously. A series of private member functions will then project the underlying prices forward and calculate the payoffs at each node moving in reverse order, arriving at the option price at $t = 0$. In the process, the underlying price on each Node element is updated moving forward in time, and then the discounted expected payoff member is calculated and set over the return trip.

This is not the only way to implement lattice models, and other methods may be out there (some proprietary) that yield better performance. The point here is that a Boost MultiArray gives you a generalized and proven underlying structure, so you don't have to implement it from scratch yourself, and its performance may very well be within the range required.

Recall from Chapter 3, we had the OptionInfo class that holds a unique pointer member to a CallPayoff or PutPayoff, determined at runtime, derived from an abstract Payoff base object. It also holds the time remaining until expiration of the option (in units of years, or a year fraction), and it will compute the option payoff for a given underlying spot price value in its option_payoff(.) member function:

```
#include "Payoffs.h"
#include <memory>

class OptionInfo
{
public:
    OptionInfo(std::unique_ptr<Payoff> payoff, double time_to_exp);
    double option_payoff(double spot) const;
    double time_to_expiration() const;
```

```
private:
    std::unique_ptr<Payoff> payoff_ptr_;
    double time_to_exp_;
};
```

For this demonstration, we are assuming that the option types are limited to European and American, defined in an enum class:

```
enum class OptType
{
    Euro,
    American
};
```

The lattice pricing class can then be summarized with its declaration. Each function is explained within the context of the class implementation that follows:

```
#include <boost/multi_array.hpp>
#include "OptionInfo.h"

class BinomialLatticePricer
{
public:
    BinomialLatticePricer(OptionInfo opt,
        double vol, double int_rate, int time_points,
        double div_rate = 0.0);

    double calc_price(double spot, OptType opt_type);

private:
    OptionInfo opt_;
    int time_points_;
    double div_rate_;

    // Will be calculated and reassigned in the constructor:
    double u_{0.0}, d_{0.0}, p_{0.0};    // up and down factors
                                         // and probability of up move

    double disc_fctr_{0.0};        // Discount factor

    boost::multi_array<Node, 2> grid_;

    void project_underlying_prices_(double spot);
    double calculate_node_payoffs_(OptType opt_type);

    // Helper functions called from calculate_node_payoffs_(.):
    double disc_expected_val_(int i, int j) const;
    void american_payoffs_();
    void european_payoffs_();
};
```

A BinomialLatticePricer object takes in an OptionInfo at construction that is stored as a data member. Because an OptionInfo object holds a unique pointer to

---

its payoff, we will need to explicitly move it in the constructor initialization in the implementation that follows.

Along with the `OptionInfo` argument, the `BinomialLatticePricer` constructor takes in the market data necessary to compute the values used in the Jarrow-Rudd discretization, as well as the desired number of time steps set by the user. The length of a time step Δt (dt), the u (u_) and d (d_) factors, and the probability p (p_) of an upward move in the underlying equity price are then calculated and set in the body of the constructor. Finally, the Boost `MultiArray` member, `grid_`, is sized according to the number of timepoints, including $t = 0$ (`time_steps + 1`). This will also be the number of terminal payoff nodes of the lattice:

```
#include "BinomialLatticePricer.h"

#include <algorithm>
#include <limits>
#include <utility>          // std::move

BinomialLatticePricer::BinomialLatticePricer(OptionInfo opt,
        double vol, double int_rate, int time_steps, double div_rate) :
        opt_{std::move(opt)}, time_points_{time_steps + 1}, div_rate_{div_rate}
{
        double dt{opt_.time_to_expiration() / time_steps};
        u_ = std::exp(vol * std::sqrt(dt));
        d_ = 1.0 / u_;
        p_ = 0.5 * (1.0 + (int_rate - div_rate - 0.5 * vol * vol)
            * std::sqrt(dt) / vol);

        disc_fctr_ = std::exp(-int_rate*dt);

        grid_.resize(boost::extents[time_points_][time_points_]);
}
```

The public member function `calc_price(.)` serves as an interface that sets the pricing computation in motion. It takes in the spot price of the underlying equity and the option type, American or European, as inputs.

At a high level, the labor is then divided between two private member functions that project the underlying prices from the initial node out to expiration (`project_prices_()`) and traverse the lattice back to calculate the payoffs at each node (`calculate_node_payoffs_(.)`), until arriving at the expected payoff at the initial node (`grid_[0][0]`), which gives us the option value:

```
double BinomialLatticePricer::calc_price(double spot, OptType opt_type)
{
        project_underlying_prices_(spot);
        return calculate_node_payoffs_(opt_type);
}
```

The `MultiArray` lattice (`grid_`) is first traversed forward in time by column, projecting the `underlying` equity price in each row element as an up move, except for the last, which is a down move. This results in the upper diagonal form as shown previously in Figures 9-4 and 9-5:

```
void BinomialLatticePricer::project_prices_(double spot)
{
    grid_[0][0].underlying = spot;          // Terminal node

    // j: columns, i: rows.
    // Traverse by columns, then set node in each row.
    for (int j = 1; j < time_points_; ++j)
    {
        for (int i = 0; i <= j; ++i)
        {
            if (i < j)
            {
                grid_[i][j].underlying = u_ * grid_[i][j - 1].underlying;
            }
            else    // (i == j)
            {
                grid_[i][j].underlying = d_ * grid_[i - 1][j - 1].underlying;
            }
        }
    }
}
```

Calculating the discounted payoffs is somewhat more complicated, as we need to take into account several steps and conditions:

1. Calculate the payoffs at expiration and assign them to each respective `payoff` member in the last column of the lattice, `grid_[i][time_points_ - 1].payoff`.

2. Iterate back in time over the lattice to compute the discounted expected payoff at each node, and in the case of an American option, compare it with the early exercise payoff at that node.

3. For an American option, set the `grid_[i][j].payoff` to the maximum payoff value in step 2, for each row i in the active column j. Otherwise, for a European option, set it to the discounted expected payoff.

4. Continue this backward iteration until reaching the initial node, and return the value of `grid_[0][0].payoff`, which is the price of the option as calculated by the lattice model.

Step (1) completes the first task of calculating the terminal payoffs as follows:

```
// Step (1)
// change name calculate_discounted_expected_payoffs_
double BinomialLatticePricer::calculate_node_payoffs_(OptType opt_type)
{
```

```
    // Set the terminal nodes with payoffs at expiration: j = time_points_ - 1
    for (int i = 0; i <= time_points_ - 1; ++i)
    {
        grid_[i][time_points_ - 1].payoff =
            opt_.option_payoff(grid_[i][time_points_ - 1].underlying);
    }

    // . . . More to come
}
```

Step (2) is conditioned on whether we are pricing a European or American option, and the respective helper function is called:

```
// Step (2)
double BinomialLatticePricer::calculate_node_payoffs_(OptType opt_type)
{
    // Set the terminal nodes with payoffs at expiration: j = time_points_ - 1
    for (int i = 0; i <= time_points_ - 1; ++i)
    {
        grid_[i][time_points_ - 1].payoff =
            opt_.option_payoff(grid_[i][time_points_ - 1].underlying);
    }

    if (opt_type == OptType::American)
        american_payoffs_();

    else
        european_payoffs_();      // OptType::Euro

    // . . . one more step to follow
}
```

For either an American or European option, we will need to calculate the discounted expected payoffs, so this is refactored out to the separate helper function disc_expected_val_(.):

```
double BinomialLatticePricer::disc_expected_val_(int i, int j) const
{
    return disc_fctr_ * (p_ * grid_[i][j + 1].payoff
        + (1.0 - p_) * grid_[i + 1][j + 1].payoff);
}
```

Step (3) is then completed for either the American or European case:

```
// Step (3) -- American
void BinomialLatticePricer::american_payoffs_()
{
    // Start from penultimate column prior to expiration: j = time_points_ - 2
    for (int j = time_points_ - 2; j >= 0; --j)
    {
        for (int i = 0; i <= j; ++i)
        {
            grid_[i][j].payoff = std::max(disc_expected_val_(i, j),
```

```
                    opt_.option_payoff(grid_[i][j].underlying));
            }
        }
    }

// Step (3) -- European
void BinomialLatticePricer::european_payoffs_()
{
    // Start from penultimate column prior to expiration: j = time_points_ - 2
    for (int j = time_points_ - 2; j >= 0; --j)
    {
        for (int i = 0; i <= j; ++i)
        {
            grid_[i][j].payoff = disc_expected_val_(i, j);
        }
    }
}
```

For an American option, optimal early exercise is checked by comparing the discounted expected payoff with the actual payoff for the underlying equity price at each node: opt_.option_payoff(grid_[i][j].underlying)).

Step (4) is the end result, when the payoff value is determined at the initial node (grid_[0][0].payoff), giving us the option price determined by the model:

```
// Step (4)
double BinomialLatticePricer::calculate_node_payoffs_(OptType opt_type)
{
    // Set the terminal nodes with payoffs at expiration: j = time_points_ - 1
    for (int i = 0; i <= time_points_ - 1; ++i)
    {
        grid_[i][time_points_ - 1].payoff =
            opt_.option_payoff(grid_[i][time_points_ - 1].underlying);
    }

    if (opt_type == OptType::American)
        american_payoffs_();

    else
        european_payoffs_();       // OptType::Euro

    return grid_[0][0].payoff;     // Option value
}
```

This option value is returned to the public calc_price(.) function, from which it is then passed to the model consumer:

```
double BinomialLatticePricer::calc_price(double spot, OptType opt_type)
{
    // . . .
    return calculate_node_payoffs_(opt_type);    // grid_[0][0].payoff
}
```

Applying the same data as in the earlier American option example, the option value is the discounted expected payoff at $t = 0$ in Figure 9-5, \$4.54. For comparison, a European option with all else being the same has the value \$3.98, so the additional premium for early exercise is evident:

```
double strike =  40.0, rf_rate = 0.06, mkt_vol = 0.2, time_to_exp = 1.0;
int time_steps = 4;
double spot = 36.0;

// ITM American put option
auto put_ptr = make_unique<PutPayoff>(strike);        // put_ptr = "put pointer"
OptionInfo put{std::move(put_ptr), time_to_exp};

// put contains a unique_ptr -- must move
BinomialLatticePricer put_pricer{std::move(put), mkt_vol, rf_rate, time_steps};

double opt_price = put_pricer.calc_price(spot, OptType::American);     // 4.54

// Compare with European case:
opt_price = put_pricer.calc_price(spot, OptType::Euro);               // 3.98
```

Convergence

The previous examples purposely used only a handful of timepoints to demonstrate how binomial pricing can be implemented using a Boost MultiArray. In practice, more nodes are necessary to ensure reasonable convergence. Using the American put option example, if we were to instead run a series of lattices out to 50 timepoints, we would see convergence to 4.49, meaning the result in the previous four-timestep example of 4.54 is off by about 1.1%.

As a side note, convergence of lattice valuations will usually exhibit an oscillating pattern. Staying with the current American put example, you can see this pattern in the results, where the number of timepoints is incremented from 45 to 50 (44 to 49 time steps). The results—out to four decimal points—are shown in Table 9-2.

Table 9-2. Projected underlying equity prices with discounted expected payoffs (ITM American put option with dividend)

Number of timepoints	Option valuation
45	4.4869
46	4.4901
47	4.4862
48	4.4910
49	4.4855
50	4.4915

Because of this effect, it is often preferred to take the average of the last two iterations as the option value, giving us 4.4885, but still resulting in 4.49 rounded to the nearest cent. For a more in-depth illustration, Section 7.3 of *Option Theory* is again highly recommended.

Extensions

A two-dimensional Boost MultiArray can be extended to accommodate a trinomial lattice, often used in the presence of stochastic interest rates or volatilities. A MultiArray can also be expanded into higher dimensions for valuing options on more than one asset. However, in this latter case, performance can be degraded with additional dimensions, so Monte Carlo–based methods might be a better alternative for valuing derivatives such as basket options.

Accumulators

The *Boost Accumulators* library provides efficient incremental descriptive statistical computations on dynamic sets of data. For example, a set of financial data (e.g., prices or returns) might be sequentially updated with new data values. Then, each time a new value is appended, a set of descriptive statistical values—such as mean, variance, maximum, and minimum—are updated as well.

The *boost/accumulators/accumulators.hpp* and *boost/accumulators/statistics/stats.hpp* header files need to be included, plus individual header files for each descriptive statistic desired, as shown in the examples that follow.

Max and Min Example

As a first example, let's apply the max and min accumulators to a set of real numbers that is updated with new data over time. Note that individual header files need to be included for both max and min:

```
#include <boost/accumulators/accumulators.hpp>
#include <boost/accumulators/statistics/stats.hpp>
#include <boost/accumulators/statistics/min.hpp>
#include <boost/accumulators/statistics/max.hpp>
```

Accumulators, accumulator sets, and extractors—for accessing each statistical metric—are scoped with the boost::accumulators namespace, but to save ourselves some typing, we can assign it to an alias:

```
namespace bacc = boost::accumulators;
```

The Boost libraries documentation (*https://oreil.ly/kyrEi*) provides the following two definitions:

- An *accumulator* "is a container that calculates a new result every time a value is inserted. The value isn't necessarily stored in the accumulator. Instead the accumulator continuously updates intermediary results as it is fed new values."

- An *accumulator set* refers to a collection of accumulators and "is specified with a sample type and a list of features," where *features* are the metrics of a sample to be calculated, such as maximum, minimum, and mean.

So now in this example, we create an accumulator set containing the max and min accumulators:

```
bacc::accumulator_set<double, bacc::stats<bacc::tag::min, bacc::tag::max>> acc{};
```

Note that `accumulator_set` is a class template, first taking in as template parameters the type (`double`), followed by the set of statistical measures, each of which is defined in the `boost::accumulators::tag` namespace, as shown in the creation of the `acc` object here.

Using `acc(.)` as a function object, data can be appended incrementally:

```
acc(5.8);
acc(-1.7);
acc(2.9);
```

To access the sample statistics, use the *extractors* for `min` and `max`:

```
cout << bacc::extract::min(acc) << ", " << bacc::extract::max(acc) << "\n";
```

The results for the minimum and maximum values at this stage are as follows:

```
(-1.7, 5.8)
```

Next, append a new value to the data and check the results on the updated set. This shows how the maximum and minimum values are automatically updated as each new value is appended to the accumulator:

```
acc(524.0);
```

The minimum value remains unchanged, but the new maximum is 524.

Because both `max(.)` and `min(.)` functions are also included in the Standard Library, the code in the previous example can show why namespaces are important. If `std` and `boost::accumulators` were imported into the global namespace with

```
using namespace std;
using namespace boost::accumulators;
```

the compiler would complain if either `max` or `min` were used without its namespace context.

Mean and Variance

We can also create `mean` and `variance` accumulator sets. Again, individual header files for mean and variance need to be included. The following example creates an accumulator set containing `mean` and `variance` accumulators, and then it extracts the corresponding values as new data is added to the data set. Note once again, the respective header files must be included:

```
#include <boost/accumulators/statistics/mean.hpp>
#include <boost/accumulators/statistics/variance.hpp>

// . . .

bacc::accumulator_set<double, bacc::stats<bacc::tag::mean, bacc::tag::variance>>
    mv_acc{};

// push in some data . . .
mv_acc(1.0);
mv_acc(2.0);
mv_acc(3.0);


// Display the results:
cout << bacc::extract::mean(mv_acc) << ", " << bacc::extract::variance(mv_acc)
    << "\n";
```

This results in a mean of 2, and a *population variance*—the sum of squared deviations from the mean divided by the entire sample size—equal to approximately 0.6667.

Next, append two additional values:

```
mv_acc(4.0);
mv_acc(5.0);

cout << bacc::extract::mean(mv_acc) << ", " << bacc::extract::variance(mv_acc)
    << "\n";
```

The mean and variance values have been updated and are now 3 and 2, respectively.

Append three more values to bring the total data set size to eight, so that the accumulators recalculate the mean and variance values again:

```
mv_acc(16.0);
mv_acc(17.0);
mv_acc(18.0);

cout << bacc::extract::mean(mv_acc) << ", " << bacc::extract::variance(mv_acc)
    << "\n\n";
```

This now yields the values 8.25 and 47.4375.

Rolling Mean and Variance

In the previous section, we looked at accumulators that returned cumulative statistical values. For example, if we have three data values, the mean is equivalent to the sum of these values divided by 3. If two new values are loaded into the accumulator, the mean is updated by summing all five elements and dividing by 5.

Typical metrics used in trading indicators and signals, however, rely on rolling values, such as a moving average over a fixed number of observations. In Boost, these values can be obtained by using *rolling window* accumulators. Before proceeding, however, it is important to note that the rolling variance accumulator computes the *sample* variance, where for a sample size of n, the sum of the squared deviations from the mean is divided by $n - 1$ rather n. The price volatility is then the square root of the variance, as there is no standard deviation accumulator in Boost.

Let's first look at a simple example to illustrate how rolling mean and rolling variance accumulators work. To demonstrate, we will define an accumulator set, roll_acc, consisting of rolling_mean and rolling_variance accumulators. The rolling period is five observations, reflected in the rolling_window::window_size parameter, as shown here:

```
// Include header files for rolling mean and rolling variance:
#include <boost/accumulators/statistics/rolling_mean.hpp>
#include <boost/accumulators/statistics/rolling_variance.hpp>

bacc::accumulator_set<double, bacc::stats<bacc::tag::rolling_mean,
    bacc::tag::rolling_variance>>
        roll_acc{bacc::tag::rolling_window::window_size = 5};
```

Next, load the first three observations (same as before):

```
roll_acc(1.0);
roll_acc(2.0);
roll_acc(3.0);
```

Note that if the rolling mean and rolling (sample) variance are extracted, their values based on these three observations alone will be computed, as five observations are not yet available:

```
cout << bacc::extract::rolling_mean(roll_acc) << ", "
    << bacc::extract::rolling_variance(roll_acc) << "\n\n";
```

The preceding code will display 2 and 1 on the screen (mean and sample variance over three observations).

Next, load two more observations and extract the values again:

```
roll_acc(4.0);
roll_acc(5.0);
```

The mean and variance are based on all five elements, yielding 3 and 2.5, respectively.

Finally, append three more values:

```
roll_acc(16.0);
roll_acc(17.0);
roll_acc(18.0);
```

The mean and variance are based on the five last elements, resulting in 12 and 47.5.

Trading Indicator Examples

In a *Bollinger Bands* trading strategy, signals are based on an indicator consisting of a rolling average of security prices (the middle band), and two outer bands defined by ± a multiple of the rolling average of the price volatility (standard deviation).

The frequency used for rolling averages of prices in trading indicators can be in terms of an arbitrary unit, ranging from high-frequency fractions of a second, to mid-frequency hourly or daily observations, and out to lower frequencies monthly or quarterly. Figure 9-6 shows daily observations of the S&P 500 SPY ETF (*https://oreil.ly/BGAVc*) from May to September 2024, with a window of 20 days, and bands of ± 1.5 standard deviations from the moving average. The dark bars indicate a net positive gain for the day, and the lighter bars a net loss.

Boost uses the term *rolling average*, but in trading parlance this is usually referred to as a *moving average*.

Figure 9-6. Bollinger Bands indicator, 20-day window, 1.5 standard deviations

Figures 9-6 and 9-7 utilize the TTR R Package (*https://oreil.ly/ K6T1h*), written and maintained by Joshua Ulrich.

Suppose now for a programming example we have a `vector` called `prices` that contains a set of daily stock-price data from an external source over a certain period of time. We will append each observed price to the `prices_acc` accumulator set, and extract the rolling mean and variance with the length set in `win_size`. As these calculations are updated with each new observation added to the accumulator, they will be extracted at each step, and the share price, moving average value, and upper and lower band values will be stored in an Eigen matrix:

```
// Data would normally come via an interface:
vector<double> prices{100.0, . . .};

// win_size = length of the inner band moving average.
// Assume win_size = 20 is chosen.

bacc::accumulator_set<double, bacc::stats<bacc::tag::rolling_mean,
    bacc::tag::rolling_variance>>
        prices_acc(bacc::tag::rolling_window::window_size = win_size);

MatrixXd indicators{prices.size(), 4};

for (size_t rec = 0; rec < prices.size(); ++rec)
{
    // Columns of matrix:  price, ma, ma + n*sig, ma - n*sig
    indicators(rec, 0) = prices[rec];
    prices_acc(prices[rec]);
    if (rec >= win_size - 1)
    {
        indicators(rec, 1) = bacc::extract::rolling_mean(prices_acc);
        double dev = n * std::sqrt(bacc::extract::rolling_variance(prices_acc));
        indicators(rec, 2) = indicators(rec, 1) + dev;
        indicators(rec, 3) = indicators(rec, 1) - dev;
    }
    else
    {
        indicators(rec, 1) = 0.0;
        indicators(rec, 2) = 0.0;
        indicators(rec, 3) = 0.0;
    }
}
```

The values stored in the `MatrixXd` object can then be used as Bollinger Bands indicators in a backtest.

For a small-scale example, suppose we have a sample of 25 daily price observations, and we set the inner band moving average to five days and the volatility multiplier to 1.5. We could put each band into a column so that the backtest can check whether either band has been crossed, and if so, where. Zeros have been placed in the accumulator value columns until five observations—the length of the moving average—has been attained:

Price	MA	Upper Band	Lower Band
100.00	0.00	0.00	0.00
103.49	0.00	0.00	0.00
102.82	0.00	0.00	0.00
106.86	0.00	0.00	0.00
104.91	103.61	107.43	99.80
107.38	105.09	108.10	102.08
107.46	105.88	108.89	102.88
111.01	107.52	110.83	104.21
112.01	108.55	112.92	104.19
114.11	110.39	114.80	105.99
116.91	112.30	117.59	107.01
121.74	115.16	121.64	108.68
120.04	116.96	123.01	110.92
120.24	118.61	123.21	114.01
120.12	119.81	122.46	117.16
120.61	120.55	121.60	119.50
121.31	120.47	121.25	119.68
119.25	120.31	121.43	119.18
118.11	119.88	121.75	118.02
120.36	119.93	121.82	118.04
117.36	119.28	121.69	116.87
119.12	118.84	120.56	117.12
119.36	118.86	120.60	117.12
123.54	119.95	123.37	116.53
123.42	120.56	124.72	116.40

As a second example, two separate moving average (MA) accumulators can be used to represent the indicators in a fast (shorter length)/slow (longer length) moving average crossing strategy. In Figure 9-7, a fast moving average over 5 days and a slow moving average over 20 days is applied to prices of the same SPY ETF, May–September 2024.

SPY   [2024-05-06/2024-09-04]

Last 550.950012207031

Figure 9-7. Dual moving average cross indicators

In code, the moving averages can be applied using two Boost accumulators—one for
the fast MA (`fast_ma_acc`) and the other for the slow MA (`slow_ma_acc`):

```
bacc::accumulator_set<double, bacc::stats<bacc::tag::rolling_mean>>
    fast_ma_acc(bacc::tag::rolling_window::window_size = fast_ma_win);

bacc::accumulator_set<double, bacc::stats<bacc::tag::rolling_mean>>
    slow_ma_acc(bacc::tag::rolling_window::window_size = slow_ma_win);

// Three columns: Price, Fast(Short) MA, Slow(Long) MA:
MatrixXd indicators{prices.size(), 3};

for (size_t rec = 0; rec < prices.size(); ++rec)
{
    // Columns of matrix:  price, ma, ma + n*sig, ma - n*sig
    indicators(rec, 0) = prices[rec];
    fast_ma_acc(prices[rec]);
    slow_ma_acc(prices[rec]);

    if (rec >= fast_ma_win - 1 && rec >= slow_ma_win - 1)
    {
        indicators(rec, 1) = bacc::extract::rolling_mean(fast_ma_acc);
```

```
        indicators(rec, 2) = bacc::extract::rolling_mean(slow_ma_acc);
    }
    else if (rec >= fast_ma_win - 1 && rec < slow_ma_win - 1)
    {
        indicators(rec, 1) = bacc::extract::rolling_mean(fast_ma_acc);
        indicators(rec, 2) = 0.0;
    }
    else
    {
        indicators(rec, 1) = 0.0;
        indicators(rec, 2) = 0.0;
    }
}
```

Again, because the moving averages are updated with each new share price, their values need to be captured and stored in a separate container. As in the previous example, we can use a matrix as shown, over which a backtest could then determine if and where one moving average line crosses over the other.

Taking the same set of prices, a fast moving average over 5 days and a slower one over 10, the results would be as follows. Note again the moving average values are set to zero until the moving average length has been reached in each of the fast and slow cases:

```
Price   Short MA Long MA
100.00    0.00    0.00
103.49    0.00    0.00
102.82    0.00    0.00
106.86    0.00    0.00
104.91  103.61    0.00
107.38  105.09    0.00
107.46  105.88    0.00
111.01  107.52    0.00
112.01  108.55    0.00
114.11  110.39  107.00
116.91  112.30  108.69
121.74  115.16  110.52
120.04  116.96  112.24
120.24  118.61  113.58
120.12  119.81  115.10
120.61  120.55  116.43
121.31  120.47  117.81
119.25  120.31  118.63
118.11  119.88  119.24
120.36  119.93  119.87
117.36  119.28  119.91
119.12  118.84  119.65
119.36  118.86  119.58
123.54  119.95  119.91
123.42  120.56  120.24
```

You can find further information on Boost Accumulators in the online documentation (https://oreil.ly/M4-ts).

Summary

Although the history of Boost library releases goes back to 1999, it ties in with modern C++ in that some of the new features beginning in C++11—such as smart pointers, distributional random number generation, and task-based concurrency—saw their start in Boost years before being adopted by the by the ISO C++ Committee.

Some Boost libraries remain separate from the current C++ specification but complement it, including those presented here that can be used in financial programming, such as statistical distributions and Boost Accumulators, which can be applied in systematic trading strategies. In some cases, Boost can extend features in standard C++, such as providing the commonly used constants $\frac{1}{\sqrt{2}}$ and $\frac{1}{\sqrt{2\pi}}$, and facilitating random number generation from a wider range of distributions, as in the Standard Library.

Finally, the `mdarray` class, the owning analog of `mdspan` (discussed in Chapter 8), might eventually provide in the Standard Library similar functionality as Boost MultiArray. This should become clearer once the proposal (*https://wg21.link/p1684*) is accepted by the ISO Committee, as should its target release, which at present is looking like C++26.

Further Reading

For more information about trading indicators such as Bollinger Bands and moving averages, see *Trading Systems (Second Edition)*, 2nd edition, by Urban Jaekle and Emilio Tomasini (Harriman House, 2019).

For a look at how an `mdarray` might be used for implementing the binomial lattice model, slides from a presentation (*https://oreil.ly/iID67*) by the author (2023) are also available online.

CHAPTER 10

Modules and Concepts

One of the most anticipated additions to C++20, *modules*, received a lot of fanfare at C++ conferences and in the blogosphere leading up to the release of the updated Standard. Modules offer potentially significant advantages over the currently employed header files with #include preprocessor statements, as will be discussed in this chapter.

Some of us had hoped that before the time this book went to press, modules would have become a common fixture in newer development projects. Unfortunately, this has not been the case, although considering that this is a major change in the C++ language, it is somewhat understandable for updated compiler implementations, as well as adoption by developers, to take time. Visual Studio provided working support for modules by around mid-2021, but implementation delays in Clang and gcc continued into 2023.

Still, as mentioned in a CppCon 2021 talk presented by Gabriel Dos Reis and Cameron DaCamara, "C++ modules were designed to bring more safety to your programs, while dramatically reducing compile time, resulting in overall increased productivity."[1] Therefore, it is probably a good idea to start becoming familiar with how modules work.

Concepts were another eagerly awaited feature in C++20. They give programmers more control over template programming. Invalid function inputs can now be more readily pinpointed at compile time, rather than being buried within the avalanche of superfluous error messages associated with templates that often obscure the location of the offending code. Concepts can also indicate the intentions behind a function

---

1 Cameron DaCamara and Gabriel Dos Reis, "Implementing C++ Modules: Lessons Learned, Lessons Abandoned" (*https://oreil.ly/La8Af*), 2021.

or class template, which in a sense make the code self-documenting. This should provide better clarity to programming teams that are responsible for maintaining a production-level codebase. All three major compilers fully support concepts.

This chapter starts by introducing modules and concludes with concepts. An overview of each is presented, along with examples that show, at least at a basic level, how convenient and useful these recent additions to the Standard can be. You should also get an idea of how they can lead to improved code quality and maintenance.

Modules

A *module* can be defined in a single file, containing both declarations and implementations. However, as you will see later, we also have the option to utilize a separate implementation file. To start with an example, our old friend SimpleClass (first used in Chapter 2) is implemented inside a module called SingleFileExample. More specifically, this defines the *primary module interface unit* for this module, as indicated by the first line of code, containing the export keyword ❶:

```
export module SingleFileModule;  ❶

// SimpleClass declaration and implementation together
export class SimpleClass  ❷
{
public:
    SimpleClass(int k) :k_{k} {}

    int get_val() const
    {
        return k_;
    }

    void reset_val(int k)
    {
        k_ = k;
    }

private:
    int k_;
};
```

The SimpleClass definition is also preceded by the export keyword ❷. This makes it available to any code that *imports* the module. For example, to use this class in a separate function, some_fcn(), residing elsewhere outside of the module, we would precede it with the import keyword, with the name of the module, as shown here:

```
import SingleFileModule;

// . . .
```

```
int some_fcn()
{
    SimpleClass sc{10};        // Exported from SingleFileExample module
    // . . .
}
```

The import keyword might remind you of using #include for a header file, but important differences exist (to be discussed momentarily). Had export not preceded the some_fcn() definition, this code would not compile, as SimpleClass would not have been visible from within the scope of some_fcn().

Similarly, modules can contain standalone nonmember functions. We can append an example to SingleFileModule to also demonstrate a non-exported function:

```
export module SingleFileModule;

import <vector>;        // Standard Library Header Units are imported...
import <algorithm>;     // to be discussed in the next section.
import <ranges>;
import <iterator>;      // std::back_inserter(.)

// . . .

std::vector<double> vector_fcn_helper(const std::vector<double>& x)
{
    std::vector<double> y;
    y.reserve(x.size());
    std::ranges::transform(x, std::back_inserter(y),
            [](double q) {return 3 * q;});

    return y;
}

export std::vector<double> vector_fcn(const std::vector<double>& x)
{
    return vector_fcn_helper(x);
}
```

In this case, vector_fcn_helper(.) is not exported, but it is called from the exported vector_fcn(.). In this sense, the latter serves as an interface, while the former holds an internal implementation. If we attempted to write the following function outside of the module:

```
import SingleFileModule;

// . . .

int vector_fcn_example()
{
    // . . .
    std::vector<double> v{1.0, 2.0, 3.0};
```

```
        std::vector<double> w = vector_fcn_helper(v);      // Will not compile!
    }
```

the code would not compile. Instead, we are forced to use the exported interface function:

```
int vector_fcn_example()
{
    // . . .
    std::vector<double> v{1.0, 2.0, 3.0};
    std::vector<double> w = vector_fcn(v);
}
```

You might also have noticed we used `import` for the Standard Library headers rather than using `#include` just after the module definition begins. Salient differences with `import`, including Standard Library headers, will be discussed next.

File Extensions for Modules

Although C++ has no standard file extensions, for years there have been generally accepted extension configurations for header files (e.g., *.h*, *.hpp*, and *.hxx*) and for implementation source files (e.g., *.cpp* and *.cxx*). When modules first started hitting the scene, however, no such consensus occurred for module interface filename extensions. In Visual Studio, the default property was an *.ixx* extension, while for Clang it was *.cppm*, which arguably was more descriptive as it could be interpreted as the common *.cpp* plus *m* for *module*. Meanwhile, the gcc compiler default was to use *.cpp* for both traditional implementation files and module interfaces.

Recent versions of Visual Studio 2022 (at least as of 4.8), however, now also recognize *.cppm* in its default properties, so perhaps some coalescing is happening around this extension format. This extension is used for module interface files in the sample code for this chapter.

You can find more details in Section 16.3.1 of *C++20: The Complete Guide* by Nicolai M. Josuttis (Leanpub, 2022).

Standard Library Header Units

Proposals to the ISO C++ Committee for reorganizing the Standard Library into Standard Modules (*https://wg21.link/p2412*) were also drafted and submitted for inclusion in C++20, but this effort was deferred (*https://wg21.link/p2465*) until C++23, and implementations for each of the three mainstream compilers are still not yet finalized as of mid-2024. In the interim, as a placeholder, Standard Library *header units* that, as described in a separate proposal, guarantee "existing `#include(s)` of Standard Library headers transparently turn into module imports in C++20."[2] What this essentially means is preprocessor statements such as

```
#include <vector>
#include <algorithm>
```

can be replaced by importing their header unit equivalents:

```
import <vector>;
import <algorithm>;
```

Note that a semicolon is required at the end of each, as these are seen by the compiler as regular C++ statements, instead of #include statements that are destined for the preprocessor.

The use of header units applies to almost all C++ Standard Library declaration files. However, because of complications arising in headers inherited from C—e.g., <cassert> and <cmath>, based on the legacy C headers assert.h and math.h, respectively—these are not covered and need to be handled with the usual #include preprocessor statements within the global fragment of a module. The *global fragment* is indicated by a simple module; statement, which must be placed above the export module statement, as shown next. Then, if we add a function math_fcn(.) that requires <cmath> functions, our module would take on something of this form:

```
module;
#include <cmath>          // Legacy C-derived headers go in the global fragment
                          // at the top of the file.

export module SingleFileModule;
import <vector>;          // Importing a Standard header unit
                          // comes after the module name is defined.
. . .

export std::vector<double> math_fcn(const std::vector<double>& x)
{
    std::vector<double> y;
    y.reserve(x.size());
    std::ranges::transform(x, std::back_inserter(y),
        [](double q) {return std::sin(q) + std::cos(q);});

    return y;
}
```

Templates in Modules

Templates can also be written in module interface files, as shown in this example:

---

2 Richard Smith, "Standard Library Header Units for C++20" (*https://wg21.link/p1502*), proposal P1502R1 (2018).

```
export module Templates;
import <iostream>;

export template<typename T>
T factored_polynomial(T a, T b, T c, T d)
{
    return (a + b) * (c + d);
}

export template<typename T>
void print(T t)
{
    std::cout << t << " ";
}
```

import Versus #include

As modules have only barely gotten off the ground at this point, including (in the #include sense) traditional header files in the global fragment will just be a fact of life for a while, not just with <cmath>, but also with popular external libraries such as Boost, Eigen, and Armadillo:

```
module;
#include <boost/math/distributions.hpp>
#include <Eigen/Dense>

export module ModuleThatUsesMathLibraries;
import <random>;        // Standard Library Header Unit

// . . .
```

When writing your own code, however, preferring modules over header files when possible can provide distinct advantages. The first is that an imported module will not "leak" other modules previously imported into it. Say, for example, module A imports another module B:

```
// Define module A that imports module B:
export module A;
import B;
```

If A is imported into another module C, B will not be imported as well unless it also is explicitly instructed to do so. If not, attempts to use exported functions in module B inside module C will fail to compile:

```
// Define module C that imports module A:
export module C;
import A;
import B;        // Must be explicitly imported if functions
                 // in B are also to be used inside module C
```

This is in contrast with a header file that contains other #include statements. If a header file is included somewhere (again, in the #include sense), it will leak anything it itself has included. For example, suppose a header file *MyHeader.h* includes another user-defined header file *YourHeader.h*, and the STL <vector> header:

```
// MyHeader.h
#include "YourHeader.h"
#include <vector>
```

. . .

If *MyHeader.h* is included, say in the translation unit containing main(), then it will also carry with it functions in *YourHeader.h* and the std::vector class, such that the following *will* compile:

```
#include "MyHeader.h"
int main()
{
    // This will compile:
    auto y = my_header_fcn(...);

    // But so will these lines:
    auto z = your_header_fcn(...);
    std::vector <double> v;
}
```

In realistic situations that might involve many more header files, losing track of what is included, and what is not, potentially leads to problems. With modules, the programmer has greater control over what is imported.

On the flip side, you might *want* to export a module imported by another module. For this, you need to use an export import statement. For example, suppose we have the following module:

```
export module VandelayIndustries;

export class Latex
{
public:
    Latex(int quantity, double unit_price) :
        quantity_{quantity}, unit_price_{unit_price} {}

    double total_sale_value() const
    {
        return quantity_ * unit_price_;
    }

private:
    int quantity_;
    double unit_price_;
};
```

And then, suppose we also have a module `ExportImportBusiness`, but we want users who import this module to also have access to the `Latex` class. This is accomplished by using `export import`:

```
export module ExportImportBusiness;
export import VandelayIndustries;
import <string>;
import <iostream>;
import <format>;

export void order(const std::string& order_code, const Latex& latex)
{
    std::cout
        << std::format("Order: {}, Total Price: {}",
            order_code, latex.total_sale_value()) << "\n";
}
```

Then, in a separate translation unit, importing the `ExportImportBusiness` module will also allow us to use the `Latex` class without explicitly importing `VandelayIndustries`:

```
import ExportImportBusiness;

void export_import_example()
{
    Latex latex{2, 10.50};        // exported from the ExportImportBusiness module
    string order_code{"X120264"};
    order(order_code, latex);
}
```

The upshot is that now you can control which modules are exported from another module, rather than having them leak by default.

Consider two final points. First, these same safeguards will also be in effect if a module is imported into nonmodule code, such as the earlier example importing the `SingleFileModule` module into the translation unit containing `main()`. And second, on the other hand, header files that are included in the global fragment of a module *will* leak to any destination where the same module is imported.

Declarations in Module Interfaces

During the preprocessor phase of the build process, with each time a traditional header file is included in a translation unit, its declarations are reparsed. Because the same header file can be included in multiple translation units, it can itself include other header files (which are leaked). In a real-world financial library or system, hundreds of header files could be in play, plus those included from external libraries, so because of basic combinatorics, these redundancies will add up and then slow the build process.

With modules, these redundancies are eliminated, as declarations in a module interface are precompiled into a single file that is reused, eliminating the repeated reparsing that takes place with traditional header files. As a result, using modules can help reduce build times. Similar results could also be obtained with traditional build methods by using precompiled headers; however, this is usually platform-dependent and hence not standard, while modules are.

Technically, these reductions in build times are tempered by the fact that modules can reduce parallelism of a build as compared to the traditional model, so at this stage, your mileage might vary. Given, however, that increasing efficiency in compilers is an active area of research, it might yield further breakthroughs down the road as the use of modules becomes mainstream, but this remains to be sorted out.

One definite positive consequence of precompiling declarations into a single file is that we can say goodbye to "ugly" preprocessor directives[3] such as include guards that are commonly used to prevent *one definition rule* (ODR) violations (*https://oreil.ly/FiX-I*), as well as to the nonstandard #pragma once that is sometimes used with compilers where it is defined.

```
#ifndef MY_HEADER_H
#define MY_HEADER_H

// Do not need these "ugly" preprocessor directives with modules.

#endif
```

File extensions used for precompiled declarations that are generated with modules for the three major compilers are as follows:

- Visual Studio: *.ifc*
- Clang: *.pcm*
- gcc: *.gcm*

Separating Declarations from Implementation

In the opening examples, we utilized a coding style similar to what you would find in Java and C#, combining a function or class declaration with its implementation (although what happens behind the scenes is completely different). This can be seen quite clearly in the previous SimpleClass example.

From an organizational point of view, writing the declarations separately from the implementation can be clearer, even though this still can be done in a single module interface file. Rewriting SimpleClass in this form, we would then have this:

---

3 Rainer Grimm: *C++20: Get the Details*, 2nd edition (Leanpub, 2022), 104.

```cpp
export class SimpleClass
{
public:
    SimpleClass(int k);
    int get_val() const;
    void reset_val(int k);

private:
    int k_;
};


SimpleClass::SimpleClass(int k) :k_{k} {}

int SimpleClass::get_val() const
{
    return k_;
}

void SimpleClass::reset_val(int k)
{
    k_ = k;
}
```

In real-life programming, of course, classes will not be this simple, so separating declarations from implementation can make the intent clearer and code maintenance easier.

We also have the option of splitting the declaration and implementation in a module into two separate files, which is commonly done. As your code increases in complexity, you will likely want to consider confining module interfaces to declarations alone, and write implementations in a *module implementation unit*, which can improve code maintenance further. One additional advantage to this separation is in cases of distributing compiled proprietary code while still providing the declarations, as is commonly done by providing header files.

As an example, we could reimplement the `BlackScholes` class from Chapter 2 as follows. First, the primary module interface would house the class declaration alone:

```cpp
// BlackScholesClass.cppm

export module BlackScholesClass;
import <array>;

export enum class PayoffType
{
    Call = 1,
    Put = -1
};

export class BlackScholes
```

```
{
public:
    BlackScholes(double strike, double spot, double time_to_exp,
        PayoffType payoff_type, double rate, double div = 0.0);

    double operator()(double vol) const;

private:

    std::array<double, 2> compute_norm_args_(double vol);     // d1 and d2;

    double strike_, spot_, time_to_exp_;
    PayoffType payoff_type_;
    double rate_, div_;
};
```

In this example, the enum class representing the payoff type and the BlackScholes class declaration are included in the module interface and exported.

We can then write the module implementation unit as shown here:

```
// BlackScholesClass.cpp        ❶

module;                         // Global fragment
#include <cmath>                ❷

module BlackScholesClass;       ❸

import <numbers>;
import <algorithm>;

BlackScholes::BlackScholes(double strike, double spot, double time_to_exp,
    PayoffType payoff_type, double rate, double div) :
    strike_{strike}, spot_{spot}, time_to_exp_{time_to_exp},
    payoff_type_{payoff_type}, rate_{rate}, div_{div} {}

double BlackScholes::operator()(double vol) const
{
    using std::exp;
    const int phi = static_cast<int>(payoff_type_);

    if (time_to_exp_ > 0.0)
    {
        auto norm_args = compute_norm_args_(vol);
        double d1 = norm_args[0];
        double d2 = norm_args[1];

        auto norm_cdf = [](double x) -> double
        {
            return (1.0 + std::erf(x / std::numbers::sqrt2)) / 2.0;
        };

        double nd_1 = norm_cdf(phi * d1);           // N(d1)
```

```
    double nd_2 = norm_cdf(phi * d2);          // N(d2)
    double disc_fctr = exp(-rate_ * time_to_exp_);

    return phi * (spot_ * exp(-div_ * time_to_exp_)
        * nd_1 - disc_fctr * strike_ * nd_2);
}
else
{
    // For std::max, the <algorithm> header unit is
    // imported in the module interface:
    return std::max(phi * (spot_ - strike_), 0.0);
}
}

std::array<double, 2> BlackScholes::compute_norm_args_(double vol)
{
    double numer = log(spot_ / strike_)
        + (rate_ - div_ + 0.5 * vol * vol) * time_to_exp_;

    double d1 = numer / (vol * sqrt(time_to_exp_));
    double d2 = d1 - vol * sqrt(time_to_exp_);
    return std::array<double, 2>{d1, d2};
}
```

Note in particular items 1–3 labeled in this code example:

❶ Module implementation files can use the same extension as existing implementation files (e.g., *.cpp*).

❷ The inclusion of the <cmath> header is placed in the global fragment of the module *implementation* unit, as it is needed only here and not in the interface. In contrast, as noted previously, *imports* of the Standard Library <numbers> and <algorithm> header units are placed in the *interface* unit.

❸ Finally, the same module BlackScholesClass; statement is applied at the outset, indicating this implementation is part of the same module. This is what associates it with the module interface. Note that the export keyword is *not* used in the implementation unit. Note that the export keyword is *not* used in the implementation unit; it can be placed only in a module interface unit.

This particular example hopefully provides a reasonable guide for writing module interfaces and implementations, but remember these two general rules:

- A module must contain one, and only one, primary module interface unit.
- A module can contain more than one implementation unit.

Namespaces

Namespaces can also be enclosed within modules. We have two basic options. First, we can export the entirety of a namespace:

```
export namespace OptionValuation
{
    enum class PayoffType
    {
        Call = 1,
        Put = -1
    };

    class BlackScholes
    {
    public:
        BlackScholes(double strike, double spot, double time_to_exp,
            PayoffType payoff_type, double rate, double div = 0.0);

        double operator()(double vol);

    private:

        std::array<double, 2> compute_norm_args_(double vol);    // d1 and d2;

        double strike_, spot_, time_to_exp_;
        PayoffType payoff_type_;
        double rate_, div_;
    };
}
```

Or alternatively, we can export individual classes and functions in a namespace, if you don't want to make an item in the namespace available outside the module:

```
namespace OptionValuation          // export not applied to the entire namespace
{
    export enum class PayoffType   // export explicitly applied where required
    {
        Call = 1,
        Put = -1
    };

    export class BlackScholes
    {
        . . .
    };

    int mystery_function(int n);    // This function is not exported
}
```

Partitions

Modules with a larger scope can be further divided into *partitions*. These can be useful for code organization, and they make it easier for different teams or individual developers to take responsibility for particular sections of the code. Implementation partitions can contain both declarations and implementations that remain internal to the module, but they cannot export anything. Interface partitions *can* export functions, but ultimately they must be imported into the primary interface and then exported to the outside world, using the `export import` designation.

Comprehensive coverage of module partitions is a more advanced topic that is beyond the intent of this chapter. You can again find an extensive discussion of the topic in Chapter 16 of *C++20: The Complete Guide* (Josuttis).

Concepts

Concepts for templates were a long-awaited and major enhancement in C++20. Just about anyone who has programmed with templates understands the agony of long and cryptic compiler error messages that obscure the reason that something went wrong, such as when a template parameter is invalid in a function template or class template.

For example, suppose we write the following function template:

```
template<typename T>
T add_them(const T& t1, const T& t2)
{
    return t1 + t2;
}
```

Then, because addition is defined for integers and real numbers, the following will compile, no problem:

```
int sum_ints = add_them(81, 84);
double sum_reals = add_them(53.15, 72.07);
```

We could also use the function to add two Eigen library matrices, as vector addition is defined by the + operator:

```
VectorXd xv(3);
VectorXd yv(3);

xv << 1.0, 2.0, 3.0;
yv << 4.0, 5.0, 6.0;

VectorXd sum_eig = add_them(xv, yv);
```

However, say we attempt to add two *Standard Library* vectors:

```
vector<double> u{1, 2, 3};
vector<double> v{4, 5, 6};
auto sum_vec = add_them(u, v);          // Error!: + not defined
```

We would get a compiler error, as expected. With the Visual Studio compiler, for example, the error message starts off with reasonably helpful information, pointing out that the + operator is not defined in this case, but what follows is a small tsunami of verbosity that does little to help us any further. The following is just an excerpt of the entire Visual Studio 2022 compiler output:

```
<source>(7): error C2676: binary '+': 'T' does not define this operator
or a conversion to a type acceptable to the predefined operator
        with
        [
            T=std::vector<int,std::allocator<int>>
        ]
C:/data/msvc/14.39.33321-Pre/include\xutility(1792): note: could be
'std::reverse_iterator<_BidIt> std::operator +(reverse_iterator<_BidIt>::
difference_type,const std::reverse_iterator<_BidIt> &) noexcept(<expr>)'
<source>(7): note: 'std::reverse_iterator<_BidIt> std::operator +
(reverse_iterator<_BidIt>::difference_type,
const std::reverse_iterator<_BidIt> &) noexcept(<expr>)': could not
deduce template argument for 'const std::reverse_iterator<_BidIt> &' from 'T'
        with
        [
            T=std::vector<int,std::allocator<int>>
        ]


. . .

Compiler returned: 2
```

Using the gcc compiler, the result isn't much better:

```
<source>: In instantiation of 'T add_them(T, T) [with T = std::vector<int>]':
<source>:14:28:   required from here
   14 |     auto sum_vec = add_them(u, v);
      |                    ~~~~~~~~^~~~~~
<source>:7:19: error: no match for 'operator+' (operand types are
'std::vector<int>' and 'std::vector<int>')
    7 |         return t1 + t2;
      |                ~~~^~~~
In file included from /opt/compiler-explorer/gcc-trunk-20240229
/include/c++/14.0.1/bits/stl_algobase.h:67,
from /opt/compiler-explorer/gcc-trunk-20240229
/include/c++/14.0.1/vector:62,from <source>:1:
/opt/compiler-explorer/gcc-trunk-20240229/include/c++/14.0.1/bits
/stl_iterator.h:627:5: note: candidate: 'template<class _Iterator> constexpr
std::reverse_iterator<_IteratorL> std::operator+(typename
reverse_iterator<_IteratorL>::difference_type,
const reverse_iterator<_IteratorL>&)'
  627 |     operator+(typename reverse_iterator<_Iterator>::difference_type __n,
      |     ^~~~~~~~

. . .

Compiler returned: 1
```

In this simple example, it's not difficult to discern the general problem from the first few lines in the compiler output. However, the remaining output—and again, this is just an excerpt—does little to help us any further. In practice, template programming can quickly become exponentially more complex, and we often end up having to search for answers obscured in cryptic output that can easily exceed what resulted in this example.

Defining Concepts

C++20 concepts help minimize the excess, resulting in more concise and helpful compiler error information. Continuing with the add_them(.) example, we can define a concept as follows:

```
template<typename T>
concept can_add = requires(const T& t1, const T& t2) {t1 + t2;};
```

A concept definition uses the same template parameter as the function, and it assigns the concept name, can_add, to the requirement (requires), which takes the form of a function itself. We then apply concept conditions to the original function by appending the requirement to the end of the function signature:

```
template<typename T>
T add_them(const T& t1, const T& t2)  requires can_add<T>
{
    return t1 + t2;
}
```

Now, when attempting to apply the can_add(.) function to two vectors, the Visual Studio compiler returns the error messages, telling us right up front what the problem is and pointing to the can_add concept evaluating to false:

```
<source>(18): error C2672: 'add_them': no matching overloaded function found
<source>(9): note: could be 'T add_them(T,T)'
<source>(18): note: the associated constraints are not satisfied
<source>(9): note: the concept 'can_add<std::vector<int,std::allocator<int>>>'
evaluated to false
<source>(6): note: binary '+': 'const std::vector<int,std::allocator<int>>'
does not define this operator or a conversion to a type acceptable to the
predefined operator

. . .

Compiler returned: 2
```

With the gcc compiler, we can again get the more relevant information up front, indicating that the constraints of the can_add concept has not been satisfied:

```
<source>:18:28: error: no matching function for call to
'add_them(std::vector<int>&, std::vector<int>&)'
   18 |      auto sum_vec = add_them(u, v);
      |                     ~~~~~~~~^~~~~~
<source>:9:3: note: candidate: 'template<class T> T add_them(T, T)
```

```
requires  can_add<T>'
    9 | T add_them(T t1, T t2) requires can_add<T>
      |   ^~~~~~~~
<source>:9:3: note:   template argument deduction/substitution failed:
<source>:9:3: note: constraints not satisfied
<source>: In substitution of 'template<class T> T add_them(T, T) requires
can_add<T> [with T = std::vector<int>]':
<source>:18:28:   required from here
<source>:9:3: note:     18 |     auto sum_vec = add_them(u, v);
<source>:9:3: note:        |                 ~~~~~~~~^~~~~
<source>:6:9:   required for the satisfaction of 'can_add<T>'
[with T = std::vector<int, std::allocator<int> >]


. . .

Execution build compiler returned: 1
```

The advantages of concepts, however, are not limited to improving compiler errors. Concepts also make the code itself clearer and more maintainable by specifying argument requirements alongside the function (or class), as should be apparent in the examples that follow.

Defining Concepts with Multiple Conditions

Suppose next we want to have a concept requiring that we can both add and subtract the parameters. This can be done by appending a subtractable condition inside the body of the requires block:

```
template<typename T>
concept can_add_and_subtr = requires(T t1, T t2)
{
    t1 + t2;
    t1 - t2;
};
```

Alternatively, we can have separate concept definitions and then combine them with *and* (&&) and *or* (||) conditions. For example, we could define a separate concept called can_subtract:

```
template<typename T>
concept can_subtract = requires(T t1, T t2) {t1 - t2;};
```

Then, we could instead use this in an *and* condition with can_add to define an equivalent "addable and subtractable" concept:

```
template<typename T>
concept can_add_and_subtr_combined = requires(T t)
{
    can_add<T> && can_subtract<T>;
};
```

Furthermore, a function template parameter can be replaced by a concept itself:

```
template<typename T>
concept can_square = requires(T t) {t * t;};

// Concept "can_square" replaces the usual function template parameter:
template <can_square T>
T square_it(const T& t)      // Can drop the "requires(.)" here.
{
    return t * t;
}
```

The examples in this book are based on a single template parameter T. Concepts can also be extended to two or more template parameters, but the process becomes more complex and can get start getting into the weeds of implicit type conversion and other matters. If you want to pursue this topic further, Item 3 (*https://oreil.ly/9lWBU*) in the online article "C++20 Concepts: Part 5 (Advanced Use Cases)", by Gajendra Gulgulia is a good place to start.

Standard Library Concepts

A set of predefined concepts, based on type traits introduced in C++11 and described in Section 5.4 (*https://oreil.ly/zjgSS*) of *The C++ Standard Library: A Tutorial and Reference*, 2nd edition, by Nicolai M. Josuttis (Addison-Wesley, 2012), is also part of the Standard Library as of C++20. For example, we can enforce the rule that a function will accept only floating-point (double, float, etc.) arguments by appending the predefined std::floating_point<T> concept (which is based on the std::is_floating_point<T> type trait). To start, consider a Quadratic *class* template that takes in coefficients a, b, and c, and that defines an operator () that computes the usual $ax^2 + bx + c$:

```
#include <concepts>  // Note we need the Standard Library <concepts> header now

template<typename T> requires std::floating_point<T>
class Quadratic
{
public:
    Quadratic(T a, T b, T c):a_{a}, b_{b}, c_{c}{}
    T operator ()(T x) const
    {
        return (a_ * x + b_) * x + c_;
    }

private:
    T a_, b_, c_;
};
```

This would now ensure that if we tried to create a Quadratic with T = int,

```
Quadratic<int> quad_int(2, 4, 2);
```

the compiler would complain, but in a good way, such that identifying the problem would be obvious, without the superfluous "extras" that might obscure it.

If we did want the class to also accept integer types (int, unsigned, etc.), this is easily rectifiable by appending an *or* condition with the integer analog of std::floating_point<T> (namely, std::integral<T>). This is done again by first defining a concept, such as the following:

```
template<typename T>
concept Number = requires(T t)
{
    std::integral<T> || std::floating_point<T>;
};
```

Then, in place of the requires statement at the top of the class definition, we can replace its single template parameter with the Number concept:

```
template<Number N>
class Quadratic
{
public:
    Quadratic(N a, N b, N c) :a_{a}, b_{b}, c_{c} {}

    N operator ()(N x) const
    {
        return (a_ * x + b_) * x + c_;
    }

private:
    N a_, b_, c_;
};
```

Now, this will compile with either floating or integral types. However, say we try to use invalid arguments at construction—for example, string types:

```
Quadratic<string> quad_string{"this", "won't", "compile"};
```

Compilation will fail (as desired), but with a descriptive yet concise error message that indicates the problem.

One last point to note is that the Number concept could alternatively be defined in a more compact form if desired:

```
template<typename T>
concept Number = std::integral<T> || std::floating_point<T>;
```

Summary

Modules were a long-awaited enhancement and are now part of C++20, but a full rollout among all three major compilers has experienced delays. Visual Studio (at the time of this writing) does have a complete implementation, while Clang and gcc appear nearly complete.

Module files have four types:

- Primary module interface unit
- Module implementation unit
- Module interface partition unit
- Internal module partition unit

We covered mainly the first two unit types, as partitions require a more advanced and detailed discussion. Still, a lot can be accomplished with primary module interface and module implementation units. Module interfaces can be used in place of traditional header files, and thus pesky leakages caused by #include, and additional compile time due to redundant parsing of header code, can be avoided. Resulting code is also cleaner in the sense that with modules there is no need for "ugly" preprocessor statements.

These interfaces also give the programmer more control over which functions and classes are to be accessible outside the module by explicit designation using the export keyword. Declarations and implementations can also be placed in separate interface and implementation files, similar to existing common practice, while still taking advantage of the safeguards and organization provided by modules.

Concepts were also a well-anticipated addition to C++20 and are fully implemented in all three major C++ distributions. They should be graciously welcomed by programmers who rely heavily on template programming, as they pinpoint errors more precisely at compile time while preventing the passage of invalid template parameter types. Concepts can be user-defined, while the Standard Library also provides a set of predefined concepts. Both categories can be combined with logical *and* and *or* conditions.

Virtual Default Destructor

So as not to disrupt the first pass through the modern context review of object inheritance in Chapter 3, discussion of the reasons for including a virtual default destructor in this context has been deferred to this appendix. We will now look at an example to demonstrate why one should be included in a base class.

Suppose we have two classes, Base and Derived, defined as follows. A virtual trig_fcn(.) on Base will compute the sine of a number, and its override on Derived will compute the cosine (objects of these classes are also used in Appendix B, where their member functions will actually be called). For this simple example, we just put the implementation inside the declaration:

```
#include <cmath>
#include <iostream>

class Base
{
public:
    virtual double trig_fcn(double x) const
    {
        return std::cos(x);
    }

    ~Base() {std::cout << "Base destructor called\n";}
};

class Derived final : public Base
{
public:
    double trig_fcn(double x) const override
    {
        return std::sin(x);
    }
```

```
    ~Derived() {std::cout << "Derived destructor called\n";}
};
```

Note that instead of the virtual destructor on the base class, each has its own destructor. The problem we encounter is related to cases where pointers to objects of these classes are defined. Supposed we define the following pointers:

```
Derived* d = new Derived{};
Base* b = new Base{};
Base* bd = new Derived{};
```

When a `Derived` object is created, a `Base` object will be constructed first, followed by its inheriting `Derived` object. When d is deleted, the objects in memory will be destroyed in the opposite order, as desired, because the destructor on d is called first, followed by that on b:

```
delete d;
```

Output to the screen is then generated by each destructor:

```
Derived destructor called
Base destructor called
```

So far, so good. If only a `Base` object is allocated, then when its pointer is deleted, the only destructor to be called is its own:

```
delete b;
```

Output from the object's destructor again verifies this:

```
Base destructor called
```

So no problem here either. But what if we delete bd, which was declared as a pointer to a `Base` but which points to an allocated `Derived` object using indirection? Now, we run into a problem:

```
delete bd;
```

In this case, only the `Base` destructor is called, leaving the `Derived` object still in memory, and with no way to deallocate it:

```
Base destructor called
```

While we usually associate raw pointers with memory leaks, and smart pointers as a way to avoid them, we will not necessarily escape this problem with a `unique_ptr` either:

```
std::unique_ptr<Base> ubd;
ubd = std::make_unique<Derived>();

ubd.reset();
```

Again, only the **Base** destructor gets called:

```
Base destructor called
```

Suppose instead we now make the destructor on **Base** virtual and override it on **Derived**:

```
class Base
{
public:

    // . . .

    virtual ~Base() {std::cout << "Base (virtual) destructor called\n";}

    // . . .
};


class Derived final : public Base
{
public:

    // . . .

    ~Derived() override {std::cout << "Derived destructor (override) called\n";}

    // . . .
};
```

Now, repeat the cases where we use indirection for both the raw and unique pointer cases:

```
Base* bd = new Derived{};

std::unique_ptr<Base> ubd;
ubd = std::make_unique<Derived>();

delete bd;
ubd.reset();
```

The result is that both the `Base` and `Derived` objects are deallocated successfully:

```
Derived destructor (override) called
Base (virtual) destructor called

Derived destructor (override) called
Base (virtual) destructor called
```

Each destructor was implemented with output for demonstration, but in practice all we need to do is declare a virtual default destructor on the base class. This ensures that the compiler-provided default destructor on the derived class (not explicitly declared) will be called as well:

```
class Base
{
public:
    // . . .

    virtual ~Base() = default;

    // . . .
};


class Derived final : public Base
{
public:
    // . . .
    // Do not need to declare a destructor -- its default is
    // provided by the compiler.
};
```

Object Slicing

Another point that was deferred from Chapter 3 is that abstract base classes can prevent *object slicing*, which will now be explained. In the result from Appendix A, both the `Base` and `Derived` classes are concrete; that is, either can be instantiated on its own:

```cpp
#include <cmath>
#include <iostream>

class Base
{
public:
    virtual double trig_fcn(double x) const
    {
        return std::cos(x);
    }

    virtual ~Base() = default;

};

class Derived final : public Base
{
public:
    double trig_fcn(double x) const override
    {
        return std::sin(x);
    }

};
```

Suppose now we create instances of each on the stack:

```cpp
Base b;
Derived d;
```

Suppose also that we have a function that takes in a `Base` argument and evaluates the `trig_fcn(.)` member function for $x = \pi$ and displays the result to the screen:

```
void slice_function(Base b)
{
    using std::cout, std::format;
    using namespace std::numbers;

    cout << format("slice_function(.): trig_fcn(pi) = {}\n",
        b.trig_fcn(pi));
}
```

Now, call this function with both b and d:

```
slice_function(b);
slice_function(d);
```

We would get as output something like this:

```
slice_function(.): trig_fcn(pi) = -1
slice_function(.): trig_fcn(pi) = -1
```

In both cases, the result is essentially −1 (this might not be exact because of floating-point arithmetic), the result of `std::cos(pi)`, even though we might have expected 0 for `std::sin(pi)` from the `Derived` object d.

If we attempt to pass a derived object to a function taking in a base object by value, the code will compile, but the derived object gets "sliced off" from its base class object. We are then left with only the functionality defined on the base class. A program may compile successfully and even appear to run without error, but with an incorrect result. These types of problems can be difficult to trace, especially in a large codebase with more realistic applications than computing sines and cosines.

Another example of object slicing is where a `Base` object is constructed with a `Derived` copy constructor argument:

```
Base bd{d};
```

In this case as well, if we write

```
cout << format("trig_fcn(pi) = {}\n", bd.trig_fcn(pi));
```

the output would be as follows:

```
trig_fcn(pi) = -1
```

So again, although we started with the `Derived` object d, the result is from calling the virtual function on the `Base` object.

If, however, a pure virtual function were declared on the Base class, the compiler would issue an error in either case, thus preventing the program from even making it to runtime, and thus protecting us from object slicing. As a very simple example, suppose we add a pure virtual function double pure_virtual_trig_fcn(.) to Base and override it on Derived, so that we now have this:

```
class Base
{
public:
    virtual double trig_fcn(double x) const
    {
        return std::cos(x);
    }

    virtual double pure_virtual_trig_fcn(double x) const = 0;

    virtual ~Base() = default;
};

class Derived final : public Base
{
public:
    double trig_fcn(double x) const override
    {
        return std::sin(x);
    }

    double pure_virtual_trig_fcn(double x) const override
    {
        return std::sin(x) + std::cos(x);
    }
};
```

Then, in this case, even attempting to create an instance of a Base class

```
Base b;
// or
Base bd{d};
```

would be prevented by the compiler. Furthermore, any function taking a Base type parameter, in this case slice_function(.), would also fail to compile.

Implementation of Move Special Member Functions

In Chapter 3, and for most of this book, we have been relying on the compiler-provided default move constructor and move assignment operator. However, for those who would like a more in-depth explanation beyond the default cases, this appendix discusses their implementations in the OptionInfo class, simply replicating their default behavior as examples.

Move operations also are related to memory allocations that are common with a vector container, discussed at a high level in Chapter 4. Reading the entirety of this section is not a prerequisite, but it is provided here in case you would like more information.

Returning to the OptionInfo class, the default settings instructing the compiler to generate default versions of the move operations are now removed. Instead, they are declared similarly to the copy operations:

```
class OptionInfo
{
public:
    OptionInfo(std::unique_ptr<Payoff> payoff, double time_to_exp);
    double option_payoff(double spot) const;
    double time_to_expiration() const;
    void swap(OptionInfo& rhs) noexcept;

    OptionInfo(const OptionInfo& rhs);
    OptionInfo& operator =(const OptionInfo& rhs);

    OptionInfo(OptionInfo&& rhs) noexcept;
    OptionInfo& operator =(OptionInfo&& rhs) noexcept;

    ~OptionInfo() = default;
```

```
private:
    std::unique_ptr<Payoff> payoff_ptr_;
    double time_to_exp_;
};
```

The first detail you will probably notice is that both special move functions have also been declared noexcept. This will also be explained.

Next, the implementation of the move constructor can be written as follows, using the std::exchange(.) function, also in the <utility> header:

```
OptionInfo::OptionInfo(OptionInfo&& rhs) noexcept:
    payoff_ptr_{std::exchange(rhs.payoff_ptr_, nullptr)},
    time_to_exp_{rhs.time_to_exp_}{}
```

The std::exchange(.) function, originally introduced with C++14, is similar in some respects to std::swap(.). It replaces its first argument with its second, and returns its first argument in its original form. Here is a trivial example to demonstrate:

```
int a = 1;
cout << format("Start: a = {},\n", a);

int b = std::exchange(a, 500);
cout << format("Now: a = {}, b = {}\n", a, b);
```

Here, a is replaced by 500, while the original value stored by a (1) is returned and is used to initialize b:

```
Start: a = 1
Now: a = 500, b = 1
```

In the OptionInfo move constructor, the memory address rhs.payoff_ptr_ is set to a null state, while the original address is returned in the initialization of the payoff_ptr_ member on the moved-to OptionInfo object. Similar to the application of std::swap(.) to memory addresses, no allocation or deallocation of memory occurs, so this is again a safe operation that will not throw an exception. However, because time_to_exp_ is a plain numerical type, it is just as efficient and simpler to copy it. This leaves the rhs object in a valid but unspecified state, per the requirement of move semantics. Thus, we can safely declare our move constructor noexcept.

As a bonus, std::exchange(.) is guaranteed by the Standard to be noexcept as of C++23.

The move assignment operator requires minimal work, as we can again use the swap(.) member function implemented earlier. Furthermore, instead of creating a temporary object with the copy constructor and swapping it, we can create one using the less expensive move constructor and swap the result with the active object as before:

```
// Implements move assignment
OptionInfo& OptionInfo::operator =(OptionInfo&& rhs) noexcept
{
    OptionInfo{std::move(rhs)}.swap(*this);
    return *this;
}
```

And finally, because the swap(.) member function is noexcept, we can declare the move assignment operator noexcept as well.

Again, for the examples in this book, the compiler-provided default move constructor and move assignment operator will be sufficient. The default move operations are noexcept if the data members' move operations are noexcept, and this was also the case for our purposes throughout the book. However, if user-defined move member functions become necessary in your code, the Core Guidelines advise making these noexcept. The guidelines state, "A throwing move violates most people's reasonable assumptions. A nonthrowing move will be used more efficiently by Standard Library and language facilities."[1]

In general, a user-defined move constructor and move assignment operator should be declared noexcept as well as the swap(.) member function, which by design is intended to be exception safe and can be useful in move assignment operator implementations (as well as copy assignment). Compile-time optimizations can also be achieved by declaring these functions noexcept.

---

1 "Make move operations noexcept" (*https://oreil.ly/OKsM_*), ISO C++ Guidelines.

Resolving Conflicts in the Initialization of a vector

This appendix is a supplement to "A potential pitfall with the meaning of () and {} with a vector" on page 121. That content requires some background on a feature added to the Standard Library with C++11, std::initializer_list. You can find more details on this topic in Section 3.1.3 (*https://oreil.ly/eN9rB*) of *The C++ Standard Library: A Tutorial and Reference*, 2nd edition, by Nicolai M. Josuttis (O'Reilly, 2012).

In the vector class, we will find multiple constructors, including the following two:

```
template <typename T /* ... this is a simplification */>
  class vector
  {
    // ...
  public:
    vector(size_type, const T&);       // number of elements, initial value
    vector(std::initializer_list<T>);  // braces with values of type T
    // ...
  };
```

For this reason, given a vector<int> type and two values of integral types, both constructors are viable:

```
// 10 ints of value -1 or two ints valued 10 and -1?
vector<int> v1{10, -1};    // two ints valued 10 and -1
vector<int> v2(10, -1);    // 10 ints of value -1
```

In C++, when using braces in a constructor, if there's a choice to be made between a constructor with an std::initializer_list (#include<initializer_list>) and another constructor, and both are viable, then the one that accepts a initializer_list takes preference. In contrast, when using parentheses, the one accepting an initializer_list is not considered (by definition). This leads to a surprising dichotomy, but it is part of the rules of the language (it would definitely be less annoying if it did not happen with vector<int>, which is arguably the poster child of containers used when teaching the language).

Suppose we add a default constructor to the Fraction class (and, say, initialize the numerator to 0 and the denominator to 1). Then, creating a vector of Fraction objects would not exhibit this difference, as there is no way to initialize a Fraction with a *single* unsigned value. The following two lines will each result in creating a vector<Fraction> object with 10 Fraction elements:

```
vector<Fraction> v_frac_braces{10};    // size() == 10
vector<Fraction> v_frac_rb(10);        // size() == 10
```

However, to make your head spin, suppose we add another Fraction constructor that takes in the numerator only (and initializes the denominator again to 1). Now, we're back to the original issue where the former has a size of 1, and the latter has a size of 10, because now we *can* initialize a Fraction with a single unsigned value:

```
// In the Fraction class, a constructor taking in a single
// int argument (the numerator) is added:
Fraction(int n) : n_{n}        // numerator only, denominator = 1

// . . .

// the sizes will now be different when creating vector instances:
vector<Fraction> v_frac_braces{10};    // size() == 1
vector<Fraction> v_frac_rb(10);        // size() == 10
```

valarray and Matrix Operations

As mentioned in Chapter 8, a Standard Library container class separate from the STL, `std::valarray`, dates back to C++98. It supports arithmetic operators and provides "for numeric computation when runtime efficiency is more important than flexibility with respect to operations and element types."[1] With slice and stride functions also accompanying the `valarray` class, it can also facilitate representation of arrays of higher dimensions—in particular, a (two-dimensional) matrix.

While `valarray` has these very useful properties that would seem to make it an obvious choice for matrix math, it has played to mixed reviews. This reaction dates back to its original specification, which was never fully complete because of debates over whether to require implementation using expression templates, a new technique at the time that could significantly optimize performance. In the end, this was not mandated. As a result, "initial implementations were slow, and thus users did not want to rely on [them]."[2]

More about the history of `valarray` is discussed in Section 27.4 of *C++ Templates: The Complete Guide* (*https://oreil.ly/ZE9R_*), 2nd edition, by David Vandevoorde et al. (Addison-Wesley, 2017). You can also find additional details about `valarray` in Section S.2 of the online supplemental chapter (*https://oreil.ly/WzCaW*) of *The C++ Standard Library: A Tutorial and Reference*, 2nd edition, by Nicolai M. Josuttis (Addison-Wesley, 2012).

At the time of this writing, however, two of the mainstream Standard Library distributions have implemented expression template versions of `valarray`—namely, those

---

1 Bjarne Stroustrup, *A Tour of C++* (*https://oreil.ly/cK17I*), 3rd edition (Addison-Wesley, 2022), Section 17.6.

2 Mark Hoemmen et al., "A Free Function Linear Algebra Interface Based on the BLAS" (*https://wg21.link/p1673*), P1673 BLAS interface proposal.

that accompany the gcc (libstdC++) and Clang (libC++) compilers. In addition, the Intel oneAPI DPC++/C++ Compiler (*https://oreil.ly/zbX7L*) ships with its own high-performance implementation of `valarray`. And incidentally, specializations of `std::begin(.)` and `std::end(.)` functions for the `valarray` class were included as enhancements in C++11.

If `valarray`'s performance is suitable for your needs, it can potentially be a convenient option for matrix/vector operations and for vectorized versions of common mathematical functions.

Arithmetic Operators and Math Functions

The `valarray` container supports the standard arithmetic operators on an element-by-element basis, as well as scalar multiplication.

For example, for two vectors (in the mathematical sense) $\mathbf{v}_1$ and $\mathbf{v}_2$, the vector sum expression $3\mathbf{v}_1 + \frac{1}{2}\mathbf{v}_2$ can be naturally transcribed from a mathematical statement into C++ by using `valarray` objects. Note that we can also use CTAD (*class template argument deduction*, introduced in Chapter 1) with `valarray`, as shown in the last line here:

```
#include <valarray>
. . .

std::valarray<double> v1{1.0, 2.0, 3.0,
            1.5, 2.5};

std::valarray<double> v2{10.0, -20.0, 30.0,
            -15.0, 25.0};

// Can also use CTAD with valarray:
std::valarray vec_sum = 3.0 * v1 + 0.5 * v2;
```

The result can be obtained with a range-based `for` loop, which is also valid for `valarray`, because of the aforementioned existence of `begin(.)` and `end(.)` functions for this type:

```
for (auto elem : vec_sum)
{
    cout << format("{} ",elem);
}
```

This gives us the following:

```
8 -4 24 -3 20
```

Element-by-element multiplication (note this is different from Eigen) is also implemented with the * operator, as shown next. Also, let's further lighten the notation by dropping the `std::` scope:

```
using std::valarray;
valarray prod = v1 * v2;
```

Now this gives us the following:

```
10 -40 90 -22.5 62.5
```

The dot (or inner) product of v1 and v2 is easily obtained by summing the elements in prod by invoking the sum() member function of the valarray class:

```
double dot_prod = prod.sum();      // Result = 100
```

In addition to sum(), valarray has max() and min() member functions, along with an apply(.) member function that applies an auxiliary function similar to std::transform:

```
// Recall:  v1 = {1.0, 2.0, 3.0, 1.5, 2.5};

double v1_max = v1.max();    // 3.0
double v1_min = v1.min();    // 1.0

valarray u = v1.apply([](double x) {return x * x;});
// Result: 1, 4, 9, 2.25, 6.25

valarray w = v1.apply([](double x) {return std::sin(x) + std::cos(x);});
// Result: 1.38177 0.493151 -0.848872 1.06823 -0.202671
```

As the apply(.) member function is nonmodifying, the contents of v1 will not be affected.

A subset of the <cmath> functions is conveniently defined for vectorized operations on the entirety of a valarray. For example, the following operations will return a valarray containing the images of the respective functions applied to each element in v1 and neg_val in the following code. Note that we can also negate each element in the same way as a plain numerical type, with the subtraction operator. The negation is also nonmodifying:

```
// Mathematical functions for valarray a la <cmath>:
valarray sine_val = std::sin(v1);
valarray log_val = std::log(v1);
valarray neg_val = -v1;
valarray abs_val = std::abs(neg_val);
valarray exp_val = std::exp(neg_val);
```

As mentioned earlier, std::begin(.) and std::end(.) functions recently provided for STL containers have also been implemented for valarray:

```
#include <algorithm>

. . .

template<typename T>
```

```
void print_this(T t) {cout << t << " ";}          // From Ch 4
```

```
std::for_each(std::begin(w), std::end(w), print_this<double>);
```

Note, however, member function versions are not provided; that is, the following will *not* compile:

```
// Don't do this!
std::for_each(w.begin(), w.end(), test_print<double>);  // Will *not* compile
```

Given the convenience of the apply(.) member function on valarray and the built-in vectorized mathematical functions that are already available, STL algorithms for_each(.) and transform(.) might not be needed as often in the case of valarray compared to STL containers.

valarray as a Matrix Proxy

The valarray container provides the facilities to represent multidimensional arrays. In our case, we are specifically concerned with representing a two-dimensional array as a proxy for a matrix. To demonstrate this, let's first lighten the notation by defining an alias:

```
using mtx_array = std::valarray<double>;
```

Then, create a valarray object val, with the code formatted in a way to make it look like a 4×3 matrix:

```
mtx_array val{1.0, 2.0, 3.0,
              1.5, 2.5, 3.5,
              7.0, 8.0, 9.0,
              7.5, 8.5, 9.5};
```

The first row can be retrieved using the std::slice(.) function, defined for a valarray, using the square bracket operator:

```
auto slice_row01 = val[std::slice(0, 3, 1)];  // Row 1 in the mathematical sense,
                                               // 0-indexed in C++
```

This code says the following:

- Go to the first element of the valarray: index 0, value = 1.0.
- Choose three elements, beginning with the first.
- Use a *stride* of 1, which in this case means to choose three consecutive elements.

Similarly, the second column can be retrieved, using in this case a stride of 3, the number of columns:

```
// The 2nd rowwise element has index 1:
auto slice_col02 = val[std::slice(1, 4, 3)];
```

It is important to note the slice(.) function returns a lighter slice_array type—which is a mutating view of the selected elements—rather than a full valarray. It does not, however, provide the necessary member functions and operators to access individual elements or compute, say, new rows comprising a matrix product. If we want to apply these functions to row or column data, we need to construct corresponding new valarray objects, copying in the elements from the slice_array. You will see this in the next example, computing the dot product of a row in one matrix by the column in another, a necessary operation in carrying out matrix multiplication.

To demonstrate this, suppose we have a 5×3 and a 3×5 matrix, each represented as a valarray. We are storing the number of rows and columns of each in separate variables:

```
mtx_array va01{1.0, 2.0, 3.0,
               1.5, 2.5, 3.5,
               4.0, 5.0, 6.0,
               4.5, 5.5, 6.5,
               7.0, 8.0, 9.0};

const int va01_cols = 3;

mtx_array va02{1.0, 2.0, 3.0, 4.0, 5.0,
               1.5, 2.5, 3.5, 4.5, 5.5,
               5.0, 6.0, 7.0, 8.0, 8.5};

const int va02_rows = 3, va02_cols = 5;
```

Applying matrix multiplication would require taking the dot product of each row of the first "matrix" by each column of the second. As an example, in order to get the dot product of the third row by the second column, we would first need the slice for each:

```
auto slice_01_row_03 = va01[std::slice(6, va01_cols, 1)];
auto slice_02_col_02 = va02[std::slice(1, va02_rows, va02_cols)];
```

However, neither element-by-element multiplication nor the sum() member function is defined on a slice_array, so we need to formally construct corresponding valarray<double> (mtx_array) objects:

```
mtx_array va01_row03{slice_01_row_03};
mtx_array va02_col02{slice_02_col_02};
```

The dot product is then computed in the usual way:

```
double dot_prod = (va01_row03 * va02_col02).sum();
```

This results in a value of 56.5.

The preceding example involved a step-by-step sequence to illustrate construction of a valarray, given a slice_array object before invoking mathematical operations on the former type. As an alternative, a `slice_array` is implicitly convertible to a `valarray`, so the same result could be accomplished in fewer lines:

```
mtx_array va01_row03_alt = va01[std::slice(6, va01_cols, 1)];
mtx_array va02_col02_alt = va02[std::slice(1, va02_rows, va02_cols)];

dot_prod = (va01_row03_alt * va02_col02_alt).sum();          // = 56.5
```

In summary, `valarray` provides the ability to conveniently apply functions on an entire array, using Standard Library mathematical functions such as `std::sin(.)`, `std::exp(.)`, and `std::abs(.)`, and an `apply(.)` member function that applies a function to each member of a `valarray`. This makes working with a `valarray` similar to working with arrays in Fortran 90, as well as in more math-focused languages such as R, Python (NumPy), and MATLAB.

As a reminder, however, there are caveats to consider. When using a `valarray` to represent a matrix, operations on individual rows and columns—each represented by a `slice_array`—such as row-by-column dot products necessary for matrix multiplication, require copies of the slice data to new `valarray` objects, introducing performance overhead. Also, overall performance can be highly dependent on the implementation provided by your Standard Library vendor.

Index

three-way comparison operator, 54-58
using keyword, 12

V

valarray, 391-396
    arithmetic operators and math functions, 392-394
    matrix proxy, 394-396
vector, 112-123
    allocation and contiguous memory, 115-118
    clear() member function, 119-120
    data() member function, 122
    default choice among sequential containers, 127
    fixed-length std::array, 126
    front(), back(), and pop_back() member functions, 120-121
    lazy evaluation, 279-282
    list sequential container, 124-126
    and polymorphic objects, 114-115
    potential pitfall with meaning of () and {}} with a vector, 121

random access: at(.) versus [.], 121
    resolving conflicts in initialization of, 389-390
    size versus capacity, 115
    storage of objects in a vector, 112-114
    uniform initialization with, 13
vector sequential container, 111
views, range-based for loops and, 173
virtual default destructor, 66, 377-380
volatility, implied, 39-42
volume-weighted average price (WWAP), 166

Y

year_month_day class, 225-245
yield curves, 249-258
    calculating forward discount factors, 252
    deriving from market data, 249-251
    discount factors, 252
    implementing a linearly interpolated yield curve class, 257-258
    implementing a yield-curve class, 253-256
    PCA and, 310-313

About the Author

Daniel Hanson worked in quantitative modeling and software development for close to 25 years, primarily with C++ implementation of option pricing and portfolio risk models, trading systems, and library development. After leaving the private sector, he held a full-time lecturer position in the Department of Applied Mathematics at the University of Washington, teaching quantitative development courses in the Computational Finance and Risk Management (CFRM) undergraduate and graduate programs. Among the classes he taught was a graduate-level sequence in C++ for quantitative finance, ranging from an introductory level through advanced. He has also mentored Google Summer of Code student projects involving mathematical model implementations in C++ and R. He currently stays active as a staff member of the annual CppCon conference (ISO C++ Foundation), primarily as chair of the conference student program.

Colophon

The animal on the cover of *Learning Modern C++ for Finance* is an Angora cat (or Turkish Angora). Originating in Turkey, Angoras were named after the Turkish capital of Ankara (formerly Angora) and are still considered a national treasure there. Angoras are a rare but highly in demand cat breed, with waiting lists often up to a year from breeders and a cost anywhere from $650 to $2,000.

Angoras are the oldest known longhair breed, dating all the way back to the 1600s. In the 1900s, breeders used Angoras to improve the Persian cat breed. This, however, almost wiped out the Angora breed. To protect them from going extinct, the Turkish government established a breeding program at the Atatürk Forest Farm and Zoo (Ankara Zoo) focusing on preserving lines producing white Angoras with blue, gold, or odd eyes (two different colors).

It wasn't until the 1950s that Angoras made their way to the US through members of the American military based in Turkey. After much hesitation from the Ankara Zoo, two Americans—Colonel and Mrs. Walter Grant—were allowed to bring two Angoras back to the US. These two cats were the foundation of the Angora breeding program in the US. Shortly after, more and more Americans were allowed to bring Angoras to the States to be bred.

Often called the "ballerina of the cat world," Angoras are long and slender with a muscular body covered in soft, silky hair. Even though they are considered a longhair breed, Angoras only have a single coat, making their fur much easier to maintain and groom. Until the 1970s, only Angoras with white fur were recognized as true Angoras. Now, Angoras can be found in a variety of colors. Even so, the most sought-after Angoras are white with blue or odd eyes.

Many of the animals on O'Reilly covers are endangered; all of them are important to the world.

The cover image is based on an antique line engraving from Lydekker's *Royal Natural History*. The series design is by Edie Freedman, Ellie Volckhausen, and Karen Montgomery. The cover fonts are Gilroy Semibold and Guardian Sans. The text font is Adobe Minion Pro; the heading font is Adobe Myriad Condensed; and the code font is Dalton Maag's Ubuntu Mono.

O'REILLY®

Learn from experts.
Become one yourself.

Books | Live online courses
Instant answers | Virtual events
Videos | Interactive learning

Get started at oreilly.com.